NO HOLDS BARRED

NO HOLDS BARRED

Ultimate Fighting and the Martial Arts Revolution

Clyde Gentry III

MILO BOOKS LTD

First published in hardback in May 2002 by Milo Books Ltd
This paperback edition published in April 2005 by Milo Books Ltd

ISBN 1 903854 30 X

Typeset by e-type

Printed and bound in the United States by
McNaughton & Gunn, Inc.

MILO BOOKS LTD
info@milobooks.com

Contents

SPECIAL THANKS

Special acknowledgment must go to Joe Silva for his guidance and the overwhelming degree of wisdom about mixed martial arts that always kept this book on track. I must also thank Dave Meltzer for his insight into the pro wrestling scene, and Peter Walsh, who allowed me to update this book for the wide release I've wanted from the very beginning.

Thanks to all the people who took time out of their day to be interviewed for a project that has been four years in the making. I finally got it right this time!

And to my parents for all their patience and support for putting up with my crazy passion.

Foreword

ONE DAY IN 1991, I was sparring with a smaller opponent in a Japanese jujutsu class. He was so much faster that there was no way I could keep his barrage of punches and kicks at bay. Since I had some high school and college wrestling experience, I picked up my opponent and threw him down to the ground.

"Stop! Stop! What are you doing? You can't do that," said my instructor.

"Well, I wasn't going to stand there and let him punch me," I responded.

I wasn't supposed to lift him up and throw him; my actions were, apparently, a violation of the "martial art" I was being taught. Afterwards, however, I felt uneasy. In a real fight, wouldn't I have reacted the same way? Wouldn't I have done anything to win? So what was the practical use of the martial art I was learning if it didn't take account of the unexpected reality?

Everything made sense when I saw the first Ultimate Fighting Championship on November 12, 1993. Watching Royce Gracie choke out and submit his opponents without recourse to flashy moves or rigidly prescribed techniques, I fell instantly in love with this empirical experiment. It helped rid me of my "mythical" perceptions of what traditional martial arts could accomplish in an actual fight. The moves were not choreographed, as in the movies, or mechanical, as in traditional fighting styles; the action was real.

Like anything you become fascinated with, I went out and learned more about these no-holds-barred contests. I found that they were not so new. And my love for the sport grew even more intense when the media and the politicians took a negative position because of ignorance and, in all honesty, the way the sport was originally marketed. After I wrote my first book, *Jackie Chan: Inside the Dragon*, I was frustrated with the fact that I did not get inside the man; I just over-analysed his work. I was determined that if I was to tell the story of this renegade sport, it would be the *inside* story, the straight dope.

What you see before you is the result of three years' work. Over a lengthy research period, I interviewed more than 120 people, spent

hours in the library and on the Internet, and attended every mixed
martial arts (MMA) show I could make. I wanted a challenging project
that would push every ounce of tenacity I had. In my research, I found
a new set of mythical perceptions that I struggled with for quite some
time. The more interviews I conducted, the more questions had to be
answered. As I dug deeper and deeper, it became quite apparent that
one book would not do the sport justice, just as 30 or even 50 interviews would not be enough either.

I finally decided to write a book that took a close look at the first
four years of the UFC's tumultuous history. To be fair, I included other
shows and other people that brought different views to the table.
Choosing the title was difficult. I did not want "martial arts" anywhere
in the title because this book is about reality fighting. Today, fighting
and martial arts can hardly be called synonymous – and yet the people
who fight in these competitions are the true martial artists of our time,
even if many of them don't have black belts to prove it. Today's fighters rarely cling to styles anymore, but they are definitely using martial
arts ... only in a realistic sense.

As for *No Holds Barred*, the term is the biggest misnomer to describe
a sport where plenty of holds are barred (thrity-one, according to rules
passed by the Nevada State Athletic Commission). As a title, however,
it does attract a wider audience that might be able to learn something
and come to an understanding of what the sport represents. It also
refers to my approach to the subject, which is a *no-holds-barred look at
mixed martial arts combat*. I tried my best to piece together tidbits of
information with the help of my subjects and the unmistakable proof
in documents and videotapes. I wanted to present the most truthful
look into a sport filled with so much misinformation.

In July 2001, *No Holds Barred: Evolution* debuted in the United States
and was met with overwhelmingly positive reviews. Though it took
awhile to find an audience (people thought it was everything from a
movie to an instructional book), I was still struggling with elements
the book didn't include. And new information from my original
subjects surfaced after they read the book and saw how in-depth it was
... or how deep it needed to be.

When Milo Books approached me about writing a UK version in
2002, it gave me the opportunity to add these elements with new interview material, including several European stars. Two years later, Milo
again contacted me about updating the UK version for a wider paperback release. Several chapters have been abridged to reflect the times
and new interview material has been added to further flesh out the
story behind the world's most misunderstood sport.

From November 1993 to December 1997, MMA struggled to evolve from a spectacle to a sport. Still in a state of flux, the grassroots movement has propelled it past the "fad" stage that nearly killed it in the late 1990s. And while MMA still has a long way to go, you'll find the history that took us to where we are now was a battle well worth fighting. I hope that anyone who reads this book will walk away with a better understanding of the relentless passion I found in virtually every person involved in this sport.

Clyde Gentry III

MMA Glossary

Here is a basic but not comprehensive list of terms used throughout the book. There were multitudes of other styles that practitioners used, but some of them (Joe Son's Joe Son Do) were highly self-serving.

BRANCAILLE: French term describing an agreement between two participants to allow strikes in what is otherwise a wrestling match.

BRAZILIAN JIU-JITSU: Brazilian Carlos Gracie adapted Japanese judoka Conde Koma's teachings to create an effective ground-based system of fighting which utilises submission and grappling techniques. His younger brother Helio later improved those techniques, which became known as BJJ.

CAPOERIA: Native Brazilian martial art that is most widely accepted as a dance, combining acrobatics and wide-ranging movements.

DIM MAK: Ancient martial art meaning "death touch." Consists of striking certain points on the body to cause illness or death. Most of what is preached is hyperbole.

FREESTYLE WRESTLING: One of two wrestling styles whereby practitioners are allowed to attack their opponents below the waist.

FULL CONTACT KARATE: Sport karate that served as a precursor for American kickboxing. Only allows for kicks above the waist and practitioners must wear eight-to-ten ounce gloves and footwear.

GRECO-ROMAN WRESTLING: One of two wrestling styles whereby practitioners are not allowed to attack the legs, so they must clinch and attempt to throw their opponents.

HIMANTES: Ancient Grecian boxers or pugilists wrapped their hands with these soft ox-hide straps to strengthen their wrists and steady their fingers.

JEET KUNE DO: Meaning "way of the intercepting fist," it was never actually a style; Bruce Lee's fighting concepts instead stressed what worked in a real situation.

JOB: Where one fighter agrees to throw a fight allowing his opponent to win. Sometimes "jobs" are company decisions where only one fighter knows what is supposed to happen, while the other fights for real. This term is normally associated with pro wrestling.

JUDO: Jigoro Kano took elements of informal jujutsu styles and created a way to use an opponent's strength against him. Judo means "gentle way" and throws, grappling and strikes were part of the style. As it gradually became a spectator sport, the real art suffered in favor of crowd-pleasing throwing techniques.

JUDOKA: One who practices judo.

JUJUTSU: By the seventeenth century, there were over 750 forms of jujutsu in Japan. This diversity meant that the term embraced everything from weapons and strikes to grappling. Jigaro Kano's judo eventually replaced Japanese jujutsu.

KARATE: Meaning "empty hand," this Japanese martial arts style was based on older striking-based styles from Okinawa. There are several systems in karate including shotokan, kenpo, and shorin-ryu.

KATA: Formal training exercise where students execute precise sets of movements that emulate real fighting situations.

KENPO: As the first Americanised martial art, the style emphasises attacking vital areas on the body with a variety of strikes. Ed Parker, known as the Father of American Kenpo, took the style to new heights and brought formality to its processes. Zane Frazier and Keith Hackney used kenpo in the UFC.

KICKBOXING: Generally accepted term for the sport that includes punches, kicks (above and below the waist), and sometimes knees.

KLIMAX: When a victor could not be declared in pankration (see below), both fighters drew lots, with the winner positioning his opponent any way he chose. With the loser remaining still, the other fighter was allowed to strike in any fashion without his opponent dodging the blow. Then, if that fighter still remained, he would do the same thing to his opponent. Seldom did it last more than a few turns.

KUNG FU: Although the name has been associated with martial arts, it actually means "skill" or "ability." Several styles of kung fu exist (wing chun, five animal, etc), but typically they are broken down into northern (long-range fighting and kicking) and southern (hand movements for shorter range fighting) schools.

KYOKUSHINKAI KARATE: Known as both a style and a sport. Fighters strike without gloves or protection of any kind but cannot punch to the head. Kicks to the head are legal.

MIXED MARTIAL ARTS: General term used to describe the convergence of striking, grappling, and submission techniques into one forum, whereby fighters can submit their opponents. Other terms include vale tudo, freestyle, no holds barred, cage fighting, extreme fighting and ultimate fighting.

MOO YEA DO: Created by Grandmaster Tiger Yang, it is a mixture of tae kwon do, aikido, and kung fu. Mark Hall used this style in the UFC.

MUAY THAI: Adapted from Thai military arts. Practitioners can punch, kick, knee, and elbow. Also known as Thai boxing. Most fighters don't last more than a few years due to injury. The term "Muay Thai kick" often describes a devastating maneuver where the shin collides with the opponent's thigh.

NINJUTSU: Feudal Japanese discipline that combined martial arts with commando tactics and alleged magical powers, among other things. Sceptics believe the ninja never existed but were just a hoax to scare up the art's large merchandising ploy with costumes and ornate weapons. Scott Morris and Steve Jennum both fought under some semblance of this style.

NO-HOLDS-BARRED: Misnomer for mixed martial arts used during the sport's infancy. Today, it is often used to separate matches with closed-fist strikes (NHB) and open-hand strikes (Pancrase style).

OCTAGON: Engineered fence used by the UFC. Once thought to be a gimmick, the octagonal shape gives structural support. The octagon is 30 feet in diameter and stands 5ft 6in (six inches were added after Tank

Abbott tried to throw Cal Worsham over the fence in Ultimate Ultimate '96).

PANCRASE: Karl Gotch supposedly coined the term (a variation of pankration) for Masakatsu Funaki's new organization, which became Pancrase Hybrid Wrestling. During the event's infancy, only open-hand strikes were allowed to the face. Because several states in the US did not allow closed fist strikes to the face for non-boxing events, Pancrase became a relative term for this style of fighting.

PANKRATION: The third combative sport added to the Ancient Olympics in 648 BC, meaning "all strength" or "all power." There were two types of pankration: ano (which only allowed for fighters to stand and was used during training) and kato (used in the games where fights could go to the ground).

PENCAK SILAT: Indonesian martial arts form where proponents fight very low to the ground with gliding movements that often attack the legs. Alberto Cerro Leon used this style in the UFC.

PIT FIGHTING: Another term for street fighting created by Art Davie for use by Tank Abbott and Scott Ferrozzo.

POINT KARATE: Non-realistic matches between karate practitioners were decided by points, and fighters were not allowed to follow through with their strikes.

PUGILISM: Derived from the Latin word "pugil," meaning to fight with fists, this term was used during the Ancient Greek Olympics and ultimately became known as "boxing."

QUEENSBERRY RULES: After the decline of bareknuckle pugilism, the English Marquis of Queensberry in 1867 established modern rules for boxing, including the introduction of padded gloves, to make it more organized and humane.

SAMBO: Russian martial art that uses a combination of grappling and submission techniques and literally means "self-defense without weapons." Much of the art resembles judo but it includes arm and leg submissions. Oleg Taktarov used his sambo training in the UFC.

SAVATE: French form of kickboxing without knee strikes. Gerard Gordeau used this style in the UFC.

SHOOT: Term generally used to describe a completely legitimate match between athletes. It is also a wrestling term for moving toward a take-down.

SHOOTFIGHTING (*aka* SHOOTWRESTLING): Bart Vale copyrighted the term "shootfighting," which describes the converged style in mixed martial arts using strikes, grappling and submission.

STAND-UP MARTIAL ARTS: Collective term used to describe martial arts styles that do not involve any ground techniques or grappling, including boxing, karate, kung fu and tae kwon do.

STIFF-WORK (see also WORK): While the match still has a predetermined ending, both fighters land harder strikes, often grappling and moving to a submission for real. The Japanese UWF matches and the Kingdom organization often employed stiff-worked bouts.

SUMO: Adapted from sumai (meaning "struggle"), this Japanese sport relies on men of gargantuan portions to push and flip their equally large opponents in a circle. While the style and its ancient tradtions are respected in the martial arts world, both Telia Tuli and Emmanuel Yarbrough could not use size to win their fights in the UFC.

TAE KWON DO: Meaning "art of kicking and punching," this Korean fighting style has become the most popular in North America and Great Britain. Unfortunately, the commercialism of the art has watered down much of its original effectiveness.

TOMATO CAN: Promoters often bring in tomato-can fighters, also known as ham-n-eggers and palookas, to build up records and/or protect budding stars. These fighters have a puncher's chance, but usually lack the skills and conditioning to beat opponents that promoters are trying to protect.

VALE TUDO: Portuguese term coined by a Brazilian newspaper journalist that means "anything goes" and was used to describe the early matches between Brazilian jiu-jitsu and other martial arts styles.

WORK: Both fighters agree on a predetermined ending for the match without undue harm; in other words, a fix. American pro wrestling matches are called "works."

CHAPTER 1

Genesis of the Warrior

AS SMOKE POURS *through a cascading flash of neon lights, the restless crowd grows louder. Two warriors emerge from the darkness. Their hands and feet are physical weapons outmatched only by minds teeming with knowledge of strategy and submission. This is the ultimate test for a fighter unbound by one-dimensional gameplay. Each man must be a tremendous athlete, versed in many fighting styles, who understands that one mistake can lead to surrender. Endurance, stamina and, most of all, courage will dictate an outcome that may take seconds or hours. The crowd roars as both combatants launch themselves forward to punch, kick, grapple and grind toward a finish.*

Many believe this sport was what the late Bruce Lee truly envisioned with his notes on martial arts, fighting, cross-training and physical fitness. In the 1960s, even before he had attained movie super stardom and sparked a worldwide craze, Lee made it his life's work to find the integral link between traditional martial arts and the unpredictability of genuine hand-to-hand combat. Lee's influential book *Tao of Jeet Kune Do* showcased his views on changing the way we look at fighting by scientifically and realistically examining its natural processes. He refused to be constrained by any single style or method of combat, preferring instead to keep an open mind, to adopt or adapt what worked and to reject what didn't.

Since the dawn of time, man has been drawn to physical challenges that dwell in a primal state. The Greeks made wrestling the first combative sport of their Olympic games; indeed many believe that Alexander the Great's conquests brought martial arts to India, which led to the creation of kung fu in China. Almost two millennia later, bare-fisted brawls for cash in the Old West were outlawed to eventually create boxing. Today television viewers may experience the same visceral thrill when watching a fiery crash in a stock car race, or a high-sticking fracas enraging two ice hockey players to duke it out. While the art of war (martial arts) has many faces, there can be no denying the power of Bruce Lee's central theme: the converging of combative styles into one forum.

The 1990s saw the emergence of a new sport that, for the first time, put this to the test. It seemed to come from nowhere and, in America at least, created impressions of the kind of bloodsport or fight to the death often featured in low-budget action films. It became known as *no-holds-barred* (NHB) when in fact there are plenty of holds that are barred, and several rules for fighter safety. It is also called *mixed martial arts* (MMA), a more appropriate term, even though "martial arts" carries plentiful definitions. Tainted by fraudulent practices, mail order black belts, chop-socky movies and Tae Bo infomercials, the collective "martial arts" could be anything and everything. Kickboxing and even professional wrestling have been called mixed martial arts. In Brazil, it is known as *vale tudo,* meaning "anything goes" in Portuguese. Even as the sport still struggles with a negative image that, in the beginning, it warranted, it doesn't have a universal name. For the purpose of this book, no-holds-barred and mixed martial arts will be used interchangeably to describe any competitive contest whereby participants can punch with a closed fist, kick, wrestle, and perform submission techniques under strict guidelines in a professionally supervised setting. Fighting sports of this type have been around a lot longer than people think; their origins can arguably be traced back as the blueprint for martial arts.

North America bore witness to the first major commercial MMA event when the Ultimate Fighting Championship (UFC) debuted in November 1993. Other organizations soon followed, though most of them died off after continued political pressure destroyed the sport's most lucrative cash stream, the US pay-per-view television market. Since that time, the sport flourished at the grassroots. Today, one can find as many as five different events occurring somewhere around the world each week. The sport has drawn martial arts back to its original form and given bored boxing fans something new to cheer about. MMA bounces in and out of the public eye, but little has kept it from growing. Thousands of competitors and hundreds of submission fighting schools around the world endeavour to produce the ultimate warrior. And as history can prove, it has always been a sport born from a need to find the perfect athlete.

IN EVERY CULTURE, in every place, in every time in history, men have fought on instinct alone, with or without proper training. There is a clear difference between fighting for cause and fighting for sport, and only the latter is the subject of this book. Sport fighting can be traced back to the Trojan War in 2000 BC, but for practical purposes, most will agree that pankration, the third combative sport of the ancient Olympics in Greece, was the first no-holds-barred contest. From 776 BC to 720 BC, the Olympics was built on running sports until wrestling was introduced in 708 BC. Combatants stripped naked, doused themselves with olive oil, and covered their oily skin with sand to gain a better grip (nudity was a way to make everyone equal, regardless of social class). In 688 BC, *pugilism* or boxing became widespread. Though men did not have gloves *per se*, they wore straps of leather called *himantes* to protect their hands. Boxing was a popular sport in the Olympics, and it created controversy as to who was a better fighter: the boxer or the wrestler.

The year 648 BC brought forth pankration, which means "all strength" or "all power", to the 33rd Olympics. No one really knows how pankration originated. Greek mythology often cited Hercules and Theseus as being the men responsible for bringing pankration to the Olympics, but that was mere fairy tale. Some historians pointed to soldiers having to use all their skills in hand-to-hand combat. Others cited civilizations dating back to 2600 BC, particularly Egypt, as being likely candidates that spawned the sport. Egypt has often been named as a source for cultural advances made by Greece, and arguably laid the foundation for Greek mythology.

The Greek author Philostratos claimed the best pankrationist would be a strong man who could be called the best wrestler amongst boxers and the best boxer amongst wrestlers. Men could strike by punching, kicking, or using other body parts, and they could wrestle and continue fighting on the ground. Eye gouging and biting were the only two illegal maneuvers in pankration, and fighters would be flogged for violation by umpires stationed close by. Combatants fought in the nude and, unlike in boxing, didn't wear gloves or himantes. The object of pankration was to submit your opponent by any means necessary. Fights continued until submission, death, or sunset; in the latter case, a *klimax* was executed to decide the victor. In klimax, each fighter drew lots, with the winner positioning his opponent any way he chose. With the loser remaining still, the other fighter was allowed to strike in any fashion without his opponent dodging the blow. Then, if that fighter still remained, he would do the same thing to his opponent. Seldom did klimax last more than a few turns.

A pankrationist could raise a hand to call an end to the fight. Joint dislocations, broken bones and primitive strangulation made pankration a violent sport, of which champion boxers and wrestlers wanted no part. Greeks elevated the pankrationist above boxers and wrestlers because he proved his prominence by doing both. Boxing, wrestling, and pankration all had one thing in common though; participants were only matched by age, not weight. Heavier men usually chose pankration as their sport. While several fights ended by knockout, the majority ended up on the ground, where fighters rolled around in the sand and mud viciously striking or strangling their opponents.

There were two types of pankration: *ano*, which was used for practice and only allowed for stand-up fighting, and *kato*, which included groundfighting and was generally used for the games. The Olympic sportsmen were not amateurs; they were professional fighters. A pankration champion was well paid, didn't have to pay taxes and was fed for life by the city. Pankration not only became an Olympic game, it became a way of training. Schools were set up, and different pankration styles evolved, all of which were held secret from other schools.

In Rome, pankration led to even more vicious spectacles, where men could not only use their hands and feet, but brutal weapons to savagely destroy their opponents. As Roman society became chaotic, gladiators moved into more dangerous forms of combat. It is believed that popular Greek pankrationists didn't compete in these types of events, for it ruined their image in the Olympics. In 393 AD, the Roman Emperor Theodosius decreed the Olympic games should stop, citing his Christian beliefs would not tolerate them. Ruler Honorius discontinued gladiatorial combat in 404 AD.

Though pankration officially ended with the ancient games, it continued in occidental forms around the world. In Europe, pankration most likely mixed with other forms of combat among several tribes, including the Celts and the Batavians. In Provence, France, a traditional wrestling match often crossed over to *brancaille*, when both men agreed that punching would be allowed. These types of matches were said to have continued through the 1940s in the south of France, only to move underground after World War II.

There is evidence to support claims that MMA matches took place in Asia in the second half of the twentieth century. Point karate fighter Ron Van Clief took part in one such event in 1969, held in Taiwan. "It involved grappling, and over ninety percent of the matches ended on the ground," remembered Van Clief. "It was a more interesting way of looking at the martial arts from a combative aspect." Van Clief competed in another event in 1982 called the World Freefighting Championships, held in Hong Kong. Though all martial arts styles could compete and grappling was legal, matches frequently stopped every time both men went to the ground or strayed from the fighting circle. Karate, kung fu, tae kwon do and other Asian stand-up martial arts were tested against one another, but the fights kept going to the ground. That event was important because it proved that two stand-ing fighters would eventually grapple and go to the ground, even if they didn't know what they were doing down there. Clearly, some form of pankration continued to exist in parts of the world since the days of Ancient Greece.

FOR YEARS, REALITY fighting existed under a veil of secrecy in the United States. Paul Smith, commissioner for an MMA promotion called International Fighting Championships, fondly remembers competing in no-holds-barred matches during the mid-1980s. There was a Texas event called the Iron Gladiator Championships that was held in Houston, Fort Worth and San Antonio. "This was a completely illegal event in the vein of Clint Eastwood's *Every Which Way But Loose,* as most of the fighters were just bareknuckle, barroom brawlers," said Smith. "The fights did go to the ground, though, and I won the tour-naments because I had submission training." Wealthy businessmen set up these events in bars and warehouses to whet their appetites for brutal action. Fighters found out about the matches just days before they were to be held from neighboring martial arts schools. Though most of these events had referees and some rules (e.g. no biting, eye gouging or groin shots), this was hardly a uniform sport.

Before the Ultimate Fighting Championship came along, arguably only two MMA matches had gained any sort of renown. On December 2, 1963, judoka Gene LeBell fought professional boxer Milo Savage. The match lasted four rounds before two-time national judo champ LeBell finally choked Savage out. The match took place in part because writer Jim Beck's article in *Rogue* magazine in August 1963, claimed judo was fraudulent and any practitioner wouldn't last against a boxer. Beck even chose Savage, a respectable middleweight, and the match took place in Salt Lake City, Utah, where Beck and Savage resided. Savage wore brass knuckles covered with leather, but he also wore a karate gi top (according to the rules set between them), making it easy for LeBell to grab him by the lapels. Years later, LeBell served as referee for one of the best-known MMA matches of all time: Antonio Inoki vs Muhammad Ali.

Held June 26, 1976, while Ali was in his second reign as world heavyweight champion, this "fight" would go down as one of the oddest – and boring – of the century. Inoki, a Japanese professional wrestler, needed a way for his organization, New Japan Wrestling, to increase ticket sales over its rival All Japan Wrestling, which had substantial ties to America's top pro wrestling stars. "New Japan had to create new stars, so one of the things they came up with was the idea of making Inoki the World's Martial Arts Champion," says David Meltzer, the premier authority on pro wrestling. "What they would do was take guys from other sports and put them in 'worked' matches with Inoki. The most famous was Willem Ruska, a multi-gold medal-list in Olympic judo." But to really put Inoki over with the crowd, he needed to beat the best, and during the mid-1970s, no one qualified more than boxing superhero Muhammad Ali.

Originally, the two had worked out a predetermined ending. "Ali would beat up Inoki, then he'd want to stop the fight because Inoki was taking such a horrible pounding," says Meltzer. "Ali was talking to the referee about stopping the fight and Inoki would come up from behind and give him a kick to the back of the head. Ali would fall down and be pinned." Ali would be paid $6 million for his troubles. Two days before the fight, Ali called it off, unwilling to lose, and they tried unsuccessfully to devise another finish. The rules were eventu-ally altered to make a real, or shoot, match nearly impossible for Inoki to win. Inoki was told he could not throw or submit Ali in any way.

Before a capacity crowd at the Budokan Arena in Tokyo, Ali threw a total of six punches and landed only two in 15 rounds. At the start of each round, Inoki ran to the center of the ring and fell on his back, from which position he would rotate back and forth, kicking Ali's legs. Ali was utterly confused and could hardly sting like a bee. The match was ruled a draw and Ali walked away with only $1.8 million. He unsuccessfully sued for the rest. Actually, Ali didn't do much walking, as he was taken to the hospital due to blood clots caused by Inoki's kicks. This was an inglorious moment in boxing history; even worse, it nearly destroyed pro wrestling in Japan. To rebuild his reputation, Inoki continued to fight in mixed matches—none of which were legit—but the plan worked and Inoki became one of the greatest legends in Japanese pro wrestling.

The masses popularized martial arts through sports competition, but in most cases, the sport siphoned the martial from the art. Since the late 1960s, the United States has staged thousands of martial arts competitions ranging from *kata* and weapons to point karate, full contact and kickboxing tournaments. Point karate tournaments were the mainstay of stand-up martial arts competition until one of its champions, Joe Lewis, voiced his concern over the unrealistic nature of these events. Lewis began his martial arts training at age 20 while stationed in Okinawa in the US Marines during the early 1960s, and earned a black belt within one year through his dedication. Training in the Orient was tough, and he often donned hard-surfaced *kendo* gear to engage in full contact sparring. Returning to the USA, he entered point karate competitions and won without even knowing the rules. But he didn't like the start-and-stop motion, especially having to pull his punches when he had been trained to strike with power. In 1969, he convinced a local promoter to host the first full contact karate match on January 17, 1970. The announcer mistakenly called it "American kickboxing" when he saw Lewis wearing boxing gloves and knew he would be kicking.

The martial arts community was outraged by this portrayal of karate, protesting it would affect enrollment and give the Japanese art a bad name. The term "kickboxing" was associated with Muay Thai in Thailand. Muay Thai is the roughest full contact, stand-up martial arts contest, where the average fighter's career lasts only a few years. Elbows, knees, clinching, and all kicking and punching techniques are legal. It is often referred to as Muay Thai "boxing" or "kickboxing," but in actuality, the Japanese abridged the Muay Thai rules to create "kickboxing." In Thailand, either name is an insult, and it is only referred to as Muay Thai. In America, even Japanese kickboxing didn't sit well with the martial arts community. "Some of my friends who owned their own karate schools came up to me, and said, 'Joe, you're ruining the karate business for all of us. Tell people that kickboxing is bad for martial arts and that people shouldn't do it,'" remembered Lewis. "And these were the guys that eventually became some of the head referees for these full contact events."

While purists fought to remove "karate" from the sport's name and call it "kickboxing," the media felt just the opposite. Karate was starting to become very popular, and kickboxing was still associated with Muay Thai, though the American rules did not allow elbows, knees, or kicks below the waist. "The reason for that was that CBS [the American television network] did an audience response survey where they put an applause meter on it and found out that the largest response was when someone got kicked in the head, the second was when someone attempted a kick to the head and the third-largest was when someone got punched to the head," said former kickboxing promoter Howard Petschler.

Lewis recalled a conversation between he and John Martin, President of *ABC Wide World of Sports* back in 1970. "He told me, 'Mr. Lewis, we have no interest whatsoever in karate. However, we will go anywhere in the world to film your kickboxing matches.'" Lewis remembered the last time martial arts was on television. "The only

time it had been on national TV was 1965 for the national championships on ABC. It was a bloodbath between Mike Stone and Pat
Worley at Jhoon Rhee's National Championships. At the end of that
match, ABC, NBC, and CBS blacklisted it. I was the one who got
martial arts back on television."

The media and the sanctioning bodies for boxing had no idea what
to make of it. "I was trying to figure out ways to generate press," said
Petschler. "What helped was when the [boxing] commission came out
and, as one commissioner said, 'We don't sanction the sport and don't
have anything to do with it, but we are watching it very closely
because it is dangerous when you kick someone in the head – you can
kill them!' And of course I sold the event out after that. Back then
(1970s), there was a big mystique about a black belt, the death touch
and all that stuff. While the general public thought we could do super-
natural things, we were just really trying to find out what worked and
what didn't, and kickboxing, like MMA, made us re-evaluate much of
the traditional technique – a mini revolution in martial arts spear-
headed by Lewis."

Unlike point karate tournaments, full contact karate contestants
needed to be in tip-top shape, as there would be constant movement.
"Many of the early fighters lacked technique. They were not used to
applying their skills in all-out, to-the-knockout fashion," say authors
Al Weiss and David Weiss in their book *The Official History of Karate in
America*. "Many fighters lacked the conditioning that kickboxing
required and the resulting contests were lackluster and brawlish."

Kickboxing sputtered along until 1974, when Lewis and promoter
Mike Anderson drummed up spectator interest for their new "international" full contact karate circuit. An elimination tournament was
held in Europe with top competitors and an agreement was made with
husband-and-wife team Don and Judy Quine to bring the event to
Universal Television. The event was broadcast on ABC's popular *Wide
World of Entertainment*, and point karate legends like Bill "Superfoot"
Wallace, Howard Jackson and Lewis all made the transition into full
contact karate. One month before, the Quines' and Anderson created a
sanctioning body called the PKA (Professional Karate Association).
Howard Petschler became one of the original PKA commissioners.

Participants wore karate pants and gloves and, to separate it from
boxing, each man had to throw at least eight kicks per round. Jhoon
Rhee, the father of American tae kwon do, added a very important
element to full contact karate when he created the "Safe-T-Chop" –
foam gear to be worn on both hands and feet. It was introduced in the
1970s and "a high percentage of the kickboxing matches in the first

decade used that gear," said Petschler. "Eventually boxing gloves for the hands and foam pads on the feet become the standard. Everybody wanted to know what worked and of course many traditional instructors refused to acknowledge the sport."

The PKA's success led to other organizations, each one claiming different stars who could be called "world champions." The sport was so well received that a full contact match preceded the famed 1975 Ali-Frazier "Thrilla in Manila" title bout in the Philippines. By the late 1970s and early 1980s, full contact karate had become widely known as kickboxing. Other events were still touted as full contact karate but were not held in a ring and bore little resemblance to full contact. Kickboxing was created to distance itself from events like *kyokushinkai karate*, which was bareknuckle but did not allow punches to the face. Since the original fighters in full contact wore gloves and could kick, the term "kickboxing" was no longer seen as a threat, and the media accepted it as such. Around 1980, knees and sometimes clinching was allowed to bring the sport closer to its Japanese cousin.

As the heyday of these matches drew to a close by the early 1990s, real martial arts competitions lost what little appeal they sustained on US cable television. For the first time, well-decorated martial artists had been given the chance to show what they could do in a fight, and the audience was unimpressed. Many fighters looked downright clumsy, failing to display the graceful moves people saw in the movies and wanted to see replicated in tournaments. Countless fly-by-night kickboxing organizations came onto the scene creating a political rivalry between promoters to keep the best matches from taking place. Most of the sport's heroes faded into the world of low-budget film or continued their martial arts careers only inside the pages of magazines. Realistic combat sports were going nowhere.

CHAPTER 2

The Origin of Groundfighting

BEFORE THE Olympic Games were outlawed, Alexander the Great and his invincible Macedonian army may have inadvertently spread pankration to the rest of the world. In 326 BC, his armies followed a successful campaign in Egypt with the conquest of India. India is said to be the birthplace of kung fu and, though no one knows for sure, some believe Alexander and his men indirectly taught the Indian monks. Alexander led his troops on long, arduous journeys, and many pankration-trained soldiers remained in the countries they had conquered. These men may well have mixed their martial skills with the fighting forms of other cultures, laying the framework for what we know today as the martial arts. In 500 BC, the Indian monk Da Mo (Boddidharma), who trained in the Indian martial arts, founded Zen Buddhism. His journeys took him across the Himalayas until he came in contact with the Shaolin temple in China. This meeting sparked the birth of kung fu. Evidence does exist of a primitive form of Chinese wrestling that took place around the same time; it is unknown whether the two were related. Though pankration is clearly not responsible for the philosophies of Eastern and Asian martial arts, it almost certainly aided the perfection of the fighting systems.

During the Choon Chu era (772-481 BC) in China, empty-hand (unarmed) fighting techniques were prevalent and filtered throughout neighboring countries such as Japan. A wrestling sport known as chikura kurabe led in 230 BC to the birth of jujutsu (known as "the gentle art"), founded on various principles ranging from empty hand and submission to weapons and wrestling. As civil unrest plagued Japan, it was necessary for soldiers to become better equipped on the battlefield. Between the eighth and sixteenth centuries, Japan's martial arts blossomed into several different styles, each with its own set of beliefs. Most of them were tested in combat. In 1532, Tenenuchi Hisamori created what is believed to be the first formal jujutsu school.

By the seventeenth century, wartime had come to a close in Japan, creating the Edo era (1603–1868). More than 750 systems of jujutsu existed during this time, and refinement was needed to expel forms and techniques based on weapons. When the power of the Shogun was given to the Japanese Emperor after the Edo period, an imperial law made practicing martial arts in the name of the samurai (the warrior class) illegal. Unarmed fighting techniques useful in everyday life became a fixed part of jujutsu, rather than the deadly aspects used in war. Jujutsu practice had to exclude weapons but, with varying philosophies employed, the term jujutsu included one school that believed only in punching and kicking, as well as another that taught groundfighting.

In 1878, a sickly, lean pacifist named Jigoro Kano began jujutsu practice as a way to better his physical condition. He studied under numerous jujutsu masters, but found that many of the techniques were not applicable in real life. He also concluded that the systems held little "spiritual balance" to govern their usage. At the age of 22, Kano learned enough to make a startling revelation. "Knowing that every one of the jujutsu schools had its merits and demerits," said Kano in an 1898 lecture, "I came to believe that it would be necessary to reconstruct jujutsu even as an exercise for martial purposes. So by taking together all the good points I had learned of the various schools and adding thereto my own devices and inventions, I founded a new system for physical culture and mental training as well as for winning contests. I called this Kodokan Judo." Kano did not like the harmful taint and violent use of jujutsu on the street. He created Kodokan Judo (meaning "a place to study the gentle way") to bring an overall philosophy to the martial arts founded on three sets of techniques: throwing, groundwork, and striking. There was also a code of conduct that had to be followed, and exhibitions for money or fights in the streets were prohibited.

Kano's judo soon become so popular that a rift between jujutsu schools culminated into a challenge in 1886. In the ensuing competition, Kano's students dominated the jujutsu practitioners, winning most of the matches. On July 24, 1905, 18 jujutsu masters joined Kano's ranks to follow his art. Jujutsu was dead, and judo replaced it with uniformity, honor and sport. Part of Kano's plan was to spread the teachings of judo to the rest of the world, and from 1889 to his death in 1938, he made ten trips to other countries including America and Europe. Japan became enamored of judo, and from 1905 to 1910, the physical focus of the art moved away from striking and dangerous techniques towards a safe yet competitive sport. In 1909, the Kudokan became an official Japanese foundation, and sport judo became an international pastime. Punching, kicking, and dangerous submissions were only taught to higher-ranking *judoka* or judo players, who could not use these techniques in competition. As a sport, judo consisted of throws and some groundfighting with submission only; highly injurious techniques such as ankle locks were often eliminated. In Europe, many judo factions still honored jujutsu and often claimed that a black belt in one system would automatically be a black belt in the other.

On one of Kano's goodwill missions, he sent one of his best students, Mitsuyo Maeda, to America in 1904 to perform a judo demonstration for President Theodore Roosevelt. When an American football player issued a challenge, Maeda put fellow student Jojiro Tomita to the task. The football player pinned Tomita in seconds, forcing Maeda to make a decision that sensei Kano would not have approved. A Japanese businessman fronted money for Maeda and fellow judoka Sanshiro Satake to enter challenge matches throughout North and South America to prove judo's effectiveness. Though only 5ft 5in tall and weighing 154lbs, Maeda competed in over 1,000 matches and never lost a jujutsu/judo competition. While on tour in Mexico, Maeda became known as "Conde Koma" (Count of Combat) in the ring, and eventually made this part of his legal name.

Maeda settled in Manaus, near the Brazilian Amazon, in December 1915, and held his first competitions early the following year. After establishing himself, he moved east to Belem, where he married in 1917. There he met a Brazilian scholar and politician of Scottish descent named Gastao Gracie. They got along well and, in exchange for Gracie's help in securing a consulate post, Maeda agreed to teach jujutsu to his teenage son Carlos. With Gracie's help, Maeda became a major force in Japanese immigration to Brazil and adopted Brazilian citizenship in the 1930s.

BORN TO A wealthy family, Carlos Gracie was the oldest of five brothers. He took jujutsu instruction from Maeda at the age of 14 for four years. Carlos continued to study under Maeda's Brazilian assistants until he moved his family to Southern Brazil from Belem. He formed his own jujutsu academy in Rio de Janeiro in 1925, and took it upon himself to teach jujutsu to three of his brothers and to friends. He had a fourth brother named Helio (the H is silent), a frail child who was eleven years younger. "At fourteen years old, my daddy was so weak and skinny that he could not even run or he would pass out," says Relson, Helio's second eldest son (all Helio's childrens' names begin with the letter R, which is pronounced as an H in

Portuguese – so Relson is "Helson," and so on). "Carlos focused on making him better by perfecting the Gracie Diet. Carlos was a doctor and went to the university for over six years. He studied plants and the combination of fruits. He [Helio] started the diet in six months and then he was playing soccer again." The Gracie Diet, something the entire family holds sacred to this day, involved eating lots of fruit and combinations of certain foods at certain times, while avoiding pork and foods high in sugar.

Helio was told not to partake in his brother's jujutsu activity until a moment of circumstance. "My dad was about sixteen years old. After spending a couple of years watching my Uncle Carlos teach classes, one day a student showed up to class and my Uncle Carlos is nowhere to be found," said Helio's eldest son, Rorion. Helio apologized for his brother's absence and told the student that if he wanted, he could take lessons from him for the day. The student agreed. When class was over, Carlos finally showed up. To his dismay, the student told Carlos that from that moment forward, he wished to take instruction from Helio. A new teacher was born, and Helio, who had once been too weak for any sport, had found something to make him only stronger. As he became more proficient in jujutsu, Helio realized that many of the things he had been taught required more energy than was needed. "Helio started changing those techniques, as a form of trial and error, gradually so that he could use them, and that is what gave birth to Brazilian jiu-jitsu," said Rorion. Instead of judo throws, Brazilian jiu-jitsu (BJJ) emphasized groundwork and submission techniques like chokes and arm bars. (Judo replaced jujutsu in Japan, while in the rest of the world it would more often assume the new spelling of jiu-jitsu and would be used more to describe groundwork than throws or striking.)

As the Gracie name became more widely known in Brazil, and associated with jiu-jitsu, challengers came out of the woodwork to discredit Helio and the family. Jiu-jitsu was virtually unknown compared to boxing and the native art of *capoeira* that ruled Brazilian martial arts. Just as Maeda had to prove himself and his art, Helio now became the defender of the Gracie name. Of all the brothers, Helio fought in most challenge matches for the family, starting with his 1931 victory over a boxer in 30 seconds. "Carlos dedicated everything to help Helio become a champion," said Relson. Soon *O Globo*, Brazil's biggest newspaper, was carrying accounts of his fights, which employed punching and kicking as well as grappling. One reporter dubbed these matches *vale tudo*, which means "anything goes" in Portuguese. "When the Gracie family first started fighting, we were looked at as traitors in Brazil," said Relson. "We were representing jiu-jitsu, which was Japanese martial arts, and we were fighting against capoeira, which was the national martial art. Every time we went to compete, people were throwing bottles and chanting, 'Traitors go away!'" Helio continued winning, and eventually, the Gracie name and jiu-jitsu spread throughout Brazil as the real deal, far more so than the colorful but less effective capoeira.

Indeed, the Gracies were to become perhaps the most remarkable family in the history of martial arts – some say in the whole history of sports. While Carlos dedicated himself to his dietary research, and Helio did most of the fighting, both spawned large families, and almost all of their children would become dedicated jiu-jitsu students, outstanding competitors and later instructors. They stressed technique above all else and preached a mantra that most genuine fights end up on the ground, so that is where they are likely to be won or lost. Develop the skills to finish an opponent on the floor and a smaller man (or woman) can defeat a much larger foe. As the Gracie offspring grew older, their children in turn would grow up to extol the family combat art as the best and most effective of all.

As headlines made big news of Helio's success in the ring, a local Japanese group that had continued Maeda's teachings sought a judoka who could knock him off his pedestal. Back in Japan, Masahiko Kimura had accomplished everything he had set out to do. Born in 1917, he had reached seventh dan in judo at the age of 29. For 13 straight years, he never suffered a single defeat. In 1950, he made the decision to leave judo to earn money in pro wrestling and judo challenge matches, just as Maeda had done before him. In July 1951, Kimura and two other judo players were asked to compete in Brazil, where Helio made an open challenge to Kimura. Believing Helio was unworthy, Kimura told him to battle one of his juniors first, so a fifth-degree black belt named Kato accepted.

One week before their match, Helio suffered a broken rib in training, but still managed to fight to a draw. Helio was ready for Kato the second time, just 30 days later. The Japanese threw him around with ease initially, and at one point began to apply a choke. Reversing the position, Gracie beat him to it and choked Kato unconscious in six minutes. Gracie's popularity surged and, having passed the test, he now wanted Kimura himself. Kimura's second and much larger *judoka*, Yamaguchi, declined for fear of injury, so Helio got his wish.

It would be Helio's greatest challenge. The Brazilian was 39 years old and 140lbs; Kimura was six years younger and outweighed him by nearly 50lbs. As in the match with Kato, Helio implemented rules dictating the fight could only be won by submission; throws did not matter.

Also, if Kimura could not beat him within the first three minutes, then Helio should be considered the winner. According to Kimura's biography, Gracie followers situated a coffin next to the ring for the Japanese fighter. On October 23, 1951, 120,000 spectators gathered inside the massive Maracana Stadium in Brazil to bear witness to the "The World Championship of Jiu-jitsu" (according to the Brazilian newspapers).

During the first of ten rounds, Kimura treated Gracie like a rag doll, throwing him around the ring. Kimura tried several submissions, but Gracie held strong and evaded his opponent's attack. Three minutes into the second round, Kimura had Gracie in an arm lock. The Brazilian would not give up until his brother Carlos threw in the towel minutes later. There seems to be some confusion as to whether Helio's elbow was actually dislocated. Rorion Gracie said it was not, but Kimura's own biography along with other accounts says otherwise. There is no doubt that Gracie suffered his first defeat, and the arm lock became known as the *kimura*, a term still used today.

Gracie's final match took place on May 24, 1957, under vale tudo rules, against former student Waldemar Santana. Santana had been a family friend for over a decade until he and Helio had a falling out that escalated into a heated tabloid-slanging exchange. The Brazilian headquarters of the YMCA in Rio hosted the fight, which lasted an exhausting three hours and 45 minutes. "At that time, more people came in and joined the Gracie Academy [jiu-jitsu school] than any other period in the Academy's history," said Rorion. A 50-year-old man fought his much younger pupil (Santana was 23), who outweighed him by 50lbs, for nearly four hours. Even though Helio finally was knocked out, how could anyone not see the advantages of jiu-jitsu in such a fight? But of course the family had to be vindicated and with Helio's retirement emerged another champion in the form of 17-year-old Carlson Gracie. Carlson, Carlos's son, fought Santana five times, winning two and drawing three.

Carlson continued fighting through the 1960s and, because of his success against Santana, which had been a huge hit on television, freestyle fighting became a true spectator sport in Brazil. As Rorion remembered, "It was called *Vale Tudo on TV* and of course it reached very high ratings; eventually other television networks were getting very political against that." These fights aired sporadically on Brazilian television throughout the 1950s and 1960s, creating heroes for the audience at home. Relson recalls another show his father Helio produced, called *Heroes of the Ring*. As more and more people learned about Brazilian jiu-jitsu, other incarnations developed, such as *luta livre* or freestyle grappling without a gi. "The name 'luta livre' comes from my daddy's event," said Relson. "My daddy promoted an event called Luta Livre Americana back in 1958 because America is wild. In Brazil, Americans were looked at as fighting very mean, like a street-fight, stemming from John Wayne movies. In Brazil, we had this image of the Americans fighting bare-fisted."

Vale tudo made heroes out of fighters other than the Gracies, such as Ivan Gomes. According to Brazilian MMA journalist Marcelo Alonso, who wrote an article about Gomes in the American magazine *Fightsport*, "[Gomes is] known in the Brazilian northeast as the best vale tudo fighter ever. [He] fought in more than 200 consecutive vale tudo matches ... not one ended in defeat." At a time when Carlson Gracie was at his best, he fought Gomes to a draw in 1963 and proclaimed it was the toughest fight of his career. Gracie befriended Gomes, who later ran one of his gyms in Brazil before competing in Japan thanks to Antonio Inoki. In August 1976, Gomes defeated three opponents and retired with a record of 199-0-6.

THE GRACIE FAMILY became legendary for their exploits. During the mid-1980s, crime was at an all-time high in Brazil and even the beaches were not a safe haven. One afternoon, Rickson and Royler Gracie (Helio's middle sons) went surfing, a common pastime for Brazilian youth. Royler was very even-tempered but got into a disagreement with another surfer. "Six guys tried to beat up Royler, but Rickson was able to get him away," said brother Relson. "Some guys were kicking Royler on the ground, so finally Rickson went to the car and grabbed a bat. Rickson laid into the guys with the bat to get Royler to safety and, as they spun away in the car, the guys were throwing rocks and broke the back windshield." The following week, a German journalist had his camera stolen and was subsequently stabbed to death. Something had to be done.

"The equivalent to the SWAT team came to my dad's [jiu-jitsu] school and the whole team was there," said Relson. "They got fifteen of us to walk with them through the beach. When the cops walk through the beach, the bad guys would hide drugs and weapons in the sand. When we walk through the beach, we were like normal people with shorts; this was to surprise the guys." Relson walked in front, Royler 30 feet behind and they had plenty of reinforcements. "I approached a group of four of the troublemakers and talked to them about coming along quietly to talk with the police," said Relson. "They didn't want to go. One guy stood up and pushed me and then punched me so I choked him out. The other guy tried to kick me so I took him down and choked him too. The third one ran into the water and then I jumped on his back and choked him out too in the water. The fourth one also got into the water and started to swim away. I swam behind him and choked him out." Relson had to bring the fourth one back to the beach with the others, and soon, his family and students surrounded them. "They resisted and some of the other bad guys showed up to make more trouble from the corner of the beach, but they were in for a surprise. The cops showed up and found weapons and drugs and arrested them."

ON NOVEMBER 30, 1984, a pivotal event called Vale Tudo No Maracanãzinho pitted Gracie students against other styles. The historic importance of this event not only shaped combat sports outside of submission wrestling but established a new hero amongst the Brazilians: Marco Ruas. A teenage Ruas had begun his martial arts training under the tutelage of uncle Zinicius, a judo black belt and well-respected teacher in Brazil. He eventually took up tae kwon do, capoeira and Thai boxing before boxing coach Santa Rosa took him under his wing. During his twenties, Ruas trained and taught steadily under the guidance of tae kwon do and Thai boxing teacher Flavio Molina. Although Ruas experimented with luta livre, he concentrated on stand-up martial arts until an incident with the Gracie family forced him to look at the bigger picture.

Sometime in early 1984, Molina's brother-in-law, a tae kwon do practitioner, got into a street fight with Charley Gracie and Gracie lost. "My cousin Renzo was in a nightclub and got into a fight with some guys from luta livre," said Relson. "Those same guys got into the street fight with Robson's son, Charley Gracie, and mobbed him up." According to Ruas, Charley went to his uncle Rolls Gracie and told him about the encounter, saying, "This tae kwon do guy was saying that jiu-jitsu was bad!" The Gracie family wielded an almost mythic power with jiu-jitsu at this point, one that few dared to challenge. While Relson was known as the streetfighter of the family, Rolls was noted as the most technically-skilled – but not on this occasion. Armed with several students, Rolls stormed Molina's school with a vengeance. "He [Molina] taught kids, but some of his students were black belts, and the jiu-jitsu guys came and put the guys to sleep," said Ruas.

"Because of these fights, it gave them [luta livre] the ego to think they can beat us," said Relson. "It created a stir in Brazil to start up the challenge matches again. For years, nobody challenged us; I only fought in the streets." Maracanãzinho was a nickname given to a smaller convention center in Brazil compared to Maracana. Originally, the Gracie family was going to face Molina's crew, but the decision was made to let Gracie students compete instead. Molina, Ruas, and others competed as "kickboxers" and fought as a team in the event, which was promoted by Robson Gracie. Just two months prior, Roberto Leito Sr. contacted Ruas and offered his services to teach him ground defense. Known as the father of luta livre, Leito Sr learned jiu-jitsu from the Gracies but built new techniques and strategies upon the art. The only chance Ruas had to defeat Carlson Gracie student Fernando Pinduka (Ruas was originally going to fight Relson Gracie) would stem from learning Brazilian jiu-jitsu. "Leito taught me some techniques and the guy could not submit me," said Ruas. "I landed a lot of punches and knocked his tooth out. Everybody around the ring was for the Gracies, and the referee was a black belt in jiu-jitsu." Though Molina was choked out by Relson Gracie brown belt Marcelo Bhering, 23-year-old Ruas fought to a draw. Pinduka controlled the pace on the ground and had the crowd behind him, but Ruas stayed out of his traps and stunned him several times standing up. This experience changed Ruas forever, and put him on the road to enlightenment about knowing both sides of the coin. (Jiu-jitsu and luta livre practitioners constantly tested themselves and their machismo attitudes against one another, not realizing that knowledge should be shared and adapted.)

Ruas developed his own following, but only fought in three other vale tudo-style matches in Brazil. "The Gracies only liked to fight guys from one style like capoeira or kung fu, guys who knew nothing about jiu-jitsu," said Ruas. "The Gracies considered me an enemy and it was hard for me to get sponsors or to get fights again. It wasn't personal; it was just about jiu-jitsu." Rorion Gracie has quite a different take on the matter. "Every single one either learned directly or indirectly from the Gracies and there was no such problem in allowing them to fight against us." At times, vale tudo became synonymous with jiu-jitsu, but the latter was more accessible and safer for public consumption. Eventually, its brutal cousin all but disappeared, relegated to underground events. As time went on, challenges made to the Gracie family became less and less; their art had proven its effectiveness and there was no point in disputing it any longer. But Helio's eldest son, Rorion, didn't want to stop there.

RORION GRACIE BEGAN learning jiu-jitsu at such an early age that he says he had a diaper on under his gi. He had grown up with a family name that meant something on the rough and tumble streets of Brazil. By young adulthood, he felt it was time to spread that fame. Against his relatives' advice, the 17-year-old Rorion journeyed to the United States in 1969 in search of a dream. He found himself sleeping on newspapers and panhandling for food instead. Returning to Brazil periodically, he graduated with a law degree from his native land and learned English. He also refused to give up. Rorion settled permanently in the US in 1978, with one thought in mind: to teach jiu-jitsu to anyone who wanted to learn the most potent system of fighting. The drive behind Gracie Jiu-Jitsu, according to Rorion, was "if these people never have access to learning jiu-jitsu, they will be forever oppressed by the big, tough guys in their neighborhood." But without any advertising, Rorion's dream of teaching the smaller guy how to defeat the bigger guy would have to wait. Instead he stumbled on an unlikely career as an actor. Over the course of the next 15 years, the tall, dark, and handsome Rorion appeared in major television series like *Hill Street Blues, Fantasy Island, Hart to Hart* and *The Love Boat.* Gracie enjoyed his new job, but that didn't prevent him from bringing people from the set to his garage to show them the family art.

Although his first dojo was basic, Rorion knew he was on to something. He believed in jiu-jitsu so much that he registered the name Gracie Jiu-jitsu. "The term Gracie Jiu-jitsu was carved by me [in the USA] and it identifies my source of instruction," said Rorion. "When the Gracie name became very famous, a lot of relatives of mine started to capitalize on the work I had done. Unfortunately, they don't have the sense of professionalism and ethics that I wished they did and because I owned the Gracie Jiu-jitsu name, I would refuse to let those guys sell and prostitute the name."

The Machado family, cousins to the Gracies, also called America home. When Rorion started conducting seminars, he brought over Carlos Machado to work with karateka and film star Chuck Norris in Las Vegas. Machado eventually moved to America and, through Norris, Carlos and his brothers dabbled in films while teaching with Rorion in his garage. According to Rorion, the Machados began teaching students behind his back, as well as undercutting his prices and changing the way the art was taught. They were eventually ousted from Rorion's group and even sued over use of the Gracie name. Rorion ended up sending several "cease and desist" letters to family members over using the name.

Carley Gracie, Rorion's nephew and son of Carlos Gracie, was a different story. He settled in America several years before Rorion in late 1972, but failed to find a niche for jiu-jitsu. When the UFC exploded onto the scene, he restarted his school and contested Rorion's registered trademark. Carley filed a lawsuit in December 1994, calling for the registration's cancellation on a number of grounds, including Carley's prior use of "Gracie Jiu-jitsu" in Florida, and an alleged "secondary meaning" because the public associated the term with the entire Gracie family as a martial arts style. A San Francisco jury tried the case in November 1997. The verdict found that Gracie Jiu-jitsu was indeed more than a teaching style, it was a style of martial arts. The District Court ordered the USPTO to cancel Rorion's service mark registration. The style improved by Helio Gracie now belonged to the world.

Issues over the name withstanding, Rorion's attempt to popularize the art in the States had not worked out as he had hoped. After all, there was no reason to venture into someone's garage to learn martial arts when one could pick and choose from countless dojos promoting every flash-in-the-pan style from the Orient. While word of mouth attracted a small though loyal following, it would take a new spin on the old family tradition to reach the masses.

CHAPTER 3

The Gracie Challenge

I N 1982, ONE of Rorion Gracie's pupils ventured into a traditional karate school and bragged of jiu-jitsu's superiority – to put it simply, how his teacher could defeat their teacher. The karate instructor responded by issuing a challenge to Gracie, with $1,000 going to the winner. Gracie was more than happy to oblige, but the instructor backed out at the last minute. However, legendary kick-boxing champion Benny "The Jet" Urquidez was a close friend of the instructor, and agreed to take on Gracie instead.

Born into a fighting family (his father a boxer, his mother a pro wrestler), Urquidez shot up through the kickboxing ranks in the mid-1970s, capturing title after title. He also paved the way for Americans to test their skills in the Orient by becoming the first Westerner to beat the Japanese at their own game. Japanese audiences were so taken by his showy performances in the ring that Urquidez became a superstar. Though doubts surround his unblemished 58-0 record, there is no doubt The Jet is one of kickboxing's greatest legends. Rorion Gracie had no idea who he was.

Gracie and Urquidez met at the local YMCA in West Valley, California, where the kickboxer frequently taught.

"Do you want to do this on mats or the hardwood floor?" asked Urquidez.

"That depends," said Gracie, "Do you want to land on the mats or do you want to land on the hardwood floor?"

They both laughed; Urquidez pulled out some mats. It was not a real fight by any means, just a sparring session between masters of two arts. With no wager in place, Gracie took Urquidez down at will; he also made him tap several times. The kickboxer was amazed with what Gracie could do, but that wasn't the point of the exercise – it was to show how good jiu-jitsu was, not the person using it. To demonstrate further, Gracie matched his student against one of his opponent's top pupils, who was 40lbs heavier. It didn't matter. Just as Gracie had instructed him, the smaller man rushed Urquidez's muscular purple belt and quickly took him to the mat where, after a struggle, he made him tap with an ankle lock. The kickboxing legend was impressed and agreed to help spread the word about Brazilian – make that Gracie – Jiu-jitsu. Rorion wondered if this would finally be the answer to his problems.

A week passed, but there was still no word from Urquidez. After repeated calls, Gracie gave up. It seemed that every time he called, The Jet was too busy with something else. A few months later a documentary filmmaker contacted Gracie at his home and asked if he would contribute to a martial arts piece he was doing. The filmmaker was intrigued by the "challenge" angle and wanted to set up a fight between Gracie and a well-known kickboxer. As fate would have it, the kickboxer turned out to be ... Benny Urquidez. The kickboxer, realizing what was at stake, drove a hard bargain. According to the filmmaker, Urquidez would fight under the following conditions: five rounds of five minutes each, but if it went to the ground, they would have to be stood back up after 60 seconds. No matter the outcome, Gracie would have to pay Urquidez $100,000. If Urquidez lost, he would give Gracie his world championship kickboxing belt. "So I'm hiring him to fight me for $100,000," said Gracie. "What would I do with a world championship belt? I'm not a kickboxer." To level the playing field, Gracie made a counter-challenge: same number of rounds and time limits, but if the fight went to the ground, it stayed there. Urquidez would put up $75,000; Gracie would put up $100,000. If the fight went to a draw, Urquidez could keep the $100,000. The filmmaker was puzzled that Gracie would concede such an apparently unfair advantage to his opponent, but told him arrangements would be made. Gracie never heard back.

News of what transpired didn't necessarily bring flocks of students to his garage dojo, but it created more hype around the Gracie Challenge. In one such match, well-known tang soo do practitioner Ralph Alegria (winner of multiple championships in tournament play) fought Rorion Gracie in a ring. Alegria tapped in less than two minutes. A watching film producer was so impressed with Gracie's abilities, he asked for his help in choreographing the fight finale between Mel Gibson and Gary Busey in the 1987 blockbuster *Lethal Weapon*. Gracie worked with both actors for two months in preparation for the sequence, which included submissions. Gracie also worked with Rene Russo in *Lethal Weapon 3*, and had a small part in the film.

TWO MORE YEARS passed before Rorion Gracie got the break he was looking for. Well-respected freelance writer Pat Jordan was working on a story about an arm wrestler when his subject recommended Gracie, having worked out with him in his garage dojo. Jordan spent three days with the jiu-jitsu master. In September 1989, his lengthy article on an "unknown sports hero" appeared not in *Black Belt* or some other karate rag, but in the mass-selling *Playboy* magazine. Headlined "BAD," it called Rorion "the toughest man in the United States" and was a compelling account of his attempt to achieve the American dream through his father's legacy. It also declared that he would fight any man in the USA for $100,000, winner-takes-all.

The "Gracie Challenge" took on a life of its own. No longer was it a singular wager made with Urquidez; it was now something the Gracie family staked its entire reputation on. A slew of letters about the article poured into the *Playboy* office, and the martial arts community soon recognized the Gracie Challenge with a follow-up in *Karate Kung Fu Illustrated*. Rorion and his brothers suddenly had their hands full with new students and new challenges.

On the other side of Los Angeles, adman Arthur Davie kept the *Playboy* article for another reason. He worked for top advertising firm J & P Marketing, and was faced with the dilemma of finding an outlet to create brand awareness for Wisdom Imports' Tecate beer. Noting the beer's Mexican/Asian appeal, an extreme sport seemed logical, but the category manager didn't think highly of Davie's idea of using kickboxing or boxing events. With money and research invested in the project, a thick folder was all that was left, waiting for someone with initiative to act on it. Davie was no stranger to taking things into his own hands, as he had already built a reputation for creating spectacles out of his ad campaigns. He had made the May 1980 issue of *TV Guide* by playing a giant motorised zucchini for Honda, and had even jumped off a ten-story building for a television commercial promoting his San Diego auto dealership at the time.

Born in Brooklyn, Davie had dabbled in amateur boxing in his youth, and kept it up when he was drafted in the Marines during the Vietnam War. In 1969, a fellow soldier returned from a lengthy R-and-R session in Bangkok full of stories about mixed martial arts bouts he'd seen in nightclubs over there. It became a never-ending source of locker room fodder, wondering if Sugar Ray Robinson could have beaten Bruce Lee. More than two decades later, that thought still lingered in Davie's mind. Rorion Gracie's newly-acquired profile was about to bring that concept to fruition – in the United States.

Davie dropped by Gracie's new school in Torrance in the spring of 1990, only to find contractors milling about with younger brother Royce, and father Helio working on the juice bar. He left his card. Two weeks later, Davie was called and asked to come down. Though the school was unfinished, Davie was invited to a challenge match held that Saturday night. He didn't know what to expect, waiting attentively in a crowded room with everyone dressed in white gis. Suddenly the door opened and a horde of karate guys based in the gang-ridden LA suburb of Compton poured in. In typical good guy *versus* bad guy fashion, they wore black gis. Their karate instructor wanted to prove himself against one of Rorion's younger brothers, Royler, who weighed a nimble 155lbs. Davie watched in astonishment as Royler choked out his man two or three times. It was clear the karate practitioners didn't have a clue what was going on. Looking around the room, Davie spotted a vaguely familiar face, Hollywood director John Milius, one of Rorion's Tinseltown protégés. Davie was a big film buff, and he and Milius hit it off immediately. Before long, Davie was taking private classes from Gracie on Tuesday nights, right after Milius. On several occasions the three would sit around Gracie's office chatting about jiu-jitsu vs karate and every type of combination in between.

After leaving the advertising company in late 1991, Davie needed a new creative outlet, and agreed to help his newfound friend promote a videotape series called *Gracies in Action*. Each tape showed several fights, from black-and-white footage of Helio to recent challenge matches held in the Gracie dojo. Hapkido experts, wrestlers and so-called masters of every conceivable martial arts style barely had time to strike a pose before being taken to the ground and tapped out. It was uncanny. Davie came up with a hot direct mail scheme that soon had the orders piling up. "When I saw the reaction to the tape from fans, I said, 'Let me see if I can come up with something to create a show around this,'" said Davie. Rorion had been approached about such an event before but nothing had ever come of it. The thought of recreating what the Gracie family had done back in Brazil was more than appealing to Rorion; it was something always in the back of his mind.

Rorion remembered the time when he was ten years old in Brazil, watching vale tudo matches at home with his family on TV. There was one long, exhaustive match where one fighter sat in the corner on the ground while his opponent loomed over him. "The guy in the middle of the ring reaches his hand down, appearing as if to let the other guy up," said Gracie. "The guy sitting down reaches up to the friendly hand that has been extended. With his hand extended, the guy standing up grabs the other guy's hand and kicks him in the face on national television. Everybody at home went crazy from the excitement. This is the type of thing that I envisioned for what would become the UFC."

Davie put together a proposal for a competition called War of the Worlds, and he and Gracie were pitching it to John Milius in under a week. Milius, who scripted *Apocalypse Now* and directed Arnold Schwarzenegger's breakout picture *Conan the Barbarian*, was excited about the idea, so Davie gathered more research to firm up the project. He found that many US states did not have boxing commissions, something that might work in their favor, as it meant there was less chance that someone would raise awkward questions about safety and licensing. He also read up on the original pankration events from Ancient Greece. By October 1992, the concept had become a detailed plan. With Milius on board, it was time to see who would bite.

By January 1993, Davie had contacted numerous pay-per-view companies like TVKO and SET. Television exposure would be essential. But no one wanted to listen; no one understood what Davie was trying to sell. At that time, pay-per-view was not making the big money everyone had hoped. Shows were expensive to produce, since cable companies were taking 50 percent, with ten percent going to the distributor and 40 percent to the producer. This was also a difficult time for sports shows that had dominated pay-per-view, like boxing and professional wrestling. The latter came under a lot of scrutiny when steroid abuse allegations led to World Wrestling Federation owner Vince McMahon being put on trial. The heyday of boxing pay-per-view, the Mike Tyson era, was gone too, with Tyson languishing in jail for rape. People weren't interested anymore in shelling out a lot of money for one headliner and two or three no-name fights.

Davie found himself with one last alternative – the small but unconventional Semaphore Entertainment Group (SEG). Based on the East Coast, SEG was a joint venture between the giant Bertelsmann Music Group (BMG) and Robert Meyrowitz, who had made his name as the foremost producer of innovative radio programming. Once described as "a riverboat gambler who sinks formidable sums into promoting concerts and other entertainment programming," the avuncular Meyrowitz had worked with Hollywood icons and had created the *King Biscuit Flower Hour*, which became America's longest-running nationally syndicated radio series and a veritable "Who's Who" of rock music. He was also behind novelty sports events such as the "Battle of the Champions," an exhibition tennis match between Jimmy Connors and Martina Navratilova. Davie thought SEG was just the kind of progressive, freewheeling company that might go for the unusual. As he'd done with all the others he had pitched, Davie gathered copies of the *Playboy* article and the *Gracies in Action* tapes and sent them to SEG's main office in New York.

Luckily, maverick programmer Campbell McLaren intercepted them. McLaren, a former film student, wasn't interested in boxing, didn't like wrestling and didn't know much about music. But he saw pay-per-view as an appealing avenue for genres previously unexplored by commercial television. At the time, he had been toying with ideas ranging from the world's biggest demolition derby to Mexican pro wrestling because of its "superhero" charm. When the *Playboy* article crossed his desk, McLaren dismissed his other ideas. He had found what he was looking for.

David Isaacs, SEG's youthful vice-president of marketing and planning, was also trying to find the right business for the firm, since all of its pay-per-view events had barely turned a profit, if they made money at all. He was shown the tapes. "I remember seeing Rickson on the beach [a match with Hugo Duarte from *Gracies in Action 2*], and the office just filled up with people watching it," said Isaacs. "And you were like, 'Oh my gosh, I've never seen anything like this!'" On April 27, 1993, Davie received a fax from McLaren inviting him to New York to talk about his proposal for War of the Worlds. When he got there he found an enthusiastic McLaren trying to win over bossman Robert Meyrowitz. "He didn't know tae kwon do from moo goo gai pan," remembered Davie. "He wasn't sure what the hell we were talking about." But one thing was sure: Meyrowitz's track record with pay-per-view wasn't cutting the mustard. Fast approaching 50, he needed something as fresh as the *King Biscuit Flower Hour*, which had put SEG on the map in radio. He trusted McLaren enough to make the right choice and move forward with the project.

IN MAY 1993, Art Davie and Rorion Gracie founded WOW Productions in Colorado. Davie and Gracie each held 45 percent, but their limited liability company needed funds. A meeting was called, and 65 students of Gracie's academy were invited to hear more about the project. After everything was said and done, ten per cent ownership was given to 28 investors. Davie and Gracie only lent their expertise – nothing out of their wallets. Campbell McLaren was in attendance; at the conclusion of the meeting, Davie turned to him and said, "By the way, this isn't just a pipedream or hypothetical." McLaren eased the WOW investors by telling them that SEG was investing $400,000 into the first show, making it a done deal. Davie established the International Fighting Council one month later to act as the show's sanctioning body, since boxing commissions were ill-equipped to licence mixed martial arts.

The first event was slated for September 1993, with SEG Sports Corp, a wholly-owned subsidiary, and WOW working in tandem to plan the essentials. SEG had just scored big with a New Kids On The Block concert that became the highest-grossing pay-per-view entertainment event ever. But while that looked great on paper, it didn't mean SEG was the one making the money, said Isaacs. "We had been doing lots of music shows where there were a lot of difficult and legal aspects to doing those deals: working with artists, recording labels, and licensing content from third parties. From a business side, it [War of the Worlds] was very appealing. Instead of being a content licensor, we would be a content creator."

But what exactly was a veteran adman, a jiu-jitsu black belt, an action film director and a fledgling pay-per-view company supposed to create? Initially, War of the Worlds was to be a 16-man single-elimination tournament for a grand prize of $110,000 and the title "The World's Hand-to-Hand Combat Champion." SEG eventually agreed on an eight-man tournament and $50,000 prize money for the winner, with varying fees given to fighters for just showing up.

The fights would be held in a circular pit some 20 feet in diameter, to be designed by John Milius. He originally devised a pit with Greek structures surrounding it. That idea was thrown out, but a conventional boxing ring was out of the question too. Rorion pointed out that a ring could not contain the fighters in this type of combat. More often than not, they ended up falling through the ropes and onto the floor; the injuries sustained outside the ring might even be worse than those in it. Campbell McLaren suggested a completely open ring with a copper panel that would be electrified for effect, or a plexi-glass enclosure with barbed wire running along the top. "Then we had a doctor tell us that if anyone landed on it and was sweaty, it could cause ventricular imputation and someone could have a heart attack," remembered Davie. Trying to add a bit of gimmickry himself, Davie envisioned a crocodile-infested moat surrounding a pit. That idea was discarded for the sake of visibility.

Eventually, SEG contracted film set designer Jason Cusson, who brought reality back into the picture by establishing parameters agreeable to all parties. He outlined a cage concept, very similar to something Art Davie and Rorion Gracie had witnessed at an underground NHB show called Kage Kombat in Irvine, California. Though refinements were made, the octagon became one of the UFC's trademarks. Cusson would be credited as the show's art director. The chain-link fencing stood 5ft 6in tall and was 30 feet in diameter. Despite popular belief, the octagonal shape was not for the sake of theatrics but a design strong enough to support the action contained inside. SEG even tried to get Kage Kombat to stop using the format, but no dice – "From the Octagon Originator! Not the Imitator," became the B-show's slogan. Little did anyone realize the cage concept would become a fixture in other MMA events produced around the world.

The name of the show, War of the Worlds, was Davie's idea, but there were others. The World's Best Fighter was one that almost ended up being adopted. It was SEG's Michael Abramson who coined The Ultimate Fighting Championship. Abramson was a longtime promotion manager with companies such as Arista Records, a solid salesman whose job was to market SEG products to affiliates. "Ultimate tested very well because it implied that there was nothing beyond that," says Davie. The logo was actually inspired by a television commercial icon, Mr Clean, and represented a character of great power but no specific ethnicity.

Though SEG was hot on the project, it was still important to get Bertelsmann interested, since they would be fronting the money. Meyrowitz and McLaren met with their German partners at a ritzy Italian eatery in Manhattan. After three vodka martinis, Meyrowitz prodded his partner to go in for the kill.

"Oh yeah, it's like the martial arts," said McLaren. "It's kind of like you had Bruce Lee fight Muhammad Ali."

"But isn't Lee dead?" asked the Germans.

It took some time for both parties to get on the same playing field, but the Germans finally committed to the event despite not understanding what it was about. What they really wanted was for SEG to get rockers ZZ Top … but that would have to wait.

With everything else in place, it was time to pitch the show to cable companies. September became October due to logistical problems, and October became November when the Viewer's Choice distribution network needed a show rundown. But how do you present a show rundown for a live event? "We couldn't for the life of us project what the quarter-hour breakdowns were going to be like because we didn't really have a clue," says McLaren. That prompted the question, "How long are these fights going to last?" Rorion Gracie claimed that fights could go on for eight hours because it sometimes took jiu-jitsu a while to "cook" a guy. Davie, on the other hand, told McLaren that guys could get their heads ripped off. "What were they talking about? Eight hours, cooking … I couldn't follow," exclaimed McLaren. Since Viewer's Choice didn't quite know what it had, the final airdate was pushed back to November 12, 1993.

Deciding on where to hold the first event was not too difficult because it had to be at a venue with no boxing commission to interfere. Colorado was a logical choice, and would be the location for the first two events. In publicity terms, the "sport" aspect was never emphasized. The show was built on a simple premise: how various martial arts disciplines would fare against one another in a realistic contest with virtually no regulations. McLaren also liked the gimmick of a man in a gi using his skills to battle an opponent from an entirely different background. After all, martial arts competitions had traditionally been intramural: karate only fought karate, and so on. "I like to think I took this circus, this pseudo-gladiatorial atmosphere, and placed it on top of the Gracie Challenge," sums up McLaren.

SEG's three-shot deal of "different programming" was about to unfold. The first was controversial comic Andrew Dice Clay's No Apologies concert, the second was a horror/magic show featuring British heavy metal band Iron Maiden, and the third was the Ultimate Fighting Championship. Clay's show did extremely well, but Iron Maiden didn't catch on big with the American public: in a test screening, one of the senior members of BMG passed out upon seeing all the blood and gore in their stage act, supplied by the same team that had handled the *Hellraiser* movies. The show did find an audience overseas, but the real question would be if the UFC would find an audience at all.

With the particulars taken care of, it was time to scout for fighters. Over the course of several months, ads were placed in martial arts magazines calling for the best fighters in the world to test their skills against each other. All of the problems with point karate tournaments, all of the martial arts styles that weren't "sport-oriented" and, quite simply, all of the frauds that turned a tidy profit from peddling their watered-down arts were in for a big surprise ... the *ultimate* surprise.

CHAPTER 4

Recruiting an Ultimate Fighter

A RT DAVIE AND Rorion Gracie began their search for seven fighters to participate in the Ultimate Fighting Championship in June 1993. They already had one recruit. After all, someone had to represent the art of jiu-jitsu and, according to the *Playboy* article, the choice was obvious. Rickson Gracie was younger than his brother Rorion by eight years and his more muscular frame marked him out from the rest of the family. He was also acknowledged as the "champion" of the Gracies, having built his reputation competing in vale tudo matches in Brazil.

However, some months earlier Rickson had been forced to leave the Gracie Academy in Torrance after a disagreement with Rorion. Rorion learned of Rickson teaching students on the side, just as the Machados had done earlier. Rorion felt he needed to protect the name Gracie Jiu-jitsu, which represented not only an art but a way of teaching that art. This rift in the family created an unlikely warrior. With little time to prepare for the first UFC, Rorion turned to 27-year old Royce Gracie, a sibling who had remained loyal to both his professional and personal aspirations.

Royce had come to the US in 1985 at the age of 17, on an invitation from Rorion to babysit his children. Like his brothers, he had been taught jiu-jitsu since birth, and now found himself part of a famous fighting family. "It was so natural to watch them [train jiu-jitsu]; it would be stranger to see someone speaking Japanese than watching a fight," remembered Royce. Upon joining his brother in America, Royce also became an important partner in the family business. But he had to learn how to speak English first; the only words he could speak were "Stop!" and "Like this," a result of assisting Rorion in teaching jiu-jitsu. He watched a lot of *Sesame Street* and went to English class for six months. As Art Davie recalled, "He was just a nice kid from the gym who would go to his brother Rorion on Saturday afternoons to get spending money for his favorite hangouts at the beach." Royce was 6ft 1in, weighed under 180lbs and, with his handsome, unmarked face, looked little like the conventional image of a vicious bruiser. He participated in dojo challenges but had no professional fighting experience. Royce never saw his participation in the UFC as being anything more than doing what his older brother asked of him.

Rickson was less than happy. "It's my fight. I've been waiting for this all my life," he told Rorion when he heard of the event. But the decision had been made. Rickson ventured off to Japan to drum up interest for himself to compete, but came back one week later after finding that no one knew who he was. Swallowing his pride for the family, Rickson began training his brother. Royce stopped teaching and put all of his energy into a combination of running, swimming, weightlifting and, of course, lots of jiu-jitsu.

Though Rorion owned half of WOW, he left the day-to-day operations to Art Davie, whose task was simply to find martial artists willing to fight. Davie sent letters to anyone listed in a legitimate martial arts organization or directory he could muster. He found most potential prospects fell into one of two groups. The first group felt the very idea of a mixed tournament broke the martial arts code of using a style's skill for sport. After all, many martial arts schools never engaged the fighting aspect but merely taught when and how these skills could be used. They proffered self-discipline, honor, respect, pacifism, and varying Eastern philosophies as valid reasons for not competing in this type of forum. The other group simply believed their style was too deadly for fighting. "They had a lot of sparring, but not that much fighting experience," said Davie. "But their system and their guru told them they were the best, that they were deadly and people would die doing this." Neither group was willing to put years in the dojo on the line, but that didn't stop Davie from eventually rounding up his magnificent seven.

Making use of his old contacts in the defunct kickboxing/advertising tie-in, Davie was able to get in touch with kickboxer Patrick Smith through Karyn Turner. Turner, the top female martial artist of 1974, had subsequently moved into promoting martial arts events. Her kickboxing promotions in Colorado with Coors beer as a sponsor were well known in the US. Smith had recently won the heavyweight championship of the Sabaki Challenge, a kyokushinkai karate event (no punching to the face). As a youngster, his only martial arts experience had been mimicking the moves of his idol Bruce Lee. In successfully using these techniques against schoolyard bullies, 13-year-old Smith caught the attention of a school security guard who was a master of an African martial art called Robotae. This was the beginning of Smith's formal training. He later earned a third degree black belt in Robotae, a first degree black belt in tae kwon do and competed in various events. At 6ft 2in and 217lbs, he had an overall win-loss record of 17-2 and was ranked seventh by the World Kickboxing Commission. He had also been working with the late Bobby Lewis, a boxing trainer who had turned ex-con Ron Lyle into a heavyweight contender who lost to Ali for the world title and gave George Foreman all he could handle in a memorable brawl. Smith's mean-spirited reputation for roughing up his opponents and even referees made him a shoo-in for the event.

To highlight the contrasts within martial arts, it was imperative to get a sumo wrestler, a man of enormous size and strength. Davie initially garnered the interest of Matsui Fata, a reigning champion from the Juryo Division of the Japanese Sumo Federation, but money became an issue and he was soon discarded. Davie eventually found Telia Tuli (*aka* Taylor Wiley, his Anglo name) via John Jacques of the American Sumo Association. Tuli, who hailed from Honolulu, made a better match for the UFC, partly because he had been thrown out of several dojos for behavioral problems. He was the first non-Japanese to win the all-Japan collegiate sumo championships and earned a slot in the Makushita Class of the Japanese Pro Sumo Association. He was also 6ft 2in and weighed a monstrous 410lbs. Tuli was paid a $5,000 premium for his participation.

While sumo, karate and professional wrestling were all popular in Japan, it was hard to classify the Universal Wrestling Federation. It was not the predordained comic book theatrics of an American pro wrestling promotion (known in the business as a "work"); much of the action looked real (termed a "shoot"). Maverick wrestler Akira Maeda had made the UWF a success in 1988 after a failed attempt years earlier, but in 1991 part of the organization broke off into Yoshiaki Fujiwara's PWFG (Professional Wrestling Fujiwara Gumi—*gumi* means group). Fujiwara had trained extensively under the tutelage of Karl Gotch, one of the original foreign talents to become a star in Japanese pro wrestling. Gotch was known as a hooker, describing his real – as opposed to faked – submission techniques. He taught this shoot style of wrestling to several of Japan's top pro wrestlers, becoming known more for his training than his wrestling exploits. The UWF style evolved from more realistic pro wrestling to very stiff-worked matches, meaning they would have predetermined endings but would "shoot" for position. Wrestlers sold their punishment to the audience and took frequent bruises, but the UWF was still a "worked" event. Frequently, "real" fighters competed for added hype, and Maeda wanted non-Japanese to be part of the crew. Masami "Sammy" Soranaka, the husband of Gotch's daughter, was the perfect man for the job since he lived in Tampa, Florida, and could recruit fighters from there.

In 1990, a professional wrestler of a different kind crossed paths with Soranaka. Kenneth Wayne Shamrock was a muscular all-American athlete who had been fashioned by his adoptive father Bob into a money-making enterprise. Shamrock competed in toughman contests and every other type of ruffian sport as an outlet for his aggressive nature. By the age of 21, he was bored with construction jobs, so his father suggested that he try pro wrestling. He joined the small-time circuit of the South Atlantic Professional Wrestling Association, among others, and rubbed shoulders with numerous wrestlers vying for a chance at the big time. Assuming the stage name Vince Torelli, Shamrock enjoyed only minor success, making as little as $50 a match when it cost more to drive to the venues, but the up-and-comer did have his share of great tag team partners, including Dean Malenko, a second-generation wrestler whose famous father was the "Great Malenko."

Shamrock's pro wrestling career was threatened when he had a run-in with another tag team, aptly named the Nasty Boys. They were moving to a larger organization and had little regard for the small-time players they were leaving behind. After a brief skirmish in a bar with Shamrock, the two Nasty Boys jumped him from behind in a neighboring hotel room later that night. Shamrock was beaten unconscious and suffered serious facial injuries, busted ribs and a broken sternum. The experience was a wake-up call: as he lay in a hospital bed the next morning, he knew he was lucky to be alive. Malenko might be his ticket to the East. "Soranaka was working out of Malenko's school, so obviously they were getting pro wrestlers and getting guys who were tough, teaching that style and bringing them to Japan," said Shamrock. "Malenko knew that I had a reputation for being tough ... so he showed me some tapes and thought I would be good at that." Shamrock was intrigued by the idea of learning something new and caught a plane to Tampa. He made his Japanese pro wrestling debut during the final months of the UWF in 1990, before joining up with Fujiwara and PWFG.

Shamrock fought several times for PWFG before that company split and pro wrestlers Masakatsui Funaki and stablemate Minori Suzuki formed Pancrase Hybrid Wrestling in early 1993. Wayne Shamrock, as he was now known, followed them. Funaki was tired of having to "put over" [deliberatley lose] to old-timers and yearned for the chance to put his skills to use in authentic matches. Karl Gotch came up with the name Pancrase, since the organization promoted itself as doing shoots, hence pankration. "You saw the change [in Pancrase] as opposed to earlier matches [in UWF] because they all ended rather quickly," said

Shamrock. Instead of systematically changing position for excitement, Shamrock defeated Funaki by choke at 6:15 in the first Pancrase event held in September 1993. He fought in one other Pancrase match before another fighter, Scott Bessac, told Shamrock about the UFC.

At first, he believed the show was an American aberration of the UWF, and had his doubts: "I thought they were definitely going to tell us we couldn't do [certain moves] or ask me to put some guy over, and I definitely would have told them that I would walk. So I was waiting for that to happen and fully expecting for the fight not to go on." But after making a call to Art Davie, Shamrock agreed, filled out an application, and sent it in. With his chiseled build and potential "hero" status, it didn't take long for Shamrock to be made one of Davie's elite eight. Still unsure if the event was going to take place, Shamrock fought in one more Pancrase match just three days before the UFC.

THANKS TO A press release that Rorion Gracie had sent out, Dutch gym owner Johan Vocsh learned of the event and had several karate players and kickboxers to pick from for a slot in the first UFC. None was interested in fighting outside his sport, however, except for Gerard Gordeau. Tall and balding, Gordeau was nearing the end of his career, having participated in competitions for over two decades. In 1988, he had even fought in a supposedly legit MMA bout in Japan against Akira Maeda for the UWF. At the time, Gordeau had competed only in karate tournaments, so he didn't have much experience fighting with gloves on. When he arrived in Japan, he was told to wear boxing gloves, while Maeda fought bare-fisted. Gordeau knocked Maeda out, but an extended count and numerous stops by the ref allowed Maeda to recover and eventually gain the upper hand, and he submitted Gordeau by leg lock. The Dutchman had learned his first lesson in groundfighting.

At 6ft 5in and 215lbs, Gordeau had a sleek build and solid martial arts credentials. He was Dutch Karate Champion from 1978 to 1985, and earned sixth place in the World Championship Karate competition held in Osaka, Japan, in 1991. Gordeau's primary style was savate or French kickboxing (without knee strikes). In savate competition, he had swept top European honors from 1988 to 1991 and had taken the World Championship in 1992. With a 27-4 fight record, he was one tough customer: Gordeau was often hired as a bodyguard and bouncer for illegal raves held around Europe, and also worked security for the underground porn business. He cites his lack of schooling (he had only five years total in grade school) and his knack for throwing a punch as reasons why he made fighting a chosen profession. Whether in the ring or on the street, Gordeau enjoyed fighting, and didn't care where he did it.

An advertisement in a run-of-the-mill martial arts mag attracted the attention of kickboxer Kevin Rosier. Rosier was a super-heavyweight in every sense, and had won several titles in kickboxing, though many were one-shot deals. "These guys would make you fight for nothing in one of their bullshit shows, promising you would get paid more for the next one," said Rosier. "Then the show would fold and I'd just throw the belt in the trash." From the age of six, he had accumulated numerous black belts in varying karate systems and Chinese forms and had fought in over 200 competitions. He retired in 1990 and found work as a bouncer and bodyguard for pop acts such as Debbie Harry and Billy Idol. Over the course of three years working some of the toughest clubs from New Orleans to New York, Rosier ballooned to a staggering 345lbs. Still, he phoned Davie and Rorion Gracie and barraged them with questions about the event. They knew who he was and didn't seem to care that he was a "little" overweight.

The only fighter Rorion recommended for the event (aside from his own brother) was Zane Frazier, a meaty, 6ft 5in kempo (an Oriental martial art) stylist. Frazier had been studying martial arts since 1980 and had been fighting for just as long. He held a fourth degree black belt in kempo and had even had the chance to study with the late Ed Parker, the father of American kempo karate. Rorion had seen Frazier take an opponent to the ground in a scuffle that ensued during a Long Beach karate tournament. Impressed that a "karate guy" knew groundfighting, Rorion sent Royce and Art to check him out at a local martial arts expo. Frazier was not there to muck it up with fellow martial artists; he went to seek out an old nemesis – Frank Dux, the man who "inspired" the movie *Bloodsport*.

As the kickboxing craze died out in the early 1990s, Frazier had needed to make some money, so a friend (Mr Tae Bo himself, Billy Blanks) introduced him to Dux, who was coming off the success of *Bloodsport* – based on the allegedly true story of his participation in a secret fighting tournament, the Kumite, held in the Bahamas in 1975. While the movie became a guilty pleasure for much of the martial arts community, its source material was mere hyperbole. However, it enabled Dux to build a promising school that needed an instructor with more time on his hands than its owner. A deal was worked out between the two, but fell apart when Dux reneged. Frazier opened up a neighboring school and took his students with him, only to face alleged death threats over the phone.

So when Frazier confronted Dux at the expo, the bad blood came to a head. Dux tried to push him away but a quick exchange of punches and kicks gave Frazier the upper hand. Royce Gracie was there to see it, while Art Davie bore witness to the aftermath. "Wow! You are definitely in the UFC. Hell, I don't need to see anymore," said Davie. "You beat the *Bloodsport* guy!"

Dux subsequently sued Frazier for the attack and the Century Plaza Hotel (where the expo was held) for failing to prevent it. The case dragged on for three years and ultimately exposed the fraudulence of Dux's claims. In fairness, he did have a martial arts background, but his vivid imagination and unbelievable fighting claims caught up with him. Frazier claimed to have found school records proving that Dux could not have been in the US, in the military, and learning to be a ninja while fighting in over 365 matches all at once. After Dux faked a seizure and postponed a deposition for not admitting to "being a fraud," according to Frazier, a court order finally made him come forward. "Frank Dux goes into the deposition and says, 'I talked to my master's second in command and if I reveal any information, my family will be killed, I will be killed and everyone in this room will be killed if I reveal anything about *Bloodsport*, the Kumite and my secret training as a ninja,'" said Frazier. Despite these ridiculous and melodramatic goings-on, Dux walked away with a half million dollars from the Century Plaza, while Frazier was absolved without further duress. Dux later authored a book entitled *The Secret Man* about his alleged career in the CIA. *Soldier of Fortune* magazine penned an article using overwhelming evidence to prove that Dux lived in a fantasy world.

IF THERE WAS to be a tournament to decide the best fighter, no style qualified more than boxing. The "sweet science" was the largest mainstream fighting sport *per se*, and many felt a boxer could knock out a martial artist with ease. The difficulty was in finding a boxer ranked in the top ten who would be willing to fight under something other than Queensberry Rules. An exhaustive search turned up notables such as James "Bonecrusher" Smith and Leon Spinks, both former heavyweight champions, but money or age proved to be insurmountable hurdles. Enter Ernest Hart Jr, former middleweight karate champion of the 1970s, who wanted to be part of the UFC any way he could. Though too old to compete himself, Hart thought that, by getting a fighter into the event, he might have a shot at announcing. Hart contacted "King" Arthur Jimmerson, a fellow St Louis native, who didn't really know what to make of the event. Jimmerson was no slouch, having been named in *Ring* magazine's fight of the year in 1988 with his KO of Lenny LaPaglia at Madison Square Garden. That win also made him the World Boxing Council's tenth-ranked cruiserweight contender. Add to that a list of impressive sparring partners, an exhibition with kickboxing Hall of Famer Don "The Dragon" Wilson, and a record of 29-5, and Jimmerson was in the show. Little did anyone know, however, that Jimmerson had recently hit paydirt when a friend who came into a lot of money made him a salaried employee at $100,000 a year, and had stopped training. He did need a fight, though, as he was scheduled for a match with Thomas "Hit Man" Hearns just a month after the UFC.

The grand prize was $50,000. The fighters would get $1,000 to show, and purses would increase as winners advanced. The total prize money was $110,000, with extra funds logged in for "commercial purposes". When he realized the lack of rules, Jimmerson backed out of the event for fear of getting hurt and possibly ruining his boxing career. After some tricky negotiating, he was offered over $20,000 just to show up, win or lose. That was the same amount he would earn for the Hearns fight, so without another thought, Jimmerson was back.

ALL OF THE fighters were required to arrive a week before showtime to acclimatize to Denver's mile-high altitude and to promote the event. As most viewers wouldn't know the fighters, Rorion Gracie wanted a name that people would recognize. He called Chuck Norris and asked him to commentate, but the TV star doubted the event would come off and declined. Instead, SEG and WOW secured Bill "Superfoot" Wallace and Kathy Long, two heavyweights in the martial arts world, to fill the bill. American football legend Jim Brown was added for good measure as a replacement for the too-expensive Marvin Hagler, the former middleweight boxing champ. To officiate the event, Rorion secured two veteran referees from the Jiu-jitsu Federation of Rio de Janeiro.

Fighters, trainers, fans, managers, and journalists showed up one by one at the Executive Tower Inn, not knowing what lay in store, much less who was supposed to fight. The day before the show, everyone convened at the Brahms conference room of the hotel to go over the rules. Most of them thought the event was "no rules" but that wasn't strictly true. Fighters would be allowed to wear clothing according to their style. In a strange rule-making anomaly, Rorion instructed that six-ounce boxing gloves were required if the fighter's usual art employed closed-fist strikes to the head; otherwise, bare knuckles were permitted. Everything else was allowed with the exception of eye gouging, biting and groin strikes. There would be five rounds of five minutes, divided by one-minute breaks. There would be no judges – no one thought the fights would go past the first round.

It was then announced that hand wraps could not be used. A wrap protects the wrist and the hand from injury, and so would favor the punchers, but Rorion allowed the wrap to be used just below the knuckles only. This launched a debate between Rorion and fighter Zane Frazier. "This is bullshit, because you are setting us up to fail by taking everything away the night before the fight," stormed Frazier. The kempo fighter had every reason to be upset. "My coaches told me that they could stop fights on cuts, so we should wrap my hands in such a way that they could act as razor blades," he said. Rorion asked if someone said something bad about Frazier's mother, would he run home and wrap his hands before fighting that person on the street? The room erupted in laughter, but Frazier was not amused, and contended to start the UFC one day early. Then the biggest man in the competition stood up. "Listen man, I came here to fight!" All eyes followed sumo wrestler Telia Tuli as he lumbered to the back of the room, signed a waiver, and left, saying, "I fight anyone who wants to fight. See you tomorrow." It was one of the few times anyone saw or heard Tuli before the event; he just sat in his hotel room and ordered plate after plate of food, according to Art Jimmerson.

The meeting in the conference room was the first time everyone saw each other. Kevin Rosier had recently had a tooth pulled; he was shot up with Novocain and sat there in a daze. Gordeau never uttered a word, having only arrived a day before via a 24-hour plane trip. Frazier played conspiracy theorist. Jimmerson had already decided Ken Shamrock would be the man to sweep the tournament when he caught him working out earlier that day. Shamrock had merely been trying to loosen up after an exhaustive flight from Tokyo to Denver the night before. Royce Gracie, the smallest fighter of the group, remained calm, pleasant – and seemed utterly unthreatening.

With all the hype, and all the experience these men brought to the table, only the following night could answer the boundless questions on everyone's mind. Would a man with 30 years of martial arts experience be able to fight for real under such conditions? Would size and strength matter? Would someone die? One thing was clear: these ten men (two alternates would fight for a shot in the next tournament) were about to change the way the world viewed martial arts forever.

CHAPTER 5

Showtime

O N NOVEMBER 12, 1993, the stage was set for the first Ultimate Fighting Championship. No one knew what was going to happen. As exterior shots of Denver rolled across televisions in homes across America, commentator Bill Wallace introduced the public to the "Ultimate Fighting *Challenge*." Wallace not only got the name of the event wrong, he did everything from belching into the mike to saying, "You could say it's an octagonal octagon." He also mispronounced several names, including announcer Rich "The G Man" Goins, whom he renamed "Ron" four times. There had been some controversy as to who would do the play-by-play, but the original UFC press materials listed Wallace, Kathy Long, and Jim Brown as color commentators. The veteran kickboxer ended up doing the job (something typically reserved for seasoned public speakers, yet this was Wallace's first time). If Wallace seemed unprepared, so was everyone else.

The first match of the evening pitted Tuli against Gordeau, the most extreme clash of styles the event had to offer. Tuli made his way to the octagon dressed in a flowery Samoan garb. Gordeau then entered and made an astonishing gesture: he turned to all four corners of the ring and, with the TV cameras on him, gave what appeared to be a series of Nazi salutes. It was an uncomfortable moment, especially given the partnership between Germany's BMG and SEG's Jewish president, Robert Meyrowitz. Gordeau, smothered in tattoos and sporting a bald, pale head, looked like an Aryan Nation poster boy. Yet he was actually giving the salutation for his art of savate. "I'm Jewish too … all my family were killed in World War Two by the Germans," he later said.

Tuli barreled toward his lofty matador and absorbed several punches to the head. Moving out of the way, Tuli then flopped to the ground, and before he could rise Gordeau planted a well-executed roundhouse kick to his face, launching a tooth into the crowd. The

Dutchman followed up with a looping right hand that connected hard and the ref stopped the action even as the bloody, confused Tuli motioned for the match to continue. A doctor called the fight off, Tuli left with blood and tears in his eyes, and the crowd had witnessed a *Streetfighter 2* game gone awry. It was all over in just 26 seconds.

As the commentators tried to make light of the quick finish, Kevin Rosier and Zane Frazier prepared for war. Rosier's hooded cloak was removed as he entered the octagon, revealing a physique that looked less than battle-ready. "He sent us this great press kit and then shows up seventy-five pounds overweight," remarked Campbell McLaren. "I saw Rosier in the gym with a pizza and a Heineken." Despite more than 50 years of martial arts experience between the two, their match looked more like a street fight between barflies than a technical exhibition between athletes. Rosier scurried clumsily at Frazier and clobbered him with a right hand, which sent them both to the ground. The fight went back and forth, until a game Rosier landed enough haymakers, dropping the kempo stylist down for the count. But there was no count. "I stomped on his head, but I pulled back like professional wrestling and put it [his foot] down so it looked more dramatic," said Rosier. "I could have driven my heel into the lower part of his spine and crippled the guy." Frazier's handlers knew when to quit and threw in the towel after the second stomp.

Sitting five rows back was boxer Art Jimmerson. He could not believe the brutality; it was unlike anything he had ever seen. Not only had he not trained for the event, he had hardly given it a thought. He had come with a large entourage, including his wife and cousin, but hadn't bothered to bring gloves. His doubts first surfaced when he entered the hotel, and heard stories about what the Gracies were capable of: "Don't get Royce mad or he'll break a limb," said one of the refs. Art Davie's kid brother managed to scrounge up a pair of eight-ounce gloves for him as the event started, but as Jimmerson walked from his seat to the backstage area to prepare, boxing gloves were the least of his worries.

As Jimmerson entered the changing area, Kevin Rosier was popping his jaw back into place. It was clearly broken. Zane Frazier was on a stretcher heading for a nearby hospital; unbeknown to everyone, he had suffered a severe asthma attack during his fight and couldn't breathe unaided after returning to the dressing room. What Jimmerson saw next was truly hard to believe. Doctors were trying to remove two of Tuli's teeth that were embedded in Gerard Gordeau's foot. They decided it would be better to leave the teeth in for the rest of the night for fear of exposing the wound anymore. On top of that, Gordeau's hand was broken in several places. Yet the savate champion, cigarette dangling from his mouth, showed no signs of quitting and had blocked the pain out of his mind.

Seeing all four men injured to various degrees was more than Jimmerson could handle. "Finally my managers came over to me and said, 'This is what we're going to do: go in there, and at the first sign of trouble, we're throwing in the towel,'" he later recalled. After all, Jimmerson's payday was locked in no matter what, so why should he risk injury?

Of the next two combatants, Royce Gracie was the first to the octagon, led by the Gracie train of Rickson, Royler, Relson, father Helio and others. "It's kind of ironic that Royce Gracie is going to wear his judo top," said Wallace, a further sign of his ignorance. The audience erupted at Gracie's introduction, while Jimmerson walked down the aisle sporting only one glove. Art Davie sat in a van outside, watching the monitor. "I almost went ballistic," he recalled. "What the fuck was he doing? What was this one glove shit?" Jimmerson's goal was to dance around for five minutes, make it to the second period and give the audience a show. Wearing a token glove was his idea, a pointless one since he was going to lie down for Royce.

Until the night of the show, no one had known who they were fighting. The brackets were left up to Art Davie, who juggled the card several times. Gracie and Shamrock were the two main variables, since he felt they were the strongest competitors. "My first match was supposed to be with Royce Gracie," remembered Gerard Gordeau, "but when I got to Denver, all the Japanese Press came to me and made pictures, and SEG asked, 'Who is that guy?' And [the Japanese] said this Gordeau was very dangerous and had a lot of fights in Japan." Gordeau believes his fight with Gracie was switched because of this, but according to all the fighters and Davie, the match-ups were changed several times.

In contrast to the previous fighters, Jimmerson and Gracie took a minute to feel each other out. The crowd groaned. "I waited and waited and he didn't come in to take the initiative, so I stepped on it," said Gracie. Without one punch thrown, the Brazilian took Jimmerson down and worked his magic. Moving into position, he headbutted the boxer to show he meant business. Jimmerson tapped, indicating surrender. Unseen by the referee, his corner had also thrown in the towel as soon as Jimmerson went to the ground, but it caught on the octagon fence. The ref was so surprised by the boxer's sudden action that he asked him if he wanted to continue. He didn't; the charade was over. Jimmerson walked away as rich as if he had lost in the finals. The boxer went on to squander his winnings, quit training, and lose most of his remaining fights. He currently works for Pepsi Cola and firmly believes the UFC cost him his career because the easy paycheck stripped him of motivation.

Kickboxer Patrick Smith against pro wrestler Ken Shamrock looked like the best match of the night. To make things even more exciting, their respective records had been beefed up. Smith now sported an unbelievable 250-0 record, and though Shamrock had only three "real fights" in anything but toughman contests, he was credited with two dozen wins. Since Pancrase was so new and he had beaten founder Funaki, Shamrock was named the number one shootfighting champion of Japan. The crowd didn't know any better and seemed happy to buy into these loaded resumes, especially that of hometown Colorado boy Smith.

What was not embellished was their dislike for one another. As Shamrock, his father and accompanying crew walked toward the entrance, Smith and an army of followers were waiting for them, dressed in black and red. They taunted Shamrock with, "You're going down! He's going to fucking kill you!" The kickboxer stared down his opponent, who didn't want to start trouble for fear of his father getting hurt in a melee. But as they moved past each other, Shamrock turned to Smith and said, "I'll see you in the ring."

With the fight underway, Smith got off one kick before Shamrock took him to the ground. Smith clung to Shamrock's underside and landed several kidney shots with the balls of his feet before the wrestler set him up and went for an ankle lock. After a brief moment of desperation, Smith screamed out in agony, violently tapping the mat with both hands. Like a lion with its kill, Shamrock had to be pulled away. "It wasn't satisfying enough that he tapped out, because he was still talking, so I didn't want to end it there," says Shamrock. "I wanted to keep going. The satisfying thing would have been to nail him in the mouth and beat on him." Smith had said earlier that his strength was his toughness, but all of the talk outside the ring couldn't save him from a kind of fight he knew little about. The crowd voiced its disapproval with profanity-laden chants. They thought their hometown favorite had been part of a fix. The absence of a large-screen monitor also prevented more than half of the 4,000 in attendance from seeing what was going on at all. Since much of the action took place on the ground, the audience's blocked view became a problem.

THE FIRST SEMI-FINAL pitted Gordeau against Rosier, with both men deserving nods for coming out with injuries. Rosier tried his patented caveman technique but it was no match for Gordeau, who produced a classic one-two combination followed by a powerful leg kick. Gordeau did this twice more, then engaged Rosier with a flurry of punches and elbows. The attack was so profuse that at one point Rosier sat down with both hands over his head. Unlike in boxing, with its eight-count, the referee let it go and, just as Rosier had done to Frazier, Gordeau began stomping. Rosier instantly tapped out and the ref stopped any further punishment. Rosier had said earlier that his strategy was to let his opponent hit him; it worked a little too well.

It was now time for the two best grapplers to mix it up. Both Gracie and Shamrock had scored very easy wins over their opponents. Shamrock thought Gracie was just another guy in a gi who practised katas: "I understood that they did some stuff on the ground, but it looked pretty slow and boring to me and it didn't look like it was effective." Though Shamrock came into the tournament not really knowing what to expect, he felt his submission training and natural athletic ability would enable him to best any man that night. And to anyone watching, it looked like a mismatch. Gracie was giving up size and strength to an opponent who knew about submission.

However, Gracie wasted no time in rushing Shamrock to get him to the ground. Shamrock positioned Gracie just as he had Smith, but the jiu-jitsu fighter followed his lead. The wrestler went for the ankle lock. Unfazed, Gracie moved with him and when Shamrock tried for the ankle again, it was too late. The Brazilian was able to get Shamrock's neck from behind and applied a rear choke. Shamrock tapped immediately but, as Gracie let go, the referee came up to them and ordered, "Fight." Shamrock grabbed the ankle again. "I didn't know what was going on. I was just reacting," he said. Gracie moved back into position. "That's when I went to his ear," said Gracie later, "and told him, 'You tapped. You tapped, Ken.'" There was no doubt that Shamrock had tapped or admitted to tapping, and the match was over. Gracie's jiu-jitsu was foreign to Shamrock's experience of grappling and, with this win, the crowd had a new hero – the small man who was able to beat the big man, plain and simple. Almost as if he had forgotten what he'd said about his match with Smith being too easy, Shamrock told the post-fight interviewer, "I'm just not used to this kind of stuff."

People have since wondered why Ken Shamrock, a man of submissions, would give his back to Royce Gracie and allow him to apply a choke with ease. Shamrock and the Japanese fighters had learned from wrestler Karl Gotch and, since the UWF was a worked organization, "they didn't emphasize chokes because it was entertainment and the action had to continue, so moving from arm bars to leg locks to rope escapes would be much more exciting than getting a guy's throat and choking him," said Shamrock. When he moved into Pancrase, chokes became more prevalent, but Shamrock didn't spend much time on them and never expected to fall victim to one. He really didn't understand the gi either and said that was how Gracie choked him, not his arm. "You're looking at adding a foot to two feet on a choke, because the position he was in with me going for the leg lock had that gi wrapped around my neck. Now without that gi, I end up with the leg lock." The rules had clearly stated shoes were not allowed if the fighter wanted to kick because they would be weapons. Ken argued a gi was a weapon too.

BEFORE THE FINALS, a qualifying match provided the audience with the type of action they had expected all along. Kung fu stylist Jason DeLucia squared off against kempo exponent Trent Jenkins to decide a slot in the next tournament. Both gave flashy performances, with well-executed high kicks. DeLucia ultimately took Jenkins to the ground and applied a rear naked choke that ended the fight. Rod Machado, a Gracie student working as commentator, called it a classic Gracie choke, as if the move was unique.

It certainly got the crowd going. As fights broke out in the audience, Jim Brown commented, "This is probably the most alive audience I've ever seen. In fact, I'm a little worried." The crowd didn't let up while a presentation was made by the Gracies to honor father Helio as the first Ultimate Fighter. Helio spoke a few words in Portuguese before it was time to see if the striker or the grappler would be crowned as the Ultimate Fighting Champion.

For the last match of the night, a visual for "round one" rolled across the television screen, signaling for the first time these fights actually had rounds. With a bandaged foot (the teeth still embedded) and broken hand, Gerard Gordeau could barely move, much less fight. He didn't get off a strike before Gracie took him to the ground. "The doctor went to the Gracie camp and told them that I broke my hand and foot and because Gracie knew everything, he blocked the good side of my body … you only see him grab my left side," said Gordeau. After a few punches had softened him up, Gordeau rolled to his stomach and solemnly whispered a string of expletives. The Dutchman felt he had been had and was angry that the "Gracie Mafia" ran the event. Gracie applied the rear naked choke, forcing Gordeau to tap not only the mat, but Gracie's arm. He wouldn't let go, because Gordeau had played a bit of funny business. "He got a piece of my ear," said Gracie.

"He didn't take a piece off, but he bit my ear and I had to pull it out of his teeth. He was trying to bite it, but it just got scratched and bled a little bit." Gracie finally let up and, as he pulled away, the blood on his ear was visible. For his part, Gordeau would need lengthy treatment in Holland for the injury he suffered kicking out Tuli's teeth: "I had to spend nine weeks in bed, and they had a drain stuck in my foot to clean it with water every hour to prevent infection for fear of blood poisoning."

Royce Gracie complained to the official about Gordeau for a few seconds, then began to celebrate, as his family clambered into the octagon. Soon he had a medal around his neck (inscribed *Per Aspera Ad Astra* meaning Through Adversity to the Stars) and a check for $50,000. Like it or not, the world embraced a different kind of martial arts superstar that night. And, despite all of the problems, the show was a tremendous success. Perhaps the concept was not entirely new, but it was new to the public, and the polish and mainstream access of the event would have the single greatest impact on the martial arts since Bruce Lee. It would be the first chapter of a legacy that even the creators behind the UFC never envisioned.

CHAPTER 6

Battle of the Styles

SEG HELD THE reins to what one pay-per-view analyst called "the first breakout franchise hit." Yet no one knew why. It had no promotion on mainstream television, no regular advertising, no on-screen build-up to its events. "The UFC succeeded without television," said pro wrestling expert David Meltzer. "When I look back at that period, there is no reason that the UFC should have ever made it." Certainly in answering the compelling question of who was the greatest martial artist, the UFC held an advantage over kickboxing, pro wrestling and toughman contests, all of which had no chance without some sort of cross-coverage on the major networks. And, at $14.95 a pop, the pay-per-view income stream promised to be substantial. To keep the momentum going, it was time to develop the sequel.

Art Davie had struggled to find martial artists to compete in the first show, but received 246 applications for the follow-up. This time he had the luxury of turning people down. "I remember this recluse from Alaska by the name of Cunningham. He sent me these pictures with him posing as if he were a monk by a river, claiming he had a death touch. I had a lot of guys who seemed more incredible than real." Many felt the first UFC's combatants had been over-the-hill veterans who didn't best represent their styles. The April 1994 issue of *Black Belt* magazine came out just before the airing of UFC II with an article entitled "Shotokan, Taekwondo and Kung Fu Challenge Jujutsu," describing how masters of these arts would dismantle Royce Gracie's techniques with their own traditional moves. The martial arts community felt Gracie deserved respect but pointed out that many arts had not been represented at all. Davie got the message, and put together a motley list of pure styles to battle it out.

With so many worthy competitors, Davie unilaterally made the decision to have a 16-man tournament, unbeknown to SEG president Bob Meyrowitz. It would throw out all of the timings for the scheduled TV slot: the preliminary round started two hours before the pay-per-view broadcast. Meyrowitz was furious when he arrived, to see his first show in person, in Denver on March 11, 1994. "We went through with it because that was the kind of organization we were," said David Isaacs. "A lot of other organizations would have just told the other guys to get back on a plane and go home." There were a total of 18 competitors, ranging from an 18-year-old tae kwon do practitioner (Sean Daugherty) to a 39-year-old karate stylist (Johnny Rhodes). Patrick Smith and Jason DeLucia returned from the first show, as did Royce Gracie, to prove BJJ was no fluke. Over ten different styles, including ninjutsu, pencak silat and sambo, were represented to quiet the naysayers.

To improve on the first show, changes were made. Rounds were out, since no fight had made it past five minutes. Matches were to be decided by drawing lots to prevent bias. "After listening to all the debate after the [first] show, with all the letters to the editor at *Black Belt* … saying that strikers were handicapped by rules like no groin shots, I pushed Rorion [who didn't like the idea] and SEG to allow them in," said Davie. "I felt that they [groin shots] answered the karate segment, which trained to use them. I thought that wearing a steel cup would minimize the real damage. Campbell loved the dramatic barbarism of allowing them, as he was still in the grip of no-rules fever." The Brazilian referees were not invited back; it had seemed that in one fight they stopped the action too soon, while in another they acted as if the man on the losing end was learning a lesson. The UFC II rulebook stated that outside interference would be kept to an absolute minimum and that only the fighter or his corner could end the match.

Bill Wallace did not return as commentator. Almost immediately after his UFC experience, Wallace slammed the show and said in a *Black Belt* column that it was bad for martial arts. "His column came out so quickly that he must have written it the day after the event and got it rushed in," said former UFC scribe Clay McBride. "I thought that was very disingenuous. Wallace had to knock this thing down immediately because it was not what he was teaching on the circuit. He knew this would impact him in his pocketbook." A tabloid war began between Wallace and the UFC. Art Davie hit back through letters in *Black Belt*, while McBride even suggested a charity match between himself and Wallace to *Black Belt* editor Jim Coleman. McBride, who wrote a column called Reality Check for *Inside Kung Fu*, was willing to put his limited jiu-jitsu experience under Rorion Gracie to the test. Neither Wallace nor *Black Belt* responded.

Fighter Kevin Rosier, for one, was scathing of the critics: "Eighty-five percent of the people that buy *Black Belt* magazine are punks that don't even go to karate dojos. They do it at home; they listen to these bullshit articles. The people that own *Black Belt* magazine don't know anything about martial arts. The people that write these articles don't know anything about martial arts. When [film star] Steven Seagal came [onto the scene], you had twenty or thirty people in the *Yellow Pages* teaching aikido. It is very hard to become an aikido instructor. When Brazilian jiu-jitsu comes out, the next year in the *Yellow Pages* you have people saying we teach jiu-jitsu, circular jiu-jitsu, linear jiu-jitsu … seventeen years of experience. Half of these instructors didn't even know what a guard or a mount was and now they're in the *Yellow Pages* selling it. They all want the mystique. People are going to train for realistic stuff, and then all these karate schools with the magazines and marketing are going to lose money. That's why they badmouth the UFC. They realize that, 'Oh shit, if our students find out that the shit we're teaching really doesn't work … that's going to be bad for karate."

Just as Joe Lewis's full contact karate had created a rift in the martial arts community decades before, the UFC started a revolution of its own. "A number of people who own martial arts schools have up to eighty percent of their enrolment as kids," said Lewis. "And when parents see an event like the UFC coming out and saying, 'These are the best of the martial arts, this is what martial arts is really all about,' and then they see people kicking teeth out of heads and blood splattering everywhere and people getting dumped upside down and breaking bones, well, that terrifies parents. And now they don't want to believe it's safe because of what they saw on TV. The complaint about mixed martial arts mainly came from the people who owned commercial schools, not necessarily spectators." The gap between fighting and traditional martial arts was being revealed before everyone's eyes – and it didn't look pretty.

SINCE NEITHER BOXING nor state athletic commissions governed the UFC, WOW Productions created its own sanctioning body. The International Fighting Commission (IFC) was essentially a one-man operation that didn't add much credibility to the UFC as a sport. Davie took over from Rorion Gracie as head of the commission after the first event. In a letter to Campbell McLaren, dated November 24, 1993, one of Davie's recommendations was: "No referees in octagon—replace with (2) IFC 'Observers' on octagon's apron in corners, who scrutinize fighters and advise the corner if fighter is in serious trouble; only the fighter or his corner can stop the fight." Fortunately, McLaren and Rorion Gracie knew that someone had to be in the octagon to officiate, even if they didn't have any power. "There was naïve thinking going on, because if you look at what he [Davie] was saying, you'd think that fighters would be reasonable, and if they get the shit kicked out of them, they'd tap or their corner would throw in the towel," said John McCarthy, who became the octagon's key ref.

McCarthy was a second-generation police officer with the Los Angeles Police Department; his father Ron had served for over 25 years. After working a gang unit for five years and putting in his time as a patrolman, McCarthy asked to become a tactical instructor for the Los Angeles Police Academy, since teaching was also part of the family tradition (Ron had become an instructor too). When a group of policeman were cleared of the brutal beating of Rodney King – despite compelling video evidence against them – Los Angeles erupted into rioting. McCarthy was subsequently asked to serve on the Civilian Martial Arts Review Board, which banded together martial artists from around the country to decide on proper "use of force" tactics for the police. Martial arts legends Benny Urquidez and Gene LeBell attended, as did Rorion Gracie. Gracie and McCarthy became friends, and swapped training tips: Gracie went through police training for a rookie; McCarthy learned jiu-jitsu. After training at the Gracie Academy and getting his wife Elaine's travel agency a profitable gig with the UFC, McCarthy was asked to take over from the Brazilians.

McCarthy had no experience refereeing, but Gracie felt his ability to make split-second decisions, learned as a police officer, was prerequisite enough. It didn't hurt that McCarthy was 6ft 4in and weighed over 250lbs. Art Davie later added the nickname "Big" John McCarthy and, though McCarthy didn't expect it, he would become as much a staple of the UFC as the octagon. He refereed in the beginning as a favor, and was unhappy at being told he was not allowed to stop fights on his own.

Just as "Are you Ready to Rumble?" had become boxing announcer Michael Buffer's calling card, John McCarthy would come to be known as the man who said, "Are you ready? Are you ready? Let's get it on!" He would start every match this way, and the crowd screamed in a frenzy just waiting to hear those familiar words to start the action. "I was thinking of something from judo, but Davie insisted that it had to be something American," says McCarthy. "I knew that [boxing referee] Mills Lane had used 'Let's get it on!' not in the fights, but in his fighter presentation in the beginning. He would say, 'Are there any questions from the challenger? From the champion? Let's get it on!' I didn't think I was infringing upon anything; I just thought that was the way to start these fights."

With no footage to market the original UFC, Campbell McLaren devised "There Are No Rules!" as its unofficial service mark. This wasn't strictly true, but was seen as a handy promotional motto to distinguish the tournament from the plethora of kickboxing and karate events that advertised in the same media. Art Davie, a veteran adman, was apprehensive about stressing the sport's harder edge "but they [Campbell McLaren and UFC producer Michael Pillot] felt the best way to reach the larger audience was to sell the blood, guts and fear aspects of it."

McLaren also drafted the official press release for UFC II. It was a document that would come back to haunt him time and again. According to this press release, "The competition has no rules – only two suggestions – no eye gouging or biting." Though the official rules said these techniques *were* forbidden, the next line nullified this: "Use of these attacks *does not* disqualify a fighter, but will earn him a $1,000 fine." Thus, someone could actually win by playing dirty and only lose a measly grand next to the big winnings of the championship. Luckily, no one took advantage of the loophole.

It was the scary remark that McLaren then added that would cause all the trouble: "Each match will run until there is a designated winner – by means of knock-out, surrender, doctor's intervention *or death*." The Press only remembered the last word, arming critics who lambasted the UFC over the next few years. "That was pure circus," admitted McLaren. "He (Meyrowitz) could have and probably should have fired me for that, but he didn't and went with it. I was vilified in the pay-per-view industry." When the UFC became the subject of a spot on *Good Morning America*, McLaren was accompanied by Jim Brown, who tried to gloss over the "or death" comment by comparing the UFC to football.

There had been other misjudgements. Between matches during the first UFC, two small children had been sent into the octagon to clean the mats. "I let my son Ryron and Rickson's son Rockson, both eleven years old at the time, wipe the blood off the octagon floor," said Rorion. "A lot of women wrote in and complained, 'How can you put kids in there cleaning up the blood from the mats?' It was a very crazy concept. I thought it was a brilliant idea at the time." Others were disgusted.

Gold's Gym had sponsored the first UFC and could have taken the event in a more lucrative direction had it not been for sumo wrestler Teila Tuli's tooth. According to UFC fighter Kevin Rosier, Tim Blind, president of human resources and public relations for Gold's Gym, was sitting ringside. The company had quite a bit of money tied up in advertising because they wanted to bring the concept of cross-training (martial arts and weightlifting) to the attention of the exercise commu-

The immortal Bruce Lee was not only a film star but also a pioneer of realistic combat training *(Warner Bros)*

Pro wrestler Antonio Inoki kicks boxing legend Muhammad Ali in an infamous mixed martial arts match in Japan. Inoki spent most of the bizarre contest scuttling on his back aiming kicks at Ali's legs. It was called a draw. *(Corbis)*

Benny "The Jet" Urquidez (left) vs Billy Jackson in a classic full contact karate contest. *(Guy Mezger)*

Enter the Gracies: (ABOVE) George, Carlos, Oswaldo and Helio make headlines in a Brazilian newspaper.

(RIGHT) An advertisement for luta livre (jiu-jitsu without a gi) giant Fred Ebert vs jiu-jitsu's Helio Gracie.

(BELOW) Helio Gracie keeps Waldemar Santana in his open guard in a four-hour fight in Rio in 1957. Helio issued challenges to fight anyone, regardless of size or weight.

(All photos Rorion Gracie)

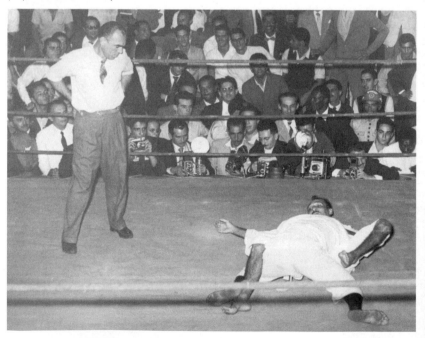

Helio Gracie and a very young Rorion Gracie, who was already starting to learn the family art. *(Rorion Gracie)*

Rorion (top) grapples with younger brother Royce. The pair would be instrumental in the early UFCs *(Rorion Gracie)*

Masakatsu Funaki, the charismatic founder of Pancrase Hybrid Wrestling, which pre-dated the UFC. *(Pancrase)*

(TOP) SEG President Robert Meyrowitz with UFC champion Royce Gracie. *(Clay McBride)* (BOTTOM) SEG's Campbell McLaren and WOW's Art Davie. *(Art Davie)*

The early publicity material for the UFC emphasised its dangers and would play into the hands of critics. *(Zuffa Entertainment)*

The heavily-muscled Ken Shamrock, one of the key competitors in UFC I, celebrates his first win in Pancrase. *(Pancrase)*

410lb sumo wrestler Teila Tuli was paid $5,000 to participate in UFC I but spent the days before ordering mountains of food in his hotel. *(Teila Tuli)*

Savate champion Gerard Gordeau worked as a bodyguard and bouncer for illegal rave parties held around Europe. *(Gerard Gordeau)*

(ABOVE) The giant Kevin Rosier worked as a bodyguard for pop stars Debbie Harry and Billy Idol before entering the UFC. *(Kevin Rosier)*
(RIGHT) Kempo exponent Zane Frasier made his name in a brawl with the man who inspired the movie *Bloodsport*. *(Zane Frasier)*

(LEFT) Sumo wrestler Telia Tuli rushes Gerard Gordeau in the first match in UFC history. Tuli was quickly despatched, minus several teeth. One of his molars flew past some prospective sponsors sitting at ringside. They decided not to be associated with the event.
(All Sport Photography)

Kevin Rosier throws a kick at Zane Frasier. The contestants fought in a fenced octagon designed by film director John Milius. *(Jose Fraguas)*

Royce Gracie signals to the referee that Ken Shamrock has already tapped out. Gracie went on to win the tournament. *(Jose Fraguas)*

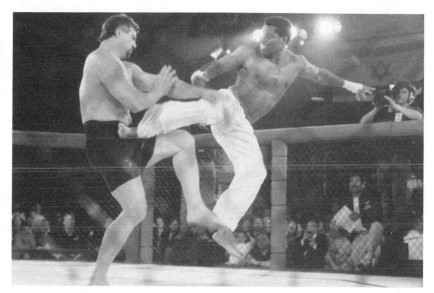

Johnny Rhodes's spinning back kick on David Levicki in UFC II didn't work out as well as he had hoped. *(Susumu Nagao)*

Kickboxer Pat Smith shows ninjutsu specialist Scott Morris the meaning of pain. *(Susumu Nagao)*

Royce Gracie wins his second UFC to prove the dominance of his family art – for now. *(Susumu Nagao)*

The third UFC was to feature the eagerly-awaited rematch between Gracie and Shamrock, but things didn't go to plan. *(Zuffa Entertainment)*

Kimo Leopoldo gives Royce Gracie all he can handle. The Brazilian won but was forced to quit the tournament with hypoglycaemia. *(Susumu Nagao)*

Ninja cop Steve Jennum pounds away on Harold Howard to win the UFC III championship. *(Clay McBride)*

nity. "When Gerard Gordeau blew out Teila Tuli's tooth, it flew right by the people at Gold's Gym whom I had dinner with later that night," said Rosier. "Right when that happened, they looked at each other and said, 'Shit! This will never fly at corporate.' So that's how you had a major sponsor like Gold's Gym all of the sudden just drop sponsorship for the next show."

If that wasn't enough, McLaren created another untruth – that the UFC was banned in 49 states. This was patently false, as the UFC took place in several states during its infancy. No one seemed to notice. Both Davie and Isaacs felt that those initial story plants by McLaren certainly went too far, but the matter was blown out of proportion. Isaacs described it as "viral marketing," wherein the Press began quoting the Press to play the bloodsport angle like a broken record. Although *TV Guide* called the UFC, "disgusting, dumb, and depraved," the second show garnered 125,732 pay-per-view buys – a 45 per cent increase.

THE SHOW WAS originally slated for an 8,000-seat auditorium but had to be moved to the 3,000-seat Mammoth Arena after the local mayor used a clause in the deed to object. Despite the name, Mammoth Arena was much smaller than the show's first venue, the 18,000-seat McNichols Arena. This presented numerous problems for the production team, as they had to put up fighters in two different hotels, turning one across from the arena into a quasi-dressing room. Jason DeLucia remembers that site well. "It was a potentially volatile situation. There were sixteen fighters, and maybe four or six of them got special treatment. The rest were stuck in a giant room, a bullpen type of thing that also housed the caterer." DeLucia claimed the disturbance caused by the caterer may have been intentional, to make the fighters lose their concentration. That wasn't the only problem. Things got so out of control that Davie asked alternate Fred Ettish if he would serve as gopher, since he wouldn't be fighting. Ettish went back and forth readying fighters to enter the octagon. What he found was a prostitute-infested motel that "didn't smell so good. Things were broken, doors didn't always lock or close, and people were making sidewalk pharmaceutical deals in the rooms."

The first round of the 16-man tournament provided some interesting matches. The third fight of the night pitted Johnny Rhodes against David Levicki, a 6ft 5in wing chun practitioner. Rhodes attempted a spinning back kick as Levicki crept up to him with showy hand movements. Neither move worked, and after a brief scramble on their feet, the remainder of the match was spent on the ground. Although he didn't know what he was doing, Levicki got Rhodes in the guard position (the bottom fighter has the top fighter positioned between his legs) and his size created enough space to take Rhodes out of striking range. The position also gave the audience a bird's eye view of Rhodes's backside, as his pants kept coming down due to Levicki's wrapped legs. Referee McCarthy had to pull them up several times during the match, but that didn't stop Rhodes, who eventually found his opening and started slugging the bigger man in the kidneys and face.

A bad cut over Levicki's left eye prompted him to call it quits. "You're the better man. I'm going to give it to you," he told Rhodes. But McCarthy didn't hear anything, and a pause gave Levicki his chance for revenge. Rhodes resumed punching as well until McCarthy finally stopped the fight, with blood streaming down Levicki's face. Levicki needed five stitches beneath and six stitches above his left eye. "I could have broken his neck using a hold I learned in the Special Forces," he said later in an article for *Penthouse*. "But I couldn't do it. I didn't come here to kill anyone." Even when reality set in, some fighters still held on to misconceptions and death touches. The match had lasted more than ten minutes, twice as long as any in the first UFC.

The now-retired Gerard Gordeau brought in Dutch sambo player Freek Hamaker as a last-minute favor to Art Davie. Hamaker was a porn theatre owner but also the Belgian Heavyweight Sambo Champion. Thaddeus Luster, a seventh degree black belt in kung fu san soo, was his opponent. Luster firmly believed his art was "the most potent fighting system on the planet," but that didn't stop Hamaker's immediate takedown and eventual submission by arm lock. Luster couldn't even get off a punch. Hamaker, who fought on three days' notice, just wanted to see what it was like to fight in one of these events; at that point he had no intention of continuing. He was fine, but told officials his hand was broken.

Fellow Dutch import Remco Pardoel had a somber face and pudgy physique but held jiu-jitsu championship titles from four countries. Pardoel took judo lessons at four years old from his martial arts instructor father. When he turned seven, he took up tae kwon do, and at age eleven trained in jiu-jitsu. He heard about Brazilian jiu-jitsu and invited well-known jiu-jitsu stylists Jacare and Fernando Yamasaki to conduct a seminar in November 1993, the month of the first UFC. Pardoel sent in his application to compete in that event, but Davie put him in the second show since the first card was full. He faced Spaniard Alberto Cerro Leon, master of pencak silat, an Indonesian martial art form that keeps the practitioner low to the ground, making him less vulnerable. "Alberto was the reason to enter the UFC for me," said Pardoel. "In Europe, the guys from pencak silat and wing chun are badmouthing all other styles by saying and writing that they are invincible, which [they're] not. So the best way to prove that they are wrong is to challenge them."

Often going by the name "El Toro," Leon had won several championships throughout Europe and Asia and claimed he once broke both legs of an opponent in a match. The Spaniard's moves were unconventional and intense, but his style was no match for Pardoel's takedown. However, the Dutchman had difficulty submitting Leon; his jiujitsu was obviously not on par with Royce Gracie's BJJ. "For me, this was the first fight in my life which wasn't a sports fight," commented Pardoel. "The UFC is sports too, but on a different level." After trying a choke and an arm lock, the big man finally submitted El Toro with a cross-arm choke. "Normally when you crank someone's arm, they will tap," said Pardoel. "He didn't and I respect him for that, but at the party afterwards, he couldn't use his arms anymore, so I think the locks were decent in a way."

Minoki Ichihara was the smallest man in the tournament. He arrived with over 200 reporters from his native Japan to represent traditional karate. He came with Royce Gracie in mind, but once again the shortcomings of stand-up arts versus ground arts became apparent. Ichihara tried to create as much distance as possible, but Gracie took him down and mounted the karate player with ease. The Japanese held on as long as he could before Gracie wrapped himself like an anaconda, performing both a choke and an arm bar simultaneously. Ichihara, out of breath, tapped before the arm was fully extended.

In the most one-sided match of the night, ninjutsu stylist Scott Morris rushed kickboxer Pat Smith in the first semi-final, only to find himself mounted and bludgeoned to a dizzying state with 14 punches and ten elbow strikes to the face. Morris staggered to his feet, blood tattooing his left eye from a gash that required 28 stitches. Morris's teacher and cornerman was Robert Bussey of Robert Bussey's Warriors International, who had been given an honorary award for his dedication to the martial arts at UFC II. During the match McCarthy looked at Bussey to throw in the towel, but when their eyes locked Bussey turned and threw the towel into the crowd, even though his fighter was taking so much abuse. Bussey believed his art was combat-tested and tough as nails, and would rather have let his fighter get hurt than protect him from unnecessary punishment. That said, the action was over so quickly that a corner stoppage would still have been too late; the referee should have been allowed to stop it. Thankfully, Smith stopped the match himself, and yelled, "What's up?" as a way of showing the crowd that he was a different fighter from the first event.

Frenchman Orlando Weit came into the UFC as a favorite and showed off his Muay Thai skills in a feverish massacre of New Yorker Robert Lucarelli. At one point, Weit turned away and raised his arms in victory, but his fallen opponent had not tapped out, so the match continued. Lucarelli's corner finally threw in the towel after Weit had slammed five hard elbows to the back of his neck. His injuries resulted in ten stitches to the head.

Weit's quarter-final match against Remco Pardoel provided a surprise, as everyone, including Pardoel, thought Weit would win. "I was sure that I would lose in a standing situation and I was nervous before the fight, as in any fight," said Pardoel. He wasted little time in closing the distance early and hip-tossing the man nicknamed "The Gladiator" to the mat. Holding him in position, Pardoel launched seven elbows to Weit's head, the third knocking him unconscious. The commentators had pegged Weit to win by sizing both men up on looks alone. They were shocked. Pardoel, who had said Weit might clinch the grand prize, was even more stunned. Weit won the 1994 Muay Thai Kickboxing Championships just eleven days after UFC II.

EVERYONE WANTED TO prove himself against Royce Gracie, but no one more so than martial arts journeyman Jason DeLucia. Though he had no formal fighting competition ranking, DeLucia was a book of knowledge on the martial arts. He had made it his life's calling to seek out styles from East to West, adding anything to better himself, and had regularly competed in backroom prizefights in Boston's Chinatown. Before the UFC in 1992, he fought Royce in a dojo challenge match (the match is shown in the *Gracies in Action* tape) at the Gracie Academy, quickly learning that five animal kung fu and his myriad honorary black belts didn't truly prepare him. "I thought that I could at least last through the fight long enough," said DeLucia, believing his stand-up base could keep the Brazilian at bay. After being submitted in less than two minutes, DeLucia contacted Rorion to fight Royce in the UFC, but all the tournament slots had been filled.

DeLucia had moved from Massachusetts to California with one thought in mind: to fight film star and aikido exponent Steven Seagal. "At that time, Steven Seagal had stated in a magazine that he would take on anybody, anytime, anywhere," says DeLucia. With very little money to his name, DeLucia made the trek to California, crashed on a friend's sofa, and went to Seagal's dojo morning, noon and night for three months. Seagal was never there. DeLucia learned a lot about aikido and ultimately found his calling when he took the Gracie Challenge instead. "It was the best single thing to happen to organized martial arts. And for that, everyone should thank Rorion Gracie because he did it. If not, we would all be working in the mill." By winning a qualifier against Trent Jenkins, he earned his chance at redemption against Royce.

DeLucia attempted a side kick during the first few seconds of the match, but broke the fibula bone in his foot when it collided with Gracie's shin. Going to the ground, DeLucia pulled Gracie off him, narrowly escaping a choke, only to leave his arm exposed for the jiu-jitsu man to finish him. DeLucia stood up, but the arm bar was locked, forcing him to fall to the ground, frantically tapping the mat. DeLucia would not be seen again in the octagon for over five years, choosing to fight in the Pancrase organization thanks to Ken Shamrock.

Patrick Smith could have worn himself out in a long stand-up battle with fellow semi-finalist Johnny Rhodes, who had punished last-minute entry Fred Ettish to a bloody pulp. Instead, Smith opted to finish Rhodes with a guillotine choke just minutes into their bout. Rhodes had to tap out with his foot. Afterward, Smith seemed as cocky as ever, muttering, "No one can really take me down!"

In jiu-jitsu vs jiu-jitsu, Royce Gracie gave up over 100lbs to Remco Pardoel to decide who would be the second finalist. Pardoel should have been able to detain Gracie and beat him at his own game. Instead, he froze and Gracie took him down early, choking Pardoel into submission by using his own gi against him. It was becoming very clear that Brazilian jiu-jitsu had something over other submission arts. In the UFC, labels, titles, records and rankings didn't mean much. "Royce is the best in the world on the ground," said Pardoel. "On that day, I was his child and he was my dad and could play with me any way he chose. After the UFC, I got enthusiastic. I devoted my life to build Brazilian jiu-jitsu in Europe, with the help of my Brazilian friends, of course."

After 13 matches, only Pat Smith and Royce Gracie remained. Both men would be fighting for the fourth time in just under three hours, though each had disposed of his opponents with relative ease. Smith had greatly improved since his first time in the octagon; with "Redemption '94" stitched across his jacket, he seemed ready to take the championship from Gracie. But as the match started, Smith got off just one kick before being taken down to the ground and mounted. Smith tapped the mat at 1:16 after Gracie threw some short punches in order to create space. The kickboxer capitulated because he felt there was nothing else he could do. "I thought he was going to put up more of a fight," said Gracie. "I was hoping that he was going to turn around so that I could get him in a choke."

In a tournament that tested so many styles, Royce Gracie affirmed his grappling art had superiority over traditional standing styles that dominated the martial arts. While the cynics retreated to magazines to snipe, there was no doubt that the quest to beat Gracie was made for a new kind of warrior. But when would this warrior emerge? After winning the $60,000 prize, Gracie smiled from ear to ear. The answer to that question would have to wait till the next event.

CHAPTER 7

"The Sport of the Nineties"

THOUGH ROYCE GRACIE swept the competition at UFC II, the WOW promoters knew that opponents would only get tougher. The decision was made to replace Royce with his brother Rickson Gracie, who had won a tournament called Japan Vale Tudo '94 on July 29. Although Rorion Gracie states that he intended merely to alternate members of the Gracie family, Art Davie emphatically believes the intention was to replace Royce with an even stronger fighter. Rickson was a legend in Brazil, where he had won numerous jiu-jitsu and vale tudo matches during the 1980s. Moodily charismatic, physically powerful and a technical master, he was considered the true fighter of the family, and WOW saw him as the next superstar in the octagon. "I always wanted Rickson for the event; he was a Brazilian Marlon Brando and I was always putting the pressure on Rorion because I was nervous about Royce," said Davie.

A month before UFC III, Rickson met with brothers Rorion and Royce, father Helio and Art Davie at the WOW office in California one Saturday morning. Art contends both he and Rorion had approached Rickson before, so this meeting laid everything out on the table. Royce sat on a couch away from where the others discussed Rickson's participation. He watched a piranha swim around in a tank that Davie had somehow inherited at the WOW office, and paid little attention to the conversation. "Rickson at some point turned to Royce and asked him in Portuguese, 'Is this what you want to do?'" according to Davie. "Royce nodded and said, 'Yes.' Rorion explained that this was in the best interest of the family."

Rickson, on the other hand, mused that it was in the best interest of Rorion and that he had other plans – his success in Japan was indication of that. Rorion and Rickson batted the matter back and forth until Helio rose to speak. He was a man of few words, but everyone listened as he pointedly told Rickson, "When I fought and when your uncle

Carlos fought, money was not our primary consideration." The room went quiet. Rickson protested that Rorion would make over $1 million from the UFC, and so he should make the same for competing. It was clear Rickson wanted to go his own way. He would no longer even work in Royce's corner in the octagon. Many Brazilians felt Rickson's spine was in Royce's body during the first two events. Could Royce succeed alone?

Though another brother, Relson, had worked out with Royce for the first two shows, he stepped up his commitment level for the third. "We had a meeting with Royce after Rickson and Royler left," said Relson. "It was my dad, Rorion, Royce and all my brothers. We agreed to keep it going. I pulled Royce aside and I said, 'You have to forget about Rickson and Royler.' They had trained him for over two months before the first fight." Now he had to do it without them. He sparred ten-minute sessions with each brother and "we would save the best for last, which was me," said Relson with a laugh. Relson was something of the tough guy in the family and had more of a name for fighting in the streets than anywhere else. "When I was training with him, every-thing was allowed and I headbutted him to prepare him for that," remembered Relson. Royce would be ready to face a whole new group of combatants.

Style against style was the original concept for the UFC, but wasn't the reason most people watched the event. In a focus group conducted by SEG, "only twenty-seven percent of the audience were martial artists," said Art Davie. "The vast majority of the audience were guys who enjoyed NFL football, monster truck pulls and professional wrestling. They wanted action." They didn't care about the nuances of martial arts, let alone what styles labelled the combatants. So a change in marketing strategy was devised, turning the third event into a real-ity-fighting contest with a pro wrestling spin.

Since pro wrestling was something people could identify with, SEG exploited the ready-made angle of Royce Gracie facing off against Ken Shamrock for UFC III. Shamrock had all the makings of a star, despite his earlier loss to Gracie, and Campbell McLaren wanted to use that. He sent Shamrock a letter after the first show stating his intention to build him up for the media. When Shamrock couldn't make the sequel due to a broken hand, he was given some interview time and spoke of a rematch. Marketing material pushed the Grace/Shamrock confrontation: two-time champion vs number one contender.

Davie, now inundated with fighter applications, packed the show with competitors who looked and acted larger than life. Sitting in his office just a few weeks before UFC III, his attention had been drawn to the roaring of a Porsche convertible pulling up out front. Out stepped a short, stocky Asian man with no shirt, while a menacing figure with tattoos adorning his muscular body fell in behind him. Joe Son announced himself to Davie as a minister who was there to bring the gospel of the Lord to the octagon by way of his student, Kimo Leopoldo. The tattooed Kimo never spoke a word, but his undeniably fierce demeanor was his first-class ticket into the show.

Born in Hawaii, Kimo was an ex-gangbanger whose life had been spinning out of control. He moved to Newport Beach, California, to escape his demons and restart a college football career. When that failed, Kimo sought refuge in religion and befriended Joe Son, who was part of an extremist Christian group. There was no mistaking his dedication; the word "Jesus" was tattooed to his stomach while a cross tattoo donned his entire back. Though just a streetfighter, Kimo was elevated to a third degree black belt in tae kwon do for the show. Aside from seeing the *Gracies in Action* tapes, Kimo was as green as they come and trained with Joe Son for only a day. Son and Kimo felt the UFC was a fad that could lead to bigger things.

Emmanuel Yarbrough was a different story. Davie had watched him in an open sumo tournament earlier that year and, for six months, had tried to get him interested in the UFC. At 6ft 8in and a truly enormous 616lbs, "Manny" was the proverbial gentle giant. Davie says Yarbrough didn't really want to fight but, after enough coaxing, agreed to enter the competition. Harold Clarence Howard was another character, a Canadian wildman with long golden hair, a beard and piercing eyes that said as much as his colorful speech. With multiple black belts and a nifty parlor trick of breaking a cement-filled bag with his bare hand (used in his promotional segment), Howard cranked up the show's bigger-than-life appeal even further.

Other so-called martial artists wanted to talk the talk without walking the walk. Wing chun stylist Emin Boztepe attacked the Gracies in martial arts magazines, pointing out how his skills could defeat jiu-jitsu. "Royce and Rorion openly challenged him to come to the show," says Campbell McLaren. "We never heard from that guy. With all the guys that we openly challenged, there was always some excuse: 'You don't do this, you don't do that.'"

SCHEDULED FOR CHARLOTTE, North Carolina, on September 9, 1994, UFC III would look much slicker and better-produced than its predecessors. The octagon canvas was changed to blue from white, since it was more photogenic. It was also made less springy, with the two-inch pad under the canvas being replaced by one of three-quarters of an inch, aiding fighter mobility. Music channel MTV introduced the UFC as "the sport of the Nineties" and different fighters hammed it up for the intro to the pay-per-view broadcast. The so-called "laws of the octagon" were announced as no rounds, no time limit, and no way out – phrases that played on the raw perceptions that had created so much heat from McLaren's UFC II press release.

Not everyone was enamored. In an article that appeared two weeks before the show in *Newsday*, sports columnist Wally Paige of the *Denver Post* referred to the previous event as "the most disgusting, horrifying thing I've ever seen. It's basically taking cock-fighting and putting it in human form." The phrase "human cockfighting," would echo over the next few years as the UFC came to wider notice and more and more objectors appeared.

There was at least one very positive difference between this show and its predecessors. John McCarthy told Rorion Gracie he would never serve as a referee again if he couldn't stop a fight, because "I knew that a fighter was going to get hurt and I wasn't going to be able to do anything about it. I cannot be in there and allow some guy [who is] knocked out to be hit if I can't stop it because there's no tap or towel." Gracie gave the go-ahead for McCarthy to use his own judgment in stopping a fight. After the brutal beating of Scott Morris, the relentless damage inflicted by Orlando Weit on Robert Lucarelli, and the "enough is enough" torture committed on Fred Ettish in UFC II, Big John was now allowed to intervene for the sake of fighter safety. This was an important step in establishing the UFC as a credible sport, but it still had a long way to go.

The first match of the evening brought out sumo giant Manny Yarbrough against Keith Hackney, a kempo stylist who had taken the place of fighter Roger Therriault on just three days' notice. To prove himself capable of competing in the UFC, Hackney had been asked to battle Thomas Ramirez in a makeshift sparring match held in a nearby North Carolina gym. If Hackney looked impressive, he would compete on the card; if not, SEG would pay for his expenses and he would watch from the front row. Hackney showed slick moves and outclassed the 350lb Ramirez (who would later lash out at Davie in *Black Belt* magazine for not getting him in the show). Hackney knew Yarbrough was a strong man; he had seen him curl 315lbs on a straight bar with relative ease. With little time to prepare, he worked on low kicks before the match to keep the sumo wrestler off him.

The crowd was bloodthirsty in the hot, dry venue as the 5ft 11in Hackney stared down his massive foe. McCarthy started the match and it didn't take long before Hackney nailed Yarbrough with a ridge hand (Hackney called it a tiger strike), much like a bat hitting a home run. The big man fell back with a resounding thud and Hackney pounced on him to finish the job. Yarbrough mounted a brief comeback, swatting Hackney's head with his huge paws. As the two staggered back up, Yarbrough's strength sent Hackney crashing through the octagon fence and into the audience. A quick restart saw the smaller man put Yarbrough down on all fours after sweeping his leg, forcing the giant to trip and fall. Without hesitation, Hackney took control and pounded his opponent's head 41 times with his fist and forearm, breaking two metacarpal bones in the process. "Realistically, I would have beat him all day just to keep him down," said Hackney. The war could have ended a lot sooner with less injury to Hackney if he had known submission or thought to use an elbow to finish it. Afterwards, Yarbrough said it "was part of the strategy to take some abuse, but you can only go so far."

Next up was Ken Shamrock vs Christophe Leininger. Leininger was two years older than Shamrock and was once ranked number two in the USA for judo. His father had been one of the originators of sport judo in Europe prior to the 1964 Olympics, and had taken the art to Arizona when he moved there with his family in 1959. Leininger learned judo from his father and understood the need to learn jiu-jitsu tactics as well. While leading the US judo team in the 1986 Olympics, he met Brazilian jiu-jitsu instructor Megaton Diaz, who gave him a better understanding of mat work as opposed to throws. The two ran a school in Phoenix for several years. After his judo career waned, Leininger thought it would be interesting to enter the UFC. He had the best credentials of any judo player who submitted a resume.

"My whole strategy was that this guy was going to try and bumrush and overpower me, and at that point, I would set up a guillotine," said Leininger. "But Shamrock didn't budge and did exactly what I didn't want him to do, which was just stand there." The match got off to a slow start, and the crowd roared in disapproval. Leininger made the first move, believing he would earn points for aggression, as in judo competition. He went for the takedown but Shamrock was ready. He cross-faced Leininger so hard that the judo man later admitted to being knocked out for a second. Down on the mat, Shamrock was in Leininger's guard. After a failed attempt at a triangle choke (where the opponent's own arm is used in the choke), Shamrock slipped out and took Leininger's back. The judoka turned to the side to prevent a choke, but was now pressed up against the fence. Lying in Leininger's guard, Shamrock stayed clear of his opponent's attempt at an arm bar, and landed some hard shots. "I got tired and had the back of my head against one of the posts and he jacked me up. With a couple of hits, I was done," said Leininger, who tapped. He suffered a minor concussion and wouldn't return to the octagon until UFC XIII.

Harold Howard's match against hometown boy Roland Payne provided much-needed fireworks. Though Payne had a background in Muay Thai, karate practitioner Howard came out blazing with more effective strikes and knocked out Payne with a devastating elbow to the back of the head.

This was the perfect warm-up for Royce Gracie's return to the octagon. Gracie made his usual entrance led by a line of his brethren, heads bowed and hands on each other's shoulders, but nothing could best the appearance of his opponent. As dried ice poured out of the backstage area, Joe Son emerged with a hooded Kimo carrying a wooden cross on his back. It was something of a surprise to the promoters. "People were buying reality, and we didn't want the taint of sports entertainment," said David Isaacs. "We wouldn't have let something like that go because we didn't want people to think we were professional wrestling." To prevent the promoters nixing his clandestine religious message, Joe Son had told Art Davie the large box shipped to the arena was "special training equipment." On his walk to the octagon, Kimo dropped to his knees and prayed. Onlookers wondered if this man was for real.

They got their answer as soon as ref McCarthy initiated the battle. Kimo rushed Gracie with ferocious intensity, barely missing with wild punches. "This match was difficult for me," said Gracie later. "I tried to match power against power instead of all my other matches, where I used technique. I just wanted to see how strong he was." Gracie and Kimo clinched, with the latter holding his own until another break in the fence forced them momentarily outside the octagon. Kimo thought they would break, as in the Yarbrough fight, and restart from their corners, but McCarthy signaled for them to continue once they were back inside. According to Kimo, this gave Gracie the chance to strengthen his grip, with Kimo losing a contact in the process as a result of a headbutt. The two finally went to the ground, but unexpectedly, Kimo took Gracie's back, and tried to sink in a rear naked choke. If he had been more astute on the ground, he might have choked Gracie out.

Unable to sink in his hooks (wrap the legs around the bottom man to tighten the grip), Gracie eventually turned to his back with Kimo hovering over him. The Brazilian landed several shots to Kimo's face, which was now bleeding, and used the bigger man's ponytail to keep him in place. "I couldn't breathe too well because of the way I was angled and I couldn't pull my head back," remembered Kimo. The clash became so intense that Gracie pulled Kimo's ponytail apart, leaving hair strewn about the canvas. As they moved to the side of the octagon fence, Gracie sunk in an arm bar. Kimo tapped as his arm barely locked out. The battle had been the toughest of Royce Gracie's career in the octagon. Victorious but exhausted, would Gracie be able to continue?

As Ken Shamrock watched the action before him, he knew he had to win one more fight before he could bury the memory of his loss to Gracie, the plague that had taken over his life. Shamrock wanted a shot at Gracie more than anything but first had to dispatch kickboxer Felix Lee Mitchell, who replaced Keith Hackney when the latter dropped out due to his broken hand. Mitchell came in wearing boxing gloves, but was forced to take them off because he didn't show them to McCarthy during the pre-fight instructions. Shamrock, who had time to change his tights in-between matches, fought cautiously and took more than four minutes to get the kickboxer to the ground. He was then able to win within seconds after taking Mitchell's back and sinking a rear naked choke. But at what price? Shamrock hobbled away with an injured ankle as his father Bob comforted him.

Harold Howard was confident about taking on Gracie. He believed he had found a way to integrate karate and jiu-jitsu to defeat the Brazilian champ – and his opponent was in bad shape. As the Gracie train made its way to the octagon, Royce felt devoid of energy. "We stopped for the cue to walk in front of the camera and I laid down. I don't remember laying down." Royce called out to older brother Relson for some watermelon juice. It was feverishly hot inside the venue and he was dehydrated. To this day, Royce doesn't remember any of this, a sign of his disorientated state. When he got inside the octagon, McCarthy asked if Gracie was okay. "I said, 'Yes,' but suddenly my vision went off, it shut down, and I couldn't see anything. That's when I turned around and said [to his family], 'Guys, I'm doing my job. Now help me out here and do your job. I can't see anything.'" McCarthy knew something was wrong and asked again if he was all right to continue. Still unable to see anything, Gracie responded just to the voice. He couldn't even see Howard, who was jumping around in his corner. Gracie pleaded with his family to do something, but after McCarthy came over a third time, the towel was thrown in and Gracie was carried out of the octagon. It turned out he was suffering from hypoglycemia, an abnormally low level of sugar in the blood.

Howard jumped for joy, though he had won only by default. As he and his manager celebrated and returned to the back, Joe Son and Kimo burst into the octagon and made a mockery of the situation, jumping up and down like something out of pro wrestling. Kimo said he didn't mean any disrespect to the Gracies; he just wanted to show he was okay and could still fight. The incident outraged Relson, who felt Son in particular needed a lesson. "I approached Joe Son and said, 'Hey motherfucker! Let me tell you something, you want to walk with me outside now because you walk like a punk,'" said Relson. "'You want to go outside with me alone. You call me names so let's go outside and see for real.' He turned to me and said, 'No! No! Royce is great. I respect you guys a lot.' I told him he didn't respect my family, my daddy, or me so let's go outside with no TV or anything and let's settle it. He grabbed both of my hands and bowed to me and apologized and said it was just for show." Kimo later wrote an apology letter to Royce for the incident. But there was something strange in the air that night. Everyone was fighting … in the stands, even out in the parking lot, where Art Davie and Joe Son almost got into it. "That show had everybody pissed off at everybody," said Davie. "Michael Pillot, Rorion and I were knocking heads because we couldn't decide on how to go forward with the show."

THE FINAL WAS to be Howard and Shamrock, but Shamrock had no more will to fight now that Gracie was out. "When something is taken from you, you lose everything," he said. "Everything I had trained for, everything I had wanted … you get so hyped up for it and now it's gone." Shamrock was not coming out. His father tried to explain how much money he would make from winning the championship, but it didn't matter: Shamrock was so stubborn that Howard could have forfeited the match, giving him a win by default, and it wouldn't have made any difference. The Lockeford, California, native would have to suffer a little longer for his revenge. He was the only one who understood that obsession.

With Gracie and Shamrock out of the picture, an alternate would have to compete in the final. Ninjutsu exponent and police officer Steve Jennum stepped up to the plate to face Howard. (Jennum was originally going to replace Gracie to fight Howard in the semis, but with time running out on the pay-per-view, they let Howard have a bye.) As the match got underway, Howard did a forward flip, either to show off or to disdain Jennum's abilities. As Jennum moved in, Howard locked him in a guillotine choke and they both fell to the ground, but Howard didn't have the choke sunk in right and had no knowledge of how to correct it. Jennum pulled out and the two went toe to toe, each landing punches. Moving to the clinch, the policeman tripped Howard and mounted him. Howard tried to protect himself, but Jennum rained down strikes until the Canadian had enough. Two towels were thrown in, and a man who had fought in only one match claimed a $60,000 check and could legitimately be called the Ultimate Fighting Champion.

The first two shows had put the effectiveness of martial arts on trial in a realistic situation. Now the competition was tougher and, for the first time, there was a problem with the tournament format. In eight matches, there had been two alternate replacements and one bye. Could this still be called the Ultimate Fighting Championship? The show left many unanswered questions, though that wasn't necessarily a bad thing. "It was like a great pro wrestling tournament. Ken didn't really lose, Kimo hurt Royce but lost and he was so big and colorful, he was a big star. Then you had this alternate win the tournament," said David Meltzer. "The marketing of pro wrestling is the only way to make this work. Many people think that's a dirty word, but it's not. It's the same with boxing. You have to create curiosity."

Spectator sports are built on curiosity and personalities, which drive the audience to watch athletes perform. Would boxing be anything without the likes of Muhammad Ali, George Foreman and Mike Tyson? All of these men were great boxers but, more importantly, they were performers who enticed crowds by clever marketing of their colorful appeal. Though the UFC sold itself as being real, it also needed those same types of performers to take it to the next level. UFC III worked off a pro wrestling model with real fights. Its success took the show to new heights.

CHAPTER 8

Changing of the Guard

WHILE THE PRO wrestling slant made the UFC more marketable, SEG wanted to focus on establishing credibility. "It took a few events until we got certain things better controlled, like what we needed from the fighters and entourages," said David Isaacs. "We wanted to run it like a sport and we wanted to treat these guys like athletes." With the tagline "Revenge of the Warriors" accompanying UFC IV, SEG wanted Kimo back. "I knew I was going to get another shot," said Kimo. "I felt that [Joe Son] and I were on a mission of God, so if it was him doing it, fine by me. We strong-armed SEG, saying if Joe Son didn't get his shot in the UFC, they would never see Kimo again." SEG made Royce Gracie vs Steve Jennum their marquee match-up.

There would also be a major shift in the production team. Producer Michael Pillot brought in Bruce Beck, a veteran Madison Square Garden staffer who had served up energetic play-by-play commentary for boxing, kickboxing, and 20 other sports in his twelve-year tenure at the famous New York venue. Beck didn't know what to make of the UFC at first, but found it compelling and, more importantly, real. He told SEG he would approach it like any other sport, calling the action like he saw it, and recommended Jeff Blatnick as color commentator. Blatnick, the 1984 Olympic Gold medallist in freestyle wrestling, had been doing commentary since 1987 for national collegiate wrestling championships. He saw the UFC as a natural extension of amateur wrestling, far removed from the bigger-than-life entertainment of the undeniably more popular pro wrestling. Ironically, Blatnick had done color for Shootwrestling, a series of US pay-per-views being passed off as real that were nothing more than old stiff-worked Japanese events.

UFC IV would be the first time a "real" wrestler tested his skills against other martial artists. "Some people wouldn't recognize wrestling as a martial art," said Blatnick. "Wrestling is a common denominator of combative sports by learning how to put someone on his back." Though the sport doesn't have karate chops, punches or fancy kicks, it is arguably the forerunner of every grappling art known to man. Yet with three UFCs in the books, no wrestler with exemplary credentials had ever entered the octagon. Ken Shamrock had done well with a wrestling background, but nothing like that of collegiate or Olympic-caliber grapplers. Campbell McLaren pushed to have them in the event, although "a lot of wrestlers thought it was interesting but didn't seem to want to get involved." He talked to Olympian Dave Schultz and even his brother Mark, who both turned him down.

Until 1988, wrestlers and other athletes had to scrape by and couldn't compete for money if they wanted to go for amateur gold. When professionalism was finally allowed and jeopardizing amateur eligibility was no longer a threat, men like Daniel Severn could finally make a better living. The Michigan native, who held over 70 amateur wrestling records, was polishing his career on the independent circuit in a pro wrestling camp in Ohio when a friend showed him a tape of the UFC. Severn found a martial arts magazine and filled out an application inside to try out for the event. He was surprised when there was not a listing for "Wrestler" among the various styles, and had to check off "Other." After sending in mug shots but not hearing anything back, Severn forgot about the event and secured a pro wrestling gig in Los Angeles instead. Phyllis Lee, a grandmotherly type who served as manager for numerous pro wrestlers, took up the slack and made calls on Severn's behalf to Art Davie, whose office was close by. Davie eventually went to see Severn in action and set up a meeting later that night.

Just days after UFC III, Davie watched Severn and pro wrestler Al Snow engage in a shoot-style pro wrestling match for Great American Mat Endeavors in the upstairs area of a Chinese restaurant. Afterwards, Davie sat down with Severn. "You realize this is real, don't you?" he asked. Severn admitted he had no professional fighting record to speak of, but he was a competitor. For over 20 years, he had wrestled in the amateur leagues all over the world from Cuba to Japan. He told Davie of an experience while in Turkey at the age of 17, where instead of wrestling another teen, he took on an ex-serviceman twice his age. His opponent grabbed the back of Severn's head and headbutted him right above the eye. "As I back-pedalled, I had my hand up beside my face, blood trickling down. I thought the match would be over with my opponent being disqualified for unsportsmanlike conduct. The referee stepped between us and cautioned me for passivity. He told me I was stalling!" This was in the first 15 seconds of the match, one that Severn ended up winning. Though it was not "anything goes," it was Severn's introduction into a foreign environment with questionable rules – and showed he had guts. Davie was not convinced, and it was over a month before Severn heard anything back.

Eventually Severn signed a contract stating, "In case of your accidental death, we are not liable." *What could possibly be accidental,* Severn thought, *if the only things I can't do are poke you in the eye and bite you?* He had only five days to prepare, and returned to Ohio to work out with Al Snow and two other pro wrestlers. None of them knew anything about fighting, but they had a pair of old boxing gloves and devised a game called "Hit Dan." In amateur wrestling, some moves can become illegal with just a turn of the wrist; Severn now practised those moves, taking down his friends and making them "scream in pain." But punching, kicking, and headbutting were not in his repertoire; Severn entered his first UFC as just wrestler, albeit a veteran one. The odds were stacked against him.

The show also featured a veteran of another kind: Ron "Black Dragon" Van Clief. As a birthday present to himself, Van Clief wanted to enter the octagon at the ripe old age of 52, still sporting the sculpted physique of his earlier days. Van Clief took martial arts in the 1950s, bounced around from style to style in the 1960s, and became the "Black Dragon" when he turned actor for the Shaw Brothers film company in the 1970s; he signed a four-picture deal for the Hong Kong company known for its over-the-top kung fu films and ended up doing 15 chop-socky flicks over a ten-year period. Van Clief also did voiceovers for Shaw films being exported to the States, usually dubbing for villains. Having competed in Hong Kong's World Freefighting Championships in 1982 and won several point karate and full contact karate matches, Van Clief saw the UFC as the epitome of what martial arts was about. Tai Mak, a student of Van Clief's and star of the film *The Last Dragon*, pushed his master to compete in the event.

But getting into the UFC was no easy task. After SEG President Bob Meyrowitz turned him down because of his age, Van Clief finagled his way into Campbell McLaren's office one afternoon. He didn't arrive alone. "Ron came in unannounced with four acolytes, these muscular, six-foot-something white guys who towered over him," said McLaren. The Black Dragon sat before him as the four men circled McLaren, making him feel uneasy. In his soft voice, Van Clief murmured, "Let me remove my shirt." As he took it off, Van Clief's men exploded in outrage and berated McLaren.

"You have humiliated our sensei!"

"You have embarrassed us!"

"How dare you make him take off his shirt!"

McLaren was perplexed, since Van Clief had acted without prompting. Then he asked McLaren to punch him in the stomach. "No, what if I just touched you," said the SEG vice-president of programming. Once again, the henchmen were indignant.

"He touched our sensei!"

"We cannot allow this."

McLaren, who was getting spooked, protested, "Guys, he asked me to do this." Finally, the veteran martial artist asked permission to perform a test of strength. "I thought he was going to karate chop my desk. It seemed like something right out of a movie. If that was planned, those guys were geniuses." Parlor tricks aside, Van Clief also said he had entered the New York City marathon. McLaren agreed that if he completed the race, he was fit enough for the UFC. Van Clief did finish the race and the Black Dragon was in.

BUDDY ALBIN PROVIDED the on-site promotion for UFC IV, and brought in two kickboxers: Anthony "Mad Dog" Macias and Dallas native Guy Mezger. WBF Intercontinental Boxing Champion Melton Bowen was the second boxer to make his way to the UFC, after the Art Jimmerson debacle. As for Royce Gracie, this would be the greatest test of his abilities in the tournament format.

After some initial problems with Oklahoma trying to ban the event before it began, UFC IV was held in Tulsa at the Expo Square Pavilion on December 16, 1994. Lots were drawn to decide the card. Van Clief smiled when he saw Gracie was his opponent in the first match of the evening. SEG, however, was far from enthusiastic about having its two-time champion mix it up with someone nearly twice his age. Though Van Clief had been involved in numerous martial arts competitions over his lifetime, he was taken down and submitted at 3:51. He was still all grins after being handed his defeat, and hugged Gracie for the experience.

"Look at him! He's scared! You're going to kill him!"

As Keith Hackney readied himself for Joe Son, the religious man's followers sought to intimidate the kempo artist. Hackney watched Son as he struggled to carry the long, balsa wood cross on his back. The act wasn't as original the second time. Son bull-rushed Hackney at the start of the match and then caught him in a guillotine choke on the ground. Hackney used groin shots to full advantage – for the first time in the UFC – punching Son six times. Though he wore a cup, Son's eyes squinted in pain. Hackney broke free, stretched out Son's 5ft 4in body, and grabbed his throat. "I was waiting for him to arm bar me, but I had a tight grip on his Adam's apple and probably would have ripped it out had he tried to push my arm out of the way," said Hackney. Son didn't go for it and subsequently tapped out.

Returning UFC champion Steve Jennum went toe-to-toe with boxer Bowen. After taking some hard shots, Jennum got the mount and pounded on Bowen, then arm-barred him for the tap out. Unfortunately, Jennum broke his hand and couldn't continue in the tournament. For the last quarter-final, amiable training partner Al Snow led Dan Severn to the octagon, and few in the crowd knew which was which. "Everyone thought that Al was me until the day of the press conference, when I was sitting up there with the rest of the fighters," says Severn. Snow always dressed in tank tops and shorts, while Severn looked like the handler in a sports jacket. Even Severn's wife and four children back home didn't know what he was doing that night; save for papers she had to sign a day before the event, his wife might never have known.

Severn vs Anthony Macias turned out to be the match of the night. Macias was an Oklahoma native and, though he had a solid wrestling background, claimed Muay Thai as his style. The 260lb Severn shot in on him "but he had so much baby oil on him that you'd swear someone had dipped him in by the ankles," said Severn. Macias threw great knees and hard elbows, but the bigger man used his Greco-Roman background and dumped the kickboxer with two devastating back *souplesses* (pro wrestling bastardized this term, calling it a "suplex"). Severn later admitted to trying a belly-to-belly throw, but Macias was too slippery. After eating plenty of good shots, Severn had his man down and choked him out without throwing a single punch. He had proven that amateur wrestling deserved to be in the UFC.

Hackney made it to the semis, though his ankle had to be injected with cortisone for the pain. He put up a tremendous fight against Royce Gracie and kept him from the takedown by throwing bombs. At one point, he even grabbed Gracie's gi and slugged away, but the Brazilian tied him up and fell to his back holding Hackney's arm. Hackney desperately tried to fight out of it and broke away momentarily, but the jiu-jitsu fighter kept his cool. By clenching Hackney's right arm, Gracie could move his hips out and wrap his leg around his opponent. It was only a matter of time before Hackney fell to the mat and tapped out to an obviously painful arm bar. The other semi was less dramatic: Dan Severn choked Jennum's replacement, Marcus Bossett, to submission in less than a minute without throwing a punch.

After a challenge match featuring Guy Mezger and Jason Fairn and 20 minutes of dead time, allowing SEG to promote its merchandising and push its website, it was grappler against grappler in the finals. The much bigger Severn easily took Gracie down and out-positioned him.

He caught Gracie with a couple of slaps to close the distance but wasn't able to finish him and both men remained up against the fence for over 15 minutes. Severn looked down at Gracie. He had him in place and knew what had to be done. But he was also having to come to grips with something his first two matches hadn't exposed: after more than 15 minutes of fighting, Severn was physically spent. Gracie locked in a triangle choke on the oblivious Severn as color commentator Jeff Blatnick noted the wrestler was in trouble. At 15:49, Severn tapped. "Did I tap because Royce Gracie beat me or did I tap because I was unwilling to hurt another individual that night?" That was the question Severn had to answer if he wanted to continue fighting. When the match was over, Severn shook his head in frustration. He felt it was his mind that had lost the fight; his body could have finished it.

Gracie hoisted the $64,000 check over his head. He was back on top, and had claimed his third title. But for SEG and WOW, disaster had struck. The show was only scheduled for a two-hour TV block, since cable companies did not treat the UFC as a legitimate sports event, which would have garnered three or more hours. With all the time wasted in the show, the final ran over by almost four minutes. People watching at home were suddenly cut off during the final crucial moments of the Gracie Severn match. They went nuts. Complaints poured in and money was refunded, costing SEG millions of dollars. What should have been the UFC's biggest-profit show was relegated to the financial status of a local event whose primary cash stream was ticket sales from a small venue in Oklahoma.

SEG TRIED SEVERAL different ventures on pay-per-view but nothing worked as well as the UFC. On June 17, 1994, they took a chance on actor David Hasselhoff's singing career by making a pay-per-view special called "David Hasselhoff and His Baywatch Friends." Any success that it might have enjoyed was cut short when O.J. Simpson took his infamous ride in the white Bronco that same evening. Despite the Hasselhoff disaster, SEG President Bob Meyrowitz became good friends with Hasselhoff's manager, Jan McCormick, a starmaker in Hollywood who had also managed the late Brandon Lee, son of Bruce.

Meyrowitz approached McCormick about the Gracie family and set up a meeting with Royce. McCormick immediately took to Gracie's charm and boyish sensibility and couldn't believe he was the one beating all these muscle-bound warriors in a cage. Anticipating something big, Meyrowitz asked Art Davie, "Can you get Rorion, Royce and yourself into a corporation for the purpose of carrying forward Royce as an entertainment property? I want ten percent, Jan wants ten percent and William Morris, as a theatrical agency, gets ten percent." Meyrowitz knew he could work with Davie but not with Rorion, who liked to call the shots. A meeting was set at William Morris early in 1995 involving all the principals, including Jeff Sheinberg, the CEO of William Morris, and Mike Simpson, president of the giant agency's TV division.

A $15 million dollar movie was discussed for Royce. Davie recalled the favoured plotline. "The yakuza are furious that Helio Gracie brought jiu-jitsu to Brazil and now with Royce becoming the Ultimate Fighting Champion, they're hijacking Japanese jiu-jitsu from Brazil, and what right does Helio have to do that? So the yakuza go and kidnap the old man from Brazil and take him to Tokyo. The Gracies, who never really got along, must band together like the Magnificent Seven and, led by Royce, go over to Japan, kick butt and get the old man back." Things seemed promising until Rorion spoke up, asking if his student John Milius could direct. Sheinberg shot that down, since Milius had not had a hit in years. "[Rorion's] with his brother in the movie, but he's not supposed to talk," said Davie later. "Things ended on that note and lot of steam came out of that meeting. Bob comes out and says, 'What the fuck was that? I thought you were going to control this guy.'"

Davie went to Rorion and tried to salvage the relationship. He told him Meyrowitz wanted a three-year management deal, but Gracie wouldn't take it. "Rorion, do you realize the magnitude of the meeting you were watching in that room?" asked Davie. "Most martial artists would give one or both of their testicles to be in that room, having someone build a $15 million dollar film for them and outline a potential career. Do you understand that?" But Gracie didn't feel comfortable with Meyrowitz, who reputedly wanted a lot more than ten percent of a film deal. "In essence, he wanted to own everything that Royce and I did," says Rorion. "I said absolutely no way. Bob said that after the agreement is made, everything that the Gracie Academy makes, he gets a percentage of that. He knew that a deal like that would affect T-shirts, classes, and videos. I said absolutely no deal. Every coin has two sides. I'm Brazilian, but I'm not stupid. Jiu-jitsu did not get this far because I'm a nice guy."

Davie went back to Meyrowitz with the bad news. "He embarrassed me in front of those people and now he's telling me he doesn't want to pay me? Fuck him," said Meyrowitz, according to Davie. A film that spun real life into art could have done a lot of big things for the UFC and the Gracie family, but it never happened. A few months later, the UFC appeared in the Russell Crowe film *Virtuosity* and came off looking like a bloodsport. It even portrayed more than two fighters in the octagon doing battle at the same time. "It took the worst elements of what the UFC was known for, which was people brawling in the ring," said Davie. At the time of writing, Rorion Gracie is finishing a book on the life of his family and hopes to turn that into a movie one day – on his terms.

MEANWHILE, ROYCE GRACIE was back on top. After winning three tournaments, the decision was made to retire him from the tournament format to compete in single "superfights." But whom would he fight? It was unfair to bring UFC II semi-finalist Pat Smith back into the loop. Marketing reports said Ken Shamrock was the most popular fighter in the UFC but he had never finished a tournament. Besides, both Shamrock and Gracie were popular, and using the pro wrestling model, two "baby faces" couldn't fight one another. Davie hatched a plan to bring in a star from the traditional martial arts realm to battle Gracie. At first, the obvious opponent was Emin Boztepe, a kung fu stylist who had blasted Gracie and the UFC in martial arts rags. Rorion Gracie was able to get Boztepe's attorney on the phone, but that was as far as it went. Next, they tried getting Bart Vale, who had made a name for himself from his stiff-worked matches in Japan. No dice.

Davie's best choice was kickboxer Dennis Alexio, because he wanted someone that martial arts purists could identify with, and Alexio's star-like quality on the mike was perfect for the UFC. "I got his home phone number and offered him $50,000 and really couldn't get him excited," said Davie. "He said he would get back to me but never responded. We were still experimenting with the format. We wanted a major name from the kickboxing world to face Royce." In the end, Davie kept coming back to Ken Shamrock. He knew the fighter wanted Gracie more than anything, even though Shamrock's adoptive father Bob no longer supported him in the event because he had pulled out of a winnable tournament in UFC III. The idea of a superfight came about to ensure both Gracie and Shamrock would fight each other. "That's the only thing that I trained for and wanted," said Shamrock. "I could have fallen apart and my life would have been over. I mean, my wife could have left me and my kids would have been destroyed because I couldn't deal with that. I was very difficult to live with. I begged Bob Meyrowitz and Art Davie not to let this go."

UFC V would return to Charlotte, North Carolina, the same setting as their proposed second meeting at UFC III. Only this time, fate had nothing to do with it; Shamrock would get his shot.

Dan Severn also felt he still had something to prove, something to conquer. He wrestled with the rules in his head and came to the conclusion that there was nothing wrong with striking his opponent. "I looked at the UFC as the ultimate challenge. It wasn't for the money or the fame," said Severn. "It was the ultimate test of spiritual, mental, and physical fortitude when you step out there. There is no room for mistakes." Severn made good on these words by dismantling judo stylist "Ghetto Man" Joe Charles in just over a minute, opening up a cut over his left eye, taking his back, and sinking in a choke. Russian immigrant Oleg Taktarov came into the show with a busted knee that popped in and out of place as a result of a training injury. Though he looked impressive in the quarter-finals, Taktarov entered the octagon against Severn believing that, since he was another grappler, there would be no striking. He could not have been more wrong. After taking him down, Severn launched several knees to the Russian's face, opening up a gash that drenched the canvas with crimson. "Gokor, he's cut!" yelled referee John McCarthy to Taktarov's trainer, even as the bloodied fighter tried to work an arm lock. The fight was stopped at 4:21 when Gokor Chivichyan threw in the towel.

Another first round match produced one of the few examples of serious foul play in the UFC. The 6ft 7in, 295lb John Hess outweighed Texan Andy "The Hammer" Anderson by 60lbs and was nine inches taller. The week of the fight, Hess had been in bully mode, pushing people and berating them with tough talk. His manager even challenged commentator Jeff Blatnick to a fight. He believed strongly in Hess's fighting style, which he dubbed Scientific Aggressive Fighting Technology of America. Anderson was a self-made millionaire who owned several businesses, including the Totally Nude Steakhouse in Longview, Texas; the place became so popular, yet offensive, that the city actually paid Anderson to shut it down. He was also a sixth-degree black belt in tae kwon do, and agreed to donate his UFC fight purse to one of three charities: School for the Blind, Feed the Children, or a cerebral palsy foundation.

As the match got underway, Hess lumbered toward Anderson throwing sloppy slaps with little technique. "Instead of hitting, he scratched my eyes while we were standing," said Anderson. "Then he continued to scratch and hit me. I finally got him on the ground and got on top of him and he shoved one thumb into my eye so that I could barely see. Then he bit a chunk out of my hand, grabbed the back of my head, and shoved a thumb in my eye, popping it out of socket. I lost twenty percent of the peripheral vision in my right eye." McCarthy stepped in to stop the bout at 1:23; Anderson was visibly disgusted when Hess's hand was raised. Hess was fined thousands of dollars for his dirty deeds, which was paid to Anderson and given to the School for the Blind. Backstage, Anderson found Hess balling his eyes out. He was exhausted, and since his hand was broken, could not continue.

A year and a half later, Hess chastized the UFC as a publicity stunt, opinions which were due to appear in *Inside Kung Fu* magazine. To prove his point, he picked an "easy" fight with an 18-year-old jiu-jitsu stylist. The match lasted 15 seconds. The jiu-jitsu man was Vitor Belfort, who demolished Hess with super-fast punches. Hess was never heard from again. Anderson continued working in the sport behind the scenes.

Though he came in as a replacement for the injured Hess, Canadian wrestler David Beneteau had solid credentials. He won the Junior Championships from 1984 to 1987 and captured the US Junior Open in 1987 as well. He had lost to Dan Severn in amateur wrestling ten years earlier. Beneteau had not competed in three years since getting his degree in sports medicine, but he managed to knock out his first two opponents with relative ease. As the finals got underway, Severn shut down Beneteau's striking game by tying up with him. The two stayed on their feet, with the Canadian barely able to land a punch. Severn eventually swept Beneteau's leg, took him to the ground, and gained side mount. Beneteau was trapped next to the fence and Severn immediately attempted an arm lock that tapped him out at 3:03.

As Severn raised his hands in celebration, the fierce look in his eyes prompted commentator Bruce Beck to dub him "The Beast." He was no longer the quiet, reserved gentleman who people had known outside the octagon. And his heavyweight championship belt for the professional National Wrestling Alliance would no longer be needed to build up his status in the real fighting realm. The Beast had been born. Daniel Severn had conquered all to win the ultimate challenge – for now.

THE PRESSURE FOR the Gracie–Shamrock superfight had been building for months, with each side predicting a consummate win come fight time. It was a match that needed to take place, but the crowd would be bitterly disappointed. Ken Shamrock had waited a year and a half to conquer his demons but, nestled in the guard of Gracie for nearly 30 minutes, he was unable to get that image of being submitted out of his mind. He didn't want to chance it, didn't want to risk a mistake. He felt uncomfortable in the guard but "all I knew was that if those legs got up around my arm or head, I was getting choked," said Shamrock later. "And he was not going to get there." The crowd booed with displeasure as all expectations for an exciting fight began to disappear. For Shamrock, it bothered him that hours before the match, he was told there was going to be a 30-minute time limit. "I think Ken respected Royce's abilities too much," said Bob Shamrock, and Ken freely admitted to being overly cautious. For his part, Gracie found a 27lb weight disparity a problem for the first time, even though he had fought and beaten heavier men. Neither man took the initiative and it went down as one of the most boring matches in UFC history.

After 30 minutes, Bruce Beck commented on the overtime: could five more minutes decide a victor? With his hands grasping the fence, Bob Shamrock was beside himself with frustration. "I don't usually cuss, but I was cussing Ken out left and right," said the elder Shamrock, who dramatically yelled out the countdown to Ken. As the five-minute over-time was instituted, Art Davie noticed the crowd getting restless, since the two seemed content with a stalemate. "I was screaming at McCarthy," he said, "and finally he looked over and saw my thumb saying stand them up." Shamrock finally landed a solid punch that made Gracie's eye swell up like a balloon. The two went back to the ground and, after 36 exhausting minutes, the match was ruled a draw, since there were no judges and no other decision could be made.

The recriminations began almost immediately. "He should be embarrassed for not beating Royce," said Rorion. "If I was as damaged from the punch as he (Ken Shamrock) said, why didn't he finish me?" said Royce. There was controversy from all sides, and both men claimed they would have finished off the other had the match contin-ued. It was an anticlimactic end to the sport's first great rivalry. The match catapulted the event into unimaginable pay-per-view buys: 286,256 at $24.95 a pop.

Rorion Gracie felt the match fell short of his vision of what the Ultimate Fighting Championship should represent; a truly realistic forum. "It [no time limit] forces the fighter to chase victory, knowing that he has to finish him off now or he might get caught later. It makes it real, like a street fight." But the UFC was not a street fight; it was a spectator sport that had to play out within a suitable time frame for a pay-per-view audience. After the fourth show ran over, time limits became a necessity. "Rorion always saw it [the UFC] as simply a means for his family's style to get over [with the mainstream]," said Davie. Davie also felt the mounting pressure of American states unwilling to hold the event. And there was growing friction between WOW and SEG. "We were always going over the expenses because we split the profits fifty-fifty and I didn't want some Jim Rockford type of deal," said Davie (a reference to the *Rockford Files* TV character, played by James Garner, who always got shafted at the end of an episode). "I felt that Bob was going to be a real problematic partner; that and the fact that we were under such political pressure. Bob Meyrowitz and I were two guys from Brooklyn who could talk, but when you got all three [including Rorion] of us in a room together, it was very strained." Davie and Gracie weren't getting along either. The Brazilian held Davie personally responsible for Royce Gracie getting punched, since he had told McCarthy to stand them up.

If the show was to move forward, something had to change. According to Rorion, "Art had gotten in cahoots with Bob and wanted me out of the decision-making process. They thought, *Let's find a way to get Rorion out of this.* So Art came to me and said, 'Let's sell WOW.' He told me he was tired of it and it wasn't going to work." Rorion didn't want to sell, knowing that more money was to be made. But he relented, if only because a new show was in the works, as he and Davie had discussed. On April 19, just twelve days after UFC V, Rorion Gracie and Art Davie sold their share of the UFC to Bob Meyrowitz. "We had an international event that spawned one of the best franchises on pay-per-view," said Meyrowitz. "We needed to step up the production and rules had to be changed." Gracie, for his part, believed that judges would never perceive that a fighter on the bottom of a ground match might possibly win.

Gracie signed a two-year non-competition clause but knew there was a way around it. "As soon as we sold WOW, Art and I went to meet with some guys in Chicago about another show. They decided not to do the deal, and Art gets hired the next day to work for SEG [as matchmaker]. It got to show me what type of person Art was and I wasn't happy about that. I felt betrayed." Davie claims Meyrowitz called him up out of the blue. Either way, it was apparent that Gracie was no longer needed. He wanted to put real fights on TV, while SEG wanted a TV show with fighting.

Gracie and Davie were paid hefty sums for their share of the UFC, even though they never put in one dime. Through a loophole, the original 28 investors, who had put in $250,000, were left with nothing. Since they were students of Gracie's, Rorion agreed to pay the principal plus ten percent to each investor. Davie bought a boat, settled in Las Vegas and was paid $25,000 per show as matchmaker. "To this day, Rorion and I are the only ones to have ever profited from the UFC," said Davie.

Naturally Royce would not continue fighting in the UFC and stepped down. He then voiced complaints about the show in numerous magazine articles, and eventually made his comeback nearly five years later for Japan's Pride organization. A party was held for Royce Gracie's triumphant reign in the octagon, at which he received a jeweled samurai sword adorned with UFC logos. The event would not be the same without Gracie, the smaller man who defeated the bigger man to collect three championship titles and only a handful of bumps and bruises. In the process, a sport had been born – and it was bigger than jiu-jitsu. The Gracies had shocked the martial art system into growing again. Now it was time to mature.

CHAPTER 9

Clash of the Titans

OLEG TAKTAROV STARED calmly across the octagon into the cold, blue eyes of a monster named Tank. It was the finals of UFC VI, dubbed "Clash of the Titans." Since the stoppage that had kept him from the finals of the previous show, Taktarov's leg had healed, he'd had more time to train and his mind was focused on the fight rather than where his next meal was coming from. Before him stood a rampaging foe who had just crushed two men in less than two minutes combined. Taktarov was unfazed. He had endured far worse.

The story of Oleg Taktarov's involvement with the UFC was something right out of a movie. He was born in Sarov, just east of the Ural Mountains in Russia, one of the ten "secret cities" of the so-called Soviet nuclear archipelago and home to one of the country's largest H-bomb research centers. Taktarov grew up inside the confines of a secret nuclear testing site, autonomous from the rest of city and surrounded by an electrical fence; like much of the populace, his family worked in the complex. At the age of ten, his father took him to a sambo/judo school nearby. Sambo is the premier Russian martial art, a mixture of wrestling and judo. For seven years, Taktarov learned sambo and spent his summer months in a special training camp. At the age of 17, he took part in a sambo match that would decide his fate. If he won, he could fulfill his mandatory two-year military service in Gorky, competing for the army in the sport division. If he lost, he would be sent to the regular army and stationed as far away as Afghanistan. During the contest, his opponent snapped Taktarov's ankle – leg locks were an integral part of sambo. Taktarov writhed in pain but would not yield and the bout continued until the referee stood them up. With only one chance to end the match, Taktarov grabbed his opponent by the gi lapels and slammed his head to the ground, knocking him out. He could continue his sambo training for the Russian military.

The army was supposed to give Taktarov the best training of his life. Instead, it was mundane, leaving the sport maniac yearning for more action. Though it was risky, he would go AWOL at 5:30am to train at his old sambo school for two hours, returning to the army camp in time for daily training. This worked out for a short while until a general caught him coming back late. Drenched in sweat, Taktarov told the officer he just wanted to make the army happy by training under his own conditions. The general didn't buy his story. Within a few days, Taktarov was shipped off to a remote forest camp for a six-month assignment as punishment for his "good intentions."

Becoming a tactical officer and learning how to read radars was not exactly what Taktarov had planned, and before long he was back training in the forest. He lifted logs, ran, and wrestled around with his comrades to build up his strength. During one session, an intense pain in his side prompted him to seek medical aid. He was told dismissively it was probably overtraining. Taktarov went AWOL again, but this time it was life or death. Trekking over five miles through the Russian countryside, he finally made his way to a doctor. It turned out he had a ruptured spleen. "If you had been twenty minutes late, it would probably have come open inside of you and you might have died," said the doctor. This time, Taktarov was not disciplined for leaving his post. He eventually resumed training and became so strong that the army felt he should represent them in weightlifting, so he was sent back to Gorky.

In a chance meeting with the general who had sent him away, Taktarov pleaded his case: "I'm different now and know what I did was wrong. I will still work hard and achieve my goals. Please let me come back and practice sambo again so I can fight in the world competitions." Taktarov was granted that opportunity, and won the nationals a couple of months later against the best in Russia. He finished his two years with the army and continued training for another two years in the top sambo school. But with nothing more to achieve, Taktarov became bored, and no longer wanted to train. For a short while he took a job teaching sambo for the government to special forces, KGB and other members of the Russian elite police. It was called counter-terrorist training. Taktarov was surprised by his students' inexperience in hand-to-hand combat.

This gave him the chance to make some money. Before long, he had opened up a lucrative training business that supported his regained interest in sport competition. Moving away from sambo, Taktarov competed in full contact jiu-jitsu events, where strikes were legal. He won four times. When news of the UFC surfaced, he went to Baltic cities in Latvia and competed in similar MMA events. After finding success there, he set his sights on fighting in America, and eventually settled in a Russian community in Los Angeles. The Russian-speaking neighborhood provided Taktarov with a safe haven, since he couldn't speak English, but his money dried up. Soon he was sleeping in a car he had rented with his last remaining dollars. He was bored of training and fighting and his childhood dream of becoming an actor seemed hopeless. That was when a dazed and confused Oleg Taktarov found himself walking into the Gracie Academy in Torrance. Returning to fighting was the only thing he could do if he was to survive in a world he did not understand.

Taktarov grappled at the academy (against Pedro Sauer) that day and later claimed he had no problem holding his own, as he was much stronger and was accustomed to wearing a gi. Rorion complimented his skills, and some other students in the school told him about the WOW office across the street. After changing into street clothes, Taktarov walked into the office to find Rorion sitting across from Art Davie. Taktarov's limited English was a problem, and after Gracie left, Davie had to get his Russian-speaking brother-in-law on the phone to translate. "I gave him some money because he was starving," said Davie. "He came back later and gave me a videotape. After looking at it, I thought, *This guy can really fight*." While having dinner with Davie over a year after his participation in the UFC, Taktarov learned the truth: "Davie told me that Gracie said, 'That guy is nothing. Do not use him. He sucks.'" Though Rorion Gracie denies this, Davie corroborated the conversation and recalled a similar story about getting Alexander Karelin into the UFC. Karelin was a Russian wrestler of superhuman strength with a long list of record-setting titles to his credit and was known as "The Experiment" for his seemingly superhuman prowess – but after wrestler Mark Schultz lasted 30 minutes with Rickson Gracie in a sparring session (Gracie finally tapped him), Rorion didn't want either one to enter the UFC. Because Rorion had taken such a stand against Taktarov, Davie decided he had to be in the show.

Davie arranged for Taktarov to train under the auspices of UFC on-site promoter and manager Buddy Albin in Texas. Though Albin took him in, the experience left the Russian with a bad taste in his mouth. Living in a rundown apartment complex in Dallas, Texas, Taktarov found he could speak more English than the rest of the tenants. "I stay in a room with a boiler behind the wall so that I could hear the water bubble all night long," he remembered. The Russian's weight dipped down below 200 and his knee was in bad shape for his appearance in UFC V. Needing help, he found it: Taktarov credits Ken Shamrock with moving him to Northern California and giving him the training he needed to fight in the UFC. He lived in Bob Shamrock's house and worked with Ken for two months in preparation for the next event, though he was still managed by Albin. Taktarov was a different man when he competed in UFC VI on July 14, 1995, in Casper, Wyoming.

THERE WAS ANOTHER man who had turned up at UFC V but hadn't got the chance to show what he could do. David Lee Abbott hailed from Huntington Beach, California, and was introduced to Art Davie by his friend Dave Thomas.

"He's kind of like that guy from the Clint Eastwood movie and the fights," he told Davie.

"You mean *Every Which Way But Loose* and Tank Murdock [a character from that film]?" said Davie.

"Yeah, except he's Tank Abbott and the guy can bench over six hundred pounds!"

How would a street fighter with no martial arts experience perform in the event? Abbott was invited to attend UFC V but Campbell McLaren and Bob Meyrowitz weren't sure they wanted him on the card because of the political pressure they were facing. It was bad enough that some traditional martial artists couldn't cut the mustard, but what about some bar brawler who tried to go in there and really hurt people? Abbott showed up and proceeded to down vodkas like water; SEG didn't know what to do with him. "When Abbott came in, he looked like the prototypical bad guy, the biker at the bar who looks like he really does want to rip your head off," remembered David Isaacs. Abbott got so inebriated at UFC V that he lost his tickets and had to be seated up in the rafters. He later used his key to get into the wrong room, the one belonging to SEG President Meyrowitz.

Sporting a pot belly and a shaven head with a contrasting bushy goatee, Abbott was a walking time bomb of testosterone, a vicious animal who was about to take the UFC to a whole new level. He called himself the "anti-martial artist," and the only true no-holds-barred fighter to ever enter the octagon. Abbott was born to a middle-class family and started wrestling at the age of nine. He wanted to try out for gridiron but his football coach father wouldn't let him, only his older brother. Abbott claimed to have been a fighter from a very early age, though he can't pinpoint where his aggression comes from. At college, he dreamed of being a champion wrestler and earning a degree in history. Only one of the two came to pass. At the age of 19, after a night of too much partying, "my buddy that was driving passed out and, while going fifty miles per hour, he hit a light pole. I woke up with my teeth knocked out and my leg almost cut off. That fucked up my wrestling career."

After graduating in 1993 from the University of California at Long Beach, Aboott planned to be a teacher "but it was a smoke screen. I knew in the back of my head that I could never be a teacher because of all my convictions for beating people up." Abbott took up boxing and found he had what are called "heavy hands", meaning his fists were like hammers. He quickly built a reputation around Huntington Beach for stirring up trouble. "A good time before I was famous was to go out, party, and then the tough guy in the bar gets his ass kicked! I'd come up to him – here I am, a kind of fat-looking guy, and didn't have a goatee then, I had hair. I'd be boogeying, going 'Woo, Woo!' and he'd go, 'Hey man, shut up.'" Baiting a guy in a bar and beating him up outside became one of Abbott's leisure pursuits.

Tank may have had a reputation as a streetfighter but SEG needed to spruce up his "legitimate" background. Davie reinvented him as a "pit fighter" and suddenly he had a record of 7-0, which remains unsubstantiated save for drunken myths from the goon crew that accompanied him to every show. When asked about the worst beating he'd ever given someone, a tight-lipped Tank only revealed the injuries. Apparently, someone had broken a pool cue over Abbott's head. The assailant ended up having "his leg broken in three places. All of his teeth were kicked out of his face – uh, did I say kicked? Well, they were missing. And he had seventy-five stitches in his face, with two and half weeks in the hospital." Abbott had also served a seven-month jail sentence before fighting in the UFC. At the time of the tourney he ran a garage door business with his brother and worked several odd jobs.

Another storm was brewing in Casper, Wyoming, as Ken Shamrock and Dan Severn faced the pre-fight press conference before their super-fight in UFC VI. After most of the attention was given to Shamrock, Severn got up and headed for the door without explanation.

Shamrock, taking Severn's gesture as a sign of disrespect, said, "We'll finish this in the ring."

"In your dreams," retorted Severn's manager, Phyllis Lee.

This made Shamrock furious. Later on in the afternoon, visitors couldn't walk through the Hyatt Hotel without stepping on copies of a nondescript newsletter explaining how Severn was going to destroy Shamrock. The flyer further enraged Shamrock, though the gentlemanly Severn insisted it was "not in my M.O." Fueled by anger, Shamrock couldn't wait to face the Beast.

It became clear on the night of the show that each fighter would also be battling the altitude in a venue 5,140 feet above sea level. It was the first show that SEG had sole control of, and from its beginning, with Michael Buffer's famous "Let's get r-r-r-eady to r-r-r-r-umble," it was a show to remember. Buffer, the undisputed king of boxing announcers, had been brought in by his brother Bruce, a lifelong martial artist with a black belt in tae kwon do whose kickboxing career was short by an adverse MRI scan. The two brothers created the Buffer Partnership and contrived to turn Michael's famous catchphrase into a multi-million dollar enterprise, with video games, movies, songs and even a TV show. After becoming a fan of the UFC, Bruce called up SEG and pitched the idea of Michael introducing the show. A three-tournament deal was cut from UFC IV to VI, but the announcer's alignment with World Championship Wrestling eventually stopped him doing future shows. "Michael would say, 'If it's not in the octagon, it's not real,' and that really upset the people at WCW and Turner Broadcasting, which is owned by Ted Turner," says Bruce. Turner, one of the most powerful media moguls in the world, usually got what he wanted.

As the lots were drawn, no one wanted Tank Abbott more than the 350lb John Matua, who was fighting to raise money for his brother in a hospital. Matua was a student of *kuialua*, the brutal Hawaiian art of bone breaking. Since no scales were used in those early UFCs, his weight was put down as over 400lbs. Abbott came in at a comparatively svelte 265lbs, wearing modified kempo gloves, the first time gloves of this type were worn in the UFC. SEG had always dithered over whether or not to allow these four- to six-ounce fingerless mitts that protect the hand but are small enough to grapple with. Abbott's usage prompted them to encourage gloves from that point on. "I have been in so many streetfights that I know that when I punch you, my hands are going to blow up," said Tank.

On McCarthy's order, Abbott wasted little time, making a beeline for Matua and mauling him with blows that sent the Hawaiian down to the mat, headfirst, with all four limbs outstretched like Frankenstein. Matua had suffered a major concussion but Tank still came down one more time with a devastating elbow to his face that bounced his head off the canvas. McCarthy pulled Tank off; it was all over in 18 explosive seconds. "John Matua was rated G; I have hit rated X," said Tank. Looking down at his handiwork, he also mimicked his prey's rigid body in a most unsportsmanlike fashion. "That bothered me, and I actually felt the swell of anger," said color commentator Jeff Blatnick.

That was the first of four quarter-final matches that each took less than a minute. The 6ft 8in Paul "The Polar Bear" Varelans laid waste to Cal Worsham, the International Taekwondo Council's number-one point fighter. It was a good little scrap, with the 5ft 10in Worsham getting in some blows before his larger opponent downed him hard with an elbow to the back of the head. Then UFC veteran Patrick Smith performed a beautiful front thrust kick to the chest of Rudyard Moncayo that took the breath out of him and set up a rear naked choke. The big match of the night was supposed to be the return of Canadian wrestler Dave Beneteau against Oleg Taktarov. Beneteau took the sambo player down to the ground with ease and was in Taktarov's guard until the wrestler pushed him up to the fence. A brief stand-up melee didn't work to Taktarov's advantage; he took some good shots with his head down and arms flailing away. The Russian survived Beneteau's onslaught and went for a single leg takedown which the wrestler countered, only to be flipped over and choked via guillotine at 0:57.

The semis produced one of the strangest occurrences in the UFC. First up were Tank Abbott and Paul Varelans. Abbott took Varelans to the fence and pounded the giant Polar Bear's face with strikes. Grabbing the fence mesh, Abbott then pressed his knee into Varelans's face and looked up with a big smile. He was enjoying the brawl and working the crowd at the same time. McCarthy finally stepped in and stopped the bout in Abbott's favor, though Varelans was still willing.

A few minutes later, Pat Smith made his way to fight Taktarov, but collapsed to his knees on the way and clutched his stomach in pain. Andy Anderson, who was escorting Smith, thought it was a response to pure fear. He told Smith to suck it up and go out anyway. Smith claimed stomach problems and abruptly left. He was seen eating ham sandwiches hours later at the after-fight party. In two alternate matches before the tournament, competitors Anthony Macias and Guy Mezger both won, and Macias was picked to take Smith's place. There was one problem: Buddy Albin managed both Macias and Taktarov, as well as Mezger.

In a locker room meeting minutes before the match, Macias made a decision that would blight his career for good: he agreed, reluctantly, to throw the fight. "I was in on the conversation with Anthony Macias, Oleg, and Buddy [Albin]," said Andy Anderson. "Everyone knew that Oleg was going to need every ounce of strength he had to beat Tank. Buddy Albin told Macias that if you don't lose this fight, you will never fight again in another no-rules fight, ever." At that time, Albin was a major force in MMA, managing several fighters, was the on-site promoter, and took as much as 40 percent of the gate receipts for the UFC. Macias obeyed his order, unbeknown to SEG: in the octagon a few minutes later, Taktarov beat him by choke in 12 seconds. Commentators Jim Brown, Jeff Blatnick, and Bruce Beck were suspicious and openly called attention to the fishy ending. Though Tank had blown through both of his opponents, Taktarov was now fresh to face him in the finals.

DAN SEVERN AND Ken Shamrock both looked to be at the top of their games for their superfight. Severn was six years older and outweighed Shamrock by 50lbs, but from the start Shamrock attempted a shoot. Severn's takedown defense kept him at bay. They clinched and worked for position to dictate the pace of the fight, but neither man was willing to chance a mistake. Moving toward the fence, Severn shot for a single leg takedown but with his head on the outside. Shamrock locked in a guillotine choke. The first one missed, but the second one cinched in tight, and when Shamrock gained leverage, Severn tapped immediately. "I proved my ability and I can wrestle," said an ecstatic Shamrock after the fight. "I wanted to see if he could throw me. I wanted to see what he had." According to Severn, he was running a high temperature and felt sluggish, but there were no signs of it in the fight. Shamrock also said that he had noticed Severn's head on the outside when going for a takedown, perfectly natural for amateur wrestling. For submission however, it leaves the head susceptible to the guillotine. The two would fight again, and their rematch would be entirely different.

It was now time for the tournament final between Taktarov and Abbott. The much stronger Tank took the Russian down early in the fight and landed several punches – Taktarov said later that he saw them coming and was unaffected – but within a few minutes began to tire. The altitude became a major factor and by the ten-minute mark, both men were gasping for air. It looked like it would come down to who wanted it more. "When you keep in mind that you still don't have a Green Card, you gotta win, and that was my motivation," says Taktarov. After 15 minutes on the ground with both men attempting chokes, John McCarthy stood them up. They worked toward the fence. Tank's head was limp. He was out of gas and in position for a guillotine choke. "He had no neck," says Taktarov, so eventually he moved to Tank's back and sank a rear naked choke that ended the fight at 17:47. Both men had fought their hearts out. No one had thought that the out-of-shape Tank could make it past the first few minutes. Afterwards, he shook his head and walked out of the octagon like nothing happened.

Taktarov, on the other hand, had a gash on his head, a bloody nose and remained still on the ground. Ken Shamrock jumped in to hold him down so he wouldn't expend energy. Taktarov claimed it was his toughest battle ever, not because of Tank, but because he felt like he was going to die after the match. "Then Buddy Albin found a gas mask, and in front of millions of people wanted to show that he knew what he was doing," said the Russian. "But they forgot to turn it on, and oxygen was not coming into the mask. So imagine that you cannot breathe and someone puts tape over your mouth! Another guy came in named Gokor [Chivichyan], who was trying to show off too, and they were both fighting over the mask." Taktarov eventually received competent attention and was rushed to the hospital, where he was told that he had lost a half-gallon of fluid. He laughed about it later, saying, "The oxygen couldn't go to my brain because my blood was dry!"

The upshot of Casper, Wyoming, was that Taktarov won the grand prize, Anthony Macias never fought in the UFC again, and there was one more fight to be had – it just wasn't on the card. Pat Smith may have bowed out on purpose without injury, but he would still get to fight, even if it was unplanned. According to Tank Abbott, Smith went into a frenzy right after the Huntington Beach bad boy returned from his match against John Matua. "I'm pretty sure Art Davie had his finger in this by saying, 'Hey, we need to disrupt the flow of what is going on.' He [Smith] came running out ... and threw a few kicks at my dad," said Abbott. Though Abbott doesn't know why he did it and Davie doesn't recall the episode, Smith certainly made an enemy by the attack. Paul Herrera, a collegiate wrestler and Tank's lackey, stood between them and got punched in the face for his troubles. Herrera wanted to get even with Smith and, later on in the show, Tank himself tried to go after the kickboxer. Campbell McLaren watched Ron Van Clief, who had taken over as IFC Commissioner from Davie, hold Tank back by grabbing his throat and telling him to stop. The streetfighter backed off for the moment, but things didn't stay cool for long. After a night of partying, Tank retired to his hotel room and crashed. Herrera and fellow wrestler Eddie Ruiz kept drinking. At one point, Herrera tried to pick up a beautiful girl who turned out to be Pat Smith's sister. She left for reinforcements in the form of Smith's crew. Herrera and Ruiz managed to get out of there and tried to wake Abbott. He was out cold.

The next morning in the hotel, Ruiz berated Herrera for not doing anything to Smith. With an evil look in his eye, Herrera put on his singlet and wrestling shoes as the whole crew got ready to go upstairs for breakfast. As the elevator door opened to the dining room, Pat Smith was standing in the entrance. He was in the wrong place at the wrong time. Herrera threw one punch that sent Smith down. "I put a boot in Patrick's ear twice and Paul beat the living hell out of him," remembered Tank. Kickboxer Maurice Smith (no relation), who had been working with Ken

Shamrock on stand-up, finally moved in and broke things up. "I saw Paul pounding on Pat because Pat was already on the ground and had been knocked down," said Maurice Smith. "I ran over there and tackled Paul to get him off, and Tank was already walking away."

Bludgeoned and bloodied, Pat Smith was carried to Andy Anderson's room. Art Davie was meeting with pseudo-star John Wayne Bobbitt, the man whose penis was severed by his enraged wife while he slept, and was interested in competing in the show. They heard the scuffle from outside. As Davie went to investigate, Abbott went one way and Herrera went the other. Davie accompanied Smith to the hospital. "He got beaten up worse than any of his UFC fights. He had stitches inside and outside his mouth." Smith never competed in the UFC again. Neither Herrera nor any of Tank's people were ever sued, but one thing was for sure: David "Tank" Abbott was a bona fide villain. He was also becoming a star for the rabid UFC fan base, and a recurring story for the press.

So popular was Abbott that he would be put under contract with SEG and paid a monthly salary instead of a per-fight purse – Randy Couture and Mark Kerr would later sign similar deals. SEG's Steven Loeb handled a lot of the fighter money and was once a bit tardy in sending out Abbott's check. To get the ball rolling, Abbott sent Loeb a bullet with Loeb's name inscribed on it. Needless to say, Tank got his money within the week.

UFC VII, HELD in Memorial Auditorium in Buffalo, New York, on September 8, 1995, broke box office records with over 8,100 in attendance. The show mixed veterans and newcomers, culminating in a dramatic finish in the tournament final between Paul Varelans and Marco Ruas. Ruas was something of a mystery man, his age kept secret, but there was no denying his stand-up and submission abilities. Fighting under the banner of Ruas Vale Tudo, he wowed the crowd with his Muay Thai skills, but despite his formidable weapons, it took him over 13 minutes to finish Varelans, causing the show to run over its allotted time once again. A power blackout also caused problems; it seemed the UFC couldn't get a break. "We had a lot of momentum going into that show, but with the time running over, it probably cost us over one million dollars," said chief operating officer David Isaacs.

No one expected the superfight between Oleg Taktarov and Ken Shamrock to go the distance either. Yet for 35 minutes, the two former training partners grappled and struck each other until a draw was declared. "I just wanted to show him that it was the wrong idea to fight, because a fight can never be exciting if two people know each other and train for many months together and you know every single move," said Taktarov. This didn't stop the Russian from bleeding (a frequent occurrence in his fights) and after the match, cut man Leon Tabbs went to work. "I go in there to stop the bleeding and he's halfway unconscious," remembered Tabbs. "He finally comes out of it and looks at me and says, 'Leon, why did you stop the fight?'" The Russian was made of stern stuff: to this day he has never tapped out from any match.

CHAPTER 10

The Age of the Wrestler

TWO YEARS AFTER the UFC had begun, it was time to decide the champion, the man who could face and triumph over the best of the best: the Ultimate Ultimate warrior. The show returned to Colorado for the third time, though it now faced opposition even there. "The mayor said he didn't know if he could do anything legally, but morally, the UFC was an abomination," recalled Art Davie. The state had its hands tied legally, however. As long as they didn't break any city ordinances or laws, the absence of a state athletic commission gave the UFC a free hand.

Ultimate Ultimate '95 featured four champions and four veterans who had made it to previous semi-finals. Unfortunately, Ken Shamrock and Royce Gracie, the two most popular fighters and obvious choices, were nowhere to be found. Shamrock had never made it beyond the semis; Gracie was tempted with everything from a new truck to more money than any fighter had ever made, but it wasn't enough. "Meyrowitz wanted to sign Royce to a multi-fight contract, which we couldn't do," said Rorion Gracie. "If Royce won, he would be worth a lot more." As it stood, champions Steve Jennum (UFC III), Dan Severn (UFC V), Oleg Taktarov (UFC VI), and Marco Ruas (UFC VII) would face off against David "Tank" Abbott, Paul Varelans, David Beneteau and Keith Hackney.

The show was held in the Mammoth Events Center, the notorious venue of UFC II. Paul Varelans was originally to be rematched with Mark Hall (Hall lost to Varelans in UFC VII) for a single fight on the card, but when Gerard Gordeau passed on his slot and Patrick Smith dropped out for no reason, Varelans moved into the main bracket. For the first time since the inaugural event, fighters would not be matched by lots, but by Art Davie's decision.

It seemed a natural for Tank Abbott, who had spent his share of time behind bars, to face the ninja police officer, Steve Jennum. Abbott walked through Jennum, much to the delight of the screaming fans. All of the quarter-final matches were over quickly as Hackney fell to Ruas, Varelans lost to Severn and, for the second time, Taktarov submitted Beneteau. Taktarov didn't waste any time, performing a crafty maneuver by rolling under the wrestler during a tie-up and going for an ankle lock. He won without suffering any damage and was fresh for his next match. Beneteau had really wanted the Russian, and thought about quitting the sport after his second loss to him. Hackney vs Ruas provided the only trump card, as both men were adequate strikers. But the kempo man had an off night and was choked into submission by the Brazilian. Grappling made the real difference in this match, since Hackney was still new to the ground game.

Both semis ended in decisions, something that had not happened before – there had been no judges. Proper judging criteria had still not been established, creating plenty of controversy. Tank Abbott could hardly get off a punch as Dan Severn got the takedown and pinned him against the fence. Abbott wondered why McCarthy wouldn't stand them up; he and everyone else had been told that if there was no action on the ground for over two minutes, they would be stood up. For 17 minutes, Severn proceeded to knee, slap, punch, and elbow the street brawler over 250 times. "Dan Severn didn't do anything," claimed Abbott later, meaning Severn wouldn't stand up and trade punches with him. The wrestler's strategy was sensible but Tank wouldn't give in or tap, and with the crowd growing restless, Severn let up, allowing his opponent to gain the advantage for three minutes. "The serious point of the match was pretty much over," said Severn later. "Nobody likes to see a grappling match, so I let him come to his feet so the crowd could get excited." The wrestler tried to perform a suplex, but time ran out. Severn was given the unanimous decision.

The first eight minutes of Taktarov vs Ruas were exciting, with the Russian getting a guillotine choke on the Brazilian and the latter throwing some good kicks and punches. When a cut opened over Taktarov's eye, John McCarthy stopped the fight to have cut man Tabbs look at it. The match continued. Then something strange happened: Ruas refused to engage. "Since he was already cut and it was getting hard for me to breathe, I just wanted to conserve my energy for Severn," he later said. For nine straight minutes, not a single punch was thrown, and at the 29-minute mark Taktarov was ruled the winner. Ruas's manager, Frederico Lapenda, was furious, charging the judges' table and voicing his anger in an interview. Lapenda had given Ruas his nickname of "King of the Streets" and had cut a lucrative deal with the UFC. "If Marco would have won, he would have won a lot more, but that wasn't good for the UFC," claimed Lapenda. The manager had already made a fuss about the judges at the rules meeting, saying, "There are no formal rules, so how could you have judges?" The lesson was that a fighter should never think he is ahead on points; he must chase victory as if victory is always within reach.

The finals rematched Severn with Taktarov. Although the Russian later claimed that doctors kept him from resting between his match with Ruas and the finals, it made little difference. Severn manhandled him, just as he had before. "This time his punches didn't land so bad and they missed a lot," said Taktarov. "He put two fingers in a scar on my face and tried to open it up." Taktarov was soon bleeding, and his opponent tried to force an early stoppage, but Tabbs twice let it go. The Russian put up a good fight, despite his mangled face, and even tried his rolling ankle lock trick again. The match lasted 33 minutes and, when it was over, Severn had won the largest purse since the first UFC: $150,000. "He was unbelievable that night," said Art Davie. "I meant it when I said to him, 'My God, you blew me away.'" Neither street brawler Tank Abbott nor sambo champion Oleg Taktarov could do anything to Severn, once again proving that wrestling was as much a martial art as anything else. The Beast had made a tremendous comeback. Soon he would face his nemesis, Ken Shamrock, one more time.

SEG DECIDED TO take UFC VIII to the Caribbean island of Puerto Rico – and unexpectedly ran into a political war. The first few tournaments had been largely beneath the radar of national politicians and the media, being staged in states without boxing commissions and airing to a tiny, though growing, audience on television. That had changed. Someone had sent a video of an event to John McCain, the Republican senator for Arizona. McCain, a former Naval Academy boxer and Vietnam prisoner of war, was disgusted. He fired off a letter to all 50 state governors railing against "a brutal and repugnant blood sport [that] should not be allowed to take place anywhere in the US."

By the time of the Puerto Rico event, McCain was moving in for the kill. He and Colorado senator Ben Nighthorse Campbell led a determined crusade to destroy the sport, and urged senator Pedro Rosello of Puerto Rico to stop the UFC from taking place in his state. The national Press corps was there in force for the first time too, sensing a story amid the palms and balmy beaches of the holiday isle. They reported that the government of Puerto Rico concurred with McCain that the event had "no place in a civilized society." SEG's lawyers fought back, contending that the authorities could not stop the event because they had no regulations governing such fights. While arguing in court, Bob Meyrowitz got word that Cablevision had dropped the event just days before it was to take place. This enraged Meyrowitz so much that he placed a $10,000 advertisement in *New York Newsday* lambasting Cablevision and its chairman, Jim Dolan. The ad prompted people to call Dolan (it included his home and office number) and demand the UFC be put back in the line-up.

The SEG legal team spent days trying to convince a District Court judge, who finally gave approval one day before showtime. The show was on. Delivering his last hurrah, producer Campbell McLaren devised the theme: David and Goliath. He had always loved the Emmanuel Yarbrough–Keith Hackney fight from UFC III and felt that a tournament with big guys against small guys would be a surefire hit. Campbell would move on to other SEG projects after this show.

A new cast of characters entered the UFC for the first time. Tank Abbott brought in fellow troublemaker Paul Herrera, a high school coach with a solid wrestling background. Gary Goodridge had won the Yukon Jack World Arm Wrestling Championships and was interested in competing; Art Davie had seen him arm wrestle on TV and didn't deliberate long about putting him in the show. Goodridge was a muscular, bald, mean-looking native of Barrie, Canada, who definitely fit the bill. Obviously, the 6ft 8in Paul Varelans was a shoo-in, and some believed that Joe Moriera, a Reylson Gracie student, would be the next big jiu-jitsu fighter to rock the event.

Though he faced Kimo Leopoldo in the superfight, Ken Shamrock brought in his first protégé to compete in the show. Just as the Gracies had their family, Ken had the Lion's Den, a submission fighting school that grew from the need to find suitable training partners for Shamrock. Enter Californian Jerry Bohlander, a former high school wrestler who was going through a tough time of working long shifts to feed his sisters and disabled mother. "I had a lot of pent-up aggression," said Bohlander, who got into numerous street fights as his form of release. When a friend turned him on to the UFC, Bohlander fell in love. He was especially fascinated with Shamrock, whom he sought out in California. Bohlander took self-defense classes from Shamrock for three months, before the UFC veteran asked him to try out for the Lion's Den. The tryouts were grueling, a crazy mixture of sparring, resistance running (carrying a guy your own weight on your back and running 160 yards), 200 squats and, after everything else, pull-ups. Buckets were on hand for triallists to throw up – then carry on. Bohlander made it through the ordeal the first time out and was more than honored when his mentor asked him to fight. "I was a poor kid and didn't have anything. I almost cried, and I had a lump in my throat that I was the first one he asked to fight, to represent the Lion's Den." With only six months of training, the 21-year-old would be part of the sport he once watched with his friends.

Scott "The Pitbull" Ferrozzo was a 350lb juggernaut who became a wealthy man selling collectible 1950s toy robots. When a collector spent over $50,000 and Ferrozzo found out he had pay-per-view ties, a few phone calls were made and he was in the show. Billed as a "pitfighter" (another Art Davie creation), Ferrozzo was a larger Tank Abbott: his tattoo-laden body featured a pitbull, stemming from a nickname he'd earned while playing college football. "In the Citrus Bowl, they have it on film where I'm ripping the quarterback's head from his neck," said Ferrozzo. "I've got his head twisted all the way around and I'm screaming at him, 'Don't get up!'" Aside from football, he boasted a record of 117-7 in high school wrestling. Remembering his violent, steroid-induced days from school, Ferrozzo wanted to see if he still had what it took.

Arizona native Don Frye was another newcomer: imagine a muscled-up Tom Selleck. Frye had wrestled for Oklahoma State and Arizona State University, where he trained under the tutelage of coach Dan Severn. He worked as a firefighter for six years and competed in pro boxing, but after compiling a 5-2-1 record, he decided to call it quits. After taking up judo, Frye saw his old coach in the UFC and ventured to Wyoming to see him lose to Ken Shamrock. The two hooked up and Frye became Severn's training partner for UU '95. Frye fought in several underground matches, one of which was held in an Atlanta dojo, to familiarize himself with mixed martial arts. Severn's new management team of lawyer Robert DePersia and trainer Richard Hamilton eventually took Frye on as their new "hot" property, and he earned a slot in the tournament. Around home, Frye was often called J.R., short for junior, but that wouldn't work for the UFC. While joking about "The Beast," Frye came up with "The Predator." It seemed like each fighter had to have a moniker that outdid the others. Though he didn't have as strong a wrestling background as Severn, Frye knew how to punch and was well aware of submissions from working with female judo teacher Becky Levi.

In the UFC, no one wants the status of hometown favorite because they never seem to do well. Puerto Rican Thomas Ramirez, whom Keith Hackney had beaten to compete in UFC III, made his debut against Don Frye in the opening round. Ramirez looked out of shape but was marketed as having won over 200 challenge matches. He became a ten-second, one-punch casualty for Frye, who didn't even break sweat. Joe Moreira's highly-touted background didn't help either as he ran from Paul Varelans, who won a boring, one-sided match by decision. Scott Ferrozzo vs Jerry Bohlander was another story. The massive Ferrozzo controlled the Lion's Den member for much of the bout. Both landed some hard shots, but stamina proved to be the key. With 52 seconds left, a gassed Ferrozzo held his head down around Bohlander's waist, allowing the smaller man to get him in a guillotine choke. "I panicked and didn't know what to do," said Ferrozzo, who tapped out.

The most spectacular fight of the night was the quarter-final between Gary Goodridge and Paul Herrera. Goodridge had a boxing background but no formal martial arts experience. His only preparation had been sparring with heavyweight friends. When word of his UFC entry spread around Canada, Goodridge met up with a martial arts master skilled in *kuk sool won*, who made an interesting proposition: "We'll give you a fourth degree black belt and buy you a gi if you represent our school." The arm wrestler accepted the offer and went to three classes but knew he was far from ready to compete. Two weeks prior to the fight, he started training with a collegiate wrestler. The only submission he learned was a maneuver called a goose neck (the legs trap one arm and the attacker's arms lock out the other, turning the victim into a human crucifix).

When Goodridge showed up in Puerto Rico, he heard rumors that Herrera was a racist (though Herrera dismisses the notion). "I got all worked up that no matter what, I was not going to lose to him," said Goodridge. He sent two of his training partners to watch the wrestler work out for a video segment used in the event's promotion. When they came back, they told Goodridge that Herrera shot in with a double leg the same way, every single time. So Goodridge remained still when their match started, and sure enough Herrera took the bait. Goodridge, in his black gi, trapped Herrera's arm and fell into the perfect position to submit him. Instead, he pounded Herrera's exposed head with eight power-bomb elbows to the face and temple, knocking him out in just 13 seconds.

Both Goodridge and Frye made it to the finals after taking out their semi-final opponents. The arm wrestler was just too powerful for Jerry Bohlander, who took a lot of punishment before referee John McCarthy stopped the fight. Frye had another easy round against Varelans's replacement, boxer Sam Adkins. Adkins looked intimidating but couldn't stop Frye's takedown and subsequent strikes, leading to a quick tap-out.

Goodridge and Frye fought a short but memorable, seesaw final. Goodridge threw Frye around with ease but took some dizzying punches in the process. In just under five minutes, the Predator finally gained an advantage on the ground and, after a couple of shots, Goodridge was done. David had beaten Goliath. "At the elite level, it is still the skill level that really dictates what goes on inside the octagon," said commentator Jeff Blatnick. UFC VIII proved that a person's physical attributes weighed heavier than black belt status; the black belts (at least those who really had black belts) were growing thin.

Shamrock and Kimo both had similar builds. Each had failed to beat Royce Gracie, and had something to prove for the superfight title. Shamrock had to show the draws to Gracie and Taktarov could be balanced by strong wins like the one against Severn, while Kimo had trained with AMC Pankration in Seattle to ready himself. As the match began, the Hawaiian ran across the octagon in typical fashion toward Shamrock, who took him immediately to the mat and gained side control. Shamrock worked to a mount position, landed a punch, and forced Kimo to his stomach, but didn't go for the obvious choke. The temperature inside the venue was a blistering 100 degrees and he felt the move would be too risky, seeing how he could slip right off his sweaty opponent. Kimo eventually overpowered him and sat in Shamrock's guard. "I know that Kimo likes to pyramid up and open for a punch," said Shamrock later. "He caught me with one, but he also opened himself up for me to go for the leg." Shamrock swung under like a pendulum and, after missing the first time, was able to get the knee bar. Kimo tried to work out of it but leg locks were Shamrock's specialty. Kimo tapped out at 4:24. The tattooed, religious zealot had suffered his second defeat in the octagon. "I was disappointed in AMC that they didn't train me in [leg locks]," said Kimo.

The night would not have been complete without another intrusion by Tank Abbott. Infuriated that his friend Paul Herrera had lost in such a devastating manner, Tank needed little prodding to be drawn into a fight. Moving out into the audience, the pitfighter noticed a vaguely familiar face in Brazilian Allan Goes. Before he had entered the UFC, the burly bad boy and his crew had visited Goes's dojo in California to study jiu-jitsu for a day. Goes, a Carlson Gracie disciple, had little trouble tapping out everyone, and was rumored to be bragging about it at the show. Elaine McCarthy sat behind Tank, his girlfriend Andrea, and manager Dave Thomas. "Here, hold my teeth," Tank said to his girlfriend as he made his way toward Goes. According to Elaine, Andrea was egging Tank on to punish the Brazilian. That was the last thing

SEG needed; they had fought tooth and nail to get permission to hold the show in Puerto Rico, and didn't need any bad publicity.

Tank got off one hit as Goes buried his head into his attacker's chest. The two were eventually pulled apart. Goes later admitted he was partly to blame; he was frustrated and angry at seeing his friend Joe Moreira lose. "Why did you do that when you know we are already in trouble?" Elaine asked Andrea. When Tank walked back toward his girlfriend, Andrea pointed toward Elaine and indicated she had insulted her. Tank marched up to Elaine, got in her face, and said, "I will kill you, you fucking whore. You don't talk to me or anyone associated with me like that." A tearful Elaine went to Bob Meyrowitz and told him that if Tank wasn't fired, she and her husband John won't be returning. "You like him and I know that, and you think he's important for your thing and that's fine, but I'm not doing anything else as long as he's around," said John McCarthy. The Lion's Den came to Elaine's aid and looked for Tank, but he was long gone, reportedly making more trouble at a Hard Rock Café. Meyrowitz called Abbott and told him to take some paid time off. Art Davie devised a "suspension" smoke screen, using the skirmish with Goes as the reason, but SEG could not afford to lose their referee and one of their most valuable team players. Tank would not return until UFC XI.

IN A DEPARTURE from previous events, SEG opted for a night of single match-ups for UFC IX. That would not be the only difference. Meyrowitz, McCarthy, and a team of lawyers were battling with the Michigan District Attorney, who was trying to prevent SEG from holding the event in Detroit. They were still in court at 4:30pm on the day of the event, when the judge issued an ultimatum: the fights could go on as long as there were no headbutts and no closed-fist strikes to the head. Meyrowitz caved in. "We had become an easy target for these small-time politicians who were looking for free publicity," he said. McCarthy looked puzzled, as the two rules were implemented just hours before the fights started, but was reassured that, if breached, they would be only "minor" infractions. Any guilty fighter would receive a $50 fine but, with a wink and a nod, everyone knew it was business as usual.

It was a small victory for the UFC, but they were losing the political war. Governor Rosello had vowed publicly that no UFC event would ever again take place in Puerto Rico. Various states, including Kansas, Mississippi, Ohio, Oklahoma and South Carolina, were reported to have banned the events, as had Chicago City Council. The sport was even sent up in an issue of the satirical magazine *MAD*; its perceived high body count and bloody carnage filled the seven-page spread. UFC fighters Dan Severn, Royce Gracie, Kimo and Ken Shamrock became Dan Septic, Royce Gravy, Chemo and Ken Wayne Amtrak. Even Campbell McLaren (*aka* Marky D. Sodd) was drawn into the piece – and subsequently bought the rights to the artwork.

A very powerful ally joined the opposition. In the run-up to Detroit, Lonnie Bristow, President of the American Medical Association, issued a ferocious statement decrying "these brutal and repugnant contests." He went on:

> Far from being legitimate sports events, ultimate fighting contests are little more than human cockfights where human gladiators battle bare-knuckled until one gives up, passes out, or the carnage is stopped by a doctor or referee. The rules are designed to increase the danger to fighters and to promote injury rather than prevent it
>
> The AMA is opposed to boxing in general as a sport in which the primary objective is to impose injury, and has worked to eliminate both amateur and professional boxing. Ultimate fighting contests are even more physcially dangerous and morally abhorrent, and it is the opinion of the AMA that these blood-filled brawls should be banned immediately.

The AMA had already provided expert testimony in legal actions to stop the UFC, and Bristow said it would continue to "support state legislatures and city officials seeking to ban these brutal and barbaric contests which are being dispensed to the public as blood-soaked, crude public spectacles."

His widely reported outburst served only to enhance the curiosity value of the event and caused a run on tickets for the 11,000-seat Cobo Arena. The venue owners admitted it was "not exactly *Sesame Street Live*" but promised "a real exciting evening." They were not entirely correct. Dan Severn's second chance at beating Ken Shamrock highlighted an otherwise hit-and-miss card. Canadian Gary Goodridge was supposed to fight fellow countryman David Beneteau, but he had a broken hand and was disqualified the night before the fight. Davie and McLaren needed an immediate replacement and couldn't think of a better choice than 1994 Olympic gold medallist wrestler Mark Schultz, who was there to corner Beneteau. Davie courted Schultz for four hours that night, but the wrestler had reservations. He was in shape but he hadn't trained for anything like this before. He didn't even have his wrestling singlet, just a toothbrush and shower shoes. But after taking the mandatory AIDS test, Schultz agreed to fight – for $50,000.

Just before the match with Goodridge began, McCarthy walked over to Schultz with a word of advice: "Try to hit him with open palms as much as you can." No one could ever doubt a wrestler's abilities again as Schultz, who was giving up 40lbs to his opponent, took Goodridge down seconds into the match. Though he knew little about submission, Schultz controlled Goodridge the entire time, and during the latter stages of the twelve-minute bout connected with several hard punches to the face. "Open hands! Open hands!" yelled McCarthy, but the wrestler paid no attention and beat Goodridge over and over again. After several stoppages to check Goodridge's bloody mug, McCarthy finally put an end to his suffering at 12:00.

Reigning jiu-jitsu champion Amaury Bitetti replaced fellow Brazilian Marco Ruas to face Don Frye. Weight was a major factor, as Frye was 15lbs heavier. Though Bitetti came out aggressively, he was not able to take Frye down. While grabbing a standing fighter above the waist and forcing him to the mat is standard for a jiu-jitsu stylist, the tactic rarely works against a seasoned wrestler. Wrestlers have great balance, and if one isn't trying to work an opponent's center of gravity (abdomen), it is very difficult to take him down. Frye chose to stay on his feet and dictated the fight against a man who could not out-grapple him. That was the least of Bitetti's problems. After tying up for the first minute, and a brief exchange, Frye battered Bitetti with punches and knees. The resilient Brazilian bounced back and even tried to take Frye down again, but the wrestler sprawled and out-positioned him on the mat. With barely two and half minutes left, Frye opened up more knees to Bitetti's head on the ground, and McCarthy finally stepped in to stop the punishment at 9:30. Bleeding and bruised, the jiu-jitsu champion had learned an important lesson.

Aside from a small circle "in the know," no one knew that closed-fist strikes were illegal for this event. "I was not going to fight," says Shamrock, who had Meyrowitz, David Isaacs, and his own father trying to convince him otherwise. "I was nowhere near confident that I could beat Dan. I didn't have the skills that night because my body and mind were messed up." In training for the fight, wrestler/body-builder Mike Radnov accidentally broke Shamrock's nose, and he had two bruised ribs and a dislocated knee to add to his problems. But the boys from his father's home for troubled teens would be watching, and *Sports Illustrated* was there to do a story on him. If he played his cards right, Shamrock was going to be on the cover of *Sports Illustrated* and be featured on *CNN Sports*. "Ken, you've broken Takashi's cheek [in Pancrase], and you've broken his jaw and nose with an open hand, so you don't need to close your fist," said Bob Shamrock. "So don't worry about any business decision that SEG makes; just don't do any headbutts, because you don't do that." It was not that simple. Shamrock had made up his mind, but reluctantly gave in to the pressure to help out the show. The cancellation of his fight could have done substantial monetary damage to SEG.

Boos from Dan Severn's hometown Michigan crowd brought Shamrock's confidence down even further, but he made good on his word. Fighting was optional, however. When Shamrock's problem with the rules got back to Severn, he devised a plan to throw him off his game. Severn went out and bought a pair of boxing gloves, indicating that he intended to punch. And for 31 minutes, the fight that would be dubbed "The Great Dance" saw neither man make a move on the other. For the first 15 minutes, Severn walked around Shamrock without a punch thrown. "I took to the center of the ring understanding that I was going to be fighting for my life, and Dan never came at me," said Shamrock. While both men agree that it was one of the most boring fights in UFC history, Severn now views it a bit differently: "the greatest, psychological match ever." After the two finally tied up and went to the ground, Shamrock had one chance for a rear naked choke. "My leg was locking out," he said later, "and if you watch the fight closely, you'll see that I had one hook in and I couldn't get in the other because my leg got locked out. That's when I lost the back mount." Shamrock lost the top position, then got hit a couple of times and started to bleed. The crowd went from hating Shamrock to plain hating the fight. Rorion Gracie, watching from home, shook his head in disgust.

The result was a decision, one Severn knew in his heart he was going to lose; after all, Shamrock was their star. But the Beast's hand was raised. Severn had redeemed himself against Shamrock, but the match cost SEG millions. Their next event saw a 33 percent drop in viewership, which was the lowest since UFC III. "Ken lost his focus on the wrong thing," said Bob Shamrock, who was upset by his son's performance. "I didn't even stay for the party; I just went upstairs, grabbed my things and got on a plane and went home." The two didn't talk for a week. Shamrock had missed his chance to shine. There would be no *Sports Illustrated* article or *CNN Sports* segment. To this day, Shamrock and Severn do not like one another. "As far as I am concerned, Ken Shamrock cannot hold my jock strap," said Severn. "And I'll bash that guy any time I get an opportunity just because I do not like what he represents." Shamrock's retort is more simplistic: "I don't like him either, and I really don't know why. There's just something about him."

Two months after the event, the Governor of Illinois signed legislation prohibiting "ultimate fighting" exhibitions. Another state had gone. SEG had also lost faith in Shamrock. He would skip two shows before making his return. And the company dropped superfights for three consecutive shows. They couldn't afford any more debacles, because the UFC was no longer the only show in town.

CHAPTER 11

Extreme Competition

OTHERS WERE BOUND to cash in eventually on the success of the UFC. Christopher Peters, 26-year-old son of heavyweight producer Jon Peters, created the first similar event of any note. One month after UFC VII, his World Combat Championship (WCC) made its debut on pay-per-view. Peters was an avid martial arts fan and had approached both Rorion Gracie and Art Davie about doing a show in 1994. When that fell through, he pulled the finances together to produce the million-dollar WCC before a 6,000-plus crowd in Salem, North Carolina. Martial artist Bob Wall helped Peters secure several fighters, including K-1 (Japan's premier kickboxing organization) stars Peter Aerts and Sam Greco. When K-1 realized what was going to take place, they pulled both from the show. That didn't seem to bother Peters, who desperately wanted to have a Gracie on the card. At one point, things looked promising for Rickson to make his debut, but money became an obstacle. Looking through *Black Belt* magazine, Peters found an ad for Renzo Gracie, cousin to Royce. Touting a $120,000 grand prize, it was easy to get him on board.

UFC event coordinator Kathy Kidd jumped ship to work with Peters on WCC. Former *Black Belt* editor Jim Coleman also went out of his way to promote the event and criticize the UFC at the same time. Was it because his journalistic integrity led him to the conclusion that WCC would be a better show? Or was it because Coleman and Kidd were now dating and she had left behind a relationship with Art Davie? Whatever the reason for Coleman's actions, Peters seemed sincere in his attempt to turn a spectacle into a sport. He used *Black Belt* as his sounding board, not realizing that Kidd and Coleman were more than just friends.

The tournament showcased decent talent like former IBF world cruiserweight boxing champion James Warring and three-time Olympic judo competitor Ben Spikjers. Its centerpiece was expected to be Renzo Gracie against American Bart Vale, who was a better marketeer than fighter and whose reputation was based on fighting worked bouts in Japan. "I didn't know about any of that," said Peters. "As far as I knew, this was some legendary guy." WCC boasted great production values and some exciting matches. Vale won his first bout, but had to pull out due to injuries. Renzo Gracie easily swept the tournament. He did face the best fighters, but the show pitted strikers against strikers and grapplers against grapplers until the final match. "It was so unfair to the strikers," said Peters. "It was a stupid mistake and I would be the first one to admit that." However, the show made money and the sequel, WCC 2: Meltdown in Mexico, was set to play just months later. Strangely, the wife of the show's investor threatened divorce if he put in another dime, so the funding went out the door. With politics making things difficult, Peters folded up shop. He would later manage fighters like Vitor Belfort and Frank Shamrock and still hopes to one day produce another MMA show.

Enter Donald Zuckerman, lawyer, boxing manager, musical talent manager (remember the group Scandal?), and former owner of the popular New York nightclub The Ritz. By 1993, several months before the inaugural UFC event, he was searching for a new avenue to flex his creative muscle. He dabbled in film production until a friend in the industry showed him a tape of some vale tudo fights, much as *Gracies in Action* had been shown to SEG. The idea was to make a film out of it, but Zuckerman felt it should be a fight show. Once described by the *Los Angeles Times* as "a raconteur ... hot after bicoastal opportunities with a phone pressed to his ear," Zuckerman had connections inside the television sports network ESPN2 and Fox International. He assembled all his money-making ducks in a row; all he needed was funds to produce the show itself. He went to Polygram and secured a deal with his friend John Sher, who headed up one of the corporation's production arms. Sher agreed to be a deficit financier to enable Polygram to pay for the show; Zuckerman would get his cut upfront and by selling video rights on the back end.

A deal was inked in April 1994 for the show to go into production just after Sher pulled off his brainchild, Woodstock II. However, when the budget of $19 million turned to $45 million for the outdoor concert – which also deteriorated into near-riot – Sher was fired, Polygram was out of the picture, and Zuckerman was left to start from scratch. The lawyer turned to a very unlikely alternative: Bob Guccione, the man who created the soft-porn *Penthouse* magazine and subsequently ran that company's parent entity, General Media Inc. The wealthy Guccione agreed to put up $750,000 and brought in his son Anthony

to aid Zuckerman in running the new sister company, called
Battlecade. (The *Penthouse* connection was no surprise: in a 1979 issue
of *Hustler* magazine, Benny "The Jet" Urquidez was featured in a
lengthy article entitled "The Baddest Dude in the World"; ten years
later, Rorion Gracie received a similar treatment in *Playboy*. It's hard to
believe, but true, that skin magazines brought more press to these two
men than any martial arts rag, and that *Playboy* sparked the all-impor-
tant union between Art Davie, Gracie and SEG.)

Zuckerman didn't know much about martial arts, or at least not
enough to produce a show comparable to the UFC. He had been trying
to pull together facts and figures about this type of show, and word
around town said Gene LeBell was the man in the know. LeBell was a
two-time Amateur Athletic Union judo champion but he was known
more as a pro wrestler and Hollywood stuntman. His martial arts
pedigree stressed groundfighting over stand-up techiques, and his
knowledge of submission holds became legendary. After several
discussions with LeBell, Zuckerman was introduced to one of his
students, John Perretti, who he invited to be the matchmaker and on-
air commentator for Extreme Fighting, the name of Battlecade's show.
Perretti, a lifelong martial artist, accepted the offer. He had studied tae
kwon do, tang soo do and other Korean forms before moving on to
wing chun kung fu, which he'd studied for 16 years. Perretti eventually moved into various competitions ranging from wushu (kung fu
forms competition) to full-contact karate (he even fought Howard
Jackson, who was ranked number ten in the world). After studying
boxing, Perretti's thirst for martial arts wisdom took him to LeBell,
"who unceremoniously convinced me that I knew nothing about fighting." He studied under LeBell, and then moved on to other grapplers
including the Machado family, cousins to the Gracies. Perretti held the
veteran in such high regard that LeBell became the middle name of his
first-born son.

With General Media's money, Zuckerman and Perretti were set to
put on Battlecade's Extreme Fighting in New York, on November 18,
1995, at the Park Slope Armory, Brooklyn. Pitching for the Big Apple
was a bold move. The pair drummed up a large amount of publicity
but, inevitably, much of it was negative. Political pressure mounted
and eventually forced litigation to stop the show. Though
Zuckerman's team ended up winning a court case that gave them
permission to go ahead in the state of New York, it had become a risky
endeavor. "Our lawyer said that no matter where we went in New
York, the police were going to take it very seriously and close us
down," said Zuckerman. Just two days before the show was due to

take place, it seemed Zuckerman's own marketing ploys had pushed him into a corner. He had little choice but to change sites.

He picked North Carolina, where the UFC had held its third show. Though a law had been passed to ban MMA in that state, it wouldn't come into effect for another month. The sellout crowd in Brooklyn was dumped and tickets were given away to fill up the North Carolina venue. With very little time to prepare, Zuckerman remembered an old client, film producer Dino De Laurentis, who had once built a sound stage there. The person who ran the sound stage just happened to be a martial artist, and welcomed Extreme Fighting with open arms. "On Friday morning, we decided that we were going down there," remembered Zuckerman. "We sent everybody by plane, and the trucks started rolling since all of the equipment was still in New York. The morning of the show, everybody started to set everything up and we just made showtime." The entire production was moved from New York to North Carolina in just 36 hours. It would certainly not be the last chapter in the story of MMA in New York.

A NEW GROUP of warriors was ready to battle in the larger, circular cage of Extreme Fighting. John Lewis was a former breakdancer who grew up in Hawaii and quickly learned that "the culture was very much streetfighting oriented." He began studying martial arts because he wanted to test his skills against better opponents. Five foot eleven and weighing 159lbs, Lewis was tattooed from head to toe, accentuating his unbelievably sculpted physique. When he wasn't practicing Japanese kickboxing, he set up mats in his backyard and fought or trained anyone who was interested. "I would always get different guys in there from different arts to see how I would fare against them, and that's how I met John Perretti," said Lewis. After sparring with Perretti in his backyard in 1991, Lewis was introduced to Gene LeBell and became his first black belt. He eventually fought in his first official MMA match in a Hawaiian event called United Full Contact Fighting. With Perretti and LeBell in his corner, Lewis won by arm bar at 1:45. That took place just two months before the first Extreme Fighting show, and Perretti used four of its fighters in his events.

Having worked with the Machados, Perretti was well aware of the Gracies, and hooked up with Carlson Gracie to secure some of his fighters for the show. Mario Sperry was a 1995 Brazilian jiu-jitsu champion, Carlson Gracie Jr was a ten-time Brazilian jiu-jitsu champion, and Marcus "Conan" Silveira was a menacing, 6ft 3in, 245lb Brazilian specimen. Silveira started judo at the age of eight and, after five years, moved on to jiu-jitsu under Carlson in Brazil: "Carlson taught more than just the fundamentals of jiu-jitsu; he brought us the knowledge of being in a street fight with technique." Silveira went to the United States in 1989 and, though he had never fought professionally, opened up a jiu-jitsu school in 1993. He was ready to test himself. Carlson gave him the nickname Conan, and he rarely went by anything else after his first professional appearance.

Perretti also found another Gracie in San Francisco: Ralph, brother of Renzo. And just as the UFC had Oleg Taktarov, Perretti had Igor Zinoviev, who had emigrated from St Petersburg to Brooklyn in 1992 purely by accident: Zinoviev was supposed to meet a business contact in America, but when he didn't show up at the airport, Zinoviev ran into a fellow Russian, who showed him around town. He has lived in the US ever since. His background in judo and sambo helped him win the heavyweight judo championship in the Empire State Games in 1995 and in 1996. When a friend introduced him to Perretti, Zinoviev became his student in kickboxing and subsequently started to learn better groundfighting.

Perretti's talent as matchmaker stemmed from his varied martial arts experience and understanding of fighters as opposed to guys with black belts. "When I watched the UFC, I was laughing as I listened to these people talk about things they had no idea about," he said. He also didn't think much of Art Davie's matchmaking. Davie's criteria was, "How much do you weigh?" Extreme Fighting had decent talent, partly because it learned from UFC's mistakes about putting in black belts who didn't know how to fight.

The action inside the circular cage, which had similar rules to the UFC, was more sport than spectacle, but with the tag line "Whatever it Takes to Win!" and pneumatic Penthouse Pets roaming the audience, there was more than a hint of the Roman Colosseum. Muscular television and film celebrity Mr T fielded questions backstage, his ignorance of the sport and cartoonish persona seeming in direct contrast to what Perretti was trying to project. One difference from the UFC was major: instead of an eight-man tournament, there would be two four-man tourneys broken down by weight class.

The first show was a lively mix of striking, controversy and competitive matches. Ralph Gracie started things off by quickly choking out Japanese karate player Makoto Murako, who was in mid-tap as he slipped into unconsciousness. Igor Zinoviev also looked impressive, knocking the wind out of Harold German with a hopping side-kick; after missing a knee bar, he punched German in the head more than a dozen times before tapping him out. Mario Sperry, who came in with an unverifiable fighting record of 272-0, finished Rudyard Moncayo with strikes, just as Silveira won his match over Zinoviev protégé Victor Tatarkin.

As Carlson Gracie Jr, known as the "Prince of Jiu-jitsu," stepped up to face John Lewis in a superfight, he probably expected a quick match. Lewis trained with jiu-jitsu practitioner Andre Pederneiras and would be competing in his second MMA match but faced a more skilled opponent. Gracie mounted an aggressive attack, but had difficulty controlling Lewis. At one point he got the takedown, but Lewis pulled guard and kicked him back with his tremendous grasshopper legs. Lewis returned with furious strikes while Gracie wanted the action to return to the mat. Working back to his feet, the Brazilian wasted his energy trying to grapple Lewis, who had his arm wrapped over the top of the fence. Gracie finally got his man down but Lewis stayed right on him and unloaded more punches. When the 15-minute time limit ran out, a five-minute overtime offered much of the same, with a clinched stalemate against the fence. The fight was ruled a draw. "A lot of people thought that I won that fight," said Lewis. "I was in control the entire time and he just kept me in his guard."

Silveira won the heavyweight tourney by beating wrestler Gary Myers by choke, despite a cut over his right eye that almost gave his opponent the win. The middleweight final was more competitive as Mario Sperry took on judo champ Igor Zinoviev. Within 40 seconds, the Brazilian took Zinoviev down and established side control – but not for long. The two volleyed for position, with Zinoviev even catching Sperry in a guillotine choke. Sperry broke free, but couldn't break the Russian's iron grip. The two eventually rose back to their feet against the fence, with Sperry behind Zinoviev. The Russian had entered the event with broken ribs, and his breathing was becoming a factor.

With three and a half minutes left in overtime, Sperry leaped on Zinoviev's back to sink in a rear naked choke, but the Russian countered by ducking. Now Sperry was in front of him on the ground, a very bad position. Sperry caught a knee to the face, but took Zinoviev down again. The fight stopped moments later when Sperry, with a huge gash over his forehead, tapped the mat once, though he was only wiping the blood away. Sperry didn't complain about referee Gokor Chivichyan's decision because of the rules. "Before the show, it was said that any cuts over the eyes would finish the fight," said Sperry. He felt the match could have continued, but when he got to his corner, he realized the cut was too severe (it required 13 stitches).

Zinoviev became Extreme Fighting's first middleweight champion. Sperry's record was allegedly now 273-1, although Perretti said later the large undefeated record was actually Carlson's idea. Records showed Sperry competing in one previous match, so his hundreds of wins were most likely in jiu-jitsu, if indeed they existed. Conan Silveira also had claimed a record of 17-0 when this was actually his first fighting experience. It's a gamble to pad resumes, and the show strained credibility by saying Rudyard Moncayo was 7-0 when he had just lost in UFC VI to Pat Smith. Sperry's loss to Zinoviev and the Lewis/Gracie draw also began to raise doubts about the strength of jiu-jitsu as a style, compared to the skill of the fighter using it.

BOB MEYROWITZ WAS unprepared. He had walked into the hornet's nest of *Larry King Live*, CNN's top-rated talk show, just ten days before the first Ultimate Ultimate in December 1995 and all he had with him was a promotional poster. Meyrowitz watched as Arizona Republican Senator John McCain entered the studio with a four-inch book entitled *UFC*; his three aides each had a copy. The nervous SEG President made a quick exit to the bathroom, where he cut up his poster to make it appear he had notes and was fully prepared. It didn't do him much good. He sensed disaster after overhearing Larry King say to McCain, "Hey John, I didn't see you at the party Friday night. I was wondering what happened to you."

Meyrowitz and McCain were there to debate mixed martial arts before the nation. In early 1995, McCain had led a rally to ban "ultimate fighting." The sports' defenders sensed a conspiracy, pointing out the brewing giant Budweiser helped finance McCain's election campaign and was also boxing's biggest advertiser – and boxing was perhaps the one sport that felt most threatened by fans switching interest to MMA. McCain wrote a letter to Wyoming Governor Jim Geringer on June 6, 1995, calling his attention to UFC VI, which was to take place in his state the following month. The second sentence of his letter read: "The 'Ultimate Fighting Championship' is a disturbing and bloody competition which places the contestants at great risk for serious injury or even death, and it should not be allowed to take place anywhere in the United States." McCain was flabbergasted that his fellow Republican, New York Governor George Pataki, had not stopped UFC VII from taking place in Buffalo. In a letter to Pataki, McCain complained, "It is very disappointing that New York State officials could not prevent this appalling event from taking place." Pataki did succeed in forcing promoter Donald Zuckerman to rethink his plan for holding an Extreme Fighting event in Brooklyn and revoked the venue's permit. He had plenty of help from Mayor Rudolph Giuliani and State Senator Roy Goodman of Manhattan.

It had all started when Zuckerman was having trouble getting press. Through a connection with the *New York Times*, he decided to create his own publicity. "I talked to this reporter, and he called Goodman and asked him if he was aware that [Extreme Fighting was taking place in New York];" said Zuckerman. Goodman held a press conference where Zuckerman offered his side of the story. To stoke the fire, the Extreme Fighting promoter felt necessary to position his event in the same "or death" vein as the UFC. Pickets lined the steps of City Hall, and Goodman felt his anti case was strong; his speech was full of sound bites. "The politicians didn't know they [pickets] were working for us," said Zuckerman. "We paid a bunch of kids to hold up signs saying that someone was going to die and to stop this now, that type of thing." The more controversy the better – or so he thought.

With the event set for Saturday, November 15, 1995, Zuckerman brought the issue to the State Supreme Court in Brooklyn on the preceding Thursday and won. The judge enjoined the state authorities from cancelling the lease, but an automatic appeal kept things in court. "They postponed their decision till the Tuesday after the fight," said Zuckerman, "and said that since the state had deep pockets, if the state was wrong, monetary damages would suffice, so they would not issue an injunction." But plenty of doubt remained in his mind. He couldn't risk the first show going under before having a chance to prove itself, so, after securing plans the day before (Wednesday), Zuckerman moved the show to North Carolina in 36 hours.

On *Larry King*, Meyrowitz was joined on a studio feed by UFC sensation Ken Shamrock, while McCain had Nevada State Boxing Commissioner Marc Ratner in his corner. The blunt speaking McCain pushed his case, arguing that the UFC "appeals to the lowest common denominator in our society." King piped in, "The object is to maim, isn't that right, Ken?" Both sides brought up good points, but the show's host cut off Shamrock before he could talk about the many deaths that had occurred in boxing. McCain pointed out that at least boxing had a referee, ignoring the fact that the UFC and other like events did too. He tried to make his case by saying that New York State Athletic Commissioner, former boxing champ Floyd Patterson, didn't like Ultimate Fighting. With sad irony, Patterson would later be relieved of duty as a result of short-term memory loss caused by brain damage suffered from boxing. McCain said he thought the event would end up overseas, since 36 states had already banned it. Neither Meyrowitz nor Shamrock could convince the panel of their case, but that didn't stop *Wild, Wild West* star Robert Conrad from calling in and chastizing the senator for worrying himself over a sport instead of balancing the budget.

From a political standpoint, the UFC and no-holds-barred was a safe issue to come out against: who wouldn't be against something dubbed a blood sport? It didn't matter that there hadn't been any serious injuries or deaths, unlike boxing; because it didn't have a true regulatory body, it was an easy target. Meyrowitz did say he was all in favor of regulation. Few people picked up on this at the time, but it would become the UFC's ticket to approval by the various state athletic commissions.

In December 1995, SEG hired lobbyist James D. Featherstonhaugh, affectionately nicknamed "Feathers" for his knack of flying under the radar to get laws passed that might otherwise have been shot down in the Senate. Meyrowitz knew that time was against him, as Pataki and Goodman were joining forces to seek outlawing the sport in New York; Zuckerman's Brooklyn show had alarmed them, and Meyrowitz's Buffalo event had come close to being shut down. In a December 5 letter to SEG, Featherstonhaugh laid out a plan to persuade key legislators to show support for the UFC by lobbying for its regulation in New York. First on his list was Senate majority leader Frank Bruno, who also happened to be Featherstonhaugh's business partner. Meyrowitz met with Bruno and, during the first two months of 1996, things were looking up for the UFC. Goodman's bill to ban the sport on January 30, 1996, did not get a hearing by the investigations committee until April of that year. By June, Goodman was looking at an entirely different picture. Some senators showed resistance toward banning these events. Goodman folded; he now sought regulation rather than banishment. By July, a law to properly regulate MMA events had passed both houses and was on its way to Governor Pataki.

ALTHOUGH THE FIRST show lost money (due to all the free tickets), the scantily-clad women, harder-edge promotion and decent fights made it a success with fans. Zuckerman didn't want to take any chances with the follow-up show. He came up with a plan to hold Extreme Fighting 2 on an Indian reservation to steer clear of the American court system altogether. After contacting several reservations without any luck, he received a call from kickboxing promoter Mike Thomas, who had been running small shows in Kahnawake, a Mohawk reservation in Quebec, Canada. Thomas was a member of the Mohawk tribe, and saw the fighters as possessing a warrior spirit, something the Indians could identify with. He became the on-site promoter and made several trips to Quebec to keep the authorities informed of what the Mohawks were doing. "There were a lot of tricks that the province [of Quebec] was trying to pull," said Thomas. "The Mohawk Council said that they were going to stand by us, which they did."

Unfortunately, the French press in Quebec played up the violence of the show and forced the Canadian Government to take the moral high road. Its first measure was to prevent participants from entering the country. "Immigration sent back nine of my fighters and my camera-man, producer, director, ring announcer and others," said Perretti. Zuckerman hired a Canadian crew, but faced with the threat of arrest they soon quit. "We ended up doing the fight with a very light crew, less than a third of what's needed," said Zuckerman. At least 27 people with the show were turned away at the border, and Perretti claimed that it wasn't entirely because of the Canadian Government: "And then Bob [Meyrowitz] or the UFC paid my fighters not to fight. I discovered all these guys, and then they got a hold of them and paid them more money than I could not to fight. Unbelievable!" Mike Thomas also learned that SEG's David Isaacs tried to rent out the same venue for the same night, an obvious attempt to block their competi-tors. The Mohawks would not go around Thomas, so Extreme Fighting stood its ground. Campbell McLaren said later that luring fighters away to compete in the UFC, and trying to gain access to the same venues, was just part of doing business and being competitive.

It was only the beginning. After spending all afternoon in court, the promoters were dealt a devastating blow when the Quebec govern-ment issued an injunction to stop Bell Canada from carrying the signal to the pay-per-view audience. Luckily for Zuckerman, they didn't enjoin anyone else. "I got an uplink truck to drive two hundred miles at breakneck speed and arrive thirty minutes before the show, and we went right up to the AT&T satellite and did it ourselves," he said.

Zuckerman and Perretti stationed all the fighters in a hotel outside of Quebec to keep them out of the limelight and decrease the possibil-ity of deportation. At the hotel, Zuckerman told the fighters not to leave any word as to where they were going – answering machine or other-wise. The police couldn't do anything on the Indian reservation, but they could try to stop people from getting there. UFC II veteran Orlando Weit was scheduled to fight Igor Zinoviev, but the pressure nixed his participation on the card. In an interview conducted that day for a German documentary on the show, Weit said, "It's not fair from the promoters' side because they didn't tell the fighters exactly what was going on." Shortly after, Weit and his wife left the hotel bound for Holland. Peretti, who had made exhaustive efforts to keep Weit at ease, fumed. "He totally chickened out and he used us as an excuse for some political nonsense." He was the only fighter who refused to go on.

Unlike the first show, this one provided few surprises save for the opener between newcomers Nigel Scantelbury and Jason Canals. Both men fought their hearts out and performed a clinic of ground techniques before the bout was ruled a draw, and deservedly so. All of the veterans on the card faced relative fighting "newbies" with genuine martial arts credentials who didn't fare too well. Newly awarded jiu-jitsu black belt John Lewis quickly out-positioned AAU National Wrestling champ Jim Teachout, who tapped after several hard elbow strikes to the back of the head. Zinoviev was left without an opponent, but Perretti matched him against wing chun exponent Steve Faulkner, who was originally supposed to face wrestler Paul Jones. Zinoviev had hardly trained for Weit in the first place and now wanted an extra $25,000 to fight his new opponent, not knowing his strengths and weaknesses. The Russian slammed Faulkner to the mat and quickly gained a rear naked choke, forcing him to tap out. Zinoviev recalled that Faulkner told him he normally fought five on one, "so this should be easy." Before the show, a tape was shown of Faulkner sparring with multiple opponents. His moves were quick and complex. Against Zinoviev, he never got off a punch, kick, or block.

Steve Nelson was a five-time national sambo champion from Amarillo, Texas, who said, "Tonight, I want to make sure that I walk out as the world champion so when I look back on this, I can say that I'm the best who ever was." After taking his back, Ralph Gracie finished him in just 43 seconds with 15 punches to the back of the head. Conan Silveira also continued his reign of terror by knocking the 5ft 8in, 218lb Carl Franks senseless at 1:17. After their opponents were turned away at the airport, Canadians Carlos Newton and Jean Riviere fought each other in an incredible seven-minute-plus bout. Nineteen-year-old Newton wore a gi and weighed 180lbs, but the promoters listed his weight as 205lbs in an attempt to match them better on paper; Riviere weighed in at 286lbs. Newton was nervous and became fatigued, but gave Riviere all he could handle before tapping out from exhaustion.

With only six bouts, and just two of them lasting more than two minutes, the show did not make the required hour and 45 minutes needed to secure the pay-per-view two-hour block. Bob Guccione added vignettes with *Penthouse* models between matches, but it didn't make much difference. The skeleton crew and short fights made for a strained relationship between Extreme Fighting and the pay-per-view operators.

As the sellout crowd began to leave, there was an immense sigh of relief backstage that the show had managed to go on despite numerous obstacles. But the following night, the Chief of the Mohawk Peacekeepers, in conjunction with the Quebec police, raided the hotel and made eight arrests. "They wanted to make it look like it was an Indian action," said Zuckerman. "The Chief [of the Mohawks] betrayed us, although we don't know that for sure." The police had a list of whom they were going to arrest, though Mike Thomas and Zuckerman were not on it. As Zuckerman recalled, Conan's brother Marcelo didn't take this very well. "His brother was three inches away from my face, telling me that if I didn't get him [Conan] out of jail tonight, I was a dead man. At one point I was going to have him arrested." The locked-up fighters would be more than okay though, as word had spread about these no-rules gladiators. The regulars behind bars were scared out of their minds, especially at the sight of Conan, who had two eyes tattooed on his back.

Other arrests were equally unpleasant. "The Texan [Steve Nelson] was in bed with his girlfriend, and they literally opened his door with a passkey and stood there and watched her dress," said Zuckerman. As Nelson was put in the squad car with Igor Zinoviev, Nelson's girlfriend said, "If these fighters had known that this was illegal, I know my boyfriend, for one, would have never fought." Nelson would later form his own fighting organization, the United Shoot Wrestling Federation, and become a major activist in legalizing the sport. He also fought a rematch with Ralph Gracie, and it took Gracie over eleven minutes to beat him. Gracie, incidentally, escaped arrest by hiding out in a friend's hotel room for three days.

When John Perretti returned to the USA and found out about the arrests, he took the next plane to Quebec and got himself arrested so that he could be with his fighters. Zuckerman worked out an agreement with the Quebec police, and all charges were dismissed after he signed an apology letter stating he had taken part in something that was illegal and not a sport. Zuckerman made sure the fighters didn't have to sign anything. Thomas was never arrested but was charged with the same violation. The prosecutors came up with a plea bargain to admit guilt that would cost him a mere $100. "I was more interested in making a statement that this was a sport, and I was prepared to spend whatever it cost to win that battle," said Thomas, who anted up $50,000 during the lengthy court case. All charges against him were dropped four years later.

The arrests confirmed the Canadian judiciary's stance on mixed martial arts, shutting down something they didn't understand. But the pioneers weren't ready to give in. They were just getting started.

Karate master Ron Van Clief during his "Black Dragon" days. He entered UFC IV at the age of 52. *(Ron Van Clief)*

Dan Severn: Unleash The Beast! A former amateur wrestling champion, the Michigan-born Severn lost to Royce Gracie in UFC IV but blazed back to win the next event. *(Dan Severn)*

Former Russian soldier Oleg Taktarov, pictured here at 19, was living rough until he walked into a Los Angeles gym. *(Oleg Taktarov)*

Ken Shamrock applies a guillotine choke to Dan Severn to win the UFC VI Superfight. *(Susumu Nagao)*

Oleg Taktarov goes for the choke on an exhausted Tank Abbott to win UFC VI. *(Susumu Nagao)*

Marco Ruas lashes a Thai kick at Paul
Varelans on his way to winning UFC VII.
(Robin Postell)

Gary Goodridge goes for the takedown on
Don Frye during the finals of UFC VIII.
(Susumu Nagao)

Dan Severn works from the top on Ken Shamrock to win UFC IX.
(Susumu Nagao)

(TOP) A young John Perretti during his martial arts competition days *(John Perretti)*. Perretti was the matchmaker for (BOTTOM) Extreme Fighting. *(Battlecade)*

Marcus "Conan" Silveira, who terrified jail inmates with his bizarre tattoos *(Battlecade)*

Igor Zinoviev (bottom) holds a crafty Ze Mario Sperry. Zinoviev became the EF's first middleweight champion. *(Battlecade)*

Ralph Gracie sprawls from Steve Nelson's takedown attempt. Gracie escaped arrest when the Canadian police tried to round up Extreme Fighting competitors by hiding in hotel room for three days. *(Battlecade)*

Andy Anderson, millionaire, promoter, fighter and referee, breaks up the action in the International Fighting Championships. *(IFC)*

Anthony Macias launches a kick at policeman Houston Dorr in the IFC, which became the premier mixed martial arts organisation in Canada. *(IFC)*

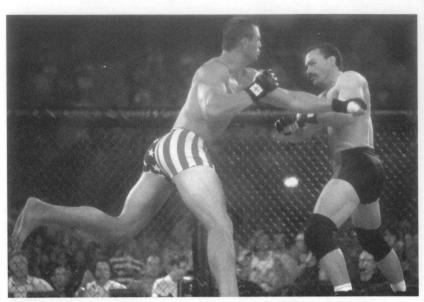

Brian Johnston fires away at Don "The Predator" Frye in a thrilling confrontation in the semi-finals of UFC X. *(Robin Postell)*

Mark Coleman dominates Don Frye in the finals of UFC X. *(Robin Postell)*

Mark Coleman wins his second UFC tournament. *(Zuffa Entertainment)*

Tank Abbott lands a haymaker on Scott "The Pitbull" Ferrozzo in a battle of the giants. Abbott became the UFC's bad boy and a firm favourite with the fans. *(Zuffa Entertainment)*

Brian Johnston suffers against Ken Shamrock.
(Robin Postell)

Mark Coleman wins his second
UFC tournament.
(Zuffa Entertainment)

Tank Abbott struts across the octagon as John McCarthy and referee Joe Hamilton help fallen Steve Nelmark. *(Susumu Nagao)*

Abbott lays into Don Frye in the finals of Ultimate Ultimate '96. Despite the power of Tank's blows, Frye won with a choke. *(Susumu Nagao)*

CHAPTER 12

The IFC Story

INTERNATIONAL FIGHTING CHAMPIONSHIPS has been one of the few franchise promotions to outlast the host of UFC clones that started in the mid-Nineties. Though it would call Canada and California home, it began with a show in Kiev, Ukraine. The story of how the IFC got there, and what took place, reads as good as any James Bond thriller. For those involved, it would be an experience they'd never forget.

Even before his defeat in UFC V, Andy Anderson was working with promoter Buddy Albin to secure on-site promotions to keep live show audiences happy. Despite Albin forcing the first "work" (Taktarov vs Macias) in UFC history, he was too useful to the company to ditch. That changed when UFC VIII came around. The two flew to Puerto Rico and began to lay the groundwork for the show a full month before it took place (February 16, 1996). Albin was a decent local promoter, having spent years in kickboxing as well as putting on underground no-holds-barred events since the 1980s. But sometime during the mid-1990s – though no one knows the full story – Albin "lost his mind to alcohol and other problems," according to Anderson.

After they had both spent a full day negotiating with a Puerto Rican company to acquire equipment for the show, Albin called Anderson later that night and began to tell him what happened, forgetting he had been with him just hours before. When Bob Meyrowitz called Albin for updates, Anderson returned the calls because his partner was too far gone to know what was going on. Anderson and Meyrowitz became friends, while Albin was relieved of his duties and subsequently fired. A week before UFC VIII, producer Michael Pillot surveyed the site and wasn't satisfied with the equipment that had been secured. He sent for all of his own equipment by boat from New York to Puerto Rico, at a $200,000-plus price tag.

In November 1995, a Ukrainian group called the International Professional Kickboxing League had invited Albin (before his dismissal), Anderson and several others to produce a show in Eastern Europe. They spent two weeks in the Ukraine sizing things up, and even after Albin's sacking they continued working together on plans to launch a show called Ultimate Warriors, to be held March 30, 1996. Albin patterned the Ultimate Warriors logo on the UFC's, and produced a poster that strikingly resembled the one used for Ultimate Ultimate '95, advertising fighters such as Marco Ruas and Oleg Taktarov. Needing more experienced help, Albin looked to his old kickboxing days. Atlantan Howard Petschler had left the PKA in 1994 and set his sights on promoting an MMA show without the bloodlust angle. He attended a few UFCs to garner the interest of investors, and when his plans to assist Martial Arts Reality Superfighting (see Chapter 17) fell through, he took a call from Albin, who he had first met at UFC III. Albin claimed he had purchased the "international" rights to the UFC, and wanted Petschler to ready a production crew bound for Kiev.

Petschler had experience producing shows for Showtime and pay-per-view in Montreal, and had worked with local promoter Victor Theriault (brother of kickboxing legend Jean Yves Theriault). He convinced Albin to bring both Theriault and Mike Thomas, the future on-site promoter for Extreme Fighting 2, to the Ukraine as well. Thomas, a Canadian native and kickboxing promoter in his own right, had spoken to Albin only over the phone. Little did anyone realize that Buddy Albin was not dealing with just another sports organization in the Ukraine. "All the sports teams over there are backed by different factions of the Mob," said Petschler. "Buddy had backed himself into a corner when he told them he was a branch of the Ultimate [UFC] and that this was going to be exactly like the UFC." The Russian mafia thought they would be making a sizeable fortune from the Americans hosting fights in their country.

Two weeks before the event, the party arrived in the Ukraine fearing the worst. Instead, Customs officials were pushed out of the way by mobsters, and the fighters were treated like celebrities, transported from the airplane to the hotel in custom vans and gleaming Mercedes and Volvos in what looked like a presidential convoy. "They were driving us through the snow on the autobahn going ninety-five miles per hour," said fighter John Lober. The city of Kiev was decked out with Ultimate Warriors propaganda, and the Russians didn't want to risk anything happening to their new American friends. "They kept us in an Olympic training center with an eleven-foot concrete wall all the way around it with barbed wire on top of that," said Anderson. Machine gun-toting guards in trenchcoats stood around the building, and no one was allowed to leave without an armed escort. "For many, this was their first experience with capitalism," said Petschler. Their contact was a man named Yuri, and apparently "a couple of peripheral players," according to Petschler.

Customs officials finally made trouble when they took the passports from several fighters, although they had by then been there for a week – with no money for food. Albin smoothed things over, borrowed $5,000 from Anderson and was rarely seen again until the night of the show. Eventually pulling all the fighters together, Albin told them, "Bob [Meyrowitz] bought the word Ultimate off of me for $1 million, so you guys are going to have no problem getting paid," according to Lober. Most of them bought it. Albin told the opposite to Petschler and everyone else: that he had paid $1 million to use the name Ultimate for the show. His lies were beginning to unravel. "If I see that logo anywhere, I will sue you for everything you've got," Meyrowitz told Albin over the phone the night before the event. Petschler had to convince Yuri to go in and paint over the title, sealed on the octagon floor in black. So what was the show to be called? Originally, Night of Diamonds (a reference to the diamond shapes of the octagon wire fence), until Petschler came up with International Fighting Championships.

The National Sports Palace was nearly full, with a house of over 18,000 on hand. Albin had promised that comedian Eddie Murphy and Muhammad Ali were going to be in attendance; a very drunk and out-of-hand Leon Spinks appeared instead. Dutch sensation Bas Rutten, who made a name for himself in the Pancrase organization, served as commentator, along with Ron Van Clief, who had been dismissed from SEG. Anderson would not be fighting but had the best view in the house as referee. Aside from being a millionaire, Anderson had refereed numerous tae kwon do tournaments and was well versed in MMA. With eleven fights on the card, he would have his work cut out.

The show comprised four single fights and an eight-man tournament. The only all-American match was John "The Machine" Lober against Eric Hebestreit. Lober was a former firefighter and had competed in sports his whole life. He became hooked on submission fighting and couldn't get enough of his new "drug," since his school ran classes only two or three times a week. In an effort to train as often as he wanted, Lober took a unique approach to finding training partners. "A friend of mine and I drove in our van down to a particular part of town. My friend would get out and hold up a sign that said, 'FIGHT MY FRIEND FOR $5 FOR FIVE MINUTES,' and all of this was in Spanish. People were accepting the offers and we were getting these big, fat guys. I got three or four off the street and [I'd] wrestle them in the garage and videotape it: me grabbing them, slapping them down, choking them, and taking their backs. There was one guy who wanted to fight me twice because I pissed him off, so I held him down and slapped him. Some turned into real fights because these guys would get pissed off because I wasn't hitting them."

When the UFC began, Lober was training in jiu-jitsu and varying fighting styles thanks to UFC alumni like Kimo and Todd Medina. He took the opportunity to fight in Kiev because he wanted to compete one time for experience and then call it quits. Lober's father, a former college wrestler, was his driving force but couldn't make the Kiev trip after a terrible car accident had damaged his health. After beating his opponent, Lober called his father to tell him the good news. His brother answered the phone; Lober's father had passed away just as his son was about to fight. The event changed Lober's life and he made the sport his calling.

THE EIGHT-MAN tournament set up four Americans against four Eastern Europeans. Paul "The Polar Bear" Varelans, Gerry Harris, John Dixson, and Fred "The Mangler" Floyd were the largest NHB fighters from the US. Outweighed by 100lbs and eight inches shorter, Russian fighter Igor Guerus knocked out Harris with the only punch thrown in a 15-second match. Both Varelans and Dixson took out their respective opponents with strikes. Valery Nikulin, Varelans's opponent, suffered a broken collarbone and a dislocated elbow that didn't hinder his attack, until the big man finally put him away.

The final match of the opening round, Floyd vs Igor Vovchanchyn, confirmed the Ukrainian fighters' ability to dish out as much punishment as they could take. Hailing from Kharkiv, Ukraine, the 22-year-old Vovchanchyn was a champion kickboxer standing 5ft 9in and weighing 207lbs. In the longest match of the evening, he systematically pounded the 340lb Floyd until the Mangler verbally submitted at 13:40. Vovchanchyn then destroyed Varelans with dizzying shots to the face. "I was sitting in my dressing room," said John Dixson, "and when Fred came back, his face looked like a watermelon. Then Paul came back and his face looked like a watermelon."

Buddy Albin picked Dixson for the IFC because he had fought for him before in kickboxing shows and was a lifelong martial artist, from praying mantis kung fu to tae kwon do to boxing. Dixson faced Vovchanchyn in the finals. Believing he was a better stand-up fighter than both of his American comrades, Dixson battled the Ukrainian with flying fists. A few minutes into the match, he threw a right hand that broke Vovchanchyn's jaw. But Vovchanchyn kept coming. Just after the six-minute mark, Vovchanchyn hit Dixson with a looping left hook that made his nose bleed like a faucet. Dixson tapped out, and later learned his nose had been broken in five places.

Conditions for the native fighters were not all they should have been. In one of the single fights, Peter Khmelev defeated Ruslan Kriviy after kicking him in the groin. Kriviy collapsed in pain; he was not wearing a hard, protective jock strap. As the night progressed, it took longer and longer for the Russian and Ukrainian fighters to emerge from their dressing rooms. "We sent someone back there to finally see what was going on," remembered Howard Petschler, "only to find that all of the Ukrainian fighters had one jock between them." Apparently, Kriviy lost the coin toss to decide who would wear the jock. In the last fight, Vovchanchyn wore a jock that had been worn seven times by five other fighters that night.

The fights inside the octagon were only the beginning of the war that took place outside. As Andy Anderson tells it, "Buddy tried to screw Yuri, Yuri tried to screw Buddy, and Yuri said, 'Well, we didn't make any money.'" Judging by the size of the crowd, that was hard to believe. Buddy told Yuri he thought the show's tape recording didn't come out; although there was no pay-per-view, Petschler and his team filmed the event and planned to produce it for the US market.

At a topless bar after the fight, Paul Varelans and Bas Rutten got carried away and Rutten threw Varelans through a glass door. "We were just playing around," admitted Rutten, though he claimed Varelans started it by biting a chunk out of his back. Later that evening, Rutten got so out of control that when a Ukrainian guard, machine gun in hand, asked him to calm down, the Dutchman slapped him across the face. In Holland, Rutten had a reputation for being a tough customer and had paid the price in jail on numerous occasions. The guard left and returned minutes later with eight other armed men, only to find that Rutten had joined the ladies up on stage. Anderson punched Rutten, grabbed him, and carried him away, knocking Rutten's head through another glass door by accident. Varelans ended up in the hospital while Rutten was taken to jail, where Anderson and Yuri managed to get him out without further complications.

The following morning, Anderson was woken by a knock at the door. It was a representative from another Russian mafia group. Anderson was told that his good job as referee the preceding night would be rewarded if he and some of the fighters stayed for an additional six to seven weeks and staged another event. Anderson declined. "I don't think you understand," said the mafioso, "you are not allowed to leave." A guard took Anderson and three others back to the hotel, but the millionaire bribed the guard into putting everyone on the next flight out. "I ended up knocking the guard out because he wanted everybody to think that we kidnapped him, otherwise he would have gotten in a lot of trouble," said Anderson. Event coordinator Mike Thomas remembered another mafia group trying to get people to stay in the Ukraine. In the event, Anderson's crew stopped off in Paris for a week before returning to the States.

As for Petschler, he stayed behind in the Ukraine with US crew member Randy Kamay to create a rough master tape in NTSC format from the original PAL (standard European video format) shoot. The two worked on the transfer, only to be interrupted by two Ukrainians, who asked to take the tapes to Customs for inspection. Things seemed fishy, so Petschler declined and called Albin to sort out the problem. The Ukrainians muscled Kamay aside and took the tapes anyway, including one of two masters. Fortunately, they left one in the machine, and Petschler had back-ups, save for the final match between Vovchanchyn and Dixson. Petschler retreated to his hotel and got on the phone to Albin, who told him to get out of the Ukraine any way possible. But leaving the country with the tapes proved impractical, as another mafia group convinced Customs that the "show" was actually an espionage attempt to film Chernobyl, the nuclear reactor site. To Albin's credit, he managed to get everyone on the next flight out, and Petschler dropped the tapes off at a Federal Express depot so they would not be confiscated. Sure enough, the IFC contingent was searched, and when the tapes didn't turn up, they were free to leave the country.

A week later, the tapes still hadn't arrived. Petschler called Fed Ex, who said that if he wanted them back, he would have to return to the Ukraine. Since Albin had not paid Petschler, going back to Kiev was the only way he could make any money. He had four men waiting for him at the airport, and was whisked away in one car with another following for protection. "I was kept hidden and moved from apartment to apartment," said Petschler. He met with another sporting group run by yet another mafia crew, who agreed to help him safely get the tapes out of the Ukraine. They drove to Fed Ex, where the rear protector car (filled with gun-toting heavies) turned back; they did not want to face what danger lay ahead.

Collecting the tapes was actually no big chore, but the Russians sped away as if it had been robbery and hid Petschler in another safe house. He then took an overnight train from Kiev to Odessa, stowing away in a sleeping compartment with a former Soviet wrestling coach of Ukrainian descent, who had arranged for the tape escape with a rival sporting club. "They were pretty slick because I didn't know we were short a tape until I got to Odessa," said Petschler. A local police captain met the intrepid IFC producer and threw him a large party. Then he was sent home without the tapes again. A Moldavian general eventually took the tapes with him and shipped them back by US mail. The missing tape contained the final match between Vovchanchyn and Dixson, so the US commercial tape abruptly ends just after the last semi-final fight.

According to John Dixson, conditions in the Ukraine were so bad that Vovchanchyn went for days without food while preparing himself for the show. Those days are over. Vovchanchyn became one of the biggest MMA stars in the world, fighting in Japan, Brazil, and Russia. Georgy Kobylyansky, the Russian mob member who had backed the event, was not left out in the cold. A year later he hooked up with Frederico Lapenda, Marco Ruas's former manager, and produced a Russian MMA series called Absolute Fighting Championship. And though Ukrainian women are among the most beautiful on the planet, Howard Petschler swears he will never return there. Insiders speculate that he has been banned and would return home in a coffin if he did.

As a footnote, MMA journalist and editor Cal Cooper, who ran an Internet site called The New Full Contact, later befriended Yuri and received the tape of the final match. His intentions to sell the tape to fans were quickly thwarted by the IFC. To this day, they have never recovered the commercial copy of that match, but Lapenda sells the entire event. It's called Night of Diamonds.

AFTER SURVIVING SUCH a bumpy ride, there was no turning back for the IFC team. Albin wanted to keep going and so did Petschler, but they needed money. Mike Thomas formed a corporation for the IFC in Montreal and, as a resident of Kahnawake – Mohawk Territory in the province of Quebec – he became the IFC president. It would be the first Indian native-owned company in the international sports television industry. Thomas and Andy Anderson invested over $70,000 for a second show, to be held in Mississippi. When Thomas and Petschler showed up to see how Albin was doing at the event site, they found themselves sharing a room while Albin stayed in a two-bedroom suite entertaining guests. Anderson flew down to referee as a favor to Thomas, only to find that he would be staying in one of the hotel's smallest rooms.

Though the second IFC didn't have the same star power as the first, Anthony Macias made his comeback and won the eight-man tournament that highlighted the event. Anderson returned to Texas to find a $26,800 American Express bill waiting for him. "Buddy told the hotel that my American Express card was a company card and to charge all the rooms to it," said Anderson. "He also charged money off the card as well." Taking a cue from Yuri, Buddy told everyone that the show hadn't made any money, when the event center had been packed to the hilt with screaming fans. One positive thing did come out of the show: Petschler secured the first legal recognition of the sport by a state's athletic commission.

A third show in Mobile, Alabama, would be Buddy Albin's last. Thomas, Petschler and Anderson read him the riot act at a meeting before the show. They still felt the IFC could continue with its original team, and when Thomas arrived at the show he gave Albin over $7,000, only to wake up the next morning to find that Albin had skipped town. Anderson and Jeff Weller had to lend money to Thomas, the investor, so that he could get back home to Montreal. To make matters worse, Albin had given Thomas the fighters' checks but they were for only half the money agreed upon. Finally, because the second show had used up all the funds, there was no money left to shoot the IFC III video.

That was the final straw. Buddy Albin was officially ousted from the organization. "To make sure he got the axe, we actually threatened to have him arrested unless he signed away [his part of] the company," says Petschler. Petschler and Thomas agreed to let Albin have all the proceeds from the sale of the Kiev video, but first they had to buy back the rights from the first two shows; Albin had apparently sold the rights to a company in Atlanta for $5,000. They gave Albin $10,000 in exchange for his part of the IFC. Months later, Albin resurfaced with another show that had IFC written all over it. He was sent a cease-and-desist order. Save for some small shows in and around Texas, Albin was rarely heard from again.

The IFC led the way for others in Canada, and has put together some great matches over the years. It also promoted the first-ever female match, on February 29, 1997, for IFC IV: Becky Levi defeated Betty Fagan in just under two minutes. After all the arrests from Extreme Fighting 2, Mike Thomas worked to secure a safe home for the IFC in Montreal, while Andy Anderson continued to referee for the IFC as well as other events. Years later, Albin called Anderson and acted like nothing had happened, claiming it was Thomas who had used Anderson's credit card for the IFC II debacle. Anderson knew better, since Thomas had put his house up for collateral to keep the show going. By Anderson's estimate, Albin embezzled over $400,000 from Thomas and his Indian reservation in just two years.

For a promotion with so many ups and downs, the IFC continued to evolve by sanctioning other events and extending its brand name. In February 1997, martial artist Paul Smith, who had fought in several underground fights during the early 1980s, became part of the IFC team and began running shows inside Indian casinos. In March 1998, he started The Warrior's Challenge, a moderately successful show held on Indian reservations throughout California. This lucrative market (the casino pays an onsite fee up front) became the blueprint for similar promotions like King of the Cage and World Extreme Cagefighting in neighboring casinos. Ironically, the IFC-sanctioned event WEC (which debuted June 30, 2001), has led the way as one of the best live shows in California, even landing a small TV deal in 2003.

In December 2000, Smith, along with Mike Thomas, made alliance with the UFC to assess favorable rules to both parties for sanctioning in California, New Jersey, and Nevada. At the time of writing, the last two had passed and were generally referred to as "unified rules." After churning out a series of smaller shows, the IFC stepped it up on September 6, 2003, for Global Domination, held in Denver, Colorado. The event featured an eight-man tournament and international talent, but failed to make much impact. The IFC continues to promote shows all over the USA, though its "international" scope may have narrowed.

CHAPTER 13

Revenge and Redemption

MARK COLEMAN WAS once again at a crossroads. The two-time NCAA Ohio State wrestling champion had just lost in the semi-finals of the 1996 Olympic trials and would be going home with his dream of glory shattered. He had faced this disappointment before. Coleman had made the 1992 Olympic team only to lose to a pair of foreign competitors he had beaten six months earlier. "I lost the eye of the tiger, and started to head down the wrong path where I stopped training," said Coleman of the 1992 debacle. "I was drinking instead." It had taken everything in Coleman's heart to bring him back four years later, and his spirits could now have sunk even lower.

As fate would have it, trainer Richard Hamilton, who had worked with both Dan Severn and Don Frye, was at the Olympic trials recruiting new talent. He told Coleman that he was one of three wrestlers (Tom Erikson and Mark Kerr were the other two) being considered for UFC X just 30 days later. Coleman convinced Hamilton that he was the man for the job. With little more than a few street fights under his belt, Coleman had only his freestyle wrestling skills to employ in the octagon – but they were considerable. From the age of six, he had been a career athlete, becoming an All-American in football, baseball and wrestling. Wrestling was what the 6ft 1in, 245lb, Columbus, Ohio native enjoyed most. Coleman knew that amateur wrestlers had few opportunities to make money on physical skills alone, and he felt the UFC would be the only chance he had to keep wrestling and provide for his future. "I watched all the UFC fights and felt that I wouldn't have any problems with anybody in the ring," said Coleman. "My confidence was believing that all those fights would be mismatches [if I had been in there]."

Coleman worked on his stand-up and trained at Hamilton's Arizona gym for submission, though he admits that Hamilton's idea of groundfighting was for Coleman to work out with beginners.

Hamilton often told people he was a minister and had a strong alliance with the North Phoenix Baptist Church, which somehow assisted him in putting on karate tournaments. By aligning himself with the amateur wrestling team Sunkist Kids (a sponsored team that competed around the world), Hamilton was the ticket for any wrestler to get into the UFC. He trained Frye and Severn in minor capacities for their UFC appearances, though lawyer Robert DePersia was their manager. "He [Hamilton] envisioned himself as someone who could control all aspects of the athlete, not just the training," said DePersia. Hamilton became Coleman's manager, but that was okay with the wrestler, who saw this opportunity as an escape from his depression. Coleman felt that taking an opponent down wouldn't be a problem, and "grounding and pounding" would be all that was required to finish him off.

UFC X: The Tournament was held on July 12, 1996, at the Alabama State Fair Arena in Birmingham. The South should have been more open to holding these events, but political pressure was building even there, and misinformation created alarm. On the night of fight, a policeman held up a video camera to film the event. "I told him he couldn't film because it was a copyrighted event and we don't allow any videography," said David Isaacs. "The officer told me he was going to arrest me if I didn't let them do it. Our local lawyer said they could arrest you and they will arrest you. I stepped aside. Every city was a battle."

There would be no superfight, since the Shamrock-Severn rematch had been so boring. SEG felt confident about their current champion, Don Frye, and had enlisted a fresh crop of fighters to vie for the coveted UFC crown. Well-rounded athlete Brian Johnston, 6ft 4in and all muscle, had been wrestling since the age of twelve, and had forged a brief career as a pro boxer and kickboxer. He wanted to make money fighting and, when kickboxing didn't pan out, the UFC was the only answer. Interestingly enough, he walked to the octagon wearing a gi, a show of respect since he had emphasised judo throws in training. Another competitor, Moti Horenstein, had served three years in the Israeli army and was a three-time karate champion in his native country. With his brawny look, he hoped that "survival" (what he called his style of fighting) would triumph.

While "Big Daddy" Gary Goodridge made his return after the loss to Schultz, traditional martial artist Mark Hall had high hopes for winning the tourney. He had destroyed Harold Howard in UFC VII, defeated Trent Jenkins in UU '95, and busted the nose of sumo wrestler Koji Kitao in the previous show. Hall was a good ole boy from

Weatherford, Texas, who had grown up with a speech impediment. His classmates knew better than to tease him since it meant an automatic fight after school. The 189-pound Hall never backed down from anyone and trained heavily in martial arts inside his father's barn. He had taken moo yea do (a Korean style) to control his temper, and saw the UFC as a better way to earn a living than bouncing at clubs or teaching self-defense.

Unlike his previous appearances, Don "The Predator" Frye came to UFC X with a little more than just plain confidence. In pre-fight interviews, he poured on the heavy-handed bravado. "I didn't train that hard for the tournament, and I made the mistake of getting too cocky," remembered Frye. "I thought there was nobody out there who could handle me." As in his college wrestling days, Frye interpreted early success as a sign that he was doing everything right and didn't need to put in the extra time to better his skills.

Frye faced Hall in the quarterfinals, and outweighed him by 25lbs. He felt sorry for Hall, and expected a quick victory over someone who lacked the strength or wrestling ability to put up a good fight. What Frye didn't count on was heart. With his traditional martial arts mentality, Hall felt he could beat his opponent with his spinning back kick. He had practiced thousands of kicks in preparation for the one perfect shot, and at the beginning of the match, Hall got his chance – and one kick was all it took before he was taken down to the ground. Frye slammed Hall to the mat and stayed in his closed guard for the duration of the match – over ten minutes. With his forearm pressed against Hall's throat, Frye battered Hall's ribs. The match dragged on, while the pair argued about stopping it.

"You need to quit," said Frye.

"No. I can't quit," Hall fired back.

The punishment continued until John McCarthy stopped it in Frye's favour. Frye had controlled his opponent, but was exhausted. He would fight Hall twice more in the next five months.

Brian Johnston gave a shaky performance against fellow kickboxer Scotty Fiedler, who had him in trouble with a rear naked choke early in their quarter-final. "I threw him and went right for the knee bar, but I didn't have experience with those techniques," said Johnston later. Fielder didn't have the choke sunk in right, and Johnston took his time and stayed calm before pulling out and reversing the position. A few hard punches to the back of Fiedler's neck led McCarthy to stop the fight. Gary Goodridge also had trouble from beefy biology teacher John Campetella, but managed to short-circuit his opponent's wrestling ability and win the match by tap out from punches.

Coleman made his way to the octagon sporting "Team Phoenix" on his shirt, an obvious advertisement for Hamilton's quasi-gym. But Coleman was there to represent freestyle wrestling in a way that had never been seen before. Though his opponent, Moti Horenstein, had been a martial artist since the age of five, it didn't make any difference. He threw one kick and Coleman went in for the takedown. The wrestler's ferocity, matched with his amateurish punching style, was too much for Horenstein, who was mounted and clobbered with a series of lefts and rights. The Israeli tried to defend, but Coleman landed enough bombs to make him cover up with both hands before tapping out. Coleman then lit up the crowd with a testosterone-injected celebration.

Frye and Coleman both had seesaw battles with their opponents in a lively semi-final round. Brian Johnston gave Frye a great fight by backing him up with his boxing skills, and it looked like an upset was in the making as the 25-year-old kickboxer trumped everything Frye could dish out. "He finally got a bear hug and ... I couldn't get out of it," said Johnston. "I tried to go for a throw, but Don was a little too experienced for that." Johnston landed on all fours, and Frye took advantage of his exhausted foe. Rolling Johnston over, Frye gained side position on his opponent and landed two sharp elbows to his forehead, which opened a small gash. With nowhere to run, panic hit Johnston. It was the first time he had ever bled in a fight, and he tapped immediately.

Coleman battled a sharper Goodridge and wrestling proved to be the bigger man's weakness. At one point, Coleman worked Goodridge over to his corner but, with a wink to Hamilton, Goodridge grabbed the fence and laterally scaled to his own corner. Coleman held Goodridge from behind and landed several uppercuts, forcing him to turn around. At five minutes, Coleman looked tired, but the two continued to work for position. Coleman took his man down several times and at just under seven minutes he moved from side mount to back mount. Opting for the rear naked choke, Coleman sunk in his hooks, but the Canadian already knew he was out of gas. He tapped before a choke or more punches could be thrown.

The UFC X final was arguably the most personal in UFC history. Richard Hamilton and Don Frye had parted on bad terms and Hamilton's foray into management was a smoke screen for his quest to find a terminator to destroy Frye. Coleman was his puppet. "He [Hamilton] made Don Frye out to be an evil person," remembered Coleman. "I have nothing against anybody, but the stuff he was telling me about Don made me want to go in there and kick his butt." Frye knew nothing of Hamilton's ruse and felt confident he could beat just another wrestler. Coleman outweighed Frye by 30lbs, and he was far from just another wrestler.

In the eleven-and-a-half minute war that ensued, Coleman set out to maul Frye. He landed countless headbutts, knees, elbows, and punches that closed both of his opponent's eyes. At one point, Coleman had Frye up against the fence in his own corner with Hamilton's face staring into Frye's. "Kill him! Make him suffer!" yelled Hamilton. "Hamilton was supposed to be some type of minister, but during the fight I heard a totally different person with the way he was talking to me," acknowledged Coleman. After pounding Frye for several minutes, Coleman eventually lost his blood lust and wondered why the match wasn't being stopped. "I felt that plenty of damage was done. I didn't like what was taking place."

Dan Severn, who had once coached and trained Frye in college, was sitting ringside as a special commentator. He looked to Frye's trainer, Becky Levi, and suggested she stop the fight, but it was trainer Steve Owen (Frye's longtime judo coach) who had to make that call. "Don told me that if he had a chance to win, do not throw in the towel," said Owen. Though Frye could do very little against Coleman, Owen felt he still had enough heart left. A cloud of concern fell over both camps. Frye's and Coleman's significant others, Molly and Tina respectively, circled the cage inches from one another. They were unable to hold back their anguish at what the men in their lives were putting them through.

Frye clung to the cage, but Coleman used all his strength to pick him up and slam him to the mat. McCarthy had stopped the bout earlier for doctors to check Frye's cuts and now, after two hard elbows to the face, a second stoppage was all she wrote. Mark Coleman was declared the winner. In his post-fight interview, he announced to the world that this was a win for wrestling. "It was important for me to promote [amateur wrestling], but now, I'm no longer a wrestler – I'm a fighter," said Coleman.

Frye had to be carried out of the octagon. He was in bad shape. "I was devastated," said Becky Levi, who sat with Frye in the triage room. He could barely move as he inclined his head toward Levi when she spoke; he could not see her because his eyes were shut. He dropped his head on her chest as she tried to stay calm. "When the doctor came in, I walked away to the shower area and cried my eyes out," she said. She rode with Frye in the ambulance to the hospital, where he spent the night with several fractured bones in his face and severe dehydration. (Mark Hall had already broken an ocular socket just below Frye's eye and Coleman's handiwork didn't make it any better.)

When Levi arrived back at the hotel, "the first thing I wanted to do was kill Richard Hamilton." Still covered in Frye's blood, she walked into a nearby bar and told Dan Severn of her intentions. As she left to find Hamilton, Severn grabbed Levi and pulled her in close. "You aren't going anywhere, have a seat," he soothed. The Beast was able to calm her down, but the elusive Hamilton had taken his revenge.

DAVID "TANK" ABBOTT was finally allowed to return for UFC XI: The Proving Ground, after SEG pleaded with Elaine McCarthy (John's wife) to let them to bring back their poster boy. For his unkind words in Puerto Rico, Abbott was supposed to write an apology letter to smooth things over with McCarthy. "I was totally and completely at fault," wrote Abbott. "I was very distraught from the events that immediately preceded the crossing of our paths. As a result, I took a very defensive position at what I perceived as a threat." Actually SEG's David Isaacs penned the one-page apology and had Abbott sign it. Everything was kosher with Elaine (she says that Tank still does all of his traveling with her company Katella and even remains good friends with her parents) and it was time for the bad boy of the UFC to get back in training. He enlisted the help of Olympic heavyweight wrestler Tolly Thompson to roll with him. Unfortunately, Thompson dropped Abbott hard to the mat one day, re-injuring his knee hurt in his previous car accident. Abbott's mother suggested anti-inflammatories, and though the remedy worked for a short while, the effects eventually wore off. The streetfighter could barely move, and ballooned to over 300lbs, but with his menacing visage emblazed across the event poster, Abbott *had* to show up.

Reigning champion Mark Coleman had been dubbed "The Hammer" and his focus and confidence were at an all time high. From a commercial viewpoint, SEG desperately hoped he and Tank would square off. UFC XI was held at the Augusta-Richmond Civic Center in Georgia on September 20, 1996, playing to a rabid crowd hungry for the return of Tank. Much like at a pro wrestling event, Tank supporters held up banners; one read, "Tank is the UFC!" Along with Tank and Coleman, the show was a mix of veterans like Jerry Bohlander and Brian Johnston and relative unknowns such as Julian Sanchez, who had no sanctioned fighting experience and faced Coleman in the quarters. Coleman blew through the flabby Sanchez, taking him down and submitting him with a side choke at 0:44.

Iranian Reza Nazri advertised a set of instructional videotapes on Greco Roman wrestling in martial arts magazines, but was pitting his skills against the formidable Brian Johnston. Seconds into the match, Johnston foiled Nazri's throw by crushing him to the mat. The impact knocked Nazri out, but Johnston was not finished. He mounted Nazri and landed a half dozen headbutts and three solid rights before McCarthy rushed in and pulled him off, bloodying Johnston's nose in the process. The kickboxer was furious, believing McCarthy had broken his nose, but he was okay.

After Abbott quickly subdued boxer Sam Adkins with a forearm choke submission, the only competitive quarter-final pitted Brazilian jiu-jitsu's Fabio Gurgel against Lion's Den fighter Jerry Bohlander. Gurgel's above-the-waist takedown couldn't match Bohlander's wrestling skill, but a solid right that opened a cut to Bohlander's face almost changed the course of the match. Gurgel took him down and mounted him, but Bohlander reversed and battered Gurgel inside his guard to win by unanimous decision.

Brian Johnston felt that he could take Coleman in their semi but, as his parents watched from the stands, Coleman hardly hesitated in taking him down after the kickboxer had landed a couple of good leg kicks. "When he shot in, I elevated him and he hit the fence," said Johnston. "I didn't know that and thought he was Superman for recovering." Coleman stayed in Johnston's half guard and launched several headbutts and punches, forcing his opponent to roll to his stomach and tap out.

Backstage, Tank Abbott and Bohlander prepared for their semi. "You're not fighting," said Ken Shamrock to his disciple; Bohlander had hurt his hand against Gurgel and Shamrock felt he was in over his head. "I told him he was too young, and there was no reason for him to go in there and get his ass beat up," said Shamrock. As SEG made the announcement with Bohlander stretcher-bound for the hospital, Abbott said in jest, "You're a pussy and your fighter is a pussy." Shamrock went ballistic. "I told him I was going to beat his fucking ass if I heard him say another word again. Jerry did not make that decision; I made that decision." The two exchanged a few more unpleasantries before going their separate ways. This marked the beginning of a longstanding feud that has never been resolved.

Abbott had trained specifically for Bohlander and had not expected to face a mirror image of himself. Scott "The Pitbull" Ferrozzo was more than ready to brawl with his fellow pitfighter. Ironically, Ferrozzo had lost to Bohlander in UFC VIII and had decided he needed better training if he wanted to continue fighting, flying Don Frye down to Minnesota to train him for four weeks. The two became good friends and Frye became Ferrozzo's manager and training partner. Before making his way to the octagon, a grinning Ferrozzo turned to Tank and said, "Now you're going to fight someone who isn't afraid of you." Tank's crew laughed it off, but Ferrozzo felt this was his day. A humble Frye accompanied him to the octagon, with everyone in the entourage sporting shirts reading "Redemption."

Both men were 31 years old but Ferrozzo outweighed Abbott by 50lbs. Their bellies bulging, the two bludgeoned each other with heavy shots during the first minute, until Abbott stopped his opponent's takedown attempt and worked him against the fence. The fence opened a cut above Ferrozzo's right eye, but he was enjoying himself. As Abbott landed punches, Ferrozzo began taunting him. Abbott, whose knee was causing him too much pain to be boxing in the center of the octagon, didn't respond. McCarthy separated the two several times, but on each occasion they gravitated back to the fence. The crowd only got glimpses of what might have been a great fight; instead they witnessed tedious fence hugging that allowed Ferrozzo to open up with a plethora of knees to Abbott's midsection. At times, Tank did nothing but hold on while his nemesis worked him over, snarling at one point, "C'mon, you fucking puss," to get Abbott to move. It didn't work. The match went to overtime, where Tank got in the better shots initially before moving back to the fence.

After 18 minutes, McCarthy raised Ferrozzo's hand as the winner by decision. "I got involved [in the UFC] for one reason, and that was to destroy Tank, and I did it," said an enthusiastic Ferrozzo. Abbott disagreed. "The guy [Ferrozzo] tries and does everything he can to beat me up, but that ain't nothing. I'm a man and can take a beating like a man, but I kicked his ass." Whatever, Ferrozzo glowed with elation instead of preparing for Coleman in the finals.

Coleman was ready to face anyone, but was anyone ready to face him? Ferrozzo had wasted all of his energy on Abbott, and was on his way to the hospital to get checked out. He was on oxygen in the back and the doctor told Art Davie he was dehydrated. "Dehydrated?" asked Davie. "The guy has enough body fat, how could that be?" But the doctor said he was gassed and couldn't go on. Brazilian Roberto Traven, who had won his alternate match, was to be his replacement, but pulled out due to a broken wrist that Davie claims was not broken. Davie and David Isaacs came up with a plan to have Tank Abbott come back out to face Coleman and give the fans their money's worth but Bob Meyrowitz couldn't make a decision and, with no other replacements, Coleman was declared the winner by default and awarded $75,000. In an attempt to give the fans in attendance some kind of treat, Coleman and Kevin Randleman, his protégé, staged a wrestling exhibition.

After UFC XI, Coleman fired Richard Hamilton as his manager.

According to Frye's trainer Steve Owen, Hamilton had brought in 25 people and paid them to be Coleman supporters out of Coleman's purse, which explains why he had so many fans with ready-made signs for his first appearance in UFC X. "I found out that he was doing some stuff behind my back," said Coleman. "I also found out that his name wasn't really Richard Hamilton. Right before UFC XI, he had been involved in a crime in New York and was in the witness protection program, so why was he on TV with me? I really didn't like the situation at all." Hamilton hit back with a breach-of-contract lawsuit, but he had other problems. He would be indicted on one count of sexual abuse and six counts of sexual conduct with a minor just a year and a half later. In June 1998, a jury in Arizona sentenced Hamilton to 78 years for those crimes. Though Hamilton's spokesman proclaimed his innocence, he sits in jail at the time of writing. He still settled out of court with Coleman on the breach-of-contract suit and received an undisclosed but substantial sum of money.

Coleman had been victorious in back-to-back events, but could he beat fellow two-time UFC champion and wrestler Dan Severn, who continually bounced back to refute his critics? Unlike any opponent he had fought in the past, Severn now faced one of his own at UFC XII's superfight. "I'm a realistic person," said Severn. "No matter who I fight, I simply write down pros and cons. I put down that he [Coleman] is younger, stronger, faster, better wrestler ... I didn't come out looking too good on paper." Severn felt the only way he could beat Coleman was to take him beyond five minutes, when conditioning became a factor. Coleman had a different take on the matter. He felt invincible. There was nothing Severn could do to him.

After a brief standup, Severn shot for Coleman's leg, but Coleman sprawled, tied up Severn's head, and pushed him back. Swinging wildly, Coleman landed a decent right, forcing the Beast to shoot for a second takedown. Coleman sprawled again and immediately took Severn's back. Now he had a difficult decision to make. "I knew Dan, and knew that he was a wrestler," said Coleman. "In the back of my mind, even though I was a grounder and pounder, I really didn't feel like going out there and punching him in the face a whole lot. We were somewhat friends, and we came from the same sport." Coleman softened him up with light body shots, but refused to use elbows and headbutts.

Severn eventually rolled to his back, and Coleman took the mount. Severn tied up his opponent's head to keep him from punching. As he had done in previous bouts, Coleman transitioned to side mount and applied a headlock that became a very effective choke. Coleman trapped one of Severn's arms and squeezed his massive arms for over a minute. Severn tried to free himself with punches to Coleman's head but at 2:59 he tapped from the pressure. The Hammer leaped to his feet with maniacal joy, scaled the octagon fence and pumped his fists. By beating two UFC champions from wrestling backgrounds, Mark Coleman was the undisputed king of the octagon.

CHAPTER 14

Tournament of Champions

T HE FIRST ULTIMATE Ultimate had failed to live up to the hype, with three back-to-back decisions instead of clear-cut victories. The second couldn't have been more different. It was an exciting tournament, full of controversy and emotion, and not one match ended by decision. Ken Shamrock was out to prove to himself and to the world that he could face his demons and finish a tournament. Don "The Predator" Frye's war with Mark Coleman had made him even more popular, and humbled him to the point of taking his training more seriously. And, after losing to Scott Ferrozzo, a leaner Tank Abbott was hungry for the fight of his life. Returning to the Alabama State Fair Arena, UU '96 was held December 7, 1996, a night no one present would forget.

Ken Shamrock had reached the end of his rope with Tank Abbott. Tank had pushed him too far with his off-color remarks toward Jerry Bohlander and himself. Since the show featured a tournament format, it was time for them to tangle. "I argued with them to put us in the first fight because Tank might not have made it to the finals, and that was a match that people wanted to see," said Shamrock. But SEG set up the brackets the same way they did for the first UU: four fighters they felt would win against four fighters who wouldn't. In other words, why put Tank vs Shamrock in the quarter-finals, when the build-up would make it more exciting to see them later? One fly in the ointment could have been Mark Coleman, but he pulled out due to a virus three weeks before the show. Ukrainian Igor Vovchanchyn and Brazilian Vitor Belfort were also supposed to fight, but for one reason or another had to be replaced.

The first match pitted Shamrock against Brian Johnston, who had started to work out with wrestler Matt Furey and Don Frye, of all people. Johnston barely got off a leg kick before Shamrock took him down and pressed him up against the fence. In Johnston's open guard, the former King of Pancrase made good on his promise to be more aggressive. Perhaps it was his way of making up for the Severn dance, but Johnston was paying the price. After being cautioned for holding the fence (a new rule to cut down on fighters using it to their advantage), Shamrock unloaded on his opponent with hard rights to the face. Shamrock believed Johnston would tap from his punches and didn't try for a submission. "He was in a terrible position, but I just didn't know enough to do anything at that point," said Johnston later. Nearly six minutes passed until Johnston's hand raised up. After a moment of hesitation, tap, tap. The match was over, leaving Shamrock the victor.

Unbeknown to SEG, Don Frye, Mark Hall, Paul Varelans and Kimo, who were all competing in UU '96, had just fought in another event dubbed U Japan less than a month earlier. It had been a way for sports agent/lawyer Robert DePersia to cash in on the fighters he represented, which was quite a few in 1996. "My presentation to [the fighters] was that because I had so many of them, it was like we were unionizing and could demand a higher wage, because they didn't want to pay anyone over a grand," said DePersia. "We were getting significant purses and it was making Meyrowitz nuts, because if he wouldn't give me what I wanted for a fighter, I would just say, 'None of my guys are coming.' So I sort of controlled his events because I controlled all the talent." The U Japan show was set up just like the UFC, in an octagon, and featured nine UFC competitors in decent matches, save for a pro wrestling bout between Dan Severn and a hardcore Japanese wrestler.

Don Frye should have been in the best shape of his life for the December show. Becky Levi (who also fought and won her first NHB match in U Japan) and trainer Steve Owen had stepped up Frye's preparation. This was to be his chance at redemption. But just one day before the show, SEG fight consultant Joe Silva witnessed one of Don's training sessions: "When I went to see Don spar, he looked terrible. He was one of the favorites going in, but I could tell something was wrong seeing him work out. He told me that he had got himself in great shape, but had caught a bad cold a couple of days before. I thought I was going to be in serious trouble."

Frye's first match would be against a new and improved Gary "Big Daddy" Goodridge. The Canadian was coming off a recent arm wrestling championship win, and trainer John Gnap slapped him across the face to psyche him up for the rematch. Goodridge and Frye tied up in the beginning, and while Frye was able to land several good knees and uppercuts, Goodridge was ready. He took the wrestler down and spent much of the match in his half guard, striking wildly. A visibly weary Frye attempted an arm bar, but his much stronger opponent pulled out of it with ease. Down on the ground, Goodridge worked his way to the front of Frye. Then, holding onto his waist, he threw a knee of his own. This was a mistake. Clutching Goodridge's knee, the Predator put the bigger man on his back. The crowd howled as the former UFC champion looked ready to take over the fight, but Goodridge was exhausted and tapped out before any damage could be administered. At 11:20, it would be the longest match of the night.

"I was so tired, they had to drag me out of the ring," said Goodridge. "He's the only fighter who, after my fights with him, I ended up crying out of frustration and disappointment. I felt I had it and then I lost it straight through my hands both times." It would be the Canadian's last appearance in the UFC for three years, but he found success in Brazil and Japan, exploiting his showmanship and distinct look. On December 31, 2003, Goodridge fought Don Frye a third time for Japan's Pride Shockwave. In 39 seconds, he delivered a devastating head kick (his first ever) and knocked out Frye. Goodridge said it was his retirement fight, but continued fighting for K-1 in kick-boxing and MMA.

Tank Abbott, who had recovered from his knee injury, faced ex-marine Cal Worsham. A doctor had shot his knee up with cortizone several times, and Tank had been able to run off some excess weight. Coming into the show, he was still a less-than-slim 273lbs but far from the 298 he had fought Ferrozzo at. In his prefight interview, Worsham said, "Tank, don't even try to hang onto the fence. This is going out in the middle, and I'm taming the Tank." As the fight began, Abbott pushed Worsham up against the fence and proceeded to throw him out of the octagon. Though Abbott denied the tactic later, he had Worsham high enough to slam him for several seconds, inviting him to counter with blows to Abbott's head. Abbott finally crushed him to the mat, moved from a side mount to the guard and punished the tae kwon do champion with strikes to the abdomen.

Worsham held on to the fence, his eyes transfixed on Abbott as his cornermen shouted helpful advice such as, "You're going to lose Tank." Abbott moved in for the kill but Worsham tapped. When McCarthy pulled them apart, Abbott got in one more shot. "I want him disqualified," Worsham screamed at McCarthy, who pushed him back to the fence and got right in his face. Unlike any other referee in combat sports history, John McCarthy has become the judge and jury in the arena, and this was one of many times he manhandled a fighter to keep the peace. Though Abbott admitted to hitting Worsham after the break, he didn't see any problem with it: apparently Worsham had stuck a finger in Tank's eye, though he claimed it was an accident.

McCarthy told Tank off but the crowd erupted with pleasure upon seeing their bar-brawling bad boy make his comeback win.

Despite losing both of his previous UFC matches, Kimo Leopoldo had become a star. His fierce looks, mysterious demeanour and brutish tattoos made him welcome on any card. Kimo had also been winning fights – just not in the UFC. In Japan, he'd defeated Patrick Smith, three Japanese fighters, and pro wrestler "Bam Bam" Bigelow. Now he faced Paul Varelans, who had replaced Mark Coleman. The Hawaiian weighed in 20lbs lighter than before, and spoke of being more of a "thinker" in the ring. As the match got underway, he wasted energy on an ankle lock and couldn't put the 340lb Polar Bear on his back. Nestled against the fence, Kimo attempted to throw his massive opponent (who outweighed him by 100lbs) but Varelans wound up on top. With blood trickling from his left eye, it looked as if Kimo would suffer his third UFC defeat – until, nearly nine minutes into the match, he reversed and mounted Varelans. He was able to do this because Varelans went unconscious for a few seconds when Kimo cut off the bigger man's circulation using his own shirt. As Varelans came out of it, Kimo landed ten dead-on shots to his face that prompted Varelan's corner to throw in the towel. An exhausted Kimo had won an emotional, gutsy battle.

Everything was set up for the match of the night: Abbott vs Ken Shamrock – but once again, Shamrock contrived to drop the ball. He pulled out with a broken hand. It was somehow typical of the emotionally-complex Shamrock, a man from a troubled background who could have been *the* star of MMA, yet never quite pulled it off. He was not at a loss for words backstage, however, telling commentator Tony Blauer, "There is one person that I really dislike for some of the things he said about one of my fighters, and I take that personally. And I would like to say right here and right now, Tank Abbott – I want him. I want him and I'm making this challenge right now."

Abbott felt the same. Over the course of three interviews for this book, he could not stop talking about Shamrock, his claims ranging from Shamrock rigging the tournament to being the envy of SEG. Abbott's assumptions were incorrect on both counts. "In the ring, Ken Shamrock was a disappointment to me as a UFC booker and promoter," said Art Davie. "You are talking about a guy who was given more opportunities to be a star in the UFC [yet] every time someone handed him a spear and asked him to throw it, he figured a way to drop it and not throw it at all." While Shamrock was quick to say he didn't like Abbott, he did respect him as a fighter. Abbott wouldn't even give that much: "He's a piece of trash. He is a poser of a warrior." Shamrock moved back to his roots with pro wrestling when he signed with the WWF in 1997, but he eventually returned to MMA. Tank scoffed at Shamrock's pro wrestling re-entry, but joined up with the competition, WCW. The two men never fought, and their rivalry became another UFC "what if?"

Shamrock did, however, meet up again with the Nasty Boys, the two wrestlers who had put him in a hospital in the late 1980s (see Chapter 4). In 1998, while on tour with the WWF, he saw his attackers in a Florida airport. "I confronted them. I was just furious. I never knew what I was going to say if I ever saw them face to face in a situation where I could do something. The blond one ran away right there in the airport and the other one came right over there with Billy Gunn standing next to me. I leaned over and said, 'I'm going to fucking kill you!' I guess he figured that because of where we were, nothing was going to happen, but I had no control. I was going to kill him … I was going to literally beat the shit out of him until there was nothing left of his body. The guy just kept saying, 'Man, chill out. What's your problem? That was a long time ago.' Yeah, for you it was a long time ago; for me, it was yesterday. He went upstairs and then came back down where all the boys were sitting, but he couldn't see me because I went away to cool off. He said, 'Man, what's up with Shamrock? He needs to take a chill pill.' That's when I jumped over the seats and went right at him. I got right up in his face and said, 'This is where I fucking kill you. You think you're fuckin' tough? Let's do it right now.' He turned his shoulder and said, 'If you hit me, it will be a federal offense and I'll press charges.' I wanted to, but I knew that I was not in the right frame of mind. At that point, I just turned away and walked."

FOR SOME REASON, Abbott got only one fight's rest before his next bout. The brackets were changed so that he would fight in the first semi-final match instead of Frye, who would get extra rest. This didn't help Shamrock's replacement, karate man Steve Nelmark. As Tank charged his beefy opponent, Nelmark circled to the left to draw away his power. Nelmark landed one punch, but Tank fired away with a big right hand at the same time, sending Nelmark across the octagon and up against the fence. Abbott wasted little time in pressing the attack, swinging wild shots that his dazed foe could not defend. An uppercut sent Nelmark staggering before Abbott knocked him out with a right hand to the jaw that took his knees from under him. It was a frightening sight, as Nelmark's folded body looked devoid of life. He had tangled with the Tank for only a minute. "I have to admit that I was always scared of seeing Tank in those early round matches; scared for the event, scared of what he might do," said play-by-play commentator Bruce Beck. Luckily, Nelmark was fine, and the fans cheered Abbott for a job well done. Just as in UFC VI, he was on his way to the finals and hardly the worse for wear.

Mark Hall sat in the dressing room, his mind cluttered by peer pressure. He had recently signed with Robert DePersia, believing the lawyer's lock on the UFC would earn him more money and better opportunities. His first match through DePersia had been at U Japan, where he fought Don Frye for a second time. "I was pissed off at myself for taking it easy on him the first time, and I felt wasting that time cost me the belt in the match against Coleman," said Frye. In the rematch, he pounded on Hall with little regard for his foe, but it still took him five and a half minutes against an opponent with two broken ribs suffered in training two weeks before. Hall had taken the fight because he needed the money. Now Frye was in bad shape; Goodridge had worn him out. He was ready to pull out of the semi-final until word came down that Kimo had dropped out due to dehydration, so he would face Hall in a rubber match.

Though it was unlikely he could beat Frye, Hall's "no quit" attitude would almost certainly fatigue the Predator even further for the finals. According to Hall, DePersia now intervened.

"Well, Mark, sometimes you do what you have to do, and we're a team. This is Don's day, not yours. Your time's coming," said the lawyer. "Mark, don't take this away from Don."

"No way," responded Hall. "I'm not going to do this [throw the fight]."

But, said Hall, it was made crystal clear that he should cooperate so Frye would be fresh to take on Abbott in the final. "Robert kind of hinted that my career would go nowhere if I didn't cooperate," he claimed. Hall walked into the bathroom to think it over, and Frye followed, lecturing him about how his dream was to win the Ultimate Ultimate. He told Hall it wouldn't make any sense for them to fight for real a third time, as Frye had already beaten him twice. Hall contemplated firing DePersia but, in the end, decided to throw the match with Frye. He was promised a percentage of Frye's purse for doing the job.

As Hall entered the octagon, he was all smiles and looked very relaxed, hardly the signs of someone about to be in a tough fight. McCarthy gave the go-ahead, and Frye ran right at Hall and took him down. The wrestler performed a heel hook and Hall tapped at 0:20. Hall sold the punishment to his ankle by wincing in pain, while Paul

Varelans stepped in to help carry him backstage. Steve Owen, Frye's trainer, claimed Frye had been working with a Russian sambo expert on leg locks, but there was no doubt this match was worked. Stylistically, Frye had never taken such a quick and risky approach in any bout, not to mention having never gone for leg submissions before. In boxing, it's illegal to manage both corners, but DePersia knew there was no such UFC rule and didn't seem to care about the ethics of the situation.

Mark Hall continued to be managed by DePersia, who would get him a fight in Brazil months later, but he never fought in the UFC again. Nine months after the event, he divulged information about the fixed bout over the internet. "I told [Frye] that I was going public with it and he pretended like he didn't know what I was talking about," said Hall. He claimed Frye never paid him his share of the money. "I asked him again about giving me even half of the money, because my school wasn't doing well and I really needed it." DePersia contended he knew nothing about the set-up and suggested Hall made the allegations only because he had lost his martial arts school, gone through a bad separation with his wife, and lost money in some other business deals with Frye. Frye said that he and Hall were supposed to hold a reality fighting seminar together (after UU '96); when he arrived, Hall was so poor that he was living in his own dojo, and the seminar only had a couple of dozen participants. Frye strongly refuted Hall's claim, saying he wouldn't need to work a fight to beat him.

In Hall's interview for this book, the subject got him so rattled that remnants of his old speech impediment resurfaced. He finished his thoughts on Frye by saying, "To this day I wake up at night thinking about that son of a bitch. I want to kill him." Hall later became a promoter and put on his own show called The Cobra Challenge. In 1999, Ken Shamrock beat him to within an inch of his life in a California casino, apparently over insulting words toward Shamrock's wife at the time.

Whatever the truth, Tank Abbott would be fighting in the finals for the second time against an opponent who, it seemed, had used a bit of funny business to get there. Undaunted, Abbott walked right toward Frye, who thought he could stand up with him. Frye quickly learned the meaning of heavy hands. With a single jab, Tank knocked him across the octagon. Frye's wife Molly screamed out in fear. *Well, dummy, that's what you get for standing up with him*, thought Frye. "I took a step and was on my heels, and he caught me at the right time. I looked up and thought, *Shit, here he comes*." Remarkably, Frye was able to get back to his feet, and the two went toe to toe. Abbott bludgeoned Frye's face, blacking both eyes and drawing blood in seconds. "I remember David Isaacs was sitting next to me, and Dave was a big Tank fan," said Art Davie. "For a minute there it looked like Tank was going to pull it off. Deep down inside, SEG would have loved to have had Tank as their champion." Frye, however, moved on the offensive and stepped on Abbott's foot by mistake, sending him to the canvas. The Predator seized the moment, taking Tank's back. After sinking in his hooks and missing a punch, Frye went for the rear naked choke. Abbott was clearly exhausted and even though the choke had not sunk in all the way, he tapped.

Despite questions about how he got there, Don "The Predator" Frye truly earned the Ultimate Ultimate '96 championship. In one of the greatest matches in UFC history, he had shown he was a true warrior. Tears streamed down his battered face like Rocky Balboa as he delivered a heartfelt speech to the crowd. Even Scott Ferrozzo was so happy to see Frye win that he lost his composure and his eyes began to water.

Tank chalked up the loss to the same politics he blamed for his other losses. Self-defense expert Tony Blauer interviewed him immediately after the match and his replies left Blauer nearly speechless.

"You said every fight's a fight," said Blauer. "Are you disappointed?"

"Well, I'd like the 'W' [win], but I don't care ... I'll go have a cocktail [and] maybe get in another fight tonight," said Abbott.

Blauer asked if Abbott respected Don Frye.

"No, I don't respect anybody, not even you!"

DON FRYE WOULD not be champion for long. He had broken his hand on Tank's head and had to have three pins inserted to hold the small, brittle bones together. He wouldn't fight in MMA again for five years. Frye interviewed with both the WWF and WCW, but felt that his tough-guy, cowboy persona came off as too cocky even for pro wrestling. Jeff Blatnick recommended Frye to wrestling champion turned pro wrestler Brad Rheingans, who was the US scout for New Japan Pro Wrestling. Frye jumped at the opportunity, and soon became a "heel" – a bad guy in the organization. His first match was against New Japan owner Antonio Inoki (Frye lost), in Inoki's retirement appearance, held at the sold-out 75,000-seat Tokyo Dome. Fellow UFC vets Brian Johnston and David Beneteau both wrestled for New Japan and, with Frye, formed a group called Club 245. Johnston came up with the name from California penal code 245: "assault with intent to do major bodily harm." The trio walked out to the Japanese crowds wearing shirts that read, "A Group of Felonious Individuals Whose Purpose is Best Served by Committing Violent, Unlawful Injury upon the Person of Another." The memory makes Johnston laugh. "The Japanese didn't know what it was and thought it was a bar. They said, 'How do you get to Club 245? I'm dying to go there.'" The group eventually broke up and Beneteau returned to Canada, while Johnston became a "babyface" or good guy on the circuit.

On August 19, 2001, Johnston collapsed from a stroke while preparing another pro wrestler for action. Doctors told his wife Teiana, who he had married just one month before, that he had a 50 per cent chance of surviving and even then would be a vegetable. Johnston had other plans. Today, given the new nickname "The Miracle," he is able to move around unassisted and is never at a loss for words. In the first quarter of 2002, he started a clothing line, Pain Inc., and has a bright future ahead. As for Frye, he returned to MMA in Japan's Pride while continuing to pro wrestle. On February 24, 2002, he faced off against Ken Shamrock, and won a gutsy decision. Frye wanted to rematch Mark Coleman more than anything else, and the pair fought on June 6, 2003, but the result was pretty much the same as their first meeting.

Although the question had now been answered about how well different martial arts would fare against one another, the new question was how the drama would play out. In storybook fashion, there would be plot twists and turns, good guys, bad guys, and wolves in sheep's clothing. The UFC had finally bridged the gap between spectator sport and pro wrestling, leaving the audience guessing what would happen next.

CHAPTER 15

Quest for the Big Apple

O N OCTOBER 30, 1996, Governor George Pataki of New York signed SB 7780 into law, placing "combative sports" under the control of the New York State Athletic Commission. It meant mixed martial arts events were "legal" in the state. Bob Meyrowitz had done it; he had won the Big Apple. "After an exhaustive investigation, they have come to recognize that ultimate fighting is a legitimate sport," he declared. 'We look forward to bringing UFC live events to our many fans in New York." SEG's home state was now ready, if not exactly willing, to host no-holds-barred tournaments and SEG immediately announced plans to hold its first sanctioned show at the Niagara Falls Civic Center on February 7, 1997.

Reporter Dan Barry of the *New York Times* began poking around on the story, and phoned both Meyrowitz and his Extreme Fighting rival, Donald Zuckerman, for quotes. "Now that it was legal in New York, [the Press] called to ask about my plans," said Zuckerman, who told the reporter he was planning a show in Manhattan on March 28. "They also called Bob, who bragged to Dan Barry that he had gotten a lobbyist to get the law changed." On January 15, Barry's feature appeared on the *Times* front page under the headline, "Outcast Gladiators Find a Home: New York." The lengthy article made the politicians look foolish. Barry quoted them saying they wanted the sport banned and were doing everything they could to prevent it from taking place in New York: so why had they signed into law a bill regulating it? How could a senator, a mayor, and a governor be so opposed to something and then pass legislation to see that "human cockfighting," as Manhattan State Senator Roy Goodman proclaimed it, was allowed?

Barry's piece dropped like a bomb. Follow-up stories in the New York media over the next few weeks stoked the controversy – and Meyrowitz and Zuckerman ate it up. Though Meyrowitz denies it, Zuckerman claimed he and the SEG president talked on a daily basis during the press frenzy and even had lunch together. Kelli O'Reilly,

Zuckerman's secretary and an Extreme Fighting associate producer, frequently received calls from Meyrowitz over the course of that week in mid-January. The rivals seemed to be acting in concert.

Though he guessed the politicians would be steamed up over the *Times* story, Meyrowitz was relatively unconcerned. After all, the new legislation was a done deal. "I was at a breakfast for [Mayor] Giuliani when his chief counsel came up to me and said, 'We've got a problem. You'll find out and I'm just giving you a heads-up.'" The *New York Times* then called Meyrowitz, but this time it was not for a victory quote; they said the law had been repealed. They went on to say that a set of rules (all of 114 pages) for the UFC had been issued by the New York State Athletic Commission, rules that would have to be adhered to for the events to go ahead. "I said, 'Well, that's not true because the only one it would affect is me, and they haven't gotten me this rulebook.'"

The *Times* did have the rulebook. Meyrowitz had them send it over, promising them an exclusive. It was true: the commission had produced a set of rules, and told Meyrowitz several hours after he received them, "We're still working on them." Meyrowitz read the fine print with mounting concern. The strict regulations were an obvious ploy to keep the "ultimate" out of the UFC. Fighters were required to wear headgear, were not allowed to kick above the shoulders, and the 30-foot-diameter octagon would now have to be 40 feet to meet the Athletic Commission's rule requirements. The rules were intended to hinder the UFC until the law could be repealed.

Just a day before the Niagara event was to take place, Donald Zuckerman issued a statement saying he was cancelling his proposed show for Manhattan. Meyrowitz wouldn't give up so easily; he had everything riding on the 7,000-seat Niagara Falls venue, which had sold out. He brought suit against the New York State Athletic Commission and took along UFC XII competitors Mark Coleman and Dan Severn for support. Meyrowitz insisted the rules were unfair and dangerous, as the mixture of headgear and grappling could create neck injuries that would otherwise be unlikely. It was too late. The judge declared the commission was allowed to make whatever rules it chose to govern any sport under its control. "The only time in the history of New York State that a law has been repealed using emergency power without a thirty-day waiting period was the UFC," said Meyrowitz. The event couldn't take place in upstate New York – or anywhere in the state for that matter.

As fighters and employees began checking into a hotel in Niagara Falls the day before the event, word came down around 2pm that the venue had been changed to Dothan, Alabama. SEG had secured

Dothan as a back-up venue only eight days before, believing there was no way they could lose since the commission and the law was on their side. New York might have won this battle, but Meyrowitz chartered three jets to take the UFC crew and the octagon to Alabama. "Many fighters saw their relationship with SEG as antagonistic, but this was the one show where everybody knew just how far we had gone, how much money we had spent, and how much effort we put into this thing," said David Isaacs. "We moved a million-dollar show in under twenty-four hours. The pressure was enormous. The sport and our business's viability hinged on our getting each event off."

Fighters were allowed to bring one person with them; friends and entourages had to either return home or pay an astronomical fee to catch the next flight to Alabama. All of the fighters arrived in the middle of the night and had to take a bus from Birmingham to Dothan. They arrived at the hotel at 6am the day of the fight. "A half hour before we were supposed to go on, we were still painting," recalled Meyrowitz. "I thought the paint was going to stick to the athletes' feet. It's remarkable that we pulled it off." Considering the fatigue factor, it was amazing that the fighters were still able to perform as expected. Yet UFC XII turned out to be one of the strongest shows in SEG's history.

To Bob Meyrowitz, Donald Zuckerman is the man who prevented SEG from cementing the success of the sport in New York, the media capital of the world. "Meyrowitz always blamed Zuckerman because he was riding on [Bob's] coattails with the Extreme event," said Art Davie. "He was trying to grandstand and pull a New York City coup. But Meyrowitz knew that you do one or two upstate in Niagara Falls, to show them they could do the event under the law. Then, once that credibility has been established, come back to Manhattan, which was Bob's market." While Zuckerman admitted he was partly to blame because "if I hadn't decided to do a show in Manhattan, none of this shit would have hit the fan in the first place," he insisted he wasn't the only one. Zuckerman claimed that Meyrowitz telling the *New York Times* about the lobbyist turned a 66-to-1 vote for the law to be passed into an Assembly vote of 134-to-1 to ban the sport. "It was just as much his fault, because we both wanted to be in New York," said Zuckerman. Nowhere in the *Times* article does it say that Meyrowitz named "Feathers" or that he bragged about getting the law passed. In fact, he praised the Senate for looking past the misinformation to pass the law. Meyrowitz did, however, have a show booked at the Nassau Coliseum one month after Zuckerman's proposed Manhattan show. Essentially, Extreme Fighting was beating UFC to the punch. Not all publicity is good publicity. If neither promoter had spoken with Dan Barry of the *New York Times*, the lobbyist's name and subsequent dealings with Senate Majority Leader Frank Bruno might never have emerged.

IN PROFESSIONAL ICE hockey, people cheer as two players throw down their gloves to fight, and the ref usually takes his time to stop it. In a stock car race, the possibility of death is always present, as any wreck can end fatally. In boxing, fans root for their favorite to knock the other guy out rather than have the fight go the distance. Many people drawn to watching full contact sports do so because of that innate curiosity to see another person injured, or worse. Few will admit it, but why else do people yell and scream for their man to "kill" or "beat" the other person when watching *mano y mano* sports? How about parents, who become unglued watching their children in Sunday league soccer? Without television or any footage to use as promotion, SEG opted initially to make the Ultimate Fighting Championship appear larger than life. To sell the concept, they had to play off that "deadly" mystique of the martial arts, and say it was a brutal display unlike anything anyone had ever seen before. Does boxing do anything different in its hyping of, for example, Mike Tyson?

From a layman's perspective, NHB appears much worse than boxing: bare-fisted punching in a cage, compared to fighting with gloves in a ring. Why? Because sports fans are comfortable with boxing; it has been around a long time as a spectator sport. What many don't understand is that boxing gloves protect the hand, not the target the gloves are intended to hit. If two people fight bare-fisted, the person throwing the punch must think of one thing: how soon before the small bones in his hand will break? Despite popular belief, the head is much harder than the small bones in the hand. In the first few UFCs, there were very few knockouts or hard punches thrown. If a fighter breaks his hand, he can't fight, plain and simple. In boxing, the fighter wears eight-ounce gloves and is permitted to have each hand wrapped in up to 18 feet of bandages held in place by ten feet of zinc oxide tape. This combination allows the boxer to pound on his opponent without the level of risk a bare-fisted fighter faces. It has been estimated that a boxer takes over 500 shots to the head in an average twelve-round boxing match (because of so many deaths and brain-related injuries from boxing, title bouts were shortened to twelve rounds from 15). Then there are the countless thousands of punches boxers take off sparring partners while training.

"The truth is, if we say, 'Safer than boxing! Men close the gap and eliminate brain-damaging blows,' that's not going to sell anything, right?" admitted Campbell McLaren. The marketing effort to portray MMA as being deadly may have worked a little too well, but the fact remains that it's safer than boxing. Since November 1993, no one has died or been seriously injured while participating in the sport in North America. Sadly, the same cannot be said for the rest of the world: American Douglas Dedge died on March 16, 1998, from injuries to the brain sustained in an unregulated Ukrainian event. He took six to seven shots before the match was stopped. Dedge collapsed and fell into a coma as the decision was being read. "We heard through guys who were with him that he was blacking out during training," says Clarence Thatch, who also competed in the event. Several reports from people who knew him said he had a pre-existing condition that should have prevented him from fighting in the first place.

Politicians have campaigned to shut down so-called no-holds-barred contests even while they have substantial proof of death in other martial arts-related sports. Twenty-three-year-old Redone Bougara died from a blood clot on the brain as a result of a draka (Russian kickboxing with wrestling and throws) match in Friant, California, in 1998. In January 1999, Michael Struve Anderson was kicked in the head during the US Open Taekwondo Championship and would be pronounced dead hours later. New York Mayor Giuliani was quoted as saying, "I happen to be a boxing fan, but this [UFC] goes way beyond boxing. This is people brutalizing each other." With an average of four deaths per year in boxing related to the cumulative damage to the brain because of blows to the head, how does MMA top death?

Every full contact sport is dangerous to some degree, but men and women make that choice and accept the responsibility for putting their bodies at risk. In the December 13, 2000, issue of *USA Today*, an article entitled "Death on the playing field" discussed the dangers of high school American football. The reason? Thirteen young men had died that year from the sport, more than from boxing and certainly more than from any other full contact fighting sport. On September 19, 1994, Joseph Estwanik, M.D., sent a letter to SEG after he had tended to the fighters' needs at UFC III. After listing the minor injuries he had come across, he had this to say:

> I believe it is appropriate to state that the Ultimate Fighting Championship III produced fewer cumulative injuries than I have medically treated from some high school football and

soccer games. Despite the apparent "brutal" image, no serious injuries were sustained and all injuries sustained were of a rather minor and non-lasting category. I found all competitors respectful, sincere and appreciated athletes. The Ultimate Fighting Championship utilizes true athletes as compared with my impressions of the Tough Man contests in which a drunken, inexperienced, and poorly trained competitor will be inappropriately mismatched.

Several anti-MMA politicians seem to be boxing fans. Yet boxing matches end much the same way as in MMA: referee stoppage, decision, towel, or fighter submission. With eight-ounce gloves and shorter rounds, fights are geared to last longer than in MMA, as knockdown rules allow the punishment to continue. Boxers who are knocked down because of a hard blow are stood back up and given an eight count. This can happen three times or more before the match is called off. A fighter can be dazed, knocked out on his feet, and then told to keep fighting even though the match should have been over at that moment. This is very dangerous, as it sets up what is generally referred to as "second impact syndrome." In an article entitled "Concussions in Sports," neurosurgeon Robert Cantu was quoted as saying, "The athlete appears stunned but does not lose consciousness and often completes the round. In the next period of seconds to a minute or two, the athlete rapidly deteriorates from a dazed state to one of deep coma."

In MMA, there are no standing eight counts; if the fighter is knocked down, the match is still in progress (in Japan, the Shooto organization has standing eight counts). He can tap and end any further damage or the referee can stop it, but either way, the match is over. Admittedly, UFC II should have never taken place, since the referee was told he couldn't stop the fight. That was a bad call: it put fighters at risk and it shouldn't have happened. Since that event, the sport has shed its circus trappings and created a systemized set of rules, with judges and a referee who can intelligently make decisions to stop a fight at any time.

In boxing, a fighter has two options: punch to the head or punch to the body. The brain takes a lot of damage as it is constantly rocked back and forth inside the skull with every hit. In MMA, fighters have an array of moves to end a fight. By adding the ground game, MMA fighters can't just stand and slug away, since a takedown from either side is imminent. Submission holds and positioning also lessen the commitment to strike aimlessly. In the Japanese promotion Rings,

Brad Kohler knocked down Valentijn Overeem and commenced to pound on him wildly. Though it seemed like Kohler had the upper hand, Overeem readjusted his position and submitted his opponent via toe hold in under a minute. In Extreme Fighting 4, Brazilian jiu-jitsu specialist Allan Goes could have traded punches with Todd Bjornethun, but caught him in a triangle choke that forced a tap without a strike being thrown. What makes MMA so appealing is the fact that every fight is different; some matches have lots of strikes, other matches have two submission fighters trying to tap the other one out. As for submissions, no one has ever been seriously injured from a choke or arm lock, but sometimes pride enters the picture. Scott Adams and Englishman Ian Freeman were "deadlocked" in trying to apply leg submissions on one another in UFC XXV. Neither man would tap until the pain became unbearable; Freeman ended up tapping after Adams broke his foot. At UFC 48, Frank Mir's arm bar was so tight on Tim Sylvia that the bone could be seen breaking as the ref stepped in less than a minute into the bout. There have been arm, knee, shoulder, wrist and leg injuries as a result of submissions, but nothing that hasn't occurred before in high school football.

The most serious injury in MMA history came in UFC IX, when Cal Worsham suffered a punctured lung from a cracked rib. In every full-contact sport, there is potential for damage by a one-time blow. Though Worsham won his fight with relative ease, Zane Frazier hit him at the right time in the right place. Worsham's adrenaline shielded any signs of the injury until he was back in the triage area, and he was fine after a trip to the hospital.

Since boxing is 100 percent striking, boxers take much more cumulative damage than people think. No one knows more about this than UFC cut man Leon Tabbs, who has spent over 40 years in boxing. He started in amateur boxing in 1945, has managed and trained professional boxers all of his life, and has been a cut man for champions such as Marvin Johnson and Bonecrusher Smith. "UFC is not as brutal as boxing, and I say that because in preparing a fighter for a fight, if he's doing a ten-round fight, he's boxing maybe six to eight rounds a day. At best, the headgear is stopping you from getting cut, but the damage is still there. There is no question about it, the training for boxing is actually more brutal than the fight. There is just no comparison between boxing and the UFC. Boxing is so much worse as far as the amount of punishment a man takes. I cannot even think of a fight in the UFC that would come close to some of the matches I've witnessed in boxing."

One of the UFC's head physicians was Dr Richard Istrico, who also happened to be a ringside physician serving the New York State Athletic Commission. In a letter dated October 24, 1995, he summed up the injuries he had seen in 53 MMA bouts. They included "soft tissue contusions, lacerations less than one centimetre in length, anterior nose bleeds and dehydration. These injuries required treatments as simple as steri strips and ice compresses."

As commisions enter the picture, some states have embraced MMA, including Arizona, which became one of the sport's biggest markets. "[John McCain] wasn't happy that I was doing shows in his backyard, much less the largest show to ever hit Arizona at the Celebrity Theater," said Gino Lucadamo, who promoted the first sanctioned event in the state in September 1998. Even McCain, who was once voted one of the "25 Most Influential People in America" by *Time* magazine, said in a documentary that while he isn't a fan of the sport, the rule changes to make it safer had drawn his attention elsewhere – such as campaigning against violence on TV.

The sport isn't completely safe yet. Toughman contests still confuse many who don't know the difference, leading to misinformation and negative press unable to distinguish between the two. Death has become commonplace in toughman events, where unskilled, ordinary people fight with little or no medical supervision. The perceived similarity between MMA and toughman has led some states to ban the lot, save for boxing. Despite overwhelming medical evidence and MMA's undeniable safety record, the general consensus remains that "ultimate fighting" is more dangerous than boxing. Perception is greater than reality.

CHAPTER 16

A Striker's Vengeance

FROM THE FIRST UFC, pure strikers from styles such as tae kwon do, karate and kempo had proven ineffective against groundfighters. While many claimed these competitors didn't truly represent their styles, it was apparent that a striker's tools could be taken from him once the fight went to the mat. Tank Abbott showed that striking could be dangerous, but against a wrestler like Dan Severn, he could do very little. Extreme Fighting also knew that grapplers would come out ahead and leaned toward the dominance of jiu-jitsu, creating stars out of Ralph Gracie, Conan Silveira and John Lewis. For the third EF, matchmaker John Perretti landed undeniably the most experienced striker to fall victim to heavyweight Conan.

With over 15 years in kickboxing, Maurice Smith had worked his way up to become champion of the World Kickboxing Association (WKA), a European version of the PKA that allowed kicks below the waist. Smith had made martial arts his calling after seeing Bruce Lee on the big screen at the age of 13. He moved from tae kwon do to karate and wing chun, and quickly realized that stepping into the ring was the only way to test himself. Smith competed in kickboxing at 18 for the WKA as one of the few Americans to fight for the organization. He claimed his first championship at 21 and, after losing a decision to Don "The Dragon" Wilson, competed for over nine years without a single loss. At 6ft 2in, Smith started out fighting at a slim 175lbs, but later moved to super-heavyweight to compete at 215.

The WKA led the way in popularizing kickboxing in Japan, and Smith made a name over there. As his popularity grew, he competed in pro wrestling in Japan for the Universal Wrestling Federation, his first match coming in November 1989 against Minoru Suzuki. Smith felt the Japanese wanted to leverage his kickboxing name to bring in more fans for the new shoot style of wrestling. From 1989 to 1995, he competed on and off for the UWF, Rings and Pancrase, familiarizing himself with groundwork, even though some of the outcomes were predetermined. Smith eventually worked with Ken Shamrock, after meeting him in Pancrase, on stand-up in preparation for the UFC. "We did more talking than training and when he went into the WWF, I got pawned off to Frank [Shamrock]," said Smith. This turned out to be a blessing in disguise. Frank – the brother of Ken in name only, having been similarly adopted by Bob Shamrock – was if anything an even more talented fighter. He and Smith became fast friends and even better training partners.

Smith remembers being contacted for a slot in the first UFC but, without predetermined endings, he passed: "I was just a kickboxer, and my credibility would have helped their sport, but I would have got my butt kicked, more than likely." After turning down an opportunity at UFC VI while helping Ken Shamrock prepare for Severn, Smith talked everything over with Frank Shamrock, and both agreed that EF 3 was the best opportunity for his MMA debut. With the help of the Lion's Den, Smith trained specifically to combat a jiu-jitsu player. "We worked on defending the side, and full mount on the ground, and [drilled] reversing the guy. If I did that, I worked to keep him against the fence and start punching him. I shouldn't worry about breaking the guard because that's not important." At 34 years old, Smith took on a whole new challenge against an opponent who seemed unbeatable: Conan Silveira.

EF was set up to have a four-man tournament to decide a definitive heavyweight champion in the fourth show. Smith and Silveira made up one bracket, Bart Vale and Murakami Kazunari the other. Vale had also started with the UWF in 1989, after 20 years of traditional martial arts, competing in point karate tournaments and local kickboxing shows in Florida. In 1983, he met Sammy Soranaka, who introduced him to the shoot style of wrestling that Karl Gotch had perfected for the UWF group. Vale was hooked from the start. On whether UWF was real, Vale said, "People often asked me that. I wished they were [worked], because that would have saved my face from getting cracked and my shoulder from getting broken." Injuries did happen in the UWF, but the truth was that it was a pro wrestling organization with fixed endings. Unlike Smith or Shamrock, Vale built his career with the UWF and later Pro Wrestling Fujiwara Gumi. When shows were held in Florida, Bart Vale became the "champion of the world" by defeating founder Yoshiaki Fujiwara for the belt.

Vale was a tenacious businessman. After copyrighting the name Shootfighting, he created his own organization, the International Shoot Fighting Association. He looked like a true champion at 6ft 4in and 270lbs, and even convinced MTV that he was legit when it aired an entire segment on him in the early 1990s. As Vale was still under contract with the Japanese, "I remember telling Perretti that there were certain opponents that I was not allowed to fight," said Vale of EF 3. "So he told me, 'Well, just get somebody from Japan that they would approve.'" The decision was made to bring in Murakami Kazunari, a 6ft 2in judo player with a solid physique. Kazunari was no stranger to MMA, as he had competed in the 1996 Lumax Cup (UFC rules except for no strikes to the face on the ground) in Japan just seven months earlier and had lost in the finals of the eight-man tournament.

In October 1996, EF 3 held its first sanctioned show in Oklahoma. For the first time since the original UFC, matches had three five-minute rounds (ridiculously called "phases") to keep the action moving. Ralph Gracie smoked karate man Ali Mihoubi and John Lewis outmatched Brazilian Johil De Oliveira for a draw (EF didn't have judges, so any fight that went the distance became a draw). The event had its first major controversy when Carlson Gracie student Allan Goes defeated Oklahoma native Anthony Macias. Goes dominated Macias, but headbutted him several times and fish-hooked (the term for hooking an opponent's mouth with a finger) him once. When the referee stopped Goes the first time for butting and tried to explain the foul to him, the Brazilian paid no attention, instead listening to Gracie in his corner. Nearly four minutes into the match, the ref stopped the action again for another butt, but Goes ended up with the win. Macias apparently was angry about Goes not getting off him when the ref stopped the action, and appeared to verbally submit. Though Goes should have been disqualified, an error in communication gave the Brazilian the win. For the rest of the night the ref frequently threatened disqualifications.

No one could predict who was going to win the Kazunari-Vale match since Vale had fought only one true MMA bout, against Mike Bitonio in the WCC, while Kazunari was an unknown. Vale was much larger but that didn't stop Kazunari from rushing in, taking Vale's back in the clinch and attempting a throw. Vale showed some skills when he tried to submit Kazunari with a straight arm bar while standing. Wincing in pain, Kazunari forced the action to the ground to take Vale's leverage away, then took full mount to open him up with punches. After rolling to his stomach and taking more punishment, Vale brought them back to their feet and landed two solid punches to Kazunari, who appeared dazed. What happened next was astonishing. The judo expert went into a frenzy, unleashing a plethora of lefts and rights that knocked Vale to the ground.

Kazunari continued punching until the ref stopped the fight and rendered a technical knockout. "I was surprised that they ended it when they did; I gassed myself out," said Vale. He went on to open his own schools around the country and, despite his questionable fighting experience, promoted Shootfighting and MMA the best he could. In the four years after EF 3, Vale would have one other legit match, against Dan Severn, who beat him soundly with punches in less than five minutes.

Maurice Smith came to the circular cage accompanied, as usual, by his 20-year manager Kirk Jenson – but this time he also had Frank Shamrock in his corner. The crowd bellowed their support for the underdog kickboxer. As the match got underway, Conan Silveira immediately went for the takedown and settled for being in Smith's half-guard. Keeping the Brazilian in close, Smith kept him from doing anything in the first round. Then, in a surprise move, the kickboxer reversed Silveira and remained in his guard for the rest of the round. Instead of exposing an arm trying to strike, Smith buried his head in Silveira's chest and punched the abdomen and head from the sides.

In the second round, Smith kept Silveira away with solid Thai kicks to his thighs. The jiu-jitsu man eventually tied Smith up but, by grabbing him just under the arms, wasn't able to take him down. A frustrated Silveira tried to finish the fight on his feet, but his flailing arm punches did very little damage to Smith, who knew how to protect himself. Just as Vale had awakened Kazunari's punching, now Smith came back and landed four perfect punches that rocked the giant. Silveira, noticeably tired, managed to recover and tied the kickboxer up again to end the five-minute round.

Tying up Smith in the third round provided an opportunity for the kickboxer to throw a hard knee to separate them. Whack! Smith landed a devastating kick to Silveira's left thigh that echoed throughout the venue. A wobbly Silveira hardly got a chance to do anything before getting kicked again. Muay Thai fighters often bait their opponents with leg kicks that over time make them drop their guard for protection; the opponent's reflexive action then sets up the finishing blow. Just a minute and a half into the fight, Maurice Smith made his move by landing a perfect high kick to the side of Conan's neck, which sent him reeling. "What ended up happening – and this has happened to me twice – was you don't feel it," said Smith. "You don't go down, but it's like the blood stops flowing to your brain for a second." The referee stepped in and stopped the bout before Smith could do anything else. Silveira claimed his knee had been injured just days before the match, but there was no sign of this. "I wasn't getting away from him and wasn't in my gameplan," said Silveira. "He did hurt me because he was throwing all these kicks and punches and I wasn't stepping out." The match became a benchmark for the sport: a kickboxer with basic grappling skills had claimed a knockout victory over a Carlson Gracie jiu-jitsu black belt.

SEG MADE TWO major changes to its tournament format for UFC XII four months later. UFC XI had seen a few injuries, so the eight-man tournament was disbanded in favor of a less-punishing four-man tournament and weight classes were instituted for lightweight (under 200lbs) and heavyweight (over 200lbs), allowing smaller fighters to take on opponents their own size and so lend more credibility to the sport. In the first-ever lightweight tournament, Lion's Den fighter Jerry Bohlander emerged the victor by scoring two easy wins in under two minutes combined.

Bohlander's only real competition would have been the victor between Carlson Gracie student Wallid Ismail and Pancrase fighter Yoshiki Takahashi. Unfamiliar with the rules, Takahashi used the fence to subdue Ismail's takedown attempts and utilize his better stand-up skills. Ismail, a native of the Amazon, had beaten both Renzo and Ralph Gracie in jiu-jitsu matches but he couldn't put anything together to beat Takahashi. "I expended a lot of energy trying to put Takahashi down, but he held the fence and I lost all my power," he said. "I knew if I put him on the floor, I'd beat him in one minute." Takahashi won by decision but was unable to fight Bohlander due to an injury. The young Lion's Den standout fought an easy final against alternate Nick Sanzo, who was submitted with a neck crank variation called a crucifix. Ismail would go on to choke out Royce Gracie in a jiu-jitsu match the following year.

For the heavyweight tournament, Scott "The Pitbull" Ferrozzo was the only veteran among newcomers Jim Mullen, Tra Telligman and Vitor Belfort. All eyes turned to 19-year-old Belfort, who came into the octagon with an Adonis-like body and choirboy face. Born in Brazil, Belfort had trained in jiu-jitsu from the age of six and dabbled in boxing and other sports. At 17, he moved to Los Angeles and stayed with his adoptive father, Carlson Gracie, who stepped up his jiu-jitsu training. Belfort was going to adopt the Gracie name, but pressure from the rest of the family, who were unsure of his skills, put a stop to it. After two years, Carlson gave Belfort his jiu-jitsu black belt and put him in his first fight in the Hawaiian promotion called Superbrawl. Belfort beat UFC veteran John Hess to a pulp in 15 seconds without even using any jiu-jitsu.

The UFC presented a more difficult test: Belfort's first opponent would be Lion's Den member and Superbrawl champion Tra "Trauma" Telligman. Telligman hailed from a rough neighborhood in Dallas, Texas, and took up martial arts for self-protection. He had already survived a terrible car accident as a 17-month-old toddler; the impact crushed his sternum and ribs and destroyed his right pectoral muscle. He never saw it as a handicap, and excelled in sports as he grew older. After training in martial arts, Telligman met Guy Mezger and joined the Lion's Den. He went on to win several fights in Russia and Hawaii before getting a slot in the UFC on two week's notice. Telligman was out of shape but knew his opponent's only skills were jiu-jitsu. "The biggest fear in my mind was that I was getting out there with this kid that didn't belong in the ring with me, and if I don't blast him out of there in six or seven minutes, I'm going to get beat by some kid," said Telligman. Color commentator Jeff Blatnick also predicted Belfort would try to take the fight to the ground. Both observations could not have been more incorrect.

In the first semi-final, Telligman circled to the left of Belfort, who bounced back and forth as if waiting for a signal. Telligman wanted him to shoot for the takedown, but Belfort had other plans. "He kind of winked at me, and then he lit me up," said Telligman. Belfort swarmed him with lightning-fast punches to close the distance and try for a takedown. Up against the fence, the Lion's Den fighter stopped the takedown, forcing the Brazilian to unload a series of accurate crosses and straight punches right out of a comic book, his back muscles flexing wildly with each punch thrown. "He was landing everything that he was throwing; he has very good timing with the distance of his punches," remarked Telligman later. Moving away from the fence, Belfort continued his attack, eventually sending the Texan to the mat. Telligman held Belfort in an open guard, but could do very little as his opponent quickly moved his leg out of the way and took side mount. After landing several elbows to the neck, Belfort looked up to John McCarthy and motioned that his opponent had sustained enough damage. McCarthy stopped the bout. Tank Abbott, watching from the sidelines, was miffed at Jeff Blatnick's praise of Belfort's hand speed.

Scott Ferrozzo's semi against kickboxer Jim Mullen was a one-sided beating. The rotund pitfighter worked on Mullen against the fence with uppercuts, knees, and punches. He seemed to enjoy hurting Mullen, who, according to Ferrozzo, had been trash-talking him the week of the fight. After one stoppage to check for a cut, the match was finally over when McCarthy realized Mullen could no longer defend himself; his face looked like a pepperoni pizza. Before the match, Ferrozzo had said, "The rule is not to get hit at all in the face," and he showed why in this match.

Ferrozzo didn't know anything about Belfort and approached the final cautiously. So did the Brazilian. After feeling each other out, Belfort landed a solid left hand flush on Ferrozzo's chin that shook him. Taking a step back to insure he didn't get trapped, Belfort fired another left. This time it dropped Ferrozzo, who fell into his arms. Belfort scooped him up and dumped him to the mat. The big man got to his knees for an escape before Belfort could do any significant damage. Holding on to Ferrozzo with his left hand, Belfort threw five hard rights to the side of his head, then two equally hard lefts. Ferrozzo protected his head with both hands, but McCarthy moved in to stop the fight at 0:45. "I thought that he would try and mount me, and I was going to try and get him up close," said Ferrozzo. "All of a sudden I felt the pressure let up, so [after the match was stopped], I got him up against the fence and then I'm accosted by the refs." The melee brought in fellow ref Joe Hamilton to calm Ferrozzo down. Later, Ferrozzo claimed he hadn't been hurt, though he admitted, "He did crack me pretty good."

ON THE DAY that UFC XII aired, Leo J. Hindery Jr was named President of TCI cable. It was the worst possible news for SEG. Cable was their lifeblood, sustaining the sport financially and helping to build its audience. But Hindery was an implacable opponent of no-holds-barred events and had refused to carry them when he ran a small cable network in San Francisco. Now he was in charge of an industry giant that could reach 14 million viewers in 46 states.

It wasn't long before Bob Meyrowitz, John McCarthy and Art Davie were flying down to meet Hindery to discuss his stance on the UFC. Meyrowitz told Hindery there would be additions to the rules: no head butts, no groin shots and mandatory gloves. "The whole reason we didn't use gloves was because the fighter couldn't hit the person as much because it hurt their hand. [Mandatory gloves] went against what we had been saying the whole time," said McCarthy. Still, in order to appease the ignorance and misinformation that had painted a negative picture for the sport, all UFC fighters were now required to wear four-to-six-ounce gloves. These are much smaller than boxing gloves and allow the fighter to hit harder without hurting his hand. Because of the politicians, the sport actually became more dangerous. Gloves became required in every MMA event in the

US that employed closed-fist strikes. The number of knockouts rose, though the risk of brain damage was minimized due to the grappling-oriented nature of these fights.

The SEG team were wasting their efforts. Hindery wouldn't budge; there was no way he was going to distribute the UFC. "I came here, found out where the bathrooms are, and I cancelled [Ultimate Fighting]," he later bragged to the *Los Angeles Times*. Worse was to follow. Time Warner followed Hindery's lead and dropped the sport. With TCI and Time Warner jointly acquiring a controlling stake in Viewers Choice, the biggest pay-per-view distributor, it effectively meant the UFC was off the small screen. The picture looked bleak. Though Meyrowitz vowed to soldier on, many muttered that this was the beginning of the end for MMA in the mainstream.

FOR UFC XIII: Ultimate Force, Vitor Belfort tested himself against Tank Abbott in the superfight. Abbott and training partner Tito Ortiz put all their energies into getting him ready for the match. "We worked so damn hard for that fight. We lifted, ran, wrestled and boxed everyday," said Ortiz. "Dave was in such good shape; he could go for twenty minutes." While Abbott's pre-fight interview followed the standard "no respect" mode, Belfort admitted his opponent was dangerous and that he had everything to lose by falling victim to him.

The fight got off to a quick start. Without wasting any time, Abbott charged Belfort and missed with a big right hand, allowing the Brazilian to go for a takedown. Abbott, pushed up against the fence, attempted a hip toss, but ended up underneath his opponent. Belfort wrapped up Abbott's left arm for a submission, but the streetfighter twirled around and drove him to the mat. Abbott then allowed him to stand, later saying he wanted to trade punches, but trainer Ortiz said he respected the Brazilian's ground skills too much. Both men tied up and started slugging away at each other's midsections until Belfort pushed Tank away and opened up with his incredible hand speed. Belfort was far too fast for Abbott, and finally decked him with a punch.

As in his match against Ferrozzo, Belfort maintained top position and dropped bombs. Ref McCarthy repeatedly yelled, "Get outta there, Tank!" Belfort moved around the back and continued his onslaught as Abbott put both hands over his head for protection. After a couple more punches, McCarthy stopped the bout at 0:53. "I go over to him [Tank] and he's sitting on the ground, and he looks up to me and says, 'That kid rocked my world!' That was his exact statement," said McCarthy. "Tank doesn't even remember that he was rattled; he was on queer street." Abbott had quite a different take on the matter later, claiming that McCarthy stopped the fight too soon, as he was just waiting for a chance to get out Belfort's trap. That said, Abbott went out of his way to shake Belfort's hand. The UFC had found a powerful new striker to take the attention away from the grapplers – a strange irony, given Belfort's grappling background.

That evening, as Abbott and company tanked it up at a bar inside their hotel, Belfort's coach Al Stankie approached Abbott and shook his hand. Stankie wouldn't let go, and the two exchanged words before Abbott pulled away, cautioning Stankie. Later that night at the after-fight party, Tank took retribution, slapping Stankie and starting an old-fashioned barroom brawl. "Wallid [Ismail] kind of came around from the side and cold-cocked Dave [Tank]," said Paul Herrera. "Eddie [Ruiz] tackled Wallid and got him under the table and started fucking him up. My brother jumped on another guy. It was a fun little go, a melee. Dave didn't even get into it." Abbott never got his licks in on Ismail, while Belfort was nowhere to be found and didn't get involved. But Abbott couldn't resist some parting words for Ismail: "He's still on the roost ... if he crosses my path the wrong time, you'll find him in the hospital. I'll catch that fucker." As in the UFC, Tank's best fights will forever be tossed back and forth in fandom rather than in real life.

UFC XIII also made Bruce Buffer its staple announcer. He has introduced the event ever since, becoming as much a fixture as his brother Michael is at boxing title fights. "Pat Miletich came up to me after a fight and said that he loves the way I announce him because it gets him so juiced up for a fight," said Bruce. "That means everything to me, when fighters praise my work and tell me this." Now known as the "Voice of the Octagon," Bruce has announced other shows as well, including King of the Cage and the Abu Dhabi Combat Championships. For the UFC, Bruce coined a slogan to match his brother's, starting off each show with, "It's time ... to begin." His likeness even appeared in the UFC video game. Bruce supports the sport in his spare time and launched a website that followed the MMA movement: Maxfighting.com. Managing Michael and doing motivational speaking engagements hasn't taken away Bruce's passion and dedication to promoting the sport he holds so dear.

CHAPTER 17

From One Extreme to Another

IMITATORS CONTINUED TO proliferate. The UFC was still going despite all of the political pressure and the collapsing cable TV deals, and others wanted a slice of the pie. They included Martial Arts Reality Superfighting (MARS), one of a select few big-budget shows with the ingredients to be a hit. Promoter John Keating learned that a great idea and a lot of money can quickly be wasted by incompetence and seedy business practices. Keating, a prominent surgeon in Atlanta, Georgia, was a lifelong martial artist who had served as a ring physician for UFC VII and numerous pro karate events. His first mistake was partnering up with William Sieglen. "He would talk about being married to Victoria's Secret models, and owning all these businesses and houses, but he lived in a little apartment here," said Keating. The list of Sieglen's unbelievable tales as a conman is lengthy, according to Keating. Despite Sieglen's questionable credentials, he and Keating staged underground pit fights in Atlanta dojos, which strongly resembled the unrefined skirmishes in UFC's early days. Few of the participants were paid, but that didn't stop one fight from lasting 90 minutes. There was, however, plenty of side betting by businessmen thirsty for action.

Using his contacts, Keating arranged a meeting with TVKO, which supplied top-notch boxing matches for pay-per-view. They responded with interest, to the point of wanting to sign a contract to put on shows in Atlantic City. Keating (who now claims to be a fool for not signing) and his lawyer felt they could make money on their own. Keating began working with a young networker named Tom Huggins who had connections with several Brazilian fighters. Having previously failed to set up shows with both Howard Petschler and John Perretti, he felt this was the perfect time for MARS. He worked with investors and "raised enough money to put on three full-fledged fights and make them better-paid fights than anyone has ever had." His vision was a show that had as few rules as possible, save for no biting or eye gouging. Lacking experience in fight promotion, he hired a showrunner in the television industry to land a quick deal with the pay-per-view companies in New York. The deal was shoddy at best, but at least MARS had a chance.

The theme for the first MARS was Russia vs Brazil. Keating has since fought hard to dispel rumors that his group wanted the Brazilians to win. "A lot of people complained that the Russians weren't well-matched for the Brazilians. That may be so, but it was not our fault. We spent a fortune trying to get the best Russians to come up and fight. There was always one excuse or another." Oleg Taktarov vs Renzo Gracie was the headliner.

Everything went wrong. Keating arrived at the venue in Birmingham, Alabama, to find dozens of people there, flown in by Huggins (according to Keating), who had nothing to do with the fight. Thousands of dollars were wasted treating these people like kings while the show suffered. Keating hired a high-priced public relations team to market the show in Alabama, but the turnout was pathetic; fewer than 2,000 people showed up. "It's almost impossible to have a fight in Alabama and not have a good crowd; we managed to do it," says Keating. Apparently, the PR firm had no idea how to promote a fight like this. On top of that, Keating put on another NHB show called Shooting Stars earlier the same day, before MARS. Hardly anyone watched it. Nearly $100,000 was spent on a state-of-the-art sound system in the auditorium, but this was a fight, not a rock concert. Oleg Taktarov's management had also created numerous problems by trying to stage his rematch with Marco Ruas twelve days before MARS. They wanted $50,000 more to nix the rematch but Keating emphatically refused; Taktarov had already signed a contract. Taktarov went ahead anyway, fought Ruas for 31 minutes (in World Vale Tudo Championships 2) and broke his hand in the process.

Shooting Stars (featuring fighters like Anthony Macias and John Dixson) went off without a hitch, despite the sparse attendance, and MARS followed with an above-average show. Olympic wrestling contender Tom Erikson, one of the few Americans in the event, made his debut by pummeling a lethargic but never-say-die Russian, while Brazilian Murilo Bustamante, a Carlson Gracie protégé, enlivened the small crowd with his submission and stand-up skills. After taking out their first and second round opponents, Erikson and Bustamante met in the finals: the proverbial David vs Goliath.

With nothing but power and wrestling skill, the 6ft 3in, 280lb Erikson had difficulty putting away Bustamante, who weighed 100 pounds less. Since the event had no time limits, the Brazilian repeatedly fell on his back in an effort to bait Erikson into a ground attack. A confused and frustrated Erikson didn't know what to make of the situation, and the two ended up fighting a slow, 40-minute battle with infrequent action. At the 30-minute mark, Keating, who was friends with many of the Brazilians, allowed the fight to continue for another ten minutes, pushing for a decisive winner since there would be no judge's decision. "The Brazilians at ringside started shrieking at me that I was an asshole for giving them another ten minutes and at this point, I'm completely puzzled," said Keating. "I thought they wanted more time, and they're screaming at me that I'm giving them too much time. They were claiming that I was trying to fuck Murilo by extending the time." Both men fought their hearts out to a draw, only to share the loser's purse. Carlson Gracie students Carlos Barretto and Ze Mario Sperry both walked over their respective Russian opponents in their superfights leading up to the headliner.

Five minutes before he was scheduled to appear, Oleg Taktarov announced he was pulling out. He wanted more money, and felt the promoters owed it to him. "I cannot remember his [exact] reason for demanding that money, but it may in fact have been money to buy him out of his SEG contract," said Keating. "Whatever it was, this was money we categorically did not owe him." In a last ditch effort, Keating walked into Taktarov's dressing room and told him that he had extended his hospitality to both Taktarov and his manager, from treating them to dinner to housing them for a stay during the Olympics. "We had an agreement, and if you don't want to come out, that's entirely up to you," Keating told Taktarov. "But I'm telling you right now, we will go on international television and announce to the world that you are afraid to fight a man that you outweigh by twenty-five pounds." The Russian finally agreed to fight. He pressed the attack early by putting Gracie down with a quick flurry, but from the bottom the Brazilian came back with a well-placed kick to Taktarov's chin that knocked him cold. The unconscious Russian instinctively sat upright as Gracie got in some licks before the match was stopped at 1:03.

It was sweet irony for Keating and MARS after all of the alleged problems with Taktarov. On the flip side, "Renzo Gracie was a total and complete gentleman and he is without question the most honorable man in the martial arts today," said Keating. Taktarov said later that he fired his manager after this match, and that part of the reason he took the fight was because his manager was broke and needed the money more than him. "Oleg's manager, Mike Flynt, made a big scene at the after-fight party," said Brett Moses, who worked with Keating the night of the show. Apparently, there was some debate over

Taktarov having to pay back $5,000 for being released from his SEG contract. "He tried to allege that the contract said that Oleg only had to pay back his share from the winner's purse and that since he lost, MARS had no right to deduct the $5,000. His interpretation of the contract proved to be incorrect."

Although the show had some great moments, large parts of the auditorium appeared deserted. "At the end of the day we spent all the money for three [events] on the one [MARS], and all of that money was wasted," admitted Keating. "It was not wasted as much on the fight as it was for flying people in who had no business being flown in, paying outrageous amounts of money on hotel rooms and airplane tickets, and spending money on public relations people who didn't do the work." Though Keating today puts in countless hours as a surgeon, he can still be found in and around the MMA scene as both a ringside physician and as a living reminder of MARS.

WITH EF AND UFC trying to tap into a dwindling pay-per-view market, smaller promotions like Iowa's Extreme Challenge evolved to capitalize on local demand. Enter Monte Cox, Quad City newspaper editor and former pro boxer, who turned his knack for marketing into a career as a boxing promoter. After working with ESPN and TVKO on numerous shows, Cox felt he couldn't go any further with them. He wasn't making much money anyway, and the thrill was turning into a routine. But when he heard of local hero Pat Miletich's upcoming MMA match in Chicago, he contacted him for a story. Cox journeyed to Miletich's gym to understand what he did, and actually rolled around with him to get a feel for submission fighting.

Miletich was a two-time All-American in high school football and wrestling and was on his way to college when he had to return home to Iowa because his mother had fallen ill. Out of shape and bored, the 21-year-old was invited to a local gym to check out traditional karate. Martial arts wasn't really his thing but Miletich wanted to learn how to fight, and the gym taught boxing and Muay Thai. Before long, he had earned a black belt and won a Muay Thai kickboxing title. He also saw the UFC and felt the early competitors were unskilled. Invited to a Renzo Gracie seminar, he decided to see what jiu-jitsu was all about. "Renzo was just going through everybody and tapping everyone out, and I knew right then that this was the real stuff," said Miletich. "I was very impressed with Renzo. That convinced me to start training in it. I knew if I could combine the Muay Thai with the wrestling takedowns I knew, and match that with good groundfighting skills, I would be tough to beat." Without anyone to further his training, Miletich bought an eleven-tape jiu-jitsu instructional series by Renzo and studied it for over a year: picture a television next to a wrestling mat and a very worn-out remote control. Miletich's kickboxing success also led him to compete in a July 1995 NHB tournament called Battle of the Masters in Chicago.

After winning the first and second Battle of the Masters, Miletich asked Cox if he would be willing to give this sport a shot. Though the boxing promoter was reluctant, he held the Quad City Ultimate to play on the "ultimate" angle initiated by the UFC. The show brought in 8,000 people, and Cox had found a new outlet for his energies. Though he still dabbled in boxing, Cox continued putting on smaller events and saw Miletich as the star. "There is no other person in this sport who can bring out that many people," said Cox. The two worked together to promote events until things got too hot for the renegade sport and it faced a ban in Iowa. Using his relationships with the boxing commission, Cox was able to get MMA regulated in the state, by doing away with certain strikes that might be considered a little too much (headbutts, kicking a downed opponent). He also made it clear that if anyone wanted to put on a show in Iowa, they had to adhere to those rules, which kept out people who didn't know what they were doing. After the first two Quad City Ultimates, Cox changed the name to Extreme Challenge. He put on four shows, then got a call from Donald Zuckerman, who needed a safe haven for the fourth Extreme Fighting event.

Though Zuckerman and his team had lost ground with pay-per-view as a result of the first two EF shows, they had come back strongly for the third. The fourth promised to be their finest hour. Taking a cue from the UFC, they added world-class wrestlers Kenny Monday and Kevin Jackson to the card. While Dan Severn and Mark Coleman had won their share of amateur wrestling accolades, their achievements paled compared to Monday's and Jackson's. Each had won Olympic gold medals in freestyle wrestling, in 1988 and 1992 respectively. Like Coleman, they ventured into the fighting sports because they could use their wrestling backgrounds and make substantially more money than any coaching job could pay. Monday faced John Lewis while Jackson faced John Lober. Could two great wrestlers defeat two submission fighters on wrestling skills alone?

While terms like jiu-jitsu, submission fighting and every variation thereof became commonplace in describing a fighter's skills, Seattle-based Matt Hume claimed the most realistic style of all: pankration. Hume's introduction to martial arts was a given, as his policeman father had actually trained under Bruce Lee for a short period of time and had taught his son boxing at the age of four. Though his father laid out a practical foundation of grappling and submission, Hume also studied traditional martial arts. If he found something that worked, he wanted that knowledge. So when a wrestler friend told him about the ancient Greek sport of pankration, Hume adopted the name and belief system. According to Hume, pankration is "the positioning of a great jiu-jitsu player, the takedowns of a great freestyle wrestler, the stand-up of a great Muay Thai fighter and boxer, and the lower body submissions of a Pancrase guy or a sambo guy, as well as being able to switch those up and go to the upper body and capitalise on everything." This powerful combination required intensive training and extensive study of the various styles involved.

Hume set up his own school and competed in Pancrase on the recommendation of fellow Washington native and kickboxing champ Maurice Smith. Like Monte Cox, Hume also moved into fight promotion and started United Full Contact Fighting, producing events in Seattle and Hawaii. John Perretti invited Hume to compete in the third EF. After two years away from serious competition, he had trouble with shootfighter Erik Paulson, but won the fight by opening up a cut on Paulson's head with a knee. For the fourth show, he took on home-town fave Pat Miletich, who had more fighting experience. Miletich predicted he would have to stop Hume from getting out of the match too early by forcing a cut. His words could not have been more ironic.

At the beginning of the first round, Hume whacked away at Miletich's legs with a couple of hard kicks. This didn't last long before Miletich took him down. Hume moved to the guard and kept Miletich in tight to keep him from striking. Just past the halfway point, Hume tried to bring the fight back to stand-up, but the Iowan took him down again. He left his head exposed and Hume attempted a guillotine choke, but Miletich pulled out of it. With less than 30 seconds left, Hume kicked Miletich back from the guard and again brought the fight back to standing. After missing with a high roundhouse kick, Hume pressed the action. "I wanted to see where his conditioning was … when I felt I was ready on the second stand-up, I went after him with punches and kicks," recalled Hume. Miletich acknowledged their effectiveness: "He threw a right hand to make me duck. That was the way I was taught in Muay Thai too – you throw a right hand and make them duck, plum their head and start throwing knees, and he did it perfect." After Hume landed four solid knees, Miletich didn't want to risk being cut so he fell to his back. Hume launched a flurry of punches until the end of the round.

As Miletich walked back to his corner, he felt his nose. Hume had broken loose some cartilage busted in an earlier training session with a boxer. The doctor examined it and ended the fight. Although a great technical match was stopped short of becoming a classic, both men have nothing but the highest admiration for one another. "To this day, Matt is the smartest fighter I've ever fought. I respect Matt a great deal because he's a Christian and a great guy, and he's just an awesome athlete," said Miletich. Though it was his first loss, he later became UFC's welterweight (169lbs) champion, Iowa's pride and joy, and a mentor and trainer to a whole class of upcoming fighters competing under the banner of Miletich Fighting Systems.

Amateur wrestlers typically had a difficult time defending submissions when they crossed over into MMA, and Olympic wrestlers Kevin Jackson and Kenny Monday faced jiu-jitsu players in their inaugural matches. After drawing with Igor Zinoviev at EF 3, Jackson's foe, John Lober, exemplified a tough opponent. It took all of 30 seconds for Jackson to gain side mount but his inexperience allowed Lober to spin underneath and attempt both an arm bar and a leg submission, without success. Lober pulled guard, but the wrestler broke free to dominate on the mat. He punched and landed knees to the head, even putting his hand over Lober's mouth to shut off his air. Lober missed another arm bar attempt, and Jackson paid him back with hard shots to end the round. In the second, the wrestler took Lober down again and disarmed his guillotine choke. Moving to the side mount, Jackson trapped one arm and sunk in an arm triangle choke, squeezing Lober tightly. Lober's grimaced face turned purple before he finally capitulated at 1:12 of the round. The battered and beaten Lober said later that he had fought with a fever, not wanting to let Perretti down by pulling out. It's doubtful it made much of a difference. Jackson claimed his first MMA victory. He said he "didn't like the brutality of it," but that was what it took to get the submission.

EF had created a personality with John Lewis, who had become the sport's poster boy by speaking up in its defense on talk shows like *Jerry Springer*. In an attempt to make Lewis look bad, one of Springer's goons jumped the gun on a planned grappling demonstration and shot in on Lewis while he was off guard. Lewis impressed the crowd by making him tap in seconds. After drawing with Carlson Gracie Jr, and beating two worthy opponents, Lewis took on Kenny Monday to cement his status. Far more aggressive than Jackson, Monday shot on Lewis as the match began and was soon in the guard position. Lewis instantly sunk in a textbook arm bar on the overzealous Monday that should have made him tap, but the wrestler seemed only irritated. He pulled out of it with his incredible strength and unloaded on Lewis as payback. After missing another arm bar and an ankle lock, Monday crushed Lewis up against the fence and landed several shots to his face. "Overall, you can't really train to have a chin, you just have to be a tough guy going in," said Lewis later. "I was knocked out on my feet. I got rocked." Near the end of the first round, Monday went head to head in Lewis's guard to keep from being arm-barred again.

As the second round started, Monday and Lewis moved right back to the same position. Monday wore Lewis down with punches until he could no longer keep the guard. The wrestler machine-gunned over 20 right hands to Lewis's head. With just under a minute left, the referee stopped the fight, since Lewis could not properly defend himself. It was another incredible victory for the wrestlers. "By the time the fight happened, he [Monday] was two hundred pounds-plus already," said Lewis. "I was one seventy-nine and pushing it, and I still fought him the way I wanted to. My problem in that fight was underestimating what it takes to be an Olympian." Monday never fought in MMA again, while Lewis took the loss in his stride and carved his future in the sport.

The final match in EF 4 pitted Maurice Smith against Murakami Kazunari, still a relative unknown even after soundly defeating Bart Vale in the previous show. He showed no fear of Smith and landed a clean palm strike that dropped the kickboxer in the opening seconds. "When he hit me, I didn't know where I was," recalled Smith. "When he was punching at me, I still wasn't absolutely coherent. If I hadn't held on out of instinct, he might have kicked my ass." Kazunari's mistake was letting Smith regain his composure enough to get back to his feet. The two circled each other for a moment before the kickboxer landed one of the hardest right hands in NHB history. WHAM! Kazunari spun all the way around and collapsed to the ground, lights out. Smith had demonstrated that an experienced striker could never be underestimated. EF 4 could not have ended on a more exciting note, but backstage, Smith's opponent wasn't looking too good. "When he went down, I was really concerned," said Smith. "I didn't find out until later that he was paralyzed for almost two hours, and I was kind of nervous about it." Kazunari fully recovered and eventually moved into pro wrestling in Japan.

DESPITE A TREMENDOUS fourth show that earned the respect of the fans and the critics, Extreme Fighting was in dire straits. The damage done by the Canadian debacle proved to be terminal.

"Donald did the math with me and we had been taken off a lot of the pay-per-view universe that the UFC was still on," said John Perretti. "So they still had buy rates for half the nation that we weren't allowed to be on because we weren't pushing enough numbers." The last show had been seen in only 45,000 homes, nowhere near enough to keep going. Another massive blow came when Request TV, the second-largest pay-per-view distributor, decided not to carry another EF show because of opposition from TCI and some other cable companies. Zuckerman and Perretti almost matched the UFC's success with half the staff, but the pressure was too much. Zuckerman was also quick to say that financial troubles at *Penthouse* (owned by his backer General Media) and Time Warner's ban on the sport made sure there was no EF 5.

Within days of EF 4, Battlecade folded. Zuckerman became a film producer in Hollywood; Perretti stuck with the fight game, working with Igor Zinoviev in Japan. But months after EF called it quits, Perretti had a new idea: staging a submission-only competition with wrestlers vs submission experts. Perretti and Zuckerman knew that politicians would leave them alone, but this time they had to bankroll the project themselves. The two met with USA Wrestling to get them on board, and after several meetings, they agreed to support The Contenders. Held on July 14, 1997, the event showcased many great athletes, including wrestlers Tom Erikson, Dan Henderson and Kenny Monday, and submission fighters Matt Hume, Carlos Newton and Frank Shamrock. Hume was especially excited to face Monday, whom he saw as the "epitome of wrestling" and an opponent he would have faced in MMA had EF continued.

With wrestling's legendary coach Dan Gable representing wrestling and "Judo" Gene LeBell representing submission, the show had promise, but failed to ignite much interest from fans of either genre. The lackluster marketing campaign featured none of the competitors, and a horrible rendition of the song "Simply the Best" didn't help either. While some of the matches were interesting, the fuzzy rules didn't give much direction on how to judge a submission-only event. Frank Shamrock and Matt Hume provided the only flashes of excitement, each man finishing his opponent in under a minute.

Before the show, a wrestling-biased female reporter, who couldn't understand how a submission fighter could possibly defeat a wrestler, taunted Shamrock. Shamrock laughed it off, then tapped out Dan Henderson by heel hook at 0:54. Hume wanted to beat that time when he faced the event's best wrestler, Kenny Monday. He engaged the Olympian and fell to his back to get things moving. "I put my leg in front of him to bait him, since he practises this technique that is basically a half Boston crab," said Hume. "I put my leg up for him and he went for it. I went up around his back and put the figure four on him." Monday tapped out in under 30 seconds. As Hume went to shake his hand, Monday pushed him away and asked for a real fight. "I told him that he was still one of my heroes regardless of what he thought of me," said Hume. "He just had a bad attitude about it." Monday never competed again. Hume won in another submission-only tournament in Abu Dhabi but, riddled with injuries, moved behind-the-scenes as a prominent manager, trainer and judge. On December 13, 2002, he resurfaced in the ring for indie-based Hook 'n' Shoot, arm-barring Canadian Shawn "Pain" Peters in less than two minutes.

The Contenders ended up being a one-time event due to a lack of interest. "I think USA Wrestling bullshitted us into believing they were going to promote it harder than they did," said Perretti. "No wrestlers watched it; no martial artists watched it. It was the worst buy rate in history, but a terrific show. If we had done four [shows], ESPN2 was going to buy it and I was going to make all my money back." To this day, only EF has ever come close to matching the UFC's early success in the States. But countless promoters try, and have taken on similar political battles in their respective states to cement MMA as a bona fide sport. Local businessmen like Denver's Sven Bean have take it upon themselves to educate commissions and properly sell them on what the sport is all about. The age of old boxing promoters with decades of experience has been replaced by ordinary people who have turned their passion for the sport into a cause worth fighting for.

CHAPTER 18

Growing Pains

THE BATTLE WAGED by SEG in New York nearly cancelled UFC XII, but the show somehow managed to live up to its potential after moving to the comparative backwater of Alabama. It would be SEG's final event to reach the masses: TCI, Cablevision and Time Warner collectively put an end to MMA on pay-per-view. Canada had been a lucrative market for the UFC, with the highest per capita viewership, but not anymore; TCI Canada also censored the event. Pay-per-view had created the UFC's appeal, but to survive SEG now had to decrease fighter purses, concentrate more on gate receipts, and re-market the show to satellite cable systems, a minuscule audience compared to the major cable players. Though the show could still be watched on a dozen or more smaller cable stations, the controversy and the media hype had come to a screeching halt. Politics had managed to bury it – for now.

But this was a sport that had no intention of dying. UFC XIII: Ultimate Force, held on May 30, 1997, at the Augusta-Richmond Civic Center, played to a capacity crowd – but penetrated less than one-tenth of its former cable reach. It was structured like the previous show, with two four-man tourneys to crown heavyweight and lightweight champions. The UFC was accumulating too many champions with little variance between them. There were tournament champions crowned at each show, and there were superfight champions crowned at each show, but no official rankings as in boxing. The confusion didn't increase fan interest. For the lightweight tourney, Christophe Leininger returned after losing to Ken Shamrock in UFC III. Leininger, who had worked with Kevin Jackson and other wrestlers in Arizona, had won an eight-man tournament as a tune-up for his UFC comeback.

Enson Inoue came into the tournament with highly touted jiu-jitsu skills and a 6-2 record while fighting for the Shooto organization in Japan. Born in Hawaii, Inoue had studied jiu-jitsu under Relson Gracie while in college. On a chance trip to Japan, Inoue, who was part

Japanese, decided to stay in the country. A Shooto promoter discovered him after Inoue wandered into a local gym to polish his jiu-jitsu training. He would become one of Japan's most celebrated stars.

Guy Mezger, who had fought in two alternate matches in the UFC, also got his chance to compete for the lightweight title. Mezger looked more like a model than a fighter, but his extensive background said otherwise. Born in Dallas, Texas, he had wrestled since the age of 14 and studied different martial arts, including chung moo kwan. Mezger blew out his knee while on a wrestling scholarship in college, ending any chance of making a career on the mat, but started competing in point karate and full contact matches, though he didn't make much money or get a title shot. Mezger's first sight of the UFC showed him the Promised Land. He had great admiration for Ken Shamrock, identifying with his marketability and athleticism. Shamrock prepared Mezger for his UFC IV debut. The two became friends and Mezger joined the Lion's Den. On the advice of Shamrock, he ventured to Japan and fought in Pancrase, since it was a more reliable paycheck and the UFC's future was in question at the time. He returned to UFC XIII with a sharper set of tools that he hoped would net him the title.

The heavyweight tournament featured four newcomers: kickboxer Dmitri Stepanov, pro wrestler Tony "The Viking" Halme (*aka* Ludwig Borga from WWF), hybrid fighter Steven Graham, and wrestler Randy Couture. Born in Littlewood, Washington, the favored Couture had made wrestling his sport of choice throughout junior high and high school, though he also played football and boxed. His collegiate honors included three-time wrestling All American for Oklahoma State University and four-time Greco Roman in the Nationals. After earning a degree in German, Couture hoped to compete in the Olympics. Then he saw an old college chum fight in the UFC.

In February 1996, Couture watched Don Frye in UFC VIII and thought it might be a new outlet for his wrestling abilities. He sent in an application to SEG, who put him on standby since they'd reached their quota for wrestlers. Couture blew off the opportunity and signed on with Real American Wrestling (RAW), an organization designed to bring national attention to amateur wrestling. Two months after signing with RAW, Couture trained with the US team in Puerto Rico in preparation for the Pan American Games. When RAW co-founder Ricco Chapirelli informed Couture that a slot had opened for UFC XIII, Couture jumped at the chance despite the event being only two weeks away. Couture spent another five days in Puerto Rico, then trained with Chapirelli in Atlanta for one week prior to the show.

"Ricco showed me what the guard was and how to pass it and what an arm lock was and how to defend against it," said Couture. With only his grappling background and some boxing (which he had done ten years before in the Army), Couture entered the event as a true greenhorn.

The lightweight semis started with Guy Mezger against Christophe Leininger. The match went the distance, with uninspiring performances by both fighters. Mezger fought cautiously, throwing jabs instead of combinations, and couldn't put Leininger away. Leininger fought in a gi, and looked sloppy and uncomfortable while standing up with Mezger. His only defense was holding onto the front of Mezger's tights, which he tugged on for most of the match, while Mezger held his opponent's gi lapel for leverage to punch. Neither man got anywhere. The only highlight came when Leininger lifted Mezger over him, but the Lion's Den member quickly recovered and took full mount. After a twelve-minute regulation and a three-minute overtime period, Mezger won by unanimous decision. "When McCarthy pulled me off of him," said Mezger, "Leininger said, 'I didn't quit! Don't stop it!' Jokingly, I said, 'Don't worry Chris, I quit. I'm tired of hitting you.'"

Enson Inoue made quick work of wrestler Royce "The Farmer" Alger, who took Inoue down and laid in his closed guard. Inoue was the only one with a gameplan. While trading strikes, he moved into position by throwing one leg over Alger's head, and locked out his arm. The best way to escape from an arm bar is to close the distance and try to finagle out of it. Alger did just the opposite by trying to pull straight out of it, thus making the submission tighter. With his arm fully extended, Alger didn't last long. He tapped the mat at 1:40.

Inoue–Mezger would have made a great match, but Inoue suffered a broken orbital bone and had to withdraw from the tournament. Alternate Tito Ortiz took his place. Ortiz was 6ft 2in, lean and muscular, and his bleached blond hair marked him out. Born and raised in Huntington Beach, Jacob Ortiz was nicknamed "Tito" by his father because he was a troublemaker. The name stuck and so did the reason it was given to him. While in high school, wrestling coach and Tank Abbott cohort Paul Herrera introduced Ortiz to wrestling. He was a natural, and saw the sport as a way to stay on the straight and narrow. His success continued through college where, as a sophomore, Ortiz racked up a 36-0 record, with 34 by pin. Ortiz prepared Tank Abbott for his UFC XI appearance, so Abbott returned the favor and got him an alternate slot in UFC XIII. Ortiz wrecked Wes Albritton with punches in 31 seconds.

In the lightweight final, Ortiz showed little respect for Mezger, charging him and throwing heavy leather. Mezger eventually shot for the single leg takedown, but Ortiz sprawled and took side mount. He used his favorite wrestling move, the inside cradle, to set up a series of devastating knees to Mezger's head. Mezger appeared to be tapping out from the damage, and was trying to defend the knees when referee McCarthy stopped the action. The referee noticed two arterial cuts to Mezger's head which spurted blood every time his heart pounded. Mezger was taken over to cutman Leon Tabbs and doctor Richard Istrico. Ortiz naturally thought he had become the lightweight champion. But the match continued after Tabbs and Istrico wiped Mezger's head and gave the okay to restart.

Mezger and Ortiz resumed from opposite ends of the octagon. Ortiz scrambled with Mezger for a few seconds before shooting in for the double leg takedown. He kept his head on the outside, allowing Mezger to sink in a guillotine choke, just as Severn had done to Shamrock in their first meeting. Mezger fell to the mat and put Ortiz in a closed guard for leverage, squeezing his opponent's neck. Ortiz could barely move, and had no choice but to tap out. Mezger was the lightweight champion. The following year, he would become the seventh King of Pancrase by defeating Masakatsu Funaki. Ortiz had been exposed to his first guillotine choke as a result of a rookie-wrestling mistake. The UFC would not see him again until January 1999 when, with polished skills and a new marketing campaign, he became one of the sport's hottest stars. Ortiz and Mezger would meet again, in a very different rematch.

For the heavyweight semis, 290lb Steven Graham manhandled 217lb Dmitri Stephanov and tapped him out with a key lock at 1:30. Tony Halme's shootfighting background was questionable, but he was an amusing pre-fight interview prior to his bout with Randy Couture: "My greatest strength is I'm not afraid of anybody. I have balls of iron. I go in there to rip the head off or die trying." As the match began, Halme dashed toward Couture (age 33, 6ft 1in and 225lbs), missed a punch, and was taken down immediately. The 300lb Halme kept a tight grip, but Couture rolled him to his stomach, submitting him via choke in just short of a minute.

Couture had a harder time with 23-year-old Steven Graham. The wrestler took Graham down during the opening seconds of the match, but he couldn't finish him with the choke. Couture moved to a front headlock, then spun around for a second choke attempt. With his opponent completely down, Couture flailed away at Graham's head until McCarthy intervened. Couture, with no professional experience, had won the heavyweight championship. "I wasn't thinking too much about fighting other than it was nice to get paid for it," said Couture. He found the experience exhilarating, partially because his interest in wrestling had grown somewhat stagnant and he'd needed a change of pace.

UFC XIV: SHOWDOWN was held in Birmingham, Alabama, at the Boutwell Arena, with 4,800 in attendance. EF champions Maurice Smith and Kevin Jackson had both been aching to get back into the mix. Smith fought for the UFC heavyweight championship by taking on Mark Coleman. Jackson competed in a four-man middleweight tournament. Beginning with this show, the classifications were as follows: lightweights (169lbs and below), middleweights (170 to 199), and heavyweights (200 and over). For the first time, four-to-six-ounce grappling gloves were mandatory for all fighters. There would also be a heavyweight tournament featuring UFC veterans Brian Johnston and Moti Horenstein and newcomers Dan "The Bull" Bobish and Mark Kerr. Kerr stood out as the darkhorse contender, and it wasn't difficult to see why.

At 6ft 1in and 255lbs, Mark Kerr had earned the moniker "The Smashing Machine" while fighting in World Vale Tudo Championships 3 in January 1997 in Brazil. With a bodybuilder physique, he destroyed Paul Varelans and Fabio Gurgel with his wrestling prowess, powerful knees and punches. Kerr had wrestled from the age of four but, incredible as it now seems, was so small that it led to high school bullying in Iowa. Luckily, upperclassman Pat Miletich was there to stick up for him. By the time he graduated from Syracuse University, his wrestling record was 98-20-2, and the university named him its 1992 Athlete of the Year. He made it to the Olympic qualifiers but lost in the first round. In 1994, Kerr won 16 straight matches without giving up a single point and, by 1996, he was one of the best wrestlers around. A series of injuries kept him out of the 1996 Summer Games, so he followed his wrestling brethren and turned to MMA as his new combative outlet.

The middleweight tournament was not as strong as previous shows. Art Davie matched two one-dimensional fighters (boxer Yuri Vaulin and karate champ Todd Butler) against jiu-jitsu's Joe Moreira and wrestler Kevin Jackson. Vaulin was clueless and defenseless against Moreira, but all Moreira could do was get the takedown. He won by decision but dropped out of the event due to a concussion. Jackson wasted little time in taking Butler down, and tapping him out with head shots. Jiu-jitsu exponent Anthony Fryklund replaced Moreira and couldn't mount much of an offense; Jackson forced the tap out by rear naked choke at 0:44.

In the heavyweights, Mark Kerr took on karate practitioner Moti Horenstein. Kerr made his octagon debut to the sound of screaming fans marveling at his hulking frame. Horenstein had said he was ready for wrestlers, but Kerr quickly closed the distance and took him down without a single punch or kick. After gaining side mount, Kerr delivered four knees to Horenstein's face before McCarthy stopped the punishment.

Brian Johnston and Dan Bobish both bombed away with fast and furious head punches in their semi-final. Bobish, 310lbs of solid beef, was much too powerful for the less-bulky Johnston. "I remember hitting him and getting no response," said Johnston. "That kind of worried me." Just as Ken Shamrock had done in Ultimate Ultimate '96, Bobish took Johnston down and applied pressure on his head up against the fence. "He was so heavy, and he was just leaning into me. I was almost ready to pass out," said Johnston. Johnston tapped out to a forearm choke after Bobish landed elbows, headbutts and punches.

The heavyweight final between Kerr and Bobish should have been exciting, but a loophole in the rules brought it to a premature end. Kerr threw two leg kicks at Bobish, who was on the attack during the opening seconds of the round. Without any set-up, Kerr then made a risky move and shot in for the double leg takedown on Bobish, a 1992 NCAA wrestling champion in his own right. Using all of his momentum, Kerr put Bobish on his back and crowded him up against the fence. Bobish landed some small shots while Kerr tried for an arm triangle choke. Just as he was in position, Bobish moved his arm out of the way, and Kerr pressed his chin down into Bobish's right eye socket. After a few seconds, the pain was too unbearable and Bobish tapped. Though the rules forbade eye gouging, a chin to the eye was never covered. "I used to talk about how great a technique it was," said McCarthy, who confirmed it was not against the rules at that time. After this match however, the eye-gouging rule was amended.

Intense heat had been created for the superfight between Maurice Smith and Mark Coleman. It would be the classic contrast in styles: the striker vs the grappler. Smith, during his pre-fight interview, even said Coleman punched like a girl. "I knew wrestlers and they weren't punching like fighters," said Smith later. "It was more of a criticism than something to tear him down." Coleman had notched two straight tournament victories and a quick submission over Dan Severn. Few people believed a kickboxer could do anything against Coleman. The buzz for this match even championed the rematch between Royce Gracie and Ken Shamrock in UFC V.

While Smith entered the octagon with a small crew, Coleman's entourage was an army of over 20 people. The 245lb, 32-year-old Coleman outweighed Smith by 25lbs and was three years younger, but Smith had been working with Lion's Den trainer Frank Shamrock on guarding against the neck crank that Coleman had used so successfully in past fights. Coleman's strategy was different: "I was going out drinking, not training, and watching Maurice Smith on film. To me, it looked like a guy that I was going to take down, punch a few times, slide off to my side headlock, and walk out of there."

Twenty-two seconds into the match, Coleman faked a left jab and shot in on Smith, taking him down with ease. In Smith's open guard, Coleman became a man possessed. For over a minute, he fired away with punches, elbows and countless headbutts as Smith tried his best to defend. "When he came into the fight, he was so pissed off [because of the punch-like-a-girl comment] that his gameplan was to kick my ass," said Smith. "He hit me about four times really hard that totally rocked me, but it took a lot out of him." For the first four minutes, Smith frustrated Coleman by preventing him from gaining side mount, while delivering several punches and elbows to Coleman's head. "After the two-minute mark, everything fell into place and I realized how dumb I was for taking on a championship fighter of Maurice Smith's caliber, and just absolutely showing him no respect," said Coleman.

Just before the five-minute mark, Coleman finally got side mount, but Smith rolled over to his stomach, opening himself up for a rear naked choke. With Coleman unable to secure it, Smith maneuvered out of danger, but not for long. Coleman took full mount and again fired punches to his opponent's head. Smith kept his composure, and volleyed from side and side, tiring the wrestler out in the process. Then he rolled back over, with Coleman trying for another choke. The kickboxer defended well from this position. "I didn't quit," said Coleman. "I was still going for the win. Everything in my whole body just seized up, and I was just hoping to get that side headlock choke on him, but he had studied it and was very slippery." At 7:30, the Coleman-heavy crowd had changed its tune, and a chant of "Maurice" was echoing through the auditorium.

At 9:00, Coleman tried for an arm triangle, but he was not in position and gave Smith the chance he'd been looking for. The kickboxer brought the fight back upstairs. Coleman, resting his hands on his knees, was gassed. He attempted a takedown, but was so tired he slipped to the ground. As he rose, Smith attempted a head kick that looked close to being a foul; it was unclear whether Coleman had more than two points of contact on the ground (to appease politicians, kicking an opponent on the ground had been made an infraction of the rules). The fight was stopped momentarily to warn Smith, and Coleman got a few seconds rest.

At the restart, Coleman was so tired he couldn't even budge from his corner, so Smith pressed the attack. He landed two leg kicks, followed them up with a solid jab, and felt confident enough to throw another leg kick. It missed, allowing Coleman to take Smith back down. Over ten minutes into the fight, Coleman clutched Smith in his guard while the kickboxer landed several hard elbows to the back of the wrestler's head. No matter what Coleman did to move from that position, Smith worked the open guard with proficiency. "I didn't want to use the closed guard like I did with Conan Silveira because a wrestler is not going to play the same game," said Smith. At just under 13 minutes, Coleman finally got the patented side mount choke that had put Severn away, but Smith slipped right out and continued throwing elbows. With 45 seconds to go in the 15-minute regulation, Smith reversed Coleman, took his back, and landed two punches before bringing the fight back upstairs.

In the rest period before the first of two three-minute overtimes, Frank Shamrock coached Smith, while Kevin Jackson yelled at Coleman to get working. "Just six more minutes," said Jackson, but Coleman was too busy catching his breath. When the overtime period started, Smith approached throwing leg kicks and even taunted Coleman with his hands to engage. Coleman was completely wasted and kept checking the clock to see when the punishment would end. In an act of desperation, he finally attempted a takedown, but it was slow and miscalculated, allowing Smith time to move out of the way. At 2:14 into the first overtime, Smith landed four hard punches and one head kick, but Coleman held on until the end of the period. Smith raised his hands victoriously before walking to his corner.

McCarthy walked over to Coleman and told him, "You gotta fight back." On resumption, Smith was even more confident and chased Coleman to chop him down, much like Marco Ruas had Paul Varelans in UFC VII. Smith even slipped and fell after missing a head kick but Coleman was too worn out to capitalize. At 1:30 of the final period, the overhead lights momentarily went out, but McCarthy pushed the action and asked Coleman if he wanted out of the fight. Despite the fatigue and the bruises on his thighs from kicks, Coleman did not quit. Smith played cautious as the final seconds wound down. "If I would have pressed it, I might have got caught on the ground again. I would have lost that fight because one judge had me losing all the way to the last minute," explained Smith.

The epic battle went to the judges, with a unanimous decision going to Maurice Smith. It was the most exciting fight of 1997, and the biggest upset in the history of MMA. Smith now claimed championships in both EF and UFC. "Winning the title was not as important to me as knowing that I could fight anyone in any style," said Smith. For the second time, a striker had defeated a well-known grappler, and conditioning won the fight. No matter how powerful, how strong or how knowledgeable a fighter is, he must be conditioned enough to go the distance. With his kickboxing background and training routines, Smith was able to pull off a major victory.

For Mark Coleman, there was a new test: to move past his one-dimensional view of a sport he felt had been tamed. "After that fight, it totally changed everything," said Coleman. "It was humbling and brought me back to the ground. It took at least two weeks before I could start using my left leg, but as soon as I was able to start working out, I was on a mission to come back." Coleman made his comeback – and it would be one of the most triumphant returns in the history of the sport. After four straight losses, he competed in Japan's Pride organization, ultimately winning the 16-man Pride Grand Prix in 2000.

UFC XV: COLLISION COURSE, held at the Casino Magic Dome in Bay St Louis, Missouri, on October 17, 1997, was another showcase for the monstrous Mark Kerr. Randy Couture took on Vitor Belfort in a heavyweight elimination superfight to decide Maurice Smith's opponent in a future event. Smith was originally slated to defend his title against Dan Severn, but Severn pulled out due to injury.

Six days before the event, a lavishly produced Japanese MMA show called Pride made its debut. Pride was created to segue between pro wrestling and MMA, and spotlighted Rickson Gracie against pro wrestler Nobuhiko Takada as the headliner. Tank Abbott was set to fight Kimo, but some trouble with the law kept Abbott from leaving the country. Severn took his place, despite his commitment with the UFC, and fought Kimo to a boring, 30-minute decision. A desperate SEG had contacted Abbott even before Pride, but called off his participation believing Severn would be fine. With less than a week, they asked for Abbott again when Severn could not make it. "I told them that I had not been training and that I had been drinking," says Abbott, who tipped the scales at 277lbs. He accepted their offer anyway.

The strikers hit back: Maurice Smith launches a Thai kick at Conan Silveira in an Extreme Fighting event. *(Battlecade)*

Wallid Ismail attempts a takedown on Yoshiki Takahashi. *(Zuffa Entertainment)*

Brazilian phenomenon Vitor Belfort blitzes Tank Abbott in UFC XIII. *(Robin Postell)*

Brazil's Murillo Bustamante (BOTTOM) tries to draw wrestler Tom Erikson into a ground game. *(John Keating)*

Matt Hume launches a knee at the popular Pat Miletich in Extreme Fighting 4. *(Battlecade)*

Renzo Gracie throws one more punch at the dazed Oleg Taktarov in a tournament called Martial Arts Reality Superfights. *(Robin Postell)*

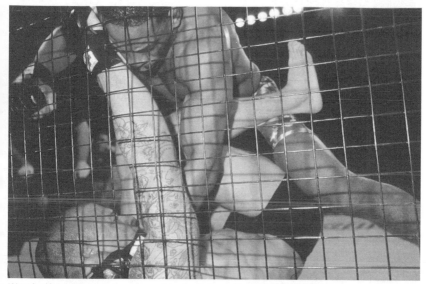

Wrestler Kenny Monday pounds on John Lewis in another Extreme Fighting event.
(Susumu Nagao)

Maurice Smith celebrates after knocking out Murakami Kazunari in devastating fashion.
(Susumu Nagao)

(ABOVE) Mark Kerr wins the UFC XV heavyweight championship. *(Cal Cooper)*

(LEFT) Wrestler Randy Couture out-strikes a dazed Vitor Belfort in the UFC XV superfight. *(Robin Postell)*

Tank Abbott feels the power of Maurice Smith's Thai kick. "I stepped off the bar stool and into the octagon," said Abbott afterwards. *(Susumu Nagao)*

Frank Shamrock (LEFT) takes on Enson Inoue In Japan Vale Tudo '97. *(Susumu Nagao)*

Kazushi Sakuraba goes for a leg submission on Conan Silveira. *(Susumu Nagao)*

Randy Couture (TOP) tries to control Maurice Smith for the UFC heavyweight championship. *(Susumu Nagao)*

Many MMA fighters appeared in films. Here Oleg Taktarov fulfils his childhood dream of becoming an actor in the thriller *15 Minutes*. *(Oleg Taktarov)*

Frank Shamrock, here celebrating his King of Pancrase win, was another to feature in movies and commercials. *(Pancrase)*

Brazilian jiu-jitsu took the United States by storm after the early UFCs, with hundreds flocking to gymnasia for lessons. *(Rorion Gracie)*

Frank Shamrock and Tito Ortiz swap punches in one of the greatest fights in UFC history *(Susumu Nagao)*

Royce Gracie made his comeback against Japanese sensation Kazushi Sakuraba during Pride Grand Prix 2000 in Japan. Sakuraba won a match lasting over 90 minutes when Rorion Gracie threw in the towel. *(Susumu Nagao)*

British MMA star Mark Weir. England saw its first UFC in the summer of 2002, a sign that the sport was taking off in Europe. *(xfuk.co.uk)*

The flamboyant Bas Rutten makes his trademark ring entrance. Rutten is perhaps the best known of the European wave of fighters. *(Pancrase)*

Gilbert Yvel kicks fellow Dutchman Bob Schrijber on his way to winning their rubber match in 2 Hot 2 Handle 4: War World 3 *(Red Devil Sports Club/Bas Boon)*

UFC XV started with two heavyweight alternate matches to decide a replacement if one was needed. Then Mark Kerr stepped in to take on Airborne Army Ranger Greg Stott. Stott talked a good game and pestered matchmaker Art Davie at every UFC with photos and business cards, trying to get a shot in the show. Davie finally gave in just to shut him up. Stott claimed to represent R.I.P. – Ranger International Performance – which he called "the most expeditious form of combat." Unfortunately, one knee from Kerr knocked him out in 20 seconds; Stott's UFC career would Rest In Peace.

By all accounts, David Beneteau was brought in to lose against Carlos Barretto. Beneteau was a solid wrestler, but with his 2-3 UFC record, most felt he hardly stood a chance against the veteran Brazilian jiu-jitsu champion. Nicknamed Carlao (meaning Big Carlos), Barretto stood 6ft 4in and weighed 235lbs of solid muscle. He was also undefeated in MMA, having bested Geza Kahlman Jr, Dan Bobish and Kevin Randleman to win the Universal Vale Tudo Fighting Championship 6 in March 1997.

During the opening minutes, Barretto took Beneteau's back for a choke, but the wrestler stood right back up. Barretto had a difficult time with Beneteau, who was able to take down the Brazilian at will; he had been training with jiu-jitsu champ Pedro Sauer. Five minutes into the match, Barretto had the wrestler against the fence and tried everything he could to pull him down to the mat. He succeeded, but Beneteau was on top, and the Carlson Gracie student paid the price with over a dozen punches to the head. As the match continued, Beneteau fatigued, but he kept a steady pace as Barretto became frustrated by having to fight standing up. He landed some leg kicks and even one head kick on Beneteau, but he wanted the fight to go to the ground. After the twelve-minute regulation period, Barretto scored a takedown, but he couldn't do anything in the three-minute overtime. In one of the closest matches in UFC history, Beneteau won by unanimous decision.

Beneteau should have taken on Kerr in the finals, but now pulled out with no explanation other than to say he would lose. "He [Beneteau] knew he wasn't hurt; he just didn't want to get his ass kicked," remembered SEG's David Isaacs. "I said to him, 'You know, I probably would have made the same decision, but I'm not a fighter.'" Beneteau thought it was the most "intelligent thing considering what I was up against," but the way he did it effectively ended his career in MMA. Although other fighters have feigned injuries to keep from losing a fight, Beneteau told the truth and was shunned for it. He made a brief comeback after attending law school, but failed to gain much attention.

The heavyweight final for UFC XV was no crowd-pleaser: Kerr choked out alternate Dwane Cason, nephew of ex-boxer Leon Spinks, in 54 seconds to win his second tournament.

Vitor Belfort vs Randy Couture turned out to be the most exciting match of the event. Couture watched tapes of Belfort and studied with boxing trainers to work on his footwork, combinations, and defense. His gameplan was to use his Greco Roman wrestling to tie Belfort up and keep him from striking. Before their match, however, it was difficult to get Belfort out of his trailer due to a mysterious intestinal virus that made him nauseous. Rumours also surfaced that he was having problems with both his girlfriend and Carlson Gracie.

Belfort fought Couture in a very low stance, anticipating a takedown attempt, but the wrestler felt comfortable standing up. He circled away from Belfort, who had positioned himself as a southpaw, and stayed clear of his onslaught of punches. "I kind of had some reach and height over him, so with that lower stance, he was right there to hit," said Couture, who landed a left jab less than a minute into regulation. After a brief exchange, Belfort crowded Couture up against the fence and clutched his left leg for a takedown. The wrestler remained calm and worked through it before going on the offensive. Couture tied up with Belfort to shut down his striking game, and at 2:41, took the Brazilian down with a double leg.

Couture latched on a front head lock, opening Belfort up with punches before the Brazilian pulled out. Pulling Couture into his guard, Belfort kept him out of punching range, but the wrestler was able to break free, finagling another front head lock. At 6:40, Couture launched knees at Belfort's head and followed up with strikes that stung his opponent. The Brazilian was tired but fired back as best he could. Couture wouldn't give him a target. At 7:32, the wrestler moved in for the kill and slugged away at Belfort with uppercuts that eventually sent him to the mat. Couture followed up with knees and more punches until referee McCarthy stopped the match at 8:17. Randy Couture had a smart gameplan that outmatched Vitor Belfort on every level. "Vitor is a single-dimension fighter who got outboxed by a wrestler because he didn't have a basic background in boxing," commented Maurice Smith.

For the heavyweight title, Tank Abbott took the fight to Maurice Smith despite the extra weight he carried from not training properly. Smith played it smart and chose not to meet Abbott head-on, instead making him expend energy. He landed a leg kick but Abbott took him up against the fence and clobbered him with punches that dropped the kickboxer. "He hit me in the back of the head and I had a pain there for at least another week," said Smith. On the ground, Smith regained his composure and pulled Abbott into his guard. Much like Coleman, Abbott swatted at Smith but few of his punches landed and he became tired. At 3:30, Abbott gained side mount, but lost it immediately when he tried to strike.

Both men worked on the ground with little success. Abbott landed some punches; Smith rained down elbows to Abbott's head and missed two arm locks. At 7:32, McCarthy stood them up. Abbott was completely out of gas, with both hands on his knees. Smith calmly walked toward Abbott, who hardly looked as if he was in the fight anymore. Whack! Abbott took a solid leg kick from Smith that nearly spun him around. A second leg kick resounded throughout the venue; the crowd could almost feel Abbott's pain. "Do you want out?" asked McCarthy. As Smith landed the third one, Abbott verbally submitted and flopped down on the mat to catch his breath.

Smith had earned a shot at Couture in UFC Japan, but Abbott ended the show with his usual honest banter. "As of last Saturday, I stepped off the bar stool and stepped into the octagon," he said. "I haven't been training; I've been partying. I came out here and went for it." Abbott later charged McCarthy with an unfair stand-up, noting that he was too gassed to continue. He said that McCarthy stood them up right after Abbott moved out of Smith's guard. But the videotape clearly shows that the match had been a stalemate on the ground, with neither man getting the better of the other.

A kickboxer beat a wrestler. A wrestler won by out-striking a jiu-jitsu player. Another wrestler defeated a jiu-jitsu champion by staving off his takedown attempts. The playing field of MMA was blurring the lines between singular styles. Grappling, submission and striking had each proven dominant alone, but now a blended system with conditioning and strategy became the next logical step. As the matchmaking improved to keep out one-dimensional styles like karate and boxing, and examine true cross-trained fighters, the crowds were also becoming more educated. Their eyes were now open to what the sport should have been all along.

CHAPTER 19

Ultimate Betrayal

THE THIRD ULTIMATE Fighting Championship was originally to have been held in Japan, a country in tune with the sport, but plans fell through. It would take SEG another three years to get there, when the company landed a deal with some of the people involved with the Japanese pro wrestling group Kingdom, to set the stage for the last show of the year in December 1997: Ultimate Japan. Superstars Ken Shamrock, Mark Kerr, Randy Couture, Vitor Belfort, Tank Abbott, and Maurice Smith headlined the card to make UFC's debut in the Land of the Rising Sun a memorable one.

Kingdom was an offshoot of the Universal Wrestling Federation International, pro wrestler Nobuhiko Takada's group, which emerged after the original UWF. Unlike other shoot-style pro wrestling shows, Kingdom permitted closed-fist strikes to the face rather than open-hand slaps, but most of the matches were worked. That said, they really hit each other and only the trained eye could tell something was amiss. UFC Japan's main event pitted Shamrock against Takada, but the latter dropped out because Shamrock refused to do a work. Officially, Takada's omission from the card stemmed from a knee injury suffered in his legit match against Rickson Gracie in Pride two months earlier.

Shamrock moved on to the WWF, and Pride claimed another casualty for Ultimate Japan when Mark Kerr pulled out of the show. A press release issued by SEG announced that Kerr was enjoined from fighting in other events because of his exclusive participation agreement with the UFC. SEG's old nemesis, Robert DePersia, was managing Kerr, and he believed there had to be a time limit on exclusivity. But Kerr was legally bound by his contract, according to SEG exec David Isaacs: "In the middle of his contract, after we had spent time and money building him up, he decided that he was just going to fight for someone else." According to Isaacs, Kerr argued in court that the UFC was not a real sport, so how could he be held in an enforceable agreement? A court battle ensued. Kerr won a release from his contract, and fought in Pride's second show. Though DePersia claims SEG lost the court case, Kerr was required to pay a steep but undisclosed price to the company so he could fight for the Japanese organization.

Kerr ultimately became one of the biggest stars in the sport, and Pride had more money to keep him happy. He would be thrust into the limelight not for his fights but for being the subject of an intense documentary dubbed *The Smashing Machine*. Filmmakers traveled with Kerr for over a year, expecting to see the rise of a modern day warrior. Instead they found a man struggling with drug addiction (painkillers), relationships and fighting itself. The program drew controversy from an MMA community unwilling to see its merits, while mainstream critics praised it for capturing the demons that haunt many athletes. People wanted to see Kerr return to the ring in tiptop shape, but in 2003 his Pride comeback was shortlived and an interview showed signs that Kerr may not have conquered his addictions.

With Shamrock and Kerr gone, all it took was Vitor Belfort dropping out of the show to prompt a Japanese ultimatum to the UFC. After his loss to Randy Couture, Belfort was no longer the fighter who had taken the MMA world by storm with his supersonic hand speed. He was still recuperating from his "worm intestinal virus" and was not feeling up to snuff for the Japan show. But SEG had no choice: either Belfort fought or the show would be cancelled. SEG brought in wrestler Brad Kohler to tangle with the Brazilian phenom in Japan, believing he would be an easy opponent, but with one week to go before the show, Belfort told SEG he didn't want to fight Kohler, especially since the wrestler had lasted an hour against Travis Fulton in Hook n' Shoot, an ambitious indie show held in a dojo in Indiana – both fighters punched and grappled in a pool of their own sweat before Kohler pulled out the victory. SEG caved in and let Belfort pick his opponent – occasional training partner Joe Charles. "If we wanted Vitor in the octagon, that was the only way to do it," said Isaacs. "It wasn't a perfect solution, but sometimes there is not a perfect solution." Kohler now faced Tra "Trauma" Telligman, who had lost to Belfort in his first UFC appearance.

Ultimate Japan was also a double header: the first-ever middleweight champ would be crowned, and Maurice Smith would defend his heavyweight belt against Randy Couture. The middleweight championship was difficult to schedule, as fellow Lion's Den fighters Guy Mezger and Jerry Bohlander obviously could not face one other. Olympic gold medallist wrestler, EF champ and

UFC winner Kevin Jackson took one slot, and fight consultant Joe Silva devised a plan for his opponent. Though Art Davie had picked Frank Shamrock for the shot, Silva pushed for the winner of Shamrock's match with Enson Inoue. The two were fighting in Japan Vale Tudo '97, held in November, and the winner would face Jackson the following month.

Frank Juarez Shamrock, the "brother" of Ken, had been adopted by and lived with Bob Shamrock during his youth. Though not related by blood, Frank had a similar physique and marketable face to Ken, and had also spent time moving from group home to group home before settling with the disciplinarian Bob. As part of the Lion's Den, Frank had walked down the aisle to the octagon on many occasions with Ken, Guy Mezger and Jerry Bohlander, but was not a recognizable name in the US, as he had been competing in Japan's Pancrase. After becoming the provisional King of Pancrase due to an injury to Bas Rutten, Frank fought his first NHB match against John Lober in a Hawaiian event called Superbrawl, promoted by ex-Chippendales dancer T.J.Thompson. Lober hit Shamrock with everything he had and won the match by decision, though Shamrock knocked Lober's teeth out in the process.

Bob never felt Frank was the right kind of fighter for NHB; Frank was too nice a guy and didn't have Ken's killer instinct. "I was used to finessing holds out of people [working with the Pancrase fighters for years] and making them work and expend energy, but when you add punching, a lot of your holds become obsolete," said Frank. "If you go for different holds, you get punched, and I wasn't prepared for that." Frank had nowhere else to turn; he couldn't go back to Pancrase, which had legal problems with Ken and didn't care about having another Shamrock in its ranks. "I hiked up on Diamond Head in Hawaii and I sat down and thought, *Am I going to do this or not?* I decided that if I was going to do it, then I was going to do it one hundred percent and be one hundred per cent honest with myself."

While in Hawaii, Frank met Angelina Brown, who had been fired by T.J. Thompson. The two fell instantly in love and later married. Angelina became a driving force behind her husband's career, something that threatened the fabric of the male-dominated Lion's Den. Ken Shamrock admits he never wanted to train Frank but, out of respect for Bob, agreed to take him in and teach him submission fighting. "What you have to understand is that Frank was not my best student," said Ken, "and that's why I held him back from NHB for a long time. Jerry Bohlander and Guy Mezger were handling him, and those guys had the opportunity in the UFC." While Frank was still living with Bob and sharing a room with Jerry, he made the decision to become his own man and make his mark. He contacted SEG about the slot against Jackson, leapfrogging Mezger and Bohlander. "It wouldn't have been such a big deal, but he was doing it behind my back," said Bohlander. "I was loyal to the UFC, but they weren't loyal to me. I felt betrayed on two ends: by the company that I worked so hard for and by one of my best friends." It did make business sense for Shamrock to get the nod, as he had already established himself in Japan, though Mezger would win the King of Pancrase title the following year.

Frank Shamrock was a determined individual and felt he had to break loose of the nest that had kept him safe for several years. Without warning, he moved out. He wanted to see if "the system that we were using really worked. So I decided to put it to the test. I just called up organizations and said, 'I want to fight. I want to fight your best guy.'" In October, Shamrock quickly submitted wrestler Dan Henderson in a submission-only match in The Contenders. The match with Enson Inoue came the following month. In front of a capacity crowd in Japan, the two fought a true brawl, with neither willing to give up. Just past the 15-minute mark, Shamrock floored Inoue with a hard knee to the chin, forcing Enson's older brother Egan to enter the ring to stop any further punishment. The match was ruled a disqualification in favor of Shamrock. There was no doubt he was a much different fighter than the one who had lost in Hawaii. Fighting in the UFC, albeit in Japan, meant audiences back home would see the other Shamrock in action for the first time, since neither Superbrawl nor Japan Vale Tudo '97 were shown on US cable.

As well as last-minute changes to the card, there were changes in SEG. Mike Goldberg replaced Bruce Beck as the play-by-play commentator, as Beck had moved on to news and other projects. More significantly, Art Davie was abruptly fired for trying to start another show behind SEG's back. Though Davie was fairly tight-lipped about the project, known as Thunderdome, he did comment on the UFC: "The show was going down. By having more rules, we were losing a big part of the audience that wasn't into martial arts and just wanted to see a good fight. And the more it would go to the ground and become a grappler's game, the more difficult it was for the core market to stay with the show." Davie also felt there was no future for the UFC, since cable had left the picture. So why would he want to start up a similar show?

Joe Silva was the one who first got wind of the project. He brought it to the attention of David Isaacs, who was shocked that his friend and co-worker would do such a thing. Bob Meyrowitz learned about it when longtime friend Andy Anderson was approached by Davie to finance Thunderdome. Meyrowitz called Davie into his office and confronted him. "I was shocked by Art's participation in Thunderdome, both that he was involved and at the deception he used to cover up what he had done, all the while acting like a member of the SEG/UFC 'team,'" said Isaacs. "Professionally and personally, he crossed the line. In the past, I had defended Art when others criticized his character or his lack of matchmaking skills. Others at SEG and I had taken over various aspects of his job and/or assisted him when deficiencies became clear. Perhaps we should have taken more seriously some of the charges, but we found them so hard to believe that we did not do so until we had hard evidence: a copy of the Thunderdome proposal." Meyrowitz phoned Davie just before he was to depart for Japan, ticket in hand, and fired him.

Davie turned into something of a Benedict Arnold the following year by lashing out at the sport in the media. He later worked with the Japanese K-1 organization to set up kickboxing shows in the US, then settled in Las Vegas for a brief time, working with ex-wife and business partner Kathy Kidd. In 2003, Davie moved to Los Angeles, where he and WVC promoter Frederico Lapenda work as TV/film producers for Mandalay Entertainment. Davie and Lapenda hoped to take MMA in a different direction with their new venture.

A CAPACITY CROWD in Yokohoma, Japan's second-largest city, was treated to hometown favorite Yoji Anjoh against the ever-colorful Tank Abbott in the first bracket of the heavyweight tournament. Just a week before, Abbott had entered Paul Herrera and Eddie Ruiz in Kingdom, and both had lost in apparently real matches, so this was a chance for Abbott to set things straight. Squeezing Anjoh's face against the fence like Playdoh, Abbott worked him over with big shots. The Japanese pro wrestler had one chance with an arm bar but Abbott was far too strong and kept pounding away until the two were stood up at the nine-minute mark. Abbott was so gassed that he rested his hands on his knees, but while Anjoh raised the ante by throwing Thai kicks, none of them had the sting of a Maurice Smith. The match went to a decision, with Abbott getting the nod. Rare as it was for Abbott to praise an opponent, he said of Anjo, "The man has heart and honor like no tomorrow."

Originally, Conan Silveira was to face UFC XV competitor Alex Hunter for the second bracket, but Kazushi Sakuraba took Hunter's place, forcing the American to take an alternate slot. Sakuraba had beaten Herrera in the Kingdom match in just three minutes, and Herrera was impressed. "He really helped me to increase my training to the way they were training," he said, "and I've come light years." Sakuraba was Nobuhiko Takada's pupil, and known for his hard work ethic, as in he could "work" a fight so well that it looked real. In 1996, Sakuraba fought his first supposed MMA match against Kimo, but due to his pro wrestling background from Kingdom, it looked like a questionably worked match. For the UFC, however, he would get a chance to prove his skills beyond doubt in a complete shoot.

The Brazilian started things off by catching the 5ft 9in Sakuraba in a guillotine choke as they went to the ground. The Japanese wrestler pulled out and shot for an ankle lock, but Silveira fired back with strikes. At two minutes, Silveira moved back to his feet and threw wild lefts and rights at Sakuraba up against the fence. Silveira landed one solid shot as his opponent covered up before dropping down for a shot at Silveira's leg. Believing Sakuraba was injured, McCarthy stopped the match as soon as Sakuraba went to the ground. The fight was over. "That's it. No more fight," he said to the stunned Japanese, who didn't seem hurt at all. The scene turned ugly, as the normally respectful Japanese crowd erupted in boos. Sakuraba threw down his mouthpiece in disgust and even tried to take the mike from announcer Bruce Buffer to voice his disapproval to the crowd. He would not leave the octagon for over 45 minutes. McCarthy said later: "I really thought he was hurt. At the time, when I made that call, I would have bet my life that he was hurt and was going down. It wasn't a good shoot that Sakuraba made, but when I looked at the tape, I made the wrong call."

It was time for Frank Shamrock to make his debut in the UFC, against Kevin Jackson for the middleweight crown. Wrestlers were back on the upswing, as both Mark Kerr and Randy Couture had won in the UFC after Mark Coleman's loss to Maurice Smith. Since his win in The Contenders, Shamrock trained with wrestlers at Stanford University, and knew he had found a wrestler's weakness. But Jackson came out smoking, flailing punches before taking Shamrock down. With the wrestler in his guard, Shamrock grasped Jackson's right arm, pushed out his hips and pulled his leg over Jackson's head. Shamrock quickly extended Jackson's arm, and the wrestler tapped out. Frank Shamrock had just won the middleweight championship in an unbelievable 16 seconds (SEG wrongly timed the bout at 22 seconds). A paradigm shift had once again occurred in MMA. The balance between wrestling, submission and stand-up had been altered yet again. It now came down to an understanding of how a fighter can use his natural skills to systematically mesh these elements together without missing a beat.

In Shamrock, the sport had a new hero. "I have more respect for Frank Shamrock than anyone else who has ever entered the octagon," said commentator and MMA Commissioner Jeff Blatnick. "To watch him be part of an entourage, break away from a shadow, create his own image, be his own man in the face of other people's criticisms, and then to display the athletic prowess and just pure sportsmanship he has and continues to have ... that's probably the brightest spot I've seen in all the UFC. If you want to legitimize this thing we call MMA, then look at Frank Shamrock."

In contrast, Vitor Belfort gave a lackluster performance in what appeared to be a straight grappling match with Joe Charles. No strikes of any kind were thrown in the exhibition-like fray, though it appeared they were shooting for position. Belfort finally tapped out Charles with an arm bar. The finals of the heavyweight tournament also appeared suspect as Conan Silveira took on Kazushi Sakuraba for the second time. SEG had been slow to label their first fight; it was later ruled a no-contest. Abbott pulled out of the finals, claiming a broken hand, but modified that decision in a later interview: "It was the hand, but I can always fight. I'll fight one-handed! They [SEG] thought they were going to work me, and I fucked the whole show up and I did it very well."

Though he felt in his mind that he'd won the first fight, Conan Silveira sat in his dressing room with several conflicting thoughts running through his mind. Dozens of Japanese Press members and other people were pounding on his door and stressing him out. "Imagine yourself in a foreign country, where you don't speak the language and don't know what is going on," said Silveira. "Besides that, I had everyone telling me that the [fate of] the UFC was in my hands. As a fighter, you don't want to have that in your mind."

Sakuraba attacked Silveira much like he had in their first meeting, but this time the Brazilian didn't mount much of a defense. "My body went out there the second time, but my mind wasn't there," he said. After missing a key lock, Sakuraba got side mount on Silveira and immediately went for an arm bar, which he achieved with relative ease. Silveira tapped just as the arm bar was extended. Though the Brazilian insisted that no one "told me anything," the whole episode looked suspicious. "For whatever reason, SEG came up with a rematch decision and one fighter changed the way he fought and the other ended up winning easily," said Jeff Blatnick. The Japanese crowd signed off with approval at the Kingdom fighter's victory. Conan

Silveira felt disgusted by the whole turn of events. "I didn't think that I wanted to fight anymore, because it didn't matter how hard you trained if people had the power to manipulate the situation." Silveira avenged his loss to Smith in 1999, but his comeback was shortlived. On June 20, 2003, he was arrested in connection with a smuggling ring importing the party drug Ecstasy.

For many, Maurice Smith had taken the sport to a higher plain, first by beating a jiu-jitsu man and then by defeating a powerful wrestler. He had won the heavyweight championship from Coleman and successfully defended against last-minute replacement Abbott. But Couture and the RAW team had worked out a gameplan for Smith: to evade his kicks and use those techniques as set-ups for takedowns. They knew Smith had been working with Frank Shamrock on the ground and that he was a very experienced competitor who was comfortable in that position. Unlike Belfort, Couture didn't want any part of Smith's stand-up game, so after a few leg kicks, the wrestler took him to the ground much the same way that Coleman had.

After attempting a key lock, Couture gained a half mount on Smith, and the two would stay in this position during the 15-minute regulation. "I thought he was going to tie me up and frustrate me so that I would expend energy," said Couture. "He would try to get me tired in the hope that he would get me back on my feet where I would not be able to protect myself." During the two overtime periods, Smith landed several good Thai kicks, but Couture kept his hands up and shut the kickboxer's game down by taking him to the mat. "[During the] last overtime, he was on top of me and had his chest across me in the choke position; he almost submitted me," said Smith. "It was really close but I thought, *man, if I get submitted by a wrestler, that's going to be bad*. I thought of what the Lion's Den would say, so I just got lucky and got out."

The fight went to a decision. "I should have risked more to try and be more dominant instead of being so controlling," said Couture, who felt he had done more than enough to win the fight at the time. Former EF matchmaker John Perretti was one of the judges, and ruled the match a draw, which he was not actually allowed to do. The other two judges gave it to Couture. He was now the UFC heavyweight champion. He later relinquished the belt over a contractual disagreement and wouldn't return to the UFC until October 2000, when he won it back. Couture would become one of the most celebrated fighters in UFC history, winning matches against men almost half his age.

Meanwhile John Perretti, after berating the UFC for its matches and publicly denouncing commentator Jeff Blatnick and ref John

McCarthy in a webzine interview, was somewhat surprisingly hired by SEG as matchmaker.

Even though riddled with problems, UFC Japan was an important step forward for the UFC and for MMA in general. Over the next three years, the UFC held two more live shows in Japan and one in Brazil. It was important to establish brand awareness for what was now an international phenomenon.

With all the controversy and intrigue, UFC Japan couldn't end without a Tank-related incident. It happened at a ritzy Japanese bar called Lexington Queen. Sitting in the VIP lounge was Andy Anderson, who had shelled out over $3,000 for liquor and wine to entertain guests at a private party. Tank, Paul Herrera, and Eddie Ruiz felt they were deserving of VIP status, and created a ruckus near the entrance when the manager felt uneasy about letting them in. Tank promised everyone would behave, but he wouldn't sit where waiters wanted him to, and found solace in some women who joined him at his table. "I had four or five bottles of liquor, two bottles of champagne and a bottle of wine," said Andy Anderson, "and out of the blue, Paul Herrera comes over and for no reason whatsoever tackles me and runs me to the end of the table against the wall and breaks all these bottles of liquor everywhere and just makes a huge mess. So I get up and drop Paul Herrera with one punch. He is laid out unconscious." Tank paid no attention, as he knew his boys had caused the skirmish and should finish it. As things began to get out of hand, Anderson walked over to David Isaacs, who seemed out of it and wanted to know if the party was over. "Yes David, that means the party is over," said Anderson, who knew that fighting in a public place in Japan meant jail time. Luckily, everyone got out okay. Herrera apologized to Anderson three years later.

CHAPTER 20

2001: A Zuffa Odyssey

B Y 1998, THE UFC had a love-hate relationship with fans, fight-ers and competing promoters. The big venues were gone, some shows didn't even sell merchandise and the cards featured few marquee names. A new crop of young fighters competed at a fraction of what their predecessors made, as SEG struggled to stay afloat. But there was still no other brand name like the UFC, and like it or not, it held the only key to the sport's salvation in America.

After holding as many as five shows a year, SEG produced only three UFCs during 1998 as they tried to build Frank Shamrock as the future of the sport. With pay-per-view out of the picture, save for emerging satellite systems, the majority of fans thought the UFC was dead. Things didn't get much better in 1999 as the UFC began to look more like an independent feeder show than the real McCoy. Some felt Monte Cox should have been called the unofficial matchmaker since he supplied up to five fighters in any given event during this time.

Shamrock may have been winning fights, but it was clear Tito Ortiz was winning fans. Savvy marketeer Sal Garcia took Ortiz to Ultimate Brazil in October 1998 to woo SEG execs into giving him a second chance. They took the bait, and Ortiz faced Jerry Bohlander at UFC 18. It was clear he had all the makings of a superstar with his brash atti-tude, aggressive fighting prowess and gimmicks: dyed hair, flame-colored shorts and a victory shirt that became his trademark. Some people discounted Ortiz as a pro wrestler wannabe, others ate it up, but no one could deny his skills. He not only defeated Bohlander but also avenged his loss to Guy Mezger at UFC 19. SEG now had all the makings of a showdown between Shamrock and Ortiz, one of the few bright spots for the company after the pay-per-view ban.

On September 24, 1999, Shamrock took everything Ortiz could dish out at UFC 24, but kept his composure and waited for the right moment to strike. Barely a minute into the fourth round, "I heard that breath; I felt that relaxation where he got weak for a second and then it came on and I went in for the kill," said Shamrock. The underdog champion unleashed punches in bunches, stunning Ortiz long enough for Shamrock to sink in a guillotine choke. With 37 seconds left in the round, blood dripped from Shamrock's forehead as he rolled him over, stood up and delivered a series of elbows, forcing Ortiz to tap out with just 10 seconds left. "I mentally broke him," said Shamrock, who relinquished the title immediately after the win.

Ortiz may have lost but his popularity soared, while Shamrock disappeared, failing to venture away from the UFC with much success. Riddled with injuries, Shamrock only fought twice in the next four years, missing opportunities by pricing himself out of the market. Ortiz, on the other hand, went on to win the title against Wanderlei Silva at UFC Japan 2, and grew in popularity. SEG used him to market the June 2000 release of the first UFC videogame, a moderate hit that spawned several sequels. But was anyone taking notice outside the small but loyal Internet fanbase?

The mecca of MMA was California, and yet it was illegal to hold events in the state. Paul Smith of the IFC and several other promoters had desperately tried to get the sport legalized in California since the late 1990s. On April 28, 2000, it appeared the California State Athletic Commission had passed "unified rules" to legally promote shows. Unfortunately, the state didn't have the budget to move forward, and for one reason or another, the rules sat in limbo. Smith convinced New Jersey athletic commissioner Larry Hazzard to test case the first MMA event in the state on September 30, 2000, using those rules. The show barely made a blip on the radar, but Hazzard was impressed nonetheless. The unified rules were amended to omit knees to the head of a downed opponent after Gan McGee's TKO of Brad Gabriel proved to be too brutal. The door was now open for SEG to stage UFC XXVIII, held November 15 of that year at the spectacular Taj Mahal casino. The show was a tremendous success, and set a standard for the UFC's live shows. It helped to reposition the event as a bona fide sport, instead of the political monster from the 1990s.

The show almost didn't go on because SEG was losing money, losing the cable war, and losing patience. "At this point, there have been so many things that have gone wrong that nothing brings tears to my eyes anymore," said SEG President Robert Meyrowitz. "I just look at it and wonder what went wrong; what got so out of hand? But it was just an injustice [the political persecution] and it was just wrong on how it played out. I really just couldn't end it like that … you couldn't let it end wrong." Moving back to his radio roots, Meyrowitz started eYada, a web-based radio program with several different channels, including one for MMA. It lasted a year, folding in July 2001, as SEG couldn't turn a profit, partly due to the technology's infancy.

Extreme Fighting's Donald Zuckerman, along with John Perretti, fight promoter Jamie Levine, and investor Dan Lambert, was rumored to be in negotiations with Meyrowitz to buy the UFC during the final months of 2000. This unlikely team didn't pique his interest, and it looked as if the SEG President would keep the show; his plan was to find investors to absorb the production costs. Then wealthy casino tycoon Lorenzo Fertitta entered the picture. As a native of Las Vegas, Fertitta grew up in the casino business. In 1977, his father started Bingo Palace, which catered to locals off the strip. The company took off over ten years later when Lorenzo and brother Frank Fertitta III exploited that model by building a string of branded casinos. The overlooked market made the family very prosperous; Fertitta Enterprises is the fifth-largest publicly traded (gaming) company, with ten properties.

Since there weren't many organized sporting events in the state, Fertitta's father took his young son to boxing matches, a passion both shared. In November 1996, Lorenzo took a post on the Nevada State Athletic Commission (NSAC), but was also becoming a closet fan of the UFC. "I thought it was very interesting, but I was also a little uncomfortable with some of the brutality of it," said Fertitta. His mindset didn't change until he saw a live event. On July 17, 1999, the NSAC was invited to observe UFC XXI in Iowa. This was SEG's final attempt to get the NSAC on their side. While the event went off without a hitch, SEG decided not to push for a commission vote to pass the sport. SEG believed there were not enough votes to pass it, so a decision was made for a "no vote at all" instead of "no," since the latter would ruin the UFC's chances at sanctioning elsewhere.

Fertitta's eyes were opened for the first time to what the UFC was truly about when he spoke to some of the fighters that night. "After meeting [Frank Shamrock] and talking with him for a few minutes, I realized that these were not guys stepping out of a bar trying to hurt each other, they were professional athletes," he said. When Fertitta learned that John Lewis, who was cornering for fighter Andre Pederneiras, lived in Las Vegas, the two agreed to meet on their return. Before long, Fertitta was taking private Brazilian jiu-jitsu lessons from Lewis, and loving every minute of it. After leaving the NSAC to take over as President of Station Casinos in July 2000, Fertitta received a call from long-time friend Dana White, who was now managing Tito Ortiz. White told Fertitta of the proposed UFC buyout, and after talking things over with his brother Frank, he approached Meyrowitz. The

SEG President wanted only an investor, but Fertitta insisted a 100 percent buyout was the only deal he'd consider.

On January 9, 2001, Zuffa Entertainment (zuffa means "to fight" or "to scrap" in Italian) bought the Ultimate Fighting Championship lock, stock and octagon. Lorenzo and Frank Fertitta were co-owners, with Dana White serving as President. White's background was in boxing, and he had popularized a boxing/aerobics program in Las Vegas. A consummate businessman, Lorenzo Fertitta became a diehard fan of the sport. Both Fertitta brothers and White are so competitive that they grapple with several fighters and keep what they learn to themselves. The Zuffa office even has a boxing ring set up where the three spar one another.

Lorenzo immediately laid plans to hold Zuffa's first show in Atlantic City, while stepping up the drive for sanctioning in other states. "Without Larry Hazzard and the New Jersey State Athletic Commission, this sport would still be dying a slow death," said Fertitta. Hazzard was once considered the man who ran boxing out of New Jersey, since he had been known for frequently changing the rules. By Hazzard taking a chance on the sport, other commissions and former naysayers were looking at the UFC with interest.

Unlike SEG, Zuffa's UFC seemed open to working with other promotions and exchanging ideas. "The problem has been that everyone has traditionally played in their own sandbox," said Fertitta. "That's like saying, 'I'm the UFC and I'm not going to recognize anyone else.' It's important for all the promoters to communicate so that we can all move in the same direction rather than fight each other." While SEG forbade anyone from using an octagon in other MMA events, Fertitta made the point that uniformity was the only way the sport could be taken seriously. He told everyone at an April 2001 New Jersey rules meeting that the octagon format was not off-limits, pushing to keep MMA safe inside of a cage, rather than the ring. Zuffa later trademarked the octagon name. Other promotions still use the format, as well as a new octagonal ring.

On February 23, 2001, Zuffa's UFC took center stage at the Taj Mahal. The show's new look and energy was hard to dismiss. SEG had become lax in many areas, from weak merchandizing to failing to treat the show as entertainment. "When I went to the show in New Orleans, I wanted to buy something; I wanted to buy a T-shirt," said Fertitta. "I couldn't find anything anywhere. I was blown away that there is this unbelievably strong brand and they [SEG] weren't taking advantage of all the items that could generate revenue." Zuffa offered full-color programs and different styles of T-shirts and posters, and the main event fight between Tito Ortiz and Evan Tanner showcased all the glitz and laser light shows of a scaled-down WWE. The fans appreciated it and, for the first time, it appeared as if the company understood that delicate balance between reality and show business. "There is a considerable consumer demand for reality-based sports," said Fertitta. "This sport has the opportunity to become as big as boxing one day because it's shown it has a tremendous following."

JOHN PERRETTI WAS relieved of his matchmaking duties after Zuffa took control. The brothers set a meeting with all former SEG employees but Perretti was unavailable while shooting a film in Japan. "I was convinced in five minutes that Joe [Silva] was going to play a key role moving forward with building the new UFC," said Fertitta. Silva wasn't a former karate champion, but his years of dedication to the UFC and insight into MMA is second to none. He has an innate talent for looking at the whole picture and evaluating a host of variables to put together smart matches. Silva became vice-president of talent relations, a position that allows him to drive ideas for the show. With new weight classes established, Silva brought prominence to the UFC titles by attracting top notch fighters.

At UFC 32 (numbers replaced the old Roman numerals), Zuffa packed over 11,000 fans into New Jersey's Continental Airlines Arena (formerly the Meadowlands). This topped previous attendance records: 9,000 for UFC IX in Buffalo, New York. "The UFC events in the past were never promoted; they never went out and did advertising or promotion," said Fertitta. "I'm not going to go from having shows at the Taj Mahal in the state of New Jersey to some very small community. Every show either needs to be a step up or a parallel step. It gives us the opportunity to show that this is the new UFC."

Zuffa launched a major ad campaign and placed ads in *Playboy*, *Maxim*, *Stuff* and other magazines focused on the 18-34 male. The new UFC wouldn't rely on old gimmicks; it would be sold as the sport of the future. Tito Ortiz assumed his poster boy image. Randy Couture also garnered a strong fan base due to his smart strategies in the octagon that netted him victory after victory. New weight classes produced more champions. In addition to light-heavyweight (186 to 205lbs) and heavyweight (206 to 265lbs), three other weight classes became fixtures: lightweight (146 to 155), welterweight (156 to 170) and middleweight (171 to 185). Taking cues from boxing, these weight classes allow stronger athletes to compete at their natural weights.

And with Zuffa, of course, came betting on fights. Gambling is a huge business, with millions of dollars bet on boxing and now MMA. MVP Sportsbook, a licensed offshore sportsbook in Costa Rica, became the first online casino to take bets for MMA matches. Several organizations have cropped up since that time, taking bets primarily on the UFC and Pride. Originally, there weren't any limits on what people could bet online, but that changed on April 28, 2002 when Wanderlei Silva fought Mirko Cro Cop in Pride 20. It was decreed that if the fight lasted all five rounds it would be declared a draw, as there were no judges. Fans bet large on the draw and nearly sank one of the online betting organizations. Now there are limits.

In July 2001, MMA won its biggest battle when Zuffa won approval to hold UFC 33 in Vegas at the $950 million Mandalay Bay mega-resort, sanctioned by the NSAC. Not only that, but the UFC regained access to 20 million homes it had lost in 1997 when In Demand cable agreed to air the event, showcasing Tito Ortiz vs Vladimir Matyushenko, on September 28. With three titles up for grabs, this was to be the show to put the UFC and MMA back on the map. Everyone watched in anticipation, hoping for the best. Unfortunately, not everything went to plan. Every match on the card went to a decision, save for two dark (unaired) matches that had decisive endings. The showy entrances and sub-par matches – though solid on paper – pushed the show past the three-hour mark, a setback the UFC and the sport could not afford. Zuffa's In Demand deal said the UFC had to generate at least 75,000 buyrates before turning a profit, otherwise a penalty would be assessed. The show never came close to that number, but Zuffa remained optimistic.

The event redeemed itself two months later at the MGM Grand in Las Vegas, when UFC 34 brought back the kind of dramatic action missing from the previous show. UFC 31's main event between champion Randy Couture and Pedro Rizzo had ended in a very controversial decision in favor of Couture; Zuffa even used footage of the match to educate judges for upcoming events. The rematch left no doubt that Couture was the heavyweight champion: he clobbered Rizzo to a TKO victory at 1:38 into the third round. All of the matches provided surprises, knockouts and submissions. Because of the previous show, Zuffa instituted a new rule allowing the referee to stand up fighters if they remained inactive on the ground. Buyrates had dropped considerably because of UFC 33, however, and Zuffa would have to spend millions in trying to recapture the audience.

Zuffa finally won the attention of the mainstream sports media when Fox Sports Net's *The Best Damn Sports Show...Period!* wanted to air a complete match. On June 22, 2002, UFC 37.5 took place in a smaller venue site at the Bellagio in Las Vegas, decked out with *BDSSP* logos. The show headlined a contender bout for the light-heavyweight title between Chuck Liddell and a new and improved Vitor Belfort. Liddell won a close decision, but three days later *BDSSP* broadcast Robbie Lawler vs Steve Berger in its entirety. It wasn't anything special, but was the first time a UFC match had been shown on a network hitting over 50 million homes. The show went through the roof and *BDSSP* continued to cover the UFC, often generating heat for the franchise's main events.

Liddell wouldn't get the chance to face Ortiz right away, since Zuffa had a blockbuster on its hands: Ortiz vs Ken Shamrock for UFC 40: Vendetta. Ever since he defeated Jerry Bohlander, Ortiz had been antagonistic towards Shamrock; the two almost came to blows after Ortiz gave him the finger after his win over Mezger. To make matters worse, Ortiz donned a derogatory shirt, infuriating Shamrock beyond belief. It was old versus new, respect versus rebellion, and big dollar signs for Zuffa. This would be the most celebrated match in UFC history. Ken Shamrock was still one of the UFC's most marketable names, and though his comeback was lukewarm in Japan, his return to the octagon was a different story.

Held at the MGM Grand, UFC 40 hosted the largest audience ever assembled for an MMA event in the US and the largest attendance that year for an event in Las Vegas: 13,770. People were split down the middle and this would be the litmus test as to whether Ortiz could cement his success by taking the torch from the 38-year-old Shamrock. In a one-sided beatdown, Ortiz mangled Shamrock's face with elbows and forearm strikes. Shamrock didn't give up but after three rounds his corner threw in the towel. Ortiz became the people's champion, especially for the UFC's core market.

The show also boasted the most extravagant live production with fireworks, but many felt the fighter vignettes pushed the UFC further into WWE territory. The fans responded positively, riding high on the official return of the UFC as sports entertainment. Even the Zuffa brass was surprised. UFC President Dana White walked into the middle of the octagon before the headliner and announced the return of a man he never thought would be invited back. And with his trademark leather jacket, a graying, slimmer Tank Abbott hyped up the crowd, announcing a three-fight deal. When Zuffa first took over the UFC, they vowed people like Abbott would never return, pushing for athletes over circus acts. Now there seemed to be a dissention in the ranks; matchmaker Joe Silva, for one, knew nothing of Abbott's return. Zuffa also hired a company that once worked for the WWE to pull off the same magic. So was the UFC moving back to its spectacle roots or not?

Zuffa had found its stride, building an action-packed event off a great headliner and a bevy of up-and-comers to develop new rivalries down the road. Unfortunately, they couldn't repeat that success. With five weight classes and only a handful of memorable showmen, the UFC had great athletes but not marketable stars. The headliner of Tim Sylvia and Ricco Rodriguez at UFC 41 didn't mean much to casual fans, just as UFC 42's main event pitting Matt Hughes against Sean Sherk failed to move people. Hughes was a formidable welterweight champion but didn't have much of a personality. His opponent had fought for the UFC in dark matches; no one had had ever seen him on pay-per-view and now he was fighting the champ. More than half of the crowd had dispersed by the time Hughes gave his victory speech after decisioning Sherk, the sound sweetened *a la* pro wrestling for extra effect. Despite Zuffa's efforts to push Hughes, the audience didn't embrace him as a star, though he was a worthy champion. Here was a conundrum: how can you build a sport but also provide entertainment? "Some fans like technical matches while others like brawlers," said Joe Silva. "It's hard to bridge the gap between sport and entertainment without alienating someone." Even with the success of UFC 40, Zuffa was losing money and was conflicted on whether to ham it up like the WWE or focus on building a sport. Even the Tank Abbott ploy failed. He lost all three matches quickly – making hundreds of thousands of dollars in the process.

On July 17, 2003, Zuffa issued a press release announcing a new format for the show. Dana White stated: "We listened to sports media experts, the analysts and handicappers who were telling us some of the over-the-top spectacle was preventing us from being taken seriously." But in reality, the fireworks and glitz cost money and Zuffa needed to cut its budgets. Perception about the UFC being a sport would hardly change by omitting the souped-up production. At UFC 44 that September, the changes took effect without much opposition as Randy Couture, who had dropped down to light heavyweight, battled Tito Ortiz for the championship. Couture had already defeated Chuck Liddell at UFC 43 and Ortiz was ready to show the world he was the undisputed champion. Over the course of five rounds, Couture battered Ortiz at will, even spanking him for good measure with seconds remaining in the bout.

UFC 45: Revolution was billed as the tenth anniversary show and Zuffa flew in champions old and new for the occasion, awarding Royce Gracie and Ken Shamrock UFC Hall of Fame plaques for their dedication to the sport. Shamrock gave a heartfelt speech about the UFC and how the fans have kept MMA alive for so long. But Matt Hughes vs fellow wrestler Frank Trigg wasn't much of a draw. It seemed more like an undercard bout than something to signify ten years of the UFC.

The light heavyweight division had become the cream of the crop for Zuffa, with Ortiz, Liddell, Couture and Vitor Belfort. Rivalries and rematches created a virtual round robin of worthy match-ups. At UFC 46, Couture met Belfort for the second time to defend his belt. Just 49 seconds into the match, the Brazilian grazed Couture's eyelid with a punch and forced a doctor stoppage to become the new champion. They get their rubber match at UFC 49: Unfinished Business. A match nearly two years in the making, Ortiz vs Liddell, took center stage at UFC 47: It's On. Both men had been trash-talking and hyping it up every chance they got on radio, TV and even in a featured documentary. With both coming off losses and with no belt on the line, it was a personal fight that generated a lot of interest, much like Ortiz vs Shamrock. Just 38 seconds into the second round, Liddell pummeled Ortiz with punches to claim the victory.

Ken Shamrock returned to the octagon a year and a half after UFC 40, knocking out previous opponent Kimo at 1:26. Tito Ortiz, who needed an angle to get back into the game after back-to-back losses, scoffed at Shamrock's victory speech. This unnecessary rematch could be another ratings bonanza for Zuffa, but at the time of writing, Ortiz was set for a rubber match against Guy Mezger – the fued that started it all.

After trying for two years to get a television deal, Zuffa signed a thirteen-week series for Spike TV. American television isn't ready for conventional MMA programming, but it is apparently ready for reality TV. A show called The Ultimate Fighter will give up and comers a chance to prove themselves – the winner in each of the two weight classes will get a contract with the UFC. The risky thirteen-week arc, no longer a staple in reality TV, was due to begin airing in January 2005 and should expose a much larger audience to the sport, acting as a one-hour informercial and raising new buyrates for UFC pay-per-views. Lion's Den standout Guy Mezger has also produced a reality show, Badass, where regular people compete in contests with real fighters. The finalists get the opportunity to compete against these fighters in the ring, the winner getting $25,000 and a contract with the Lion's Den.

At the time of this writing, Zuffa had managed to broadcast the UFC all over the world via pay-per-view and remained the top name brand in the sport. Pay-per-view buyrates have generally been getting stronger, but are still nowhere near the heyday of the franchise. Zuffa was able to renegotiate a better deal with In Demand. At UFC 46, Zuffa landed its first Fortune 500 sponsor, Miller Lite, showing that MMA has a chance against boxing. UFC live gates pull in over a million dollars per show, selling out the MGM Grand and the Mandalay Events Center. Now the company is examining movie projects, looking to diversify the UFC name even further. It's merchandising and video game products have done increasingly well, all in the hopes of building brand loyalty among consumers. With its extra financial clout, Zuffa will hopefully keep the UFC in the mainstream long enough to become profitable.

CHAPTER 21

Real Fighting versus Martial Arts

Bruce Lee Was Right All Along

"Some martial arts are very popular, real crowd pleasers, because they look good, have smooth techniques. But beware. They are like a wine that has been watered. A diluted wine is not a real wine, not a good wine, hardly the genuine article.

Some martial arts don't look so good, but you know that they have a kick, a tang, a genuine taste. They are like olives. The taste may be strong and bitter-sweet. The flavor lasts. You cultivate a taste for them. No one ever developed a taste for diluted wine."

Bruce Lee, *Tao of Jeet Kune Do*

NOTE: This chapter is in no way trying to belittle the men and women who have made martial arts a part of their lives. It is meant to enlighten those who have perhaps taken martial arts under a false pretense. An entire book could be written on this subject alone, but this will only be a general overview of how martial arts has lost its realistic beginnings.

POLITICS AND BUSINESS aside, the Ultimate Fighting Championship opened the eyes of a world blinded by a centuries-old mystique shadowing martial arts. This was a devastating revelation for those who had bought into that false sense of security taught by their so-called masters. With over ten million people studying martial arts around the world, it was time for the truth to be told about the synergy between martial arts and reality fighting.

Most martial arts can be traced back to a lawless time when they were crucial to preserve life and limb. They evolved from real-life experiences and became an integral part of cultures that often invested the arts with a spiritual power. Historical warriors were enshrined in folklore, lending their martial arts an almost superhero quality. Traditional techniques were passed down from generation to generation with little regard to practicality.

But something was lost in the translation, making perception greater than reality. Some of the arts ossified over time. They became formal, rigid and, in truth, ineffective. Many were blatantly commercialized to appeal to the new and wealthy constituency when fighting schools flourished in the United States and Western Europe from the 1960s. They became a money-making enterprise. Westerners were curious, open and naïve; masters from the Orient were an unknown commodity. Many of their claims were taken at face value; students believed what they were told. Movies were partly to blame. They showed unbelievable feats of physical prowess and fighting techniques foreign to most people on the street. High-flying kicks and the ability to beat several – sometimes dozens – of opponents at once were staples of the martial arts presented on the big screen.

As these arts were being taught in the United States, there was a need to make them accessible to the public. And there was no better way to do this than to turn them into competitive sports, adding credibility and uniformity. The founder of judo, Jigoro Kano, had ended up making his overall self-defense system less effective when he popularized the art as a sport. With countless jujutsu forms being taught in Japan, Kano combined the best elements and formed a very effective *do* system. Judo has now been relegated to throwing movements because the sport dictated those movements would be the most enjoyable to the crowd. Sport karate was also a product of the twentieth century, and became the most popular of all martial arts. Tae kwon do competitions and the flashy stylings of kung fu demonstrations were also well received. The ultimate parlor trick, of course, was breaking a soft balsa wood board that was often baked to ensure it could be torn in half by a karate chop.

Did anything positive develop from the modern-day martial arts movement in America? With schools growing by the thousands and entire federations being built on particular styles, the essence of martial arts became lost in the shuffle. Masters passed along their knowledge to the masses, but how much of this knowledge truly prepared someone for an actual fight? Most Korean systems concentrated on elaborate and often impractical kicking techniques. There's nothing wrong with that, so long as students know what they are getting. "Everyone wants something different from martial arts – not everyone wants to be a no-holds-barred fighter," said kenpo stylist and UFC competitor Keith Hackney. "There are still people who only want to do forms, and don't want any kind of physical confrontation. They just want to do it as an art form, which is fine as long as they don't pretend that they are doing this for self-defense on the street."

What works on the street is quite different from what works in a dojo because the latter is derived from a precise set of movements carved out by a particular style practiced in a relatively safe environment. In tae kwon do, stances, kicks and punches dictate a fight. In judo, grappling and throws dictate a fight. But a real-life, hand-to-hand confrontation is something that has no form or dictation and follows no particular set of rules. It is an act of aggression built on numerous variables, not formal rules; the true no-holds-barred contest, where a person's morality and judgment as well as their physical prowess will dictate the amount of harm inflicted. While the UFC and other similar competitions are not real fights as they might occur in a bar or in the street, they are as close to a real fight as one can acceptably get between two willing athletes in a sporting context.

The myth of the martial arts says that a man with a black belt can defeat almost any opponent with his "empty hand" tools – usually fists and feet. While it's true there are countless examples of martial artists protecting themselves effectively in real fights, how many of these situations involved opponents who also knew how to fight, possibly from another system? That was the intriguing scenario that drew so much attention to the early UFCs. It quickly provided as many answers as it raised new questions. Most people knew, of course, the hole in martial arts teaching: the fact that years of learning one style could not possibly *guarantee* domination over an opponent from another discipline. "Some guys still believe that their kung fu and karate is so deadly that they can't compete," says former kickboxing champ and MMA star Maurice Smith. "I don't believe that. I think that the smart instructors realize that a lot of stuff that you're taught in traditional martial arts is bullshit."

One man brought the truth about martial arts to the attention of the media, and his name was Bruce Lee. Lee started his martial arts training in Hong Kong at the age of 13, when he learned wing chun kung fu from Master Yip Man. He would have only five years of formal instruction before immigrating to the United States. Lee's greatest strength was his thirst for knowledge in everything he did. Though he adopted wing chun as his base, Lee was left with questions about his style after a real fight against another kung fu exponent. He discovered that much of what he had learned was not truly effective. He knew it would be too time-consuming to try to learn all styles of martial arts, since he found questionable techniques in them as well. Physical conditioning was also a variable he had overlooked up until that point. By applying the philosophy he had been introduced to in college, Lee became a martial arts innovator by creating a concept known as jeet kune do, the "way of the intercepting fist."

Lee made copious notes that were published well after his death as a book, *Tao of Jeet Kune Do*. It is made up of Lee's findings from his own experimentation and from his collection of martial arts books. He came to the conclusion that formlessness keeps one from defining a limited pattern of attack. "It is the artistic process, therefore, that is reality and reality is truth," said Lee. Lee discussed varying stand-up and ground techniques, as well as the importance of being physically fit. The book serves as a basis for enlightenment about an approach to combat, and it's clear the "Little Dragon" was onto something revolutionary. "I thought his principles were the most advanced stuff out there, and I still use a lot of those principles," said karate legend Joe Lewis.

Ironically, Bruce Lee's films were just as responsible for the divergence of martial arts teaching from combat reality as they were for its commercial success. Millions worldwide have seen his films; less than a million bought his book. Many who saw the films swallowed the myth of this tiny, blur-fast dervish, smashing foe after foe with his kicks, punches and back-fists. It was wildly exciting, but hardly realistic. His writings were different, and from them we can assume that, if Lee were alive today, he would revel in the UFC. It broke stereotypes and allowed us to re-evaluate the martial arts by defining it as a sum of many parts that otherwise might never have co-existed.

So where does fighting fit into martial arts? "That's really impressive, but would you mind knocking that off," said Campbell McLaren as Bill "Superfoot" Wallace balanced himself on one foot and swept the other over McLaren's head, toying with him. McLaren was working with Wallace to prepare him for the first UFC (which obviously didn't work out).

McLaren asked Wallace, "Do you think we'll see any of this in the Ultimate fights?"

"Are you kidding?" answered Wallace. "If you tried to kick someone like this, they'd rip your balls off!"

"But isn't this what you teach?" said McLaren.

"Yeah, I teach to make money. It has nothing to do with fighting," admitted Wallace, according to McLaren.

"I think that's one of the things that really got the martial arts world involved because so many people were teaching stuff that really had nothing to do with reality," says McLaren.

After the second UFC, it was clear that seasoned martial artists could not perform many of their ornate techniques in an actual fighting situation against formidable opponents. There has been a lot of debate on whether the Gracies stacked things in their favor, but the fact is that most people were clueless early on as to the effectiveness of groundfighting. Though the Gracie family tried to treat the UFC as a living infomercial for Gracie Jiu-jitsu, it did prove their contention that the majority of fights would go to the ground. "I had never been on the ground in my life with all the martial arts training that I had," said Kevin Rosier years after his UFC appearance. Some styles of traditional martial arts, such as karate and tae kwon do, include groundfighting, but instructors chose to emphasize the flashier aspects portrayed by the media. Thus, self-defense became hit-or-miss offense based on the high kicks and karate chops people felt they had to learn.

The Gracies proved that an experienced ground fighter can defeat an experienced stand-up fighter simply because it is easier for the stand-up artist to have his tools taken from him. In the *Gracies in Action* videos, there are countless scenes of hapkido, kung fu and other stand-up styles collapsing against the rudimentary takedowns and eventual submissions of the jiu-jitsu fighters. Once everything goes to the ground, the stand-up martial artist doesn't have the distance or leverage necessary to properly execute kicks or punches. Then, trapped in an unfamiliar environment, he falls victim to the superior ground skills of his opponent. Conversely, wrestlers proved difficult for jiu-jitsu practitioners, as they were able to neutralize jiu-jitsu takedowns, thus taking the submission tools away from them.

Stand-up martial arts account for most of what is taught in dojos, so they collectively were not supportive of the UFC. In an effort to keep their myths alive, many stand-up arts like karate and tae kwon do claimed that eye-gouging and biting were part of a real fight, thus proving that the UFC – which banned them – was not realistic. But would anyone need martial arts to learn how to do these techniques? How many fights have ended up with someone being eye-gouged? In Japan Vale Tudo '94, Gerard Gordeau eye-gouged opponent Yuki Nakai, but Nakai still pulled out the win. Someone in a street fight could eye-gouge his opponent, step and break his neck, or just kill him. But is every fight life-threatening enough to go to that extreme, and wouldn't the person who took it to that level go to prison?

(Incidentally, Gordeau's eye-gouging permanently ended Nakai's MMA career. Aside from some stiff-worked matches in Japan,

Gordeau never competed in these types of events again. He offered no explanation for biting or gouging, except to say that these acts were all part of fighting in a no-rules event. Today, he works as a repairman in Holland, teaches karate with his two brothers, and frequently pro wrestles for Japan's UFO organization. Gordeau even promotes real MMA events in Amsterdam under the UFO banner. Aged in his forties, Gordeau has officially retired from fighting, but still gets into an occasional street fight.)

Martial artists also said that going to the ground was not representative of a real fight, despite the men in the octagon doing what came naturally. When Johnny Rhodes faced David Levicki in UFC II, both men stayed on the ground for the entire duration of the match, even though neither one knew anything about groundfighting. The 1981 Kung Fu and Freefighting Championships held in Hong Kong showcased nothing but stand-up martial artists, but time and again they ended up in a clinch and went to the ground. Clearly, two stand-up fighters can become groundfighters even if they don't know what they are doing down there.

Johnny Rhodes was one of those who questioned the authenticity of the UFC. When he entered the tournament, he had not seen tapes of the first UFC and assumed "THERE ARE NO RULES!" meant just that. "I think that [rules] really hurt it because people don't want to see grappling," said Rhodes. "They want to see blood. People want to see you get beat up. Had the rules been a little bit different, the stand-up fighters would have won back then too because you couldn't bite. If I would have gotten you in a lock and you would have put your teeth into me, I would have let go. That's how I expected it to be because it said no rules. When I got there, I was not aware that you couldn't bite."

If nothing else, NHB competitions laid to rest the stereotypes surrounding martial arts. Martial artists were finally able to throw punches and kicks at their discretion without any regard for rules germane to their disciplines. The mystique of the black belt, the *dim mak* (death touch) and the lightning-fast kicks that break dozens of boards is a powerful one, often leading followers to believe the performers are deadly. This perception also gives us an unrealistic view of how a real fight unfolds. Would it look as pretty as the movies? Would a martial artist be throwing these beautiful kicks and taking his opponents out with ease? Lee said the martial artist should fight and spar often, just as a swimmer can't practice on dry land. The cold, honest truth lied in the unscripted contests between experienced martial artists who dared to step into the octagon.

Minutes after Alberto Cerro Leon's defeat at the hands of Remco Pardoel in UFC II, Art Davie came across Leon, "crying in the dressing room. He and his manager left the hotel and got on a plane. I had to mail the check to him. The guy was psychologically devastated." He could not believe his art had failed. In a time when Tae Bo exercising and martial arts are said in the same breath, and styles are promoted as "self-defense" by showing one man kick another in the head, it is apparent that the art of war has lost its meaning. How much of martial arts has anything to do with self-defense versus an impractical offense? Many martial arts masters frown upon those who go and learn from other schools. They forget that art is not bound by singularity – especially martial arts. The true martial artist will arrive at his own conclusion that may start from anywhere, but take him on a road to clarity. The truth of what works and what doesn't work lies beneath a vale of commercialism, greed, and ignorance. Martial arts is a process whereby one must learn "simply to simplify."

Don "The Dragon" Wilson was brought in to serve as color commentator for the UFC based on his name in the martial arts world. Though he had been successful at making the transition from kung fu to full contact karate, that hardly made Wilson an expert in MMA. "Well if I was in there ... " became a Dragonism, so to speak, and many felt he would never have done that well in the octagon. Play-by-play commentator Bruce Beck finally got tired of Wilson's musings after one UFC event. "He would tell us how he would beat these guys, and I would turn to him later at night at a cocktail party and say, 'Dragon, you would have got your ass kicked and you know it!' And he would go, 'Bullshit! You don't know how quick I am. Have you ever seen me with my spinning backfist?' I would just say, 'Dragon, you would kick your leg up once and if you missed, you would be down on the ground and they would be bashing your head in!' 'I can beat any of these guys ... I can kill any of them!' he would tell me. He was always talking about having a big fight for a hundred grand or something – 'If they give me a million, I'll fight' – and I said, 'Yeah, and you'll get your ass kicked.'" Wilson actually did try to get in the UFC for a million-dollar payday, knowing full well he would price himself out of the market and would never get to perform his spinning backfist. But just because a technique appears improbable, it doesn't mean it's ineffective. Losing his match against Matt Serra at UFC 31, Shonie Carter dropped his opponent with a spinning backfist. He followed that up with a second one to seal one of the most memorable victories in the franchise.

Art Davie was swamped with requests by traditionalists who had no fighting experience but wanted to prove themselves in the octagon.

Mitch Cox was a former Army Ranger who taught "realistic combat" martial arts. Davie agreed to see Cox in action, but only on his terms. He took kung fu exponent Tai Bowden to Cox's dojo to set up a makeshift match in Los Angeles, with the winner to fight in UFC IX. Davie drove down in a limousine with Koji Kitao, reporters from Japan's *Baseball* magazine, and Bowden. "Bowden beat the fuck out of him three times and in front of his own students," said Davie. "It wasn't sparring. After the first time, Cox wanted to go again and again, but Bowden would just take him down and pound him out." Bowden got the shot in UFC IX and lost to Steve Nelmark at 7:25. Another fighter desperate to compete was Thomas Ramirez, who openly complained in magazines that Art Davie wouldn't let him in the show. Don Frye knocked out Ramirez in ten seconds in UFC VIII.

FRED ETTISH: HONOR NOT LOST

KEN SHAMROCK HAD to pull out of UFC II due to a broken hand sustained in a training session. Two weeks before the event, Art Davie called Johnny Rhodes and Fredrick Ettish. Rhodes, an alternate, was nursing a broken finger after a bareknuckle fight, but still moved into Shamrock's slot, while Ettish took over as the alternate. Ettish had expressed interest in the event months earlier but was told the card was full. He accepted the invitation and intensified his training.

Fred Ettish began his martial arts education in 1969 with Chinese kempo, moving into Okinawan karate ten years later. He eventually adopted shorin-ryu matsumura kempo (a Japanese/Okinawan hybrid) as his style and has stuck with it ever since. Thirty-eight year old Ettish wanted to enter the UFC because it was a sport that was "a bit more raw, more real and more honest, that allowed two fighters to be two fighters." He was not interested in point karate tournaments and believed this would be a good test for his art, though he hadn't seen the first event.

When he arrived in Denver, SEG arranged for Ettish to have some gym time even though he was unlikely to compete. Because there were 16 fighters, an alternate match was unnecessary, so the only way Ettish was going to compete was if someone pulled out before fight time. By 5:30pm, everyone was healthy and ready to go, so Ettish agreed to help Davie and show producer Michael Pillot with various backstage duties. With all the commotion, the fifth-degree black belt didn't even have time to watch any of the matches.

Ettish and Rorion Gracie passed on a stairway. Gracie asked, "Are you ready to fight?" It would have been an easy question to answer for any fighter in the show, except one whose mind was now elsewhere. Freek Hamaker pulled out of the event after realizing that NHB wasn't for him. An exhausted Johnny Rhodes was going to pull out too until his cornerman rushed to tell him that a much smaller alternate would be taking his opponent's place. Fred Ettish was in; Rhodes took the gamble.

Ten minutes after hearing the news, Ettish donned his traditional gi and made his way to the octagon, trying to keep calm and ready his mind for the battle at hand. For an introverted man who ran a small dojo back in Minnesota and fought with the blessing of his sensei in Okinawa, this was the moment of truth. As for thirty nine year old Rhodes, he was no longer going to use his shorin ji-ryu karate background, which had failed to live up to his expectations against Levicki, his first-round opponent. Instead, he decided to fall back on his street-wise bravado and bareknuckle fighting experience.

The match started with a few light kicks from each man until a big right hand from Rhodes sent Ettish reeling, struggling to regain his composure. It was already too late. Rhodes followed that up by grabbing Ettish and forcing him to the canvas after three more hard punches. On the ground, Ettish held one hand up and one hand down trying to keep Rhodes' attack at bay. He absorbed a brutal punch to the face. "I ended up losing the vision in one eye," said Ettish. "It was like trying to look through a glass of milk; everything was very white and totally clouded over." He rolled to his stomach with both hands over his head. Rhodes pounded Ettish unmercifully, landing four knees and scrambling back to his feet.

With Rhodes circling him like a shark, a bloodied Fred Ettish was in serious trouble. "Pride wouldn't let him submit," remembered Rhodes. "I felt bad because I knew if I was in that same situation, it would have been hard for me too." Rhodes eventually took Ettish's back, pulled his hair, and sunk in a basic choke. Ettish, still showing some fight, resisted all he could before finally tapping the mat at 3:07.

It would be two hours before Ettish could see out of both eyes again, but he had learned a powerful lesson. "I was trying to focus on what I was trying to do and not be distracted by the events going on around me. And that's where I was not successful. In my opinion, there are three things that a person needs to be successful in something like that: you need to be physically fit, you need to have a good fighting heart, and you need to have the right psychological mindset going in. I was two for three."

A month later Ettish sent Art Davie a letter. "It was one of the greatest experiences of his life. He would willingly come back and fight again," said Davie. "That to me says a lot about the competitors who applied to get in the UFC. Some of them didn't actually have a lot of fighting experience, but they came and went all out. And Fred Ettish summed it all up. He had to switch gears so quickly and all of the sudden be a fighter. He wasn't prepared for it; I had him working up to five minutes before that bout. To me, he really typified what the event was all about. I still think about that."

But as the memory of the fight faded, an unconceivable assault beset Ettish and his family, an insult to every man who has the courage to step into the ring. Sometime in 1995, a rogue website was erected to embarrass Ettish, dubbing his style "The Fetal Fighting System" in reference to Ettish's defense from the down position. Many other fighters have fought from this position; in fact many jiu-jitsu fighters have simply fallen to their butts to tempt their opponents into a ground game. Yet Ettish was persecuted for the action. "We've had [the site] taken down more than once, but it's like a dandelion … you pluck one out and another pops up somewhere else," said Ettish. "We contacted the hosts of the site and confronted them. After bantering back and forth on the computer, it would go down. Then someone else would pop back up with the exact same website." Ettish fought his heart out, while others have cracked under pressure and given up. Yet he was mocked and stripped of the basic respect he wholeheartedly deserves.

"I've been tried, convicted and sentenced all on the performance of one night. I think it's a shame to be judged that way," said Ettish. "I've been doing martial arts for decades, and on one night when I step out of the box and do something in a venue foreign to me, and I don't come through, it seems a little harsh. I readily admit that I didn't do well, there is no doubt about that. I bear full responsibility. But I've been misquoted in magazines. There were interviews attributed to me that were in no way, shape or form things that I said. And that ridiculous website! It goes against everything I believe in and what a martial artist should be. I think I've paid my price and don't need to be subjected to any more of that."

Ettish also feels it's unfair to label him as the sacraficial lamb of traditional martial arts. "I didn't do what I should have done, but does that mean all traditional martial arts are bad? No, it certainly doesn't. I regret that my fight might have tainted traditional martial arts in a lot of people's eyes." Ettish believes most people do not invest the time and hard work needed to harvest the rewards of traditional martial arts, opting instead for quick satisfaction.

Nearing the age of fifty, Fred Ettish still lives in the forest ranges of Bemidji, Minnesota, where he runs a school with thirty-plus students inside his own house, part of which has been converted to a dojo. He is now a seventh-degree black belt in shorin karate and acts as the United States director and vice-president for the Matsumura Kempo Association. Ettish leads a humble life, and admits the experience has made him a better teacher. Though he still considers himself a traditionalist, he and his students train in a wide variety of submissions. Not a day goes by that he doesn't think about fighting one more time under better conditions, but he still ventures out to watch local events. At UFC 45: Revolution, Ettish was flown to Atlantic City and signed autographs alongside many UFC veterans. He may have been written off as an early MMA casualty in the beginning, but Fred Ettish truly exemplifies a modern martial artist.

Footnote: WOW Promotions presented Helio Gracie with an award in the first UFC for his contribution to the martial arts. Ninja Robert Bussey got one in the second event and Don "The Dragon" Wilson received one at UFC III. Art Davie was going to honor Frank Dux as well, until the truth came out about his past. From then on, awards were no longer given out. Bruce Lee, who made the biggest contribution to martial arts, never received the recognition he deserved. To this day, almost every fighter attributes their love of fighting and martial arts to the Little Dragon.

CHAPTER 22

My Life as a Fighter

I'M IN THE *dressing room, pacing back and forth, wondering if all the months of preparation will pay off. The tension builds as I realize that one small mistake can end the fight with hardly a scratch to show for it. Now I'm in the middle of the cage and there's no escape. The crowd is much too loud for me to think. Maybe that's my problem – should I let instinct take over? He doesn't look so tough: the tattoos are window dressing. I stand there with eyes locked on my opponent's. There's a stillness in the air and now everything seems quiet. As the ref motions us to begin, I ponder how this real life chess match will play out, and in whose favor ...*

HOW AND WHY does one become a mixed martial artist? Obviously, it's not by answering an advertisement: WANTED. *Quick thinkers to work in a fast-paced environment with few benefits and the propensity for bodily injury.* Most of the fighters interviewed for this book credit Bruce Lee as their inspiration for getting involved in martial arts. They enjoyed watching Lee onscreen and yearned to attain that athletic body and those powerful yet graceful moves. For John Lober, the *Tao of Jeet Kune Do* outlined a philosophy that combined what worked with one's own physical prowess; he chose to compete under "Jeet Kune Do Concepts" (the name of Lee's methodology). "Just look at the opening scene from *Enter the Dragon*," said Zane Frazier. "He [Lee] fought with gloves for striking, and there were takedowns and a submission." From kickboxer Maurice Smith to jiu-jitsu player Royce Gracie, Bruce Lee is a symbol of excellence that transcended style, culture, and race.

UK fighter Dexter Casey grew up in Hong Kong and saw Bruce Lee as the apex of martial arts. Though he knew most martial arts styles were ineffective in a real situation, "I still wanted to believe in an ultimate warrior-type person, so I continued." Casey yearned for knowledge of something practical, believing Thai boxing was the answer until he saw the UFC. "Royce Gracie was my new Bruce Lee. The idea that someone the same size as me [at the time] could beat these big monsters was amazing."

STYLE

The commercialism of traditional martial arts tainted much of its original value by moving away from realistic combative aspects in favor of movie-inspired flashiness. Many sought the true essence of what they had been studying. That truth led them to the belief that one style couldn't beat all, and style was only part of the puzzle. While karate instructors were preaching to their students that they held the answer, Lee professed the opposite. He knew the key was finding that link between one's physical attributes and the gradual process of discovering which fighting concepts worked in reality.

In the first few UFCs, Brazilian jiu-jitsu proved its dominance, because the mainstream martial arts were unfamiliar with ground-fighting, nor had anyone expected a tae kwon do black belt to lose in such a manner as a choke or arm bar. To answer that early question of what style was best, jiu-jitsu won because much of the martial arts community, with their rigid, contained ideals about combat, was asleep. But jiu-jitsu fooled itself in believing its style was superior when it merely supplied a more practical base on which to build on. Once the riddle of jiu-jitsu was solved, people took notice, seeking out new knowledge to sharpen their own fighting skills.

Things have changed since then. "In the beginning, the guy training in jiu-jitsu wouldn't have to train in boxing or wrestling because no one knew about jiu-jitsu," said Wallid Ismail. "I hold the guy and make the guy like a baby. For a no-holds-barred fight, I have to train boxing and wrestling because everyone already knows jiu-jitsu." Rorion Gracie prescribes jiu-jitsu as the basis for effective fighting. "The fight is going to boil down to the ground. So if you know how to get into the clinch, all of that stand-up stuff is going to be gone." Out of jiu-jitsu emerged the submission or hybrid fighter, a relatively new term that jiu-jitsu practitioners felt was a ruse to avoid giving credit to the Brazilians. "I think it's ridiculous because they want to start their own little trend," said Rorion. "They don't want to admit that jiu-jitsu is the one that is doing it for them. They want to be originators of their own styles. Joe Son Do? What the heck is Joe Son Do?"

Not so, says submission expert Frank Shamrock. "What I do and what I teach is a bit of wrestling, a bit of sambo, a bit of judo, a bit of jiu-jitsu – a bit of everything because it's a bit of everything that works. Anybody that does jiu-jitsu is very simple. I want a complete fighting system. There has to be more than jiu-jitsu; jiu-jitsu is just a base, like karate. Yeah, they [Gracies] got this thing started, but they're old news now. People just need to understand that. They can call it whatever they want and do whatever they need. Jiu-jitsu is now just another martial art." By 1997, the lines between styles were blurred to such a point that everyone did "a little bit of everything" to be successful in MMA. Stand-up fighters learned the ground, just as ground fighters learned stand-up and the synergy of those two styles enabled MMA to become a more strategic and complex battle. Today the sport insists on base styles with free-flowing elements, to make complete fighters.

Some fighters learn the ground game only for defense. Dutch kickboxer Bob Schrijber could no longer rely on just his fists and feet when he transitioned to MMA. "I am not training for getting to the ground to submit somebody," said Schrijber. "I train [groundfighting] only for defense, and blocking takedowns is a thing I work on right now." Schrijber doesn't like training jiu-jitsu because that is not his game, but the thrill of the fight is, and he's defeated experienced ground players before by sprawling, keeping it standing, and knocking them out.

"You are a really good martial artist when you can compete under any rules and fight anyone in any style," said Frank Shamrock. Chicago-born Shonie Carter is one such example, a soft-spoken, martial arts enthusiast who competes in everything: freestyle and Greco Roman wrestling, judo, jiu-jitsu, boxing, kickboxing, point karate, submission wrestling and pankration. He competes in different arenas because he sees each one as an individual challenge, acting as a personal release that keeps the non-fighting Carter grounded. He has fought in top MMA promotions from the UFC to Pancrase, but often mixes it up in local Chicago nightclubs under not-so-normal rules. One time, Carter and another fighter engaged in a two-on-three match inside a makeshift ring, held for special customers at a bar just after midnight.

TEAM SPORT

Ken Shamrock's Lion's Den emerged as the first American team to prepare fighters for MMA. Single entrants in the UFC just didn't have the same support structure afforded to Royce Gracie with his jiu-jitsu family in tow. Styles for jiu-jitsu, wrestling and kickboxing formed many teams in the beginning, but eventually the team philiosophy rested on the harmonious union of its members striving to become better athletes. Today's teams are more like brotherhoods, as members rely on one another for training, advice, and sometimes rent money. In pro boxing, a fighter brings his trainer, cut man, manager and assistants to their bouts. In MMA, a fighter brings as many as a dozen teammates to cheer him on and show their support. The manager is often another team member or team leader, not a management company.

In America alone, there are over 30 major teams that have produced champions at all levels of the game. In Iowa, Pat Miletich's Miletich Fighting Systems has spawned Matt Hughes, Jens Pulver, Tim Sylvia and Robbie Lawler. In San Jose, California, Frank Shamrock student "Crazy" Bob Cook and kickboxer Javier Mendez run American Kickboxing Academy, which has produced several stars including Josh Thomson, Paul Buentello and Richard Crunkilton. Florida has the American Top Team (a sister team to the Brazilian Top Team), Massachusetts has Team Elite and Oregon has Team Quest. Teams not only prepare their students for MMA, but they also train them for jiu-jitsu and submission matches, kickboxing and boxing as well.

A CAREER CHOICE

Earning a living as a fighter is very difficult. You must train at your own expense, even travel to different countries just to learn a particular choke, new positioning or way of putting the pieces of the puzzle together. "I got guys who drive three hours so they can train, and they don't see their families because they stay all weekend," said Frank Shamrock. As others were born to play golf or be pro basketball players, these athletes were born to fight. "I had aspirations of going into boxing or kickboxing, but when I saw the UFC, that is what I wanted to do," said Aaron Riley. Travis Fulton bought into the fantasy of the film *Bloodsport*, but made it his goal in life to compete in the UFC when he saw the truth. Today, Fulton has fought in more matches than anyone else – over 100, and he's still in his twenties. "If I had my way, I would fight everyday. I'm doing this because this is what I like to do," he said. He sees fighting as a paid vacation that will help him rack up a lot of stories by the time he's 30. Yet the largest purse Fulton has made has been $3,000, while most of his matches were fought for mere hundreds of dollars.

Unlike boxing, MMA doesn't really have an amateur league. To gain experience, most fighters put it on the line for as little as $100 in front of an audience. Many of these shows don't even have insurance, but the fighters are willing to chock it up to experience. Outside of the UFC and Japanese promotions, fighter purses are generally below par considering reward vs risk. Putting things into perspective, the UFC's normal rate for a first-time entry is $2,000 to show and $2,000 to win. Without long term contracts, that fighter may have to compete for gradual increases in purse money, and IF he becomes a big name, only then can he negotiate for enough pay to fight fulltime. It's sad these professionally trained athletes, who must sacrifice so much, can't make a decent wage doing what they do best.

Worst of all, several athletes have destroyed the sport by agreeing to compete for next to nothing. Lion's Den fighter Mikey Burnett was pretty candid about his thoughts on this matter. "Any fighter that fights for that cheap [$100] is cheating the fuck out of himself and cheating the fuck out of everybody. He's cheating me, cheating Mikey! We do this for a living and anyone who knows about training for ultimate fighting knows it takes a long time, every damn day. I have to work at it everyday, four to six hours a day." With very few managers and no regulations about purses, the fighter is the one who suffers. In most of the regional shows, slots are plentiful, and the promoter has the luxury of looking elsewhere if someone isn't willing to fight for chump change. Often times, the show will value the fighter's purse on the number of tickets he can sell in the region. Instead of spending his time training, the fighter must now put in the time to sell tickets; otherwise the opportunity isn't worth it.

If the fighter is good enough to make it to the next step, he probably won't stay in America too long. The UFC has had to pay over $100,000 to its heavyweight and light-heavyweight talent just to keep them from moving to Japan's Pride and K-1 organizations. As for everyone else, a fighter that normally makes $5,000 to show and $5,000 to win in the US could make five times that amount for a match in Japan. According to Ivan Trembow, who researched fighter salaries for MMAweekly.com, only eight out of sixteen fighters made more than $10,000 at UFC 46 and six out of sixteen fighters made more than $10,000 at UFC 47. Through sponsorship deals and large fighter purses, someone competing in Japan could make as much as $250,000 per match.

MMA is a dream many fighters hope will turn into something more. Like bodybuilding, only a handful of people make any money;

the rest must look at the sport as a supplement to other forms of income. It is a difficult sport to master, as so many elements come into play, and personal satisfaction must be the overriding factor for doing it in the first place. The sport gave martial artists a way to make real money in competition, but the money is very little relative to pro boxing, where a single Mike Tyson paycheck is more than the combined salaries for five current UFCs.

MOTIVATION

Money isn't always the motivator behind fighting, as Iowa-born Bobby Hoffman can attest. Hoffman says he has always been a fighter, from as far back as he can remember. At five years old, he was accidentally hit in the head with a garden hoe. The hoe had to be removed by a doctor, and Hoffman spent seven months in a hospital. Hoffman's adulthood didn't fare much better, after a brief stint with the Cleveland Browns football team. "By 1996, I had racked up fourteen assault charges in four years. I was actually facing eight years [for assault to commit bodily injury], but served ninety-two [days] and got out." The gym was the only thing that kept his mind off violence. As fate would have it, Hoffman met a local NHB fighter who was about to turn his life around for the better. Hoffman had no martial arts or boxing background, but as he put it, "My old man was rough on me and boxed me around a lot. I had no type of fight training whatsoever except for barroom brawls." On two days' notice, the 265lb, 6ft 3in Hoffman entered his first MMA fight, Bare Knuckle Brawls. After competing all over the world with great success, his vices got the best of him and in 2001, he was sentenced to prison for several crimes. He made his comeback the following year, but wasn't the same fighter as before.

Most career MMA fighters never thought they'd be doing this for a living. Wrestler Mike Van Arsdale saw it as bringing wrestling back to its foundation: "Wrestling was turned into a sport where college kids wouldn't get hurt, so this is just going back to a place in time where wrestling was different." When wrestlers reach that pinnacle and feel they have no more to learn, MMA allows them to apply those skills in a fresh environment. Frank Shamrock needed something in his life to give him perspective. He thought football was too hard and wasn't interested in wrestling, so volleyball and hackey-sack became his only physical solace. When Shamrock was given the opportunity to be part of the Lion's Den, he seized it as a way to put his life on track. "I never saw myself as a fighter, nor did I want to be a fighter. It was something that was just given to me, so I took it," said Shamrock. It took a couple of years for Shamrock to feel comfortable with the idea, but he learned quickly and became one of the most well-rounded, athletic fighters in MMA. After becoming King of Pancrase, he was able to write his own meal ticket in a sport with little money to go around and a lot of risk to be had.

MENTAL EDGE

The mindset of a fighter is a hard thing to gauge. Unlike a street-fighter, a professional mixed martial artist must always keep a cool head, since overzealousness might cost him the match. "You have to separate yourself from what you're doing," said Shonie Carter. "A lot of guys get psyched up before a fight, but I'm not like that … you can't have an emotion about fighting because that person has done nothing against you personally. They're just competing to earn money or to test themselves as a fighter." But sometimes a personal element does enter the picture, as in the case of Hawaiian fighter Jay R Palmer and Brazilian Maurice Corty. According to Palmer, Corty had the gall to walk up to Palmer's wife and say, "Sorry, I'm going to have to break his arm and send him out on a stretcher." Palmer was beside himself with anger when his wife told him. A camera close-up of Palmer's face revealed a man possessed, marked by heavy breathing and wild eyes. Palmer attacked Corty in the first two and half minutes with an onslaught of good old-fashioned streetfighting that resulted in the Brazilian being stomped unconscious.

For others, such as Mark Kerr, fighting affects the emotions in a different way. "I brought my brother to the first UFC that I fought in and these are so emotional for me that I broke down after the fight. I was in tears, and I've probably cried three or four times after a fight. It's just so emotional for me to get it over with and there is so much tension." Ultimately, each man must find what works best for him, but having the proper mindset is key.

British fighter Dexter Casey finds he can control the tension – some-times too much. "I have seen fighters crying before getting in the ring due to the adrenaline running through them," he said. "They think they are scared but they aren't, it's adrenaline. Being able to control your response to all this adrenaline is the mental aspect. I am a natural performer and adrenaline does not bother me. This can work against you, as I have recently been going into the ring too relaxed and because of that, I have been beaten. A bit of tension and edge can keep you alive."

As boxers have long recognized, physchology can be crucial in *many y mano* contests. Vale, a neanderthal Russian bouncer, had made quite a name for himself on the east coast of England. Whether it was competing in illegal prizefights or throwing people out on their butts, he was certainly someone to be feared. As MMA events sprouted up around Europe, Casey got the chance to fight him in the ring. "When I got to the arena I was treated like a celeb," he said. "Everybody wanted me to smash his face in, patriotically of course." Meeting for the first time at the weigh-in, Vale claimed Casey was too small to fight him, vexing the Brit in the process. "He was basically assuming, because he outweighed me by thirty pounds, that he was going to run right over me," said Casey, who was a solid 210lbs.

Two hours before the fight, Casey's mind was elsewhere. Vale's comments enraged him. Devising a strategy, he and his pad man began working Thai kicks just outside of Vale's changing area. "The sound reverberated through his door and it was really loud. After about ten minutes of this, I knew he must be wondering what the sound was." Casey knew Vale was a good puncher and solid grappler, but wasn't much of a kicker. The sound of Casey's kicks could only plant question marks in Vale's head.

The Brit was the first one to the ring and he stomped around to let people know he meant business. "When [Vale] came out, I stared at him so hard that he had to break eye contact. I stood in his corner and made him go around me to get in. All these little things made him stiff and nervous." With the sound of the bell, Vale came out just as nervous as his brain and "threw a big right hand that came all the way from Moscow. I slipped the punch and threw a hard low kick. He backed up and I threw another low kick. He looked at me scared and I threw three more low kicks really fast with complete commitment." Vale crumbled in the corner and the fight was over with in just 18 seconds. Though Casey was disappointed that eight weeks of training led to 18 seconds of ring time, the mental aspect won the fight.

Perhaps there is also a spiritual side to fighting, as many Christians and other religious people also claim MMA professions. "There's certainly nothing wrong with it," said Matt Hume, a devout Christian and head of AMC Pankration in Seattle, Washington. "I'm available to talk with anyone, and even point them to scripture verses if it helps them get their mind right before they step in the ring. There are a couple of scriptures that I use." Texas native Paul Jones, who once worked for a boy's home for troubled teens, came up with the slogan, "Christians Aren't Wimps!" to promote his views. In Hawaii, there is even a professional fighting team called Jesus is Lord. And who could forget the sight of Kimo and Joe Son both carrying crosses and spouting scripture during their debuts in the UFC? UK competitor James Zikic had to wrestle with his Christian beliefs before accepting in his heart that fighting in MMA was something he was born to do. By studying under Frank Shamrock and others, Zikic made a name for himself as one of best up and coming fighters to come out of Britain.

PHYSICAL EDGE

On the other side of the coin is the physical aspect: readying a body to perform in an environment full of exhaustive grappling, danger-ous striking and brutal time limits. Successful fighters must train like Olympic athletes to achieve the level of endurance and stamina needed for the profession. Fighters like Tank Abbott, who relies on his one-to-two-minute window to knock his opponent out, often tire well before the end of the round due to lack of conditioning. Even Olympic-caliber wrestler Mark Coleman had trouble with Maurice Smith because he didn't have enough gas in the tank to finish with the same level of intensity as he'd started. A fighter can have all the knowledge in the world, but how can he employ this knowledge if his conditioning prohibits him? "Karate people are not athletes," said kempo exponent Zane Frazier. "Karate, tae kwon do, jiu-jitsu, and kung fu are martial arts disciplines. The reason we are not winning in NHB is simply because our techniques are not trained in the manner that a professional athlete trains." Thus, a world-class athlete with adequate skills can defeat a sub-par athlete with above average skills.

Fighters must go through a strenuous program of resistance train-ing, plyometrics [jumping], weight training, and running, and be able to separate as well as blend all of the elements in a fight (grappling, submission, striking). This training takes the MMA fighter out of his domain and forces him to look at singular elements. Frequently, he will train with a Muay Thai coach, then spar at a professional boxing gym, before rolling with a jiu-jitsu master. Between running and lifting weights, these athletes put in a tremendous amount of training in preparation for one fight.

Like athletes in other sports, they study their diet and adjust accordingly for weak spots, to maximize their potential in the ring.

After losing to Ricco Rodriguez at UFC 36 as a heavyweight, Randy Couture moved down to light heavyweight and worked with a nutritionist to better his conditioning in later rounds. The nutritionist prescribed ample amounts of green, leafy vegetables, which increases the alkalinity of the blood, while increasing endurance levels and longevity. Couture's conditioning improved two-fold as a result. Some fighters experiment with energy drinks and over-the-counter stimulants like Xenedrine and Ripped Fuel to see how it will affect them in the ring—certainly not the best solution, especially when someone doesn't understand the real problem.

In the past 30 years, sports have been plagued by steroid abuse, and MMA is unfortunately no different. "There are anabolic (stimulates tissue growth and repair) and androgenic (stimulates growth of secondary male sex organs and the synthesis of cellular protein) steroids," said Dr John Keating, longtime ringside physician and surgeon. "Most sports have moved to outlaw performance enhancing substances of all kinds, not so much because of the damage it does the athletes, but rather in an effort to keep the playing field level." MMA fighter Travis Fulton was one of the few who commented on his use of steroids. "My wind went downhill big time, and I'm still recovering," said Fulton. "I got good steroids; it wasn't like I was doing bad stuff. My body started looking better and I got a lot stronger and much bigger. It's one of the reasons I got into the UFC, because I was a heavyweight. But to this day, my body aches all the time." Some, like Dan Severn, are adamantly against steroids, even to the point of lobbying for drug-free competitions.

John Keating has this to say about the dangers of steroid use: "The various performance-enhancing agents [in steroids] certainly do enhance performance up to a point. They are extremely effective at developing bulk and strength. Obviously, you can massively over-develop muscles that create more of an oxygen debt than can be met in sports such as MMA, which require a mix of aerobic and anaerobic capacity. But it's not the short-term oxygen debt problems that concern sports physicians. It is the broad band of side effects that move us to urge athletes to eschew steroid use. They poison your liver, create significant heart changes (both to the muscle itself and to the arteries supplying the heart), promote hypertension, male pattern baldness, and suppress immune function (increasing the likelihood of infection and compromised response to tumour). In fact, long-time steroid users have five thousand times the incidence of liver cancer as the general public."

Benching over 600lbs, self-proclaimed natural fighter David "Tank"

Abbott was also outspoken on the topic. "The first use of steroids was by the Nazis on the front lines so they would be more aggressive. Those guys have to take drugs to think like me. I've taken so many drug and steroid tests, and I have never taken a steroid. Obviously, by looking at my body, you can tell I don't. Steroids ruined real fighting; they ruined the UFC." Though some athletes have used them to become more powerful, there have been too many cases where all they've done is decreased the endurance and stamina needed to finish a fight.

So if steroid abuse exists, what is to be done about it? "Educate the athlete," said Keating. "Blood testing is expensive and ineffective. I believe the only person harmed by the steroids is the user himself, so the final responsibility lives with the athlete. In the short term, steroids may add some marginal additional risk during the event of a hyper-tensive episode, but whatever these risks are they do not substantially add to the danger of what goes on inside the ring."

The first steroid case in MMA occurred on April 22, 2002, when the NSAC filed a complaint against Josh Barnett after winning the heavy-weight championship over Randy Couture at UFC 36. The NSAC alleged two positive tests for anabolic steroids from samples taken on November 2, 2001 and March 22, 2002. Barnett was ultimately stripped of the title and given a six-month suspenion despite Barnett's camp protesting any usage of anabolic enhancements. Barnett never competed in the UFC again, opting instead to pro wrestle and fight for Antonio Inoki in Japan. Lightning struck again at UFC 44 when Tim Sylvia admitted to steroid use after defending the heavyweight crown. He was also stripped and suspended for four months, but contends to stay with the UFC. A title shot at UFC 47 was postponed when anabolic agents were still found in his bloodstream; he was cleared two days later.

Similar to what can be found in other professional sports, some fighters also use painkillers to combat the myriad of problems these athletes face, especially in the knee and shoulder joints. It's also not uncommon for fighters to partake in recreational drugs, as part of an extremist lifestyle that's hardcore in every respect. Fighters know they can use their occupation to their advantage in social situations. Fighter gyms and teams have their share of groupies much like one would see with rock stars.

PERFORMING ARTISTS

MMA is a spectator sport and fighters are performers. They must entertain the audience while trying to win the fight. Upon seeing Tank

Abbott's phenomenal success with the crowd, Gary Goodridge became "Big Daddy," giving colorful interview soundbytes before walking out to the octagon. Quinton "Rampage" Jackson, with his trademark chain around his neck, howls into the air before trotting down the ramp to fight for Pride. His no-bullshit interviews and perceived player lifestyle have made him a huge fan favorite. Heath Herring, known as "The Texas Crazyhorse," comes out with a different hairdo every time and hams it up in the ring – it made him a star in Pride. Genki Sudo has come out as everything from a samurai warrior to a geisha girl for his UFC matches. The audience has grown to look forward to his unpredictable behavior in and out of the ring.

No doubt MMA fighters are a different breed. Some have quirks and mannerisms that set them apart from everyone else, and it's the lack of that red tape found in, for example, boxing that allows everyone to see the natural character each fighter possesses. Pride, and several Japanese organizations, rely more on characters than actual fighting ability, while US promotions take the opposite approach. The US market is perhaps too focused on legitimacy, just as the Japanese promotions are free to please a much larger fanbase that mostly comes from pro wrestling. Either way, every fighter must find what makes him unique, and physical skill isn't always the primary factor.

Case in point is Matt Lindland and Phil Baroni, the two most diametrically opposed fighters in the UFC. Lindland is an Olympic silver medallist who trains with Randy Couture in Oregon. His all-business demeanor and physical features don't necessarily fit the stereotype of a UFC fighter, compared to the mouthy, brash Phil Baroni, a former bodybuilder and pin-up model who hypes it up every chance he gets. Both men represent extremes of perception about what a star is all about, but Baroni has carved a niche for himself as being the controversial, unapologetic "New York Badass"—his justified nickname. Baroni's reputation includes a suspension for punching a ref, dropping f-bombs on the mike and being kicked off fight teams for being too uncooperative. Lindland and Baroni have met twice in the octagon, and both times, Lindland has reigned supreme. Lindland says he can't do anything about "public perception," as people form their opinions by a myriad of ways. "After much thought, planning, and input from my brilliant staff of 'war room' image makers, I have come up with a spectacular strategy to hold the fan's attention: it's called winning fights," says Lindland. And no matter what people think, he has proven himself time and time again as one of the best fighters in the middleweight class.

Building a star in the ring can also have its problems. Dan Severn used "The Beast" and his pro wrestling experience to create a character the audience would remember. After winning a match, Severn will raise his large hands up into the air and let out a roar to get the crowd going. Out of the limelight, Severn is a family man who used to speak frequently of his long-time devotion to his wife (married since 1984) and five children. But not anymore. "I had one of my children almost abducted after my first two years of being involved in this," said Severn. The Beast promotes himself as a bachelor to the media these days. He runs his own promotion, the Danger Zone, and his office and training camp sit only 40 yards from his house.

PART-TIME FIGHTERS

More than 90 per cent of all MMA fighters have full time jobs, allowing them flexibility to train for fights on the weekend. Gary Goodridge worked a 40-plus hour week for Honda of Canada Manufacturing in the vehicle quality division. He made fighting a hobby until Japan made him a superstar, affording him the opportunity to fight full-time. Russian immigrant Roman Roytberg is a licensed dentist, but competes in kickboxing and MMA. Matt Lindland owns a used car lot in Oregon. Australian standout Elvis Sinosic works in the telecommunications industry, and takes time off work to train and fight. Jason Godsey, Phil Johns and Ron Waterman are high school teachers. Eugene Jackson runs a trucking business; Genki Sudo and Nicholaus Hill are actors.

Here is a partial list of MMA fighters who have appeared in film, television and commercials:

Tito Ortiz (*The Crow: Wicked Prayer, Cradle 2 The Grave*)
Joe Son (*Austin Powers*)
Oleg Taktarov (*Air Force One, 15 Minutes*)
Bas Rutten (*The Eliminator, Shadow Fury, Martial Law*)
Ken Shamrock (*Virtuosity, The Champions*)
Frank Shamrock (*Walker, Texas Ranger, Burger King* commercial, *No Rules*)
Lance Gibson (*Rumble in the Bronx, Romeo Must Die*)
Kimo (*Ultimate Fight*)
Dan Severn (*Rudy*)
Tank Abbott (*Friends*)
Randy Couture (*Nike* commercial, *Cradle 2 The Grave, No Rules*)
Maurice Smith (*Bloodfist II, Fist of Glory*)
Pete Spratt (*Thugs 2*)

So what advice can be given to the aspiring mixed martial artist? "Get your head examined!" said Guy Mezger. "And if you get your head examined and find out that you're crazy enough to still do this, it's important that you get well-rounded training and that you get really good quality training."

"The sport has evolved from a lack of knowledge in the beginning, to a knowledge of submission, to a knowledge of grappling, to a knowledge of striking, and now a knowledge of conditioning," said Maurice Smith. "This is truly a martial art, what these guys are doing now by cross-training and becoming hybrid fighters. There will be a guy in the future who is going to have excellent grappling, submission, striking, and strategy skills." Ironically, many of the fighters interviewed for this book spoke of a similar fighter, an almost mythical figure who would emerge to supplant the best of the best today. Even in the world of reality fighting, people still believe in mythic heroes and legends. But until they step into the ring, that's all they'll ever be.

CHAPTER 23

Fighting for a Renegade Sport

FOR MOST CASUAL viewers, MMA was a beer-induced fad that came and passed during the mid-1990s. After major pay-per-view companies dropped the UFC, the media had no cause to persecute or milk it anymore: it was a "win" for the moral majority. Press coverage died, just as the masses yearned for something else "too taboo." The UFC had breathed new life into a market bored with boxing and pro wrestling, but with MMA out of the spotlight, Vince McMahon of World Wrestling Entertainment came back strong to promote an improved pro wrestling that reclaimed its profitable pay-per-view days. Marketed as sports entertainment, the WWE revamped its programming with raunchy storylines, more scantily clad women, funnier archetypes, and less actual wrestling. The media now had a new villain: sex and violence on television. In the midst of war in the Middle East and risque reality television, MMA looked rather tame by comparison. Can it survive by being perceived as a sport rather than entertainment?

UFC vice-president Joe Silva remembers, while serving as a fight consultant, the time he spoke to programming director Campbell McLaren at Ultimate Ultimate '95: "I told Campbell that we needed to be more like a real sport, and Campbell said, 'The last thing we want to be is a sport.'" Silva became enchanted by MMA after seeing the UFC. "At the end of that first show, I was so happy that I was practically in tears. This is the reality I've been trying to tell people about, what would happen in a real fight. This is not just people running their mouths; this is people putting it on the line." Silva, who had made martial arts a large part of his life, began calling the SEG office, offering up his opinions on how to better the show. His dedication and insight led him to trade ideas for posters and other fan paraphernalia. Silva has been part of the UFC since the third show, from fight consultant to matchmaker.

Despite inaccessibility on pay-per-view, MMA created a paradigm shift in the martial arts worldwide. One can't walk into a conventional martial arts school without seeing "submission", "freestyle", "vale tudo" and "jiu-jitsu" bandied about as a way to attract people outside traditional styles. MMA schools often do the opposite by bringing in karate instructors to teach kids classes – the cash cow of the business.

Brazilian jiu-jitsu has been an underlying factor for popularizing MMA. While the sport has been hit and miss with state legislators around the US, jiu-jitsu tournaments take place almost every weekend somewhere around the world. Arnold Schwarzenegger's "Arnold Classic" bodybuilding and fitness event even added the Arnold World Gracie Submission Championships to its growing list of competitive sports. Headed up by Relson Gracie, over 4,000 people compete each year. People of all ages train jiu-jitsu, much to the delight of Rorion Gracie, who has kept his dream alive in more than one way. His three sons, Ryron, Rener and Ralek, are "part of the next generation and are teaching and training at the academy now," said Rorion. "It's in their blood; they want to do MMA." Rener Gracie is also a state champion wrestler; his jiu-jitsu game sharpened his wrestling and *vice versa*. Rorion even started his own submission event in California.

If there was to be one reason why MMA has stayed around as long as it has without free television, it would be the Internet. "[It] has been amazingly resilient," said Cal Cooper, who has worked on two major MMA websites. "It's a vast, convoluted community, made up of news sites, forums and the Combat List, an exhaustive e-mail list disseminated to thousands of in-boxes per day." Without mainstream sports media, fans, fighters and promoters rely on the Internet as its biggest source for information. Most Internet journalists write for free and webmasters keep their sites going by selling merchandise.

Kirik Jenness and David Roy run mma.tv, the definitive sounding board for the sport. The site's infamous Underground Forum is the most up-to-date source of information, where insiders and outsiders are free to post anything about the sport and do so regularly. With over 50,000 members, "the mixed martial arts audience is very well rounded – people in their seventies to a twelve-year-old girl," said Jenness, whose site was started as a vehicle to sell *The Fighter's Notebook*, an instructional book on submission grappling techniques. "I took martial arts for twenty years before watching the UFC and after that, I came to the realization that I don't know anything." Today, The Forum is a rite of passage for every MMA fan and becomes an obsessive daily, sometimes hourly, fix to see what's happening in the sport.

Joel Gold is perhaps the ultimate enterprising fight fanatic. He turned his love for MMA into an empire comprising a newspaper, website, and clothing line. Everything is collectively known as *Full Contact Fighter*. In 1993, Gold was training in a local New York boxing gym when he saw the UFC and criticized the stand-up abilities of the first few UFC participants. Intrigued by Brazilian jiu-jitsu, he took up the art and before long, the 155-pound Gold was challenging anyone who would put their skills to the test. After taking on guys twice his size, Gold experienced sharp pains in his neck that continued for months. He woke one morning to find the right side of his body paralyzed. Gold went to a sports medicine clinic and discovered his neck had accumulated three herniated discs. He keeps the X-ray as a reminder.

Yearning to be part of the fight game somehow, Gold took up photography at boxing and kickboxing events. *Full Contact Fighter* started with a website and a twelve-page newspaper when Gold covered UFC XIII. The entrepreneur had a knack for asking tough questions at interviews, packing them tightly into the newspaper with his photos. The paper took off, gained a solid subscription base and became required reading for hardcores. Gold eventually diversified the brand name to include merchandising, namely to meet the demand from fighters. (Gold wasn't the only one to break into this market, as companies like Tap Out produced quality clothes with raw appeal for fans and fighters alike.) In March 2000, Canadian TV producer Brian Sobie launched a short-lived televison show around *Full Contact Fighter*. Full color magazines, such as *Ultimate Athlete* and *Fightsport*, soon entered the market but couldn't sustain enough revenue to keep going. Today, *Full Contact Fighter* has grown in page count, added color and stands as the most reliable news source outside the Internet.

IN ALMOST EVERY conceivable place around the USA, and even the world, MMA promotions continue to exist in some form. These shows give opportunities to up-and-coming fighters, who perform in front of crowds from 300 to 6,000. Since athletic commissons are often ill equipped or uninformed, promoters have swarmed the market by holding shows on American Indian land and under a veil of secrecy in small, off-the-map venues.

It's been a mixed blessing for a sport trying to find its way, with solidarity being the key issue. No neutral body oversees MMA, as there are too many promotions with too many individual ideas on how it should be governed. Some matches are held in a ring, some in a cage. Rules change with each show. Sometimes participants can hit with a closed fist to the face, sometimes they can only strike with an open hand. There are variations in weight class categories and glove sizes. There is no official ranking system. Websites offer a primitive semblance of ranking by having journalists decide who is the best of the best on that day. Promoters often manage fighters in their own shows. Some fighters take their lives in their hands by competing in as many as ten matches a year, even after knockouts. Without an organization to police the entire sport, most fighters are left to do as they please. It's a close-knit society that lacks structure and remains territorial. This every-man-for-himself approach will hinder MMA from ever being recognized as a true sport unless everyone unites to form a governing body establishing standard rules.

Most promotions have a set of formal rules, but only for their shows. SEG set up the Mixed Martial Arts Council (MMAC) to act as the credible, formalized version of Art Davie's defunct Ultimate Fighting Alliance and International Fighting Council. To his credit, Davie drafted five rulebooks and contends that 85 percent of those rules are still in place today. But the Ultimate Fighting Alliance was nothing more than a trade association trying to exploit the UFC brand name. It did nothing to further the sport.

The April 3, 2001, meeting called by Larry Hazzard of the New Jersey State Athletic Commission can be called one of the most important steps toward legitimacy. This epochal meeting set standards on several issues, while Marc Ratner, representing the NSAC, listened via conference call to report back to the commission. Boxing is king in Nevada, and the state's commission is the most prominent in the country. All eyes were on legislation passing in this state, which finally put MMA back on the map with the cable industry and the rest of the world in 2001. When the NJSAC sanctioned the UFC, the MMAC was disbanded. The "unified rules" created by this meeting was one of the few instances of solidarity among the top promoters in the country, and even those rules were changed slightly by the Nevada commission. Fighters now have to compete without shoes for uniformity and safety. Yet many promoters continue to operate as they please. Other sanctioning bodies promote themselves as being politically neutral but have failed to make an impact. Vanity keeps some promoters from working together, believing "they know" what the rules should be without thinking of the bigger picture. It's improbable that every promoter will get on the same page.

Education is the most important element in legitimizing the sport. Guy Mezger worked with the Texas Boxing Commission to pass the first fully sanctioned event in the state in late 2000. Monte Cox drafted his own rules in Iowa for MMA. Anyone coming into the state must abide by those rules, including the UFC, who held an event there in June 2000. Former kickboxing promoter Sven Bean brought the sport full circle by getting it legalized in Colorado. Arizona has also become a hotbed of activity with shows produced in Phoenix and Tucson, all under the watchful eye of the Arizona State Athletic Commission.

Hawaii can possibly be called the best site to host an indie promotion in the US. TJ Thompson hosted NHB events in bars in 1996 using the name Futurebrawl, capitalizing on the UFC's hardcore image. Eventually he became a crusader for the sport, working with politicans to institute rules and hold events in major venues like the Blaisdell Arena. Operating out of Honolulu, Thompson now calls the event, Superbrawl, and has attracted as many as 9,000 fans for one show. On August 1, 1998, Thompson held Superbrawl 7 in Guam, and it became the first MMA event to ever be aired on a major free television network – and NBC affiliate. Fighter BJ Penn has also started a successful promotion in Hilo, Hawaii, called Rumble on the Rock. In California, the unified rules are still awaiting acceptance by the floundering California State Athletic Commission. The tortuous deregulation of water in California (which bankrupted businesses and upset the economy) buried any new legislation in 2002 but many hope with Arnold Schwarzenegger running the state, a pro-MMA bill could pass in 2005.

Unfortunately the sport is not out of the water yet. Matt Hume worked to pass legislation in Washington to hold events back in the mid-1990s. But on March 26, 2004, a bill was passed to ban all MMA events, partly due to misinformation and the inability to distinguish MMA from crude toughman contests that claim lives every year. Also in 2004, North Carolina banned all MMA events, and Georgia might be the next state to fall. And while UFC fighter Keith Hackney worked with others to bring MMA "back" to the Olympics, and more than 40 countries committed to it, the 2004 Games in Athens declined to include pankration.

Countless MMA promotions have come and gone from the sport, much like kickboxing's early days. Champions were crowned one night, then their belts were worth nothing. In lieu of originality, most of these promotions combined any of the following to create a name: ultimate, extreme, rage, king, world, cagefighting, international and championship. Sherdog.com has the best record of fight statistics anywhere, and its survey of 400 MMA promotions from around the world provided some interesting results. Only 145 promotions were still active at the time of writing, compared to 255 that remained inactive (i.e. not produced any event within the eight months prior to the survey). Of those inactive promotions, 50 percent promoted only one show before folding. So many inexperienced promoters have come onto the scene, spent thousands of dollars, lost thousands of dollars and vanished from sight.

There are a few exceptions. Since 1999, KOTC has promoted shows on Indian land in California and New Mexico, and through commissions in Nevada, Florida and Ohio. The promotion has continued to strive, thanks in part to Brentwood Communications, a video distribution company that has pushed the product out to the masses. The promotion started out strong, but fell victim to quantity over quality of shows. In May 2002, they held their first show in Reno, Nevada, and joined the ranks of the UFC and Pride by getting on pay-per-view. Unfortunately a lot of promoters come out too strong, letting vanity overtake reason. After the sport became legal in Las Vegas, it was only a matter of time before Vegas native John Lewis promoted his own show: World Fighting Alliance, in association with club promoter John Huntington. The WFA held three events before folding due to money problems. Several promotions have tried to enter the Vegas market, but only the UFC has succeeded.

On March 31, 2004, the US Senate passed a bill by Arizona senator John McCain establishing the United States Boxing Administration, which would ensure safety and health standards for the sport. With many of boxing's top figures having endured FBI investigation, "[boxing] is dying," said promoter Lou DiBella for an article in *Parade*. "It's like a cancer patient on chemo." Many of the problems plaguing MMA have been going on far too long in boxing. Without boxing's pedigree, can MMA last under similar conditions? With the sport still in its infancy, it needs form and structure if it is too survive.

JEFFREY OSBORNE DIDN'T make his way into MMA as a promoter and journalist because of money. With his long black hair in a ponytail, skinny stature, deep voice and round-rimmed glasses, it was hard to believe that Osborne was once a hardcore pro wrestler. Unlike the showy WWE, hardcore pro wrestling relies on the use of barbed wire, fire, and other props that could damage the body. In April 1994, Osborne nearly lost his life due to a bad fall. He reconsidered his career and got out of the business: too much attitude, too much drug abuse (Osborne himself never used drugs), and two close friends dying.

Osborne knew about MMA through Japanese promotions like Shooto and Rings. In 1995, he started Hook 'n' Shoot as a small-time venture in Evansville, Indiana. "The thing I like about MMA is that if you have an ego, it can be crushed at anytime," said Osborne. Along with partner Miguel Itturate, Hook 'n' Shoot has been running strong for ten years. It continues to be one of the best independent shows. In 2001, one Hook 'n' Shoot attracted over 3,000 fans, besting some of the early UFCs. Osborne has worked diligently to make it accessible to people at home via local TV networks. He handles pretty much every duty, including commentary, camerawork and post-production editing. "If I see someone knocked out or hurt, I will leave the production booth and get up to the ring because I'm genuinely concerned," said Osborne, who has even fought in MMA himself.

He and Itturate produced documenatries called *Fight World* and formed alliances with Japan's Shooto and a submission-only organization called Abu Dhabi Combat Club during the late-1990s. Before the horrible terrorist attacks on September 11, 2001, the Abu Dhabi World Submission Wrestling Championship was held in the United Arab Emirates for the sole purpose of entertaining Sheik Tahnoon and other wealthy oil tycoons who enjoy the competition. The show became a who's who in the submission world and paid large purses, since the Sheik had enough money to get any fighter he chose. In 2001, Osborne took over from Jeff Blatnick as color commentator for the UFC. He cut his ponytail, replaced his glasses with contacts and wore a suit, but comedian Joe Rogan replaced him a year later.

On April 13, 2002, Hook 'n' Shoot took its biggest gamble yet by staging the first all-women MMA event in the US. Its success sparked more support for female mixed martial artists. Fighter Debi Purcell, started a website called fightergirls.com where promoters can contact women around the world to book for their events. Erica Montoya, who started competing in MMA at age 15, even serves as the Spanish color commentator for the UFC. Today, Osborne and Iturrate are no longer partners; Osborne kept the Hook 'n' Shoot name. Both men continue promoting shows in Indiana, Florida and Atlantic City.

THE DVD/VIDEO AFTERMARKET has become the only way of seeing many of these smaller shows, as well as the majors who have larger distribution deals. The average person on the street may have heard of ultimate fighting and perhaps the Gracies, but without the pay-per-view universe and readily available videotapes and DVDs, the sport would peak with each show and lose considerable steam. SEG unwisely licensed much of their video rights to Trimark, which did a competent job in releasing UFC videos but could never put them out fast enough. Even SEG's homegrown *Secrets of the Octagon,* a five-videotape instructional set featuring Ken Shamrock and Oleg Taktarov, never made it to stores and racked up shoddy numbers. At that time, proper cross-training had yet to enter the picture and, while the set had some merit, it is laughable today compared to numerous other training tapes that effectively teach submission fighting.

Trimark also ignored the DVD market, with the exception of a two-disc release of *Biggest Hits* that showcased knockouts. "Our plan is to have the product out as soon as possible after the event is over," said Lorenzo Fertitta, co-owner of Zuffa's UFC. He made good on his word when Zuffa signed with Ventura, a major distribution label, releasing every show starting with UFC 39 as a special two-disc set. For the week of February 25, 2004, *UFC 44: Undisputed* ranked ninth among all sports titles on DVD, evidence of a strong market. Unfortunately, when Zuffa bought the UFC from SEG, a lot of footage from the early shows came up missing. Some preliminary matches from the SEG period may never be seen again. Fans don't have to resort to bootlegging UFCs, but international and indie shows can't meet the demand in the States, so illegal videos unfortunately become a fan's only choice.

Brentwood Communications was proactive enough to release its two American promotions, King of the Cage and Gladiator Challenge, on DVD at a low price just months after live shows. "The first KOTC has sold more than 40,000 units," said KOTC promoter Terry Trebilcock. Other promotions are following their lead, but it will undoubtedly saturate the market. For now, bootlegging is the only way to obtain most shows from other countries. While Pride has solid distribution in America, consumers are brand-conscious and many don't even know the promotion exists. Some rabid fans own over 500 MMA videotapes from around the world. For now, the home video market is the only way to reach people that don't otherwise know the sport exists. With free television, movies and documentaries, the sport should eventually break out of its pay-per-view shell into larger territory.

LOOKING AT TEN years of MMA, the jury is still out on whether it will take off. Many promoters sell their shows on brand name alone, instead of pushing the athletes. Regional shows hold as many as twenty bouts in one evening, selling the brutality and violence of "extreme fighting." These fight-centric promotions don't even bother listing the complete fight card so the audience is left with watching violence without caring about who or what is involved. When Zuffa took over the UFC, they even eliminated fighter interviews, but eventually brought them back to a degree. It's important to constantly push the fighter's names and faces to maximize retention. Even the UFC pay-per-view commercials are beginning to reflect more about the fighters and their stories instead of just promoting a night of action. What takes place in the ring is only a small part of the equation.

The audience must have an emotional connection to what they are watching before MMA can become a mainstream success. In theory, it has little to do with fighting or anything connected to a sport. Can one imagine if football or basketball did away with promoting the athletes and just put numbers on their shirts? Football, baseball and basketball fans are drawn to bigger-than-life heroes who can do something the average person cannot. Sponsorship deals, TV appearances and mass media help the mainstream audience become enamored of sports stars; some people go to games less for the action than to see their heroes in the flesh. Over the past few years, golf and tennis have attracted a large number of fans outside the hardcore fanbase due to breakout stars transitioning into mainstream media.

The current audience for MMA can be broken down into two categories: casual fans and diehard fans. The casual fans buy on name brand only, may know of a few fighters, but merely want a quick fix of blood and violence. The diehard fan combs the Net for information, has a steady supply of tapes and is picky about what he will pay for. Even combining casuals and diehards, the fanbase remains small by comparison to what most nations consider major sports.

From November 1993 to the end of 1997, a sport-in-the-making evolved from the concept of testing martial arts in a reality-based setting. After initial exposure, the grassroots movement kept MMA going in the USA, while the new millennium brought it back to the mainstream. Granted, potential MMA fans will need to look past the old engimas to claim new heroes and educate themselves on the sport. For any fight fan or martial artist, this sport provides a unique forum for two properly trained athletes to show what works and what doesn't. The ultimate in combative sports, it has just as much right to exist as boxing or pro wrestling, and the horizon has never looked brighter. Its supporters have shown they are willing to sacrifice much to fight for it. They certainly aren't about to tap out now.

CHAPTER 24

Japanese MMA: History and Beyond

THE GENESIS OF MMA as a sport can arguably be traced to Japan, when pro wrestlers like Antonio Inoki and Akira Maeda put themselves over by beating top fighters from other martial arts in worked bouts. Though Brazilian jiu-jitsu paved the way for the UFC and similar events in the US, pro wrestling served as the springboard for MMA in the Land of the Rising Sun.

In the 1960s and 1970s, American pro wrestler Karl Gotch, known for his legit submission wrestling abilities, was invited by Antonio Inoki to teach wrestlers for his New Japan Pro Wrestling (NJPW) organization. Gotch and Inoki even faced off in the inaugural NJPW show on March 6, 1972. The Japanese pro wrestlers really liked the shoot style of pro wrestling as compared to the theatrics embraced by the American scene. Gotch taught Inoki, Akira Maeda, Satoru Sayama and Yoshiaki Fujiwara, four men whose legacy was the Japanese MMA scene.

While Inoki continued to wrestle shooters with NJPW, Akira Maeda had other plans. Maeda started pro wrestling at age 18 in 1977. At 6ft 4in and well over 200lbs, a giant by Japanese standards, he quickly became one of the group's most popular wrestlers. Maeda eventually left New Japan and started Universal Wrestling Federation (UWF), where the new shoot style could have its own forum. When he was joined by rising star Satoru Sayama – better known as the original "Tiger Mask" – Yoshiaki Fujiwara and Nobuhiko Takada, the organization flourished, developing a harder style of stiff-worked matches using solid ground techniques with open hand strikes. Dissention in the ranks, however, built to a head when a pro wrestling match between Maeda and Sayama turned into a real fight. The company folded soon after and Maeda, Fujiwara and Takada eventually returned to NJPW in 1986. In November 1987, Maeda was involved in another ruckus with pro wrestler Riki Choshu and was kicked out of the organization.

Sayama moved out on his own and began prepping fighters for a new organization called Shooto. Though Sayama had been one of the most flamboyant Japanese pro wrestlers, the organization that debuted in 1989 promoted shoots only – the first of its kind in Japan. Maeda and Takada restarted the UWF in 1988 and Maeda, following in Inoki's footsteps, put himself over by fighting legit outsiders. His first big match was against Holland's Gerard Gordeau in August 1988. After defeating another Dutchman, Chris Dolman, in May 1989, he beat judo silver medallist Willie Wilhelm in November 1989 in what became the first Tokyo Dome sellout of any combat sport. Even Mike Tyson vs Buster Douglas couldn't sell out the venue, but despite its initial success, the promotion folded on December 1, 1990.

Nobuhiko Takada formed Union of Wrestling Forces International (UWFI) using leftover UWF talent soon after. Using his contacts from Europe, Maeda created Rings, which debuted on May 11, 1991. It looked similar to UWF, but Maeda made enough slight changes to sell the show as being completely legit. In reality, most of the matches were stiff works, save for the occasional shoot involving non-Japanese. Maeda spun off the Rings name for incarnations in Holland, Russia and Georgia for starters. Most of the matches that took place in these countries were completely shoot, building up talent to crossover to Japan.

On March 4, 1991, Yoshiaki Fujiwara stepped into the spotlight by starting Pro Wrestling Fujiwaragumi (PWFG). The organization enjoyed great success, partly due to the addition of Masakatsu Funaki and Minoru Suzuki, who had both wrestled for NJPW and the UWF. While American Bart Vale had close ties with Fujiwara in the new organization, Ken Shamrock's impressive debut in 1992, made him one of Japan's few non-Japanese breakout stars. (Ken initially went by the name Wayne Shamrock because he had worked on tour for All Japan Pro Wrestling using his real name, and the UWF didn't want Japanese fans thinking he was a pro wrestler.) Eventually, Funaki became tired of putting over older wrestlers like Fujiwara, and he too wanted to branch out on his own. On September 21, 1993, Funaki launched Pancrase with Suzuki and Shamrock. Pancrase looked like Rings and employed similar rules, but it promoted mostly shoot fights.

After the success of the UFC, Satoru Sayama and investors promoted Japan Vale Tudo '94, a gala MMA event with Rickson Gracie competing in an eight-man tournament. Gracie tore through the competition to take the top prize, establishing himself in Japan just as Royce had done in the States. Yoji Anjoh, Takada's UWFI stablemate, thought he could become a star by fighting the Brazilian so he flew to Los Angeles with press in tow for an impromptu challenge. On December 7, 1994, Rickson beat Anjoh down for three minutes inside his local gym. The press wasn't allowed to view the fight, only the aftermath – Anjoh waking up from being choked out.

Back in Japan, "everyone expected Takada to seek revenge as the head of the stable in Japanese martial arts tradition," said pro wrestling expert David Meltzer. "Takada's fans thought he was the real deal since UWFI was sold as being legit and Takada was the star of the group. When he didn't work to make the Rickson match happen, and didn't challenge him, UWFI fans lost [respect for] Takada." The UWFI suffered as a result, and ended up needing NJPW to bail the company out of debt in exchange for Takada losing the world championship to NJPW's Keiji Mutoh on May 3, 1995.

AFTER REBUILDING HIMSELF, Takada fought Rickson Gracie for a new organization called Pride on October 11, 1997. The show featured several UFC alumni with Gracie vs Takada headlining. It took Gracie less than five minutes to submit the pro wrestler with an arm bar. KRS, the company that produced Pride, wanted to take up where Japan Vale Tudo left off by creating an ongoing promotion to topple the fledgling pro wrestling scene. Realizing both Renzo and Rickson Gracie would win their matches, they cut deals with John Dixson and Nathan Jones (who played the giant that Brad Pitt kills at the beginning of *Troy*) to work their bouts against Japanese opponents, according to Dixson.

Frequently Japanese promotions will bring in outsiders to serve as tomato cans for Japanese fighters, throwing money at them on late notice to make the journey. Often the outsider hasn't had time to prepare and succumbs to the readied Japanese fighter. KRS needed to build Takada back up with another bout and weren't about to take any chances. They were assured American Kyle Sturgeon would lose. "We had all the details worked out for Kyle to lose the match against Takada around the ten-minute mark," said Sturgeon's former manager Clint Dahl. "I remember getting a call from him in Japan the night before the fight. He told me the Brazilians were egging him on to beat Takada anyway and deviate from the plan. I informed him that KRS had make it very clear that if Sturgeon doesn't do the job, he won't be coming back home." During the fight, Sturgeon threw a high kick a little too hard and dropped Takada to the canvas. Nervous that he would not get up, Sturgeon danced around, wasting enough time for

Takada to regain his composure. Takada submitted Sturgeon with a heel hook less than a minute later.

The win set up the rematch between Takada and Rickson Gracie; it took nearly ten minutes for the Brazilian to submit him this time. Despite over 30,000 people in attendance, Pride 4 would be the final event for KRS. The company sold Pride to Dreamstage Entertainment, which has driven the franchise to record attendance numbers, American pay-per-view and steady merchandise sales. Dreamstage knew it had to make an impact by leveraging the pro wrestling fanbase with real fighting. Takada was obviously someone they had to protect, but Kazushi Sakuraba became an unexpected star. His first Pride wins over Vernon White and Carlos Newton proved the victory over Conan Silveira at UFC Japan was no fluke. Though Sakuraba wasn't a big draw in Takada's wrestling promotion Kingdom (which replaced the failed UWFI), his skills as a shooter made him Pride's poster boy. He also has the distinction of defeating several Brazilian jiu-jitsu stylists like Vitor Belfort and four Gracies: Royler, Renzo, Ryan and Royce. Eventually, Sakuraba burned himself out by not maintaining his health (bad smoking and drinking habits) and fighting in too many matches against tough opposition.

Dreamstage follows a traditional pro wrestling strategy by building fighters up against tomato cans until they are ready to fight for a belt. Most cards are one-sided fights mixed with a couple of well-matched bouts. But the colorful characters, production design and raw energy are hard to dismiss. When Dreamstage first took over the organization, it relied on using Japanese pro wrestlers to drive ticket sales, but outside of Sakuraba, most couldn't cut it against top opponents. Dreamstage even tried promoting a pro wrestling bout between Takada and Alexander Otsuka at Pride 8, but it didn't seem to work. Now Pride has stars from Brazil, Russia and the US, along with a few Japanese thrown in for good measure. The organization, which changed to Pride Fighting Championships, has been unable to tap into the American market with weak PPV buys.

On August 28, 2002, Dreamstage pulled off its biggest show to date by cross-promoting with K-1, Japan's premier kickboxing organization. Shockwave 2002 or K-1 Dynamite (the promotion went by both names) drew 71,000 fans, the largest audience ever assembled for an MMA promotion. Since Dreamstage came onto the scene, it has signed several former UFC stars to its line-up, attempting to break ground with the US market. Pride even started hosting tournaments that became a big hit for new fans, who missed the drama of the early UFC format. But K-1 had a plan of its own and Pride found competition right in its own backyard.

*

MASTER KAZUYOSHI ISHII established seidokan karate schools around Osaka in the 1970s and staged countless karate tournaments during the late 1980s. In 1991, he worked for one year in the front office for Maeda's Rings organization, learning about pro wrestling angles and marketing stars – the missing ingredients to take his own promotion aspirations to the next level. In 1993, Ishii invented K-1, a splashy kickboxing show with colorful athletes and world-class production. "K" represented many martial arts styles (karate, kung fu, kickboxing) while "1" represented only one weight class: heavyweight. The K-1 Grand Prix became the hot ticket in Japan, where year after year the elite eight fighters from around the world met in tournament format. Dutchmen Ernesto Hoost and Peter Aerts became superstars, and with Fuji Television on board, the organization sold out shows all over Japan and in European countries. K-1 failed twice to break into the American market before establishing a smaller scale, successful production in Las Vegas in 1999.

Moving into 2000, the organization faced trouble as K-1's stars were getting old, Master Ishii was looking at jail time for tax evasion and Pride was gaining momentum. Enter Bob Sapp, a 377-pound, 6'4" former pro football player whose injuries sidelined a promising career. Sapp was spotted in a toughman contest against ex-Chicago Bears William "The Refrigerator" Perry. His sloppy skills beat the out-of-shape Perry, and K-1 liked his look. Taking a gamble, they decided to transform him into a fighter. Sapp was flown to Seattle, Washington, and began training kickboxing under the tutlege of K-1/UFC alumni Maurice Smith and submission wrestling under Matt Hume. K-1 allowed Sapp to fight for Pride first, and after destroying his opponent, Norihisa Yamamoto, he competed in several kickboxing matches with great success. The audience couldn't get enough of Sapp and loved his over-the-top personality and superhuman girth.

Nicknamed "The Beast," he bounced between Pride and K-1 until the latter made him their signature star. Sapp resurrected the K-1 franchise with dozens of sponsorship tie-ins and TV appearances, becoming a national icon in Japan. He even released a record entitled *Sapp Time*; the album cover ripping off Michael Jackson's *Thriller*. Sapp's unbelievable success transformed K-1 into something of a circus act by bringing in over-the-hill boxers like Francois Botha (who lost his first four K-1 bouts) and old sumo wrestlers like Yokozuna Akebono in the hopes of creating another Sapp. Unfortunately, K-1 lost all credibility as a kickboxing promotion in the process. (K-1 Max, featuring lightweight fighters, did earn the respect of honest kickboxing fans throughout the world.)

In 2003, K-1 signed a promotional contract with Mike Tyson, putting the company in the spotlight with a debut set for 2004. Even K-1 isn't safe from scrutiny and misinformation, as evidenced by this April 2004 quote from World Boxing Council president Jose Sulaiman. "The World Boxing Council deeply regrets the fact that the great world ex-heavyweight champion Mike Tyson is thinking of the possibility of contending in a sport known as K-1 which represents a huge and regrettable return to the most savage times in which respect to human life did not exist at all – as this 'sport' is one of the most violent and less humane practices anyone can ever witness." One week later, K-1 announced that Tyson would stick with boxing, under their new banner – Fighting Entertainment Group.

From a business standpoint, K-1 is the clear winner, becoming a profitable powerhouse relying on pro wrestling gimmickery over conventional sports wisdom. On December 10, 1994, K-1 promoted its first MMA bout between UFC alumni Kimo and Pat Smith, held in an octagon. K-1's top stars commented on the fight, saying it wasn't a real sport. Nearly a decade later, K-1 was promoting MMA-only cards, luring fighters from other organizations with top dollar purses. Ishii eventually stepped down from K-1, but never served a day in jail.

Despite decent ratings, Pride had its share of problems, and on January 8, 2003, a bombshell dropped on the MMA community. Pride President Naoto Morishita called a press conference to announce both a middleweight and heavyweight grand prix to be spread out over the coming months, then returned to his hotel room. At 12:20 AM, Morishita was found dead from an apparent suicide. Rumors surfaced that his death could be attributed to everything from a romantic affair gone awry to continuing pressure from Dreamstage brass to improve revenue figures. No one knew for sure and many thought Pride was offically dead. Nobuhiko Takada took over for the interim before Dreamstage hired Nobuyuki Sakakibara, who was Morishita's right hand man, to be the new president. Takada would now serve as General Director for the organization, but his role is rumored to be largely that of a public figurehead. With the change, Pride put plans to enter the US market (Dreamstage obtained a NSAC license in 2003.) on the backburner and started a sister organization called Pride Bushido showcasing lighter weight fighters.

December 31, 2003 will be a day that all Japanese fight fans remember. Pride Shockwave 2003 headlined Royce Gracie vs former Olympic judo medallist Hidehiko Yoshida; K-1 promoted its first MMA-heavy show with Sapp vs. Akebono; and Antonio Inoki assembled a lacklus-ter card borrowing stars from Pride and K-1. In the end, K-1 won the ratings war and made a statement that Pride wasn't the only show in town. As for Inoki, to this day, no one really knows just how much power he wields in Japan. Despite nearly destorying pro wrestling with the Ali debacle, his name has reached iconic proportions. After promoting MMA bouts in three separate promotions, Inoki took a formal position with K-1 after the company created a new organiza-tion, Romanex, to hold MMA-only shows on a regular basis.

ON FEBRUARY 15, 2002, Maeda officially promoted the last Rings Japan show. Rings couldn't compete with Pride and made the error of moving to shoots with closed-fist strikes. Most people thought this added credi-bility to the organization by enriching the promotion to compete against Pride, but Rings fans were pro wrestling fans. When stars like Kiyoshi Tamura could no longer be protected, the fanbase dried up. Rings Japan went through many ups and downs, but ended on a high note by producing two of the most interesting 32-man tournaments in the sport's history. Rings wasn't completely dead and continued to produce regular shows in Holland and Lithuania. Pride was more than happy to take Rings talent, cleaning them out with Brazilians Rodrigo "Minotauro" Nogueira and Ricardo Arona, Russian Fedor Emelianenko, and Dutchman Gilbert Yvel. Pride destroyed Tamura by having the 185-pounder face Wanderlei Silva and the monstrous Bob Sapp back to back, instead of rebuilding him as their new star.

Japan's Pancrase turned out many great champions under founder Masakatsu Funaki, including Ken and Frank Shamrock, Bas Rutten, Guy Mezger, Semmy Schilt and Yuki Kondo. In the late 1990s, the promotion lost steam and money, and even changed its rules to incor-porate closed fist strikes. By that time, the stars were gone and the fans were tuning into Pride. Founder Masakatsu Funaki competed in a retirement match against Rickson Gracie in Coliseum, a joint effort between Pancrase and Rings. Though Funaki lost by choke, he stayed on with the organization he created and became a film actor to boot. Today, Pancrase no longer sells out the major venues and is desper-ately trying to stay afloat.

The country's longest running and most consistent series, Shooto, stayed active by focusing on the lighter weight classes. Fighters like Rumina Sato, Hayato Sakurai, Takanori Gomi and Caol Uno became legends, but the promotion's appeal is strictly for hardcore fans. Sayato Sayama eventually left Shooto and turned back to his roots in pro wrestling, but Shooto has never promoted a worked match in its history.

FOOTNOTE: Japan is also responsible for paving the way for women in MMA. In August 1996, the U-Top Tournament assembled women from all over the world to fight. Despite rumored works, it set a precedent for the fairer sex to have their day in the ring. On December 5, 2000, Japan hosted the ReMix World Cup 2000, a 16-woman tournament with fighters from Japan, Russia, the US and Holland. The openweight class event showed just how far women had come in the sport, drawing over 6,500 attendees. Holland fighter Marloes Coenen swept the event by beating Japan's Megumi Yabushita by decision. The real showstopper saw Coenen, a nimble fighter weighing 150lbs, employ a flying arm bar to dispatch undefeated 200lbs-plus Becky Levi at 1:24. ReMix promoted one more show in 2001 before folding, while a smaller promotion, Smack Girl, continues to be the only all-woman MMA series in the world.

CHAPTER 25

MMA Around the World

BRAZIL

Brazilian vale tudo had dried up during the early 1990s until the UFC came along. The controversial decision in the Marco Ruas–Oleg Taktarov fight in Ultimate, Ultimate '95 prompted Frederico Lapenda to rebuild Ruas by starting the World Vale Tudo Championship (WVC). Debuting August 4, 1996, the first show was held in Japan, implementing the standard eight-man heavyweight tournament with few rules and bare fists. The headliner pitted Ruas against UFC III champ Steve Jennum. The ex-cop didn't stand a chance, while Taktarov, who faced Joe Charles, also won his match with ease.

Lapenda set up the rematch between Ruas and Taktarov for WVC 2 in Brazil, just eleven months after their first meeting. This time Ruas pummeled Taktarov for 30 minutes. The two battled toe to toe with no groundwork, but this was by design. "[Lapenda] wanted to make this fight look so good that he paid me extra money at the time," said Taktarov. "We reached an agreement where I would not fight Marco on the ground." According to Ruas, Lapenda told him he was not allowed to kick the Russian. "He said that if I kick, I have to pay Oleg $1,000. Then he said that I would have to fight with open hand. I refused, but said I wouldn't kick. Then during the fight, Oleg kick me first, so I kicked [back]. After the fight, Oleg's manager tried to sue and there were a lot of problems. Oleg agreed not to take me down." For 29 minutes, Taktarov stood and took a beating. As the final minute ticked away, Taktarov's corner said the word and the Russian took Ruas down immediately and established half mount just to show he could.

The match was ruled a draw under their agreement, since Ruas couldn't knock him out and the fight went the distance. "That fight was a draw because both of our hands were up when I was there," said Taktarov. "When everyone left, [Lapenda] raised Ruas's hand while he stood by himself." Only the shot of Ruas as the winner appeared on the video. Taktarov wanted to set up a third fight, but no one was interested. Ruas split with Lapenda soon after, but later befriended the Russian. The WVC promoted three events in Aruba and showcased world-class talent like Igor Vovchanchyn and Amar Suloev. On March 7, 2002, the WVC promoted its final show in Jamaica. Lapenda produced several documentaries, including the immensely popular *Smashing Machine*, starring former WVC star Mark Kerr. He currently lives in Los Angeles, working as a producer for Mandalay Entertainment.

Lapenda's original referee, former kickboxer Sergio Batarelli, started the International Vale Tudo Championship (IVC) when personal problems forced him to leave after WVC 4. Batarelli employed similar rules and built the show around Brazilian talent, but brought in several Westerners for the first event, held July 7, 1997. In the eight-man tournament, Gary Goodridge made it to the finals to face Pedro Otavio, who wore down his larger opponent on the ground. During the 16-minute match, Goodridge held Otavio in his guard, using his feet to keep him out of striking range. Goodridge's tactic worked until his toes started wiggling inside Otavio's trunks. "My foot slipped out the back of his pants, so I'm trying to pull them back and I felt his jock, so I thought, *why don't I just kick his jock out and I'll freakin' knee him in the nuts?*" remembered Goodridge. After a brief restart, the two fell into the same position, where Otavio complained to ref Batarelli about Goodridge's actions. Batarelli let them continue and Goodridge finally gained the upper hand, tapping out Otavio with strikes. Rumors circulated that Goodridge was playing footsie with Otavio's balls. "Sergio owed me $22,000 and told me that I ruined his show," said Goodridge. "I told him to keep the money and let's get a doctor to inspect his testicles. If there's anything wrong with them, you keep the money. They didn't want to go that route." On October 16, 1998, Batarelli co-promoted UFC Brazil, giving Americans their first glimpse at Brazilians Pedro Rizzo and Wanderlei Silva. The UFC never made it back to the country, but Batarelli pressed on, producing IVCs in Venezuela, Yugoslavia and Croatia. Eventually, he took a post heading up K-1's MMA shows in Brazil.

Two months after the inauguaral IVC, Pentagon Combat took place in Rio de Janeiro, setting up a grudge match between luta livre's Eugenio Tadeu and jiu-jitsu's Renzo Gracie. Ill will between these two fighting factions put this event in the history books for a different reason. According to event promoter Nelson Monteiro, ten minutes into their battle, "members of the luta livre group invaded the outer ring area and also started climbing the ring's lighting structure.

Because of the weight of the people, the light structure started collapsing." As tension built, the angry luta livre mob got out of hand, and someone stabbed Renzo in the back with a sharp object. "A riot broke out, complete anarchy, chairs were flying, fists were flying, even gunshots were being fired and all coming from the luta livre side," said Monteiro. Talk of banning vale tudo in Brazil worried fans, but eventually subsided after safer security measures became prevalent in future shows.

The rivalry between jiu-jitsu and luta livre eventually peteredout, but a milder rift surfaced between the Brazilian Top Team and the Chute Boxe Academy. Both Brazilian schools turned out top talent and Pride Fighting Championships had their hooks in both, keeping the conflict in the ring. Top Team emerged from a fallout between Carlson Gracie and his students. Under the leadership of Mario Sperry, the team consists of Murilo Bustamante, Ricardo Arona and identical twins Rogerio and Rodrigo Nogueira. Rodrigo can arguably be called the best heavyweight submission fighter in the world, using his long arms and legs to trap his opponents when they make a mistake. Hailing from Bahia, Brazil, he hungered for sports growing up, until a life-threatening accident at age 11. A bus plowed into the youngster, first leaving him in a coma, then without hope of walking for nearly two years. With badly scarred lungs that required thirteen operations, Rodrigo defied the odds, taking up boxing as part of his recuperation. Eventually he began training jiu-jitsu with Carlson Gracie disciples. In his twenties, he moved to Florida to join his mother and Rogerio. When Rodrigo started competing in Japan, first in Rings and then in Pride, he moved back to his native land and joined Brazilian Top Team. After becoming the 2000 Rings King of Kings champion, he moved over to Pride, defeating several marquee names to ultimately become the Pride heavyweight champion. Though he lost the title in 2003, Rodrigo sported (at the time of writing) an incredible record of 22-2-1, with 15 wins by way of submission. His favorite move is the triangle choke, but Rodrigo continually surprises his opponents by pulling submissions from any position.

In 1980, Rudimar Fedrigo opened the Chute Boxe Academy (Chute Boxe means Muay Thai in Brazil) in Curitiba, and assembled one of the toughest groups of fighters to ever come out of the country. Unlike most Brazilian teams, the Chute Boxe Academy relied more on striking as its base, though jiu-jitsu was part of the program as well. A war with capoeira fighters prompted Fedrigo to stage his first vale tudo event in 1991; Chute Boxe won all their matches. On November 1, 1996, Campeonato Brasileiro de Vale Tudo saw Chute Boxe student

Jose "Pele" Landi-jons win a four-man tournament, ending with a defeat over BJJ black belt Jorge "Macaco" Patino. The back and forth action lasted nearly 15 minutes, and it became one of the most talked about fights in Brazilian vale tudo history. Both men developed a hatred for one another, and Pele won the rematch at WVC 4 after Patino's overzealous efforts forced him out of the ring, stopping the fight on a cut. Though he was one of Fedrigo's first students, Pele left Chute Boxe in 2002, while strangely enough, Patino joined a year later. The team has fielded great fighters, including Murilo and Mauricio Rua and Anderson Silva (who eventually left), but when people think of the team, only one name comes to mind: Wanderlei Silva.

Without a doubt, he is the most ferocious specimen to ever step in the ring, with his menacing scowl, shaven, tattooed head and vicious fighting style. Silva earned his nickname "The Axe Murderer" from former UFC matchmaker John Peretti. As of this writing, he has never lost in Pride, racking up 15 wins, 12 by knockout, since his April 2000 decision loss to Tito Ortiz at UFC Japan 2. The current Pride middleweight champion grew up in Curitiba, and started training with the Chute Boxe Academy at age 13. Silva fought in several, bloody battles in Brazilian shows, and learned discipline with a brief tour in the army. At UFC Brazil, he wanted to show off his skills against Vitor Belfort, but didn't get the chance, as "The Phenom" crushed him in 53 seconds with strikes. Silva recommitted his work ethic, and at Pride he improves with every fight. His big test came at Pride 13 when he faced Kazushi Sakuraba, who had dispatched many top Brazilians, including Belfort. At 1:38 into the first round, Silva stomped Sakuraba's face into mush. He has since defeated Sakuraba twice, Guy Mezger and Quinton Jackson. Silva's popularity carried over to signing endorsement deals and doing Japanese commercials. After winning the Pride Grand Prix middleweight tournament, he seems content to punish whoever is brave enough to step in the ring with him.

Although Brazil has produced many top stars that have moved abroad, the scene within the country is stronger than ever. Brazilian shows eventually started adopting Pride rules to better prepare their athletes for the big time. Rudimar Fedrigo started Meca Vale Tudo in Curitiba in 2000, which became one of the country's top shows. His Chute Boxe student, Rafael Cordeiro, co-promotes Storm Samurai, a Muay Thai event. Wallid Ismail worked with Antonio Inoki to produce Jungle Fights in the Amazon. Rodrigo Nogueira got into the promotion game by starting Conquista Fight in Bahia. In July 2003, Heat Fighting Championship debuted in Natal, stepping up the Brazilian scene with better production value. Now some Westerners are gaining experience by competing in Brazil, further proof the sport has become a worldwide affair.

EUROPE

In January 1990, Akira Maeda traveled to Holland and met up with Chris Dolman, a multi-time sambo champion who carved his name by competing in stiff-worked pro wrestling matches in Japan. The two hatched an idea to take Maeda's Rings to the next level, and by March 1991, the Rings Fighting Network was born. Starting with Rings Holland run by Dolman, the promotion branched out to Russia, Georgia, Bulgaria, Australia and the US. Dolman is considered the godfather of European MMA, as he paved the way for homegrown talent to cross over into Rings, whether it be Holland, Russia or otherwise. The European Rings shows rarely promoted works, but the rules were the same, allowing for open-hand strikes, rope escapes and submissions.

Even with Rings taking off, the more brutal style of MMA reared its head in Europe. Headbutts, elbows and bare fists were commonplace. Men like "Dirty" Bob Schrijber, who had well over 100 kickboxing matches, didn't care; it was just another fight. In June 1993, Schrijber competed in his first Rings match upon winning the European Kickboxing Championship. He competed in one of the first closed-fist MMA bouts in Europe, called the Cage Fight Tournament, held in Belgium in January 1995. Due to lack of alternates and lack of submission experience, Schrijber fought twice and lost twice in the same night. He began training with Dolman, Remco Pardoel and others to understand the submission game. Schrijber's ring prowess was outmatched only by his looks, which included polka dot dye in his hair before he shaved it bald. As one of Holland's biggest stars, he hung up his gloves in October 2003 upon losing five of his last six matches.

Fellow kickboxer Gilbert "The Hurricane" Yvel also emerged as a household name among Dutch MMA purists. Though he never seriously studied traditional martial arts, he took up Thai boxing at age 16, and after winning the European Full Contact Karate Championship, he signed on with Rings Holland. There he enjoyed much success, knocking out opponents left and right, mostly using his long legs and knees. Schrijber handed Yvel his first major loss to win the finals of a European promotion called KO Power Tournament. Yvel had met his real mother for the first time two days before their fight and his mind was elsewhere. Schrijber had just lost to Yvel two months prior, and five years would pass before meeting a third time. In 2002, Yvel knocked his fellow countryman out after a gutsy war.

Yvel, along with brothers Valentijn and Alistair Overeem, Remco Pardoel and Semmy Schilt, formed Golden Glory. As Holland's premiere fighting team, they have competed in the US, Russia, Japan, Brazil and Aruba in the West Indies. "We train hard and we have the best trainers in Holland, who have produced many world champions," said Yvel. "Dutch people in general are pretty tall compared to fighters in other countries; it's a big advantage."

The man behind Golden Glory, Bas Boon, has also been the brain trust behind the Cage Fight Tournament events that broke new ground in Europe. He created Golden Glory after World Vale Tudo Championship 9 sparked interest in Dutch fighter Gilbert Yvel. He also took on American Heath Herring, whose B-level fighter status became a thing of the past after some time spent with the rest of the crew. Boon has put Golden Glory fighters in the UFC, Pride, and of course, several Holland promotions. 2 Hot 2 Handle is the flagship promotion in Holland, complete with laser light shows, a magic act and even a minature blimp that flies over the crowd. Boon has co-promoted shows in several European countries, including Germany and Russia. Georgy Kobylyansky, who co-promoted the inaugural IFC, started up the first Russian organization, Absolute Fighting Championship, but M-1 Mix-Fight has been the country's top show since 1997. The promotion builds fighters for the Red Devil Team, taking its name from a popular energy drink that also sponsors M-1, allowing Boon to cross-promote using his fighters.

CHRIS DOLMAN AND Rings also heavily influenced the UK scene. Bob Schrijber turned Lee Hasdell onto Rings after his pro kickboxing career grew stagnant. "Maeda saw me and invited me to study with him in Japan, so two months later I went to Rings Japan," said Hasdell The softly-spoken Brit eventually formed Night of the Samurai, one of the UK's first promotions using rules similar to Rings, but it didn't last long. As British fighters began learning submission, other promotions came along. Since December 5, 1999, Andy Jardine's Millennium Brawl has given rising British talent an opportunity to compete at home. Cage Warriors Fighting Championships debuted in 2002, and promises to step things up to an international level. While Jardine admits he hasn't become wealthy from his shows, he's committed to doing anything to further the sport and has showcased top UK talent including Dexter Casey, Ian Freeman, James Zikic and Lee Murray.

Mark Weir is something of an anomaly. He took up martial arts for the most basic need: survival. Growing up in a racially biased neighborhood, Weir needed protection and took up boxing, judo and later tae kwon do. Martial arts was something that made his life complete, not just a hobby or an extension of childhood rage. After winning two tournament championships, Weir lost his motivation and tae kwon do lost its luster. Everything changed after he saw the UFC. "Anybody who's looking to actually improve in martial arts as a whole will eventually end up in MMA, no matter what foundations or background you have."

Britain is not that influential in the MMA world, as few competitors have fought abroad in bigger shows. The country is far behind Russia and Holland, which have both produced top names. Weir notes that part of the problem lies in the fact that martial arts never really took off as a whole in Britain: unlike judo's wide acceptance in France, and Thai boxing's popularity in Holland, Britain never really claimed an art or a system of its own. Boxing is still the king of combat sports in Britain, where the Queensberry Rules originated. "[MMA] is new to this country; [Britain] is only beginning to accept it and they're airing more about the sport on national TV," said Weir. He also notes that jiu-jitsu wasn't an attractive sport to the British, who mistakenly linked it to no-holds-barred fighting instead of seeing it as a stand-alone art. Only when UFC and MMA videotapes surfaced in the country did more people want to learn submission fighting.

Weir admits that expecting to make money from fighting in MMA is not the best way to look at it. He started martial arts to improve himself and his self-confidence, and chose to take things further by continually testing himself against world class opponents. "If I can hold my own against them I know that my skill level and my outlook in martial arts has been justified." Weir's goal is to stay in the sport, not just as a fighter but as a coach and role model to others following a similar path.

Britain's most active fighter is Ian Freeman, who has competed in Japan, Holland, Russia and the US. He never really had a martial arts background *per se*, but learned boxing at age 20. "I was more of a brawler than a boxer," said Freeman, who migrated to jiu-jitsu after his fists failed to subdue an opponent when he was 32 years old. He never really understood groundfighting until real life showed him what he was missing. Freeman was even puzzled by watching the early UFCs, wondering why they weren't standing up and fighting. After taking jiu-jitsu and finding success in his club, Freeman ventured out to test himself: part martial arts, part machismo practice. He found there was still much to learn.

On March 10, 2000, Freeman became the first Brit to compete in the UFC, fighting submission specialist Scott Adams on four days' notice. Freeman even paid for his own airfare. The match stayed competitive until both men went for leg locks. "Scott snapped the ligaments in my ankle three times in that fight and afterwards I had to have a cast put on my leg," said Freeman. "I never knew how far the UK was behind the USA in terms of fighting until I entered the UFC. I was beating the best in the UK in under five minutes, but it's a big step when you fight in America."

Freeman admits that Britain needs a wake-up call if it wants its fighters to get ahead of the game. His fights all over the world have prepared him for the best and worst competition. After losing to Adams, he had varied success worldwide. Freeman later chronicled his exploits in an autobiography, *The Machine*, in 2001, which described his moving from a nine-to-five job as a salesman to an ultimate fighter. "Along the way I was beaten up by a gang of skinheads and spent a long time in the hospital, going into deep depression. I gained acceptance as a streetfighter in my hometown and began to lead an army of doormen. It is funny, [contains] horrific fight scenes and most of all, it's enjoyable to read." Freeman loves fighting all over the world and gets the opportunity to meet so many different types of people. In 2004, he started his own fight promotion, Pride & Glory. The fans keep him going as well. Nothing will stop "The Machine."

BRITAIN AND THE rest of Europe is growing more supportive of MMA. In 2001, the British Association of Mixed Martial Arts was established to bring attention to the sport. The rising number of European competitors means the sport's popularity will no longer be anchored by the US, Brazil and Japan alone. The grassroots movement, along with promoters and pioneers like Bas Boon, Lee Hasdell, Bas Rutten, and Andy Jardine, has sustained the growth of a sport whose flame has no chance of dying out … not now, not ever.

In 2002, Zuffa introduced a regular TV program on the UFC to the UK market (on Sky). It failed to find an audience, but Zuffa was able to secure a pay-per-view deal for their shows. On July 13, 2002, UFC 38 was held at the famous Royal Albert Hall in London. The show was a huge success, with Mark Weir defeating Eugene Jackson with the fastest knockout in UFC history: ten seconds. Ian Freeman shocked everyone by beating down Frank Mir, forcing a ref stoppage, and dedicated the fight to his father, who was in a nearby hospital, only to learn his father had passed away the night before the match. His family didn't want to upset him with the news, knowing Freeman's father would have wanted him to do his best.

The event ended with an after-fight party that once again supplied extra fireworks. At a nearby bar, a friendly bit of rough-housing escalated into a streetfight involving then UFC light heavyweight champ Tito Ortiz and Britain's Lee Murray. "Tito came right at me and hit me in the ear," said Murray, who gave his account to Dutch journalist Wiggert Meerman. "We clinched, and I punched him two straight ones, two uppercuts, and then he went down, and I kicked him in the face." Murray, who had a rep for his powerful hands, made a name for himself in the States, but it didn't get him any offers. He knocked out Jose Landi-jons in a local event exactly one year after UFC 38, earning his shot in the UFC six months later and a long-term contract.

In 2003, Granada, the UK company responsible for the infamous Michael Jackson exposé, produced Ultimate Warriors, a thirteen-hour look at MMA and other combative sports. Camera crews were dispatched to the US, Japan, Thailand and throughout Europe, interviewing hundreds of people. To date, it is the most comprehensive documentary series ever produced on the subject.

CANADA

Two years after Extreme Fighting 2's debacle, Mike Thomas worked with Quebec's gaming commission to bridge the relationship with the Mohawks. Thomas, a Mohawk native, befriended the commission and gained clearance for the IFC to hold the first sanctioned Canadian event on May 30, 1998. Dubbed Montreal Cage Combat, the show was a success, ending with Vladimir Matyushenko defeating Anthony Macias in fifteen seconds. The rules disallowed punching with a closed fist to the head on the ground, but the commission reinstated the tactic for future events.

Quebec-born Stephane Patry was soon approached to serve as director of operations for the company, since Thomas needed someone who could speak French and understood the game. Patry had successfully lobbied the Canadian Radio-Television and Telecommunications Commission to bring the UFC back to pay-per-view. He had also worked with SEG to translate press releases into French for the Quebec press and serve as the French color commentator for UFC PPVs. Patry managed several French fighters, who participated in the Montreal IFC events. After working on two shows, he left the organization over "creative differences," and in February 2000, co-founded the Universal Combat Challenge. (The IFC never promoted another event in Canada after its January 2000 show.) Patry teamed up with New York-born Pete Rodley, whose passion for the sport was just as strong. After moving to Ontario, Rodley took up karate at the same school that produced the UFC's first Canadian entry, Harold Howard. Later Rodley managed fighters who competed against Patry's in the IFC, for which he also worked as an Ontario liason. "We wanted to build the sport so we could pay them what they could be paid," said Rodley. "We wanted to give the fans what we felt they deserved and there were no bigger fans than me and Stephane."

With Patry as President and Rodley as VP, the UCC held its first show on June 2, 2000. Their headliner fell apart when Kimo no-showed due to injury and Canadian Kristophe Midoux pulled out after a car accident. The main event of Australian Elvis Sinosic vs Canada's own Dave Beneteau ended up being a snoozer, but the first UCC was a learning experience. The organization had its work cut out in rebuilding the relationship with fans miffed over Kimo's absence.

UCC 6: Redemption, held October 19, 2001, was the turning point for the promotion when Patry signed former ranked pro boxer Stephane Ouellet. Quebec rallied behind the boxer and Patry felt the big name could double his audience. Ouellet destroyed Jeff Davis in six seconds, and the UCC sold out a venue of 6,000 compared to 3,000 from previous shows. The ploy worked to familiarize fans with UCC stars like David "The Crow" Loiseau, Shawn "Pain" Peters and Justin Bruckman. Ouellet was no match for Peters in the following event, however, and disqualified himself with illegal headbutts. The crowd embraced Peters, who everyone thought would be another Ouellet casualty. With his frazzled beard, crazied eyes and off-the-wall antics (riding a motorcycle down to the ring while wearing a *Halloween* Michael Myers mask), Peters surfaced as one of the country's biggest stars. Loiseau, with his lightning fast hands, also become a breakout hit with the audience. Born in Montreal, the bilingual Loiseau would rev up the crowd saying, "What time is it? It's Crow Time!" Despite the promotion's lack of heavyweights, it compiled a stable of lighter weight fighters, each with their own style and appeal that works for the culturally diverse audience.

Gary Goodridge and Carlos Newton are Canada's most well-known fighters. While Goodridge made waves all over the world with his colorful persona, Newton's path was guided by something more spiritual. At age 16, Newton, who emigrated from the British Virgin Islands to Vancouver, Canada, was introduced to *The Book of Five Rings*, written by a samurai warrior named Miyamoto Musashi in 1645. "I was drawn to seeking the path of the warrior and being a fighter by living my life through contest," said Newton. A break-up with his girlfriend and lack of concentration in the ring sent him on a worldwide quest to find himself. At age 20, he assumed the role of ronin, or masterless samurai, and lived in Japan, Australia, Thailand, Greece and Egypt over a two-year period. In May 2001, Newton was a changed man and stepped up to face Pat Miletich for the UFC welterweight title. He caught Miletich with a side choke in the third round, and joyously performed his trademark move by firing an imaginary energy ball – a reference to the Japanese animae *Dragonball Z*. While Newton lost his first title defense, his graceful demeanor and skills have made him a hot property in both Pride and the UFC for years. Preparing to enter medical school, Newton, whose nickname is Ronin, is the epitome of dedication, heart and showmanship.

With pay-per-view, a sister show building new fighters, frequent coverage on free TV, a bevy of high-profile sponsors (Coors Light, Pepsi) and a fighter-centric website, the UCC was hailed as arguably the second best promotion in North America behind the UFC. But outside of Canada, no one was really paying attention. The UCC brought in a few fighters from America and Brazil, and even held a cross-promotion in Hawaii, but couldn't turn heads outside of Quebec. That changed on January 25, 2003, when the UCC took a chance by headlining its twelfth show with two big American names: Duane Ludwig vs Jens Pulver. The rest of the event was packed solid with top Canadian talent like Georges St. Pierre and Steve Vigneault, along with four other Americans. For the 3,500 in attendance, it was the best UCC ever produced, lighting up message boards and MMA Internet news sites, talking up Ludwig's demolition of Pulver at 1:13 into the first round.

Ironically, the show everyone touted as a major achievement also sent shockwaves through the MMA community over allegations of unpaid fighters and unreturned phone calls. MMA forums were used as a virtual battlefield for President Stephane Patry to defend his position against countless people wanting answers. Joe Ferraro was co-founder of Showdown Fight Wear, one of UCC's first sponsors. He eventually served under Patry in several capacities, from commentator to VP of Talent Relations. As time went on, he felt the heat of what he called "shady" business practices. "I was the clean-up man for years, for various 'messes' [Stephane] would create," alleged Ferraro. "From manager Monte Cox to a DVD replication house to everyone in between, I would be the sound board of how everyone and their brother was owed money." Patry didn't want to comment on specific allegations, but says, "The UCC was losing money, a lot of money especially after the UCC 8 and UCC 12 fiascos. I was the only one in this company putting money in show after show right after UCC 3." (After all the momentum built from UCC 7, the eighth show was held in Rimouski, Quebec, ten hours north of Montreal; attendance was less than 1,000.)

Pete Rodley, who didn't even attend UCC 12, was fed up and wanted out. "[Stephane] was surprised I didn't attend the show, but I told him it would be a good idea if I did not see him person at this time," said Rodley. He says Patry frequently contradicted him behind his back and could no longer take it. "For over three years I would defend his actions and make good for his lies. After realizing this trend was not going to end, I had to preserve my reputation and bow out of the project." Rodley left the organization and sold his shares of the company to Patry. Ferraro unwillingly took over as VP, despite being owed money himself.

On September 6, 2003, the UCC became TKO Communications and started promoting events as usual. But the problems didn't go away and some of Patry's most trusted employees were finding it difficult to stay on board. By November 2003, color commentator JT McCarthy and Joe Ferraro had resigned. Canadian MMA forums were swamped with threads concerning Ferraro's departure, and subsequent defection to a new Canadian promotion—Shut Up and Fight (SUAF). "Rumors floated around about money, dirty politics and shady relationships," said Ferraro, "but the big one concerned a merger between two bitter enemies, Patry and Mark Pavelich." Pavelich had set up shop in Alberta, and promoted Maximum Fighting Championships since March 2001. Despite 2,300 miles separating them, Pavelich and Patry allegedly tried to put eachother out of business through fighter exclusivity contracts, forum trolling and personal bickering. Strangely enough, both men set aside their differences, forming a relationship to own Canada's MMA scene. Pavelich took over for Ferraro as VP of TKO, and Patry became VP of MFC.

Their first order of business, according to Ferraro, was to shut down Shut Up. Ferraro says Pavelich, on advice from Patry, began contacting authorities, sponsors, local papers and local radio stations that an illegal, unsanctioned event was taking place in British Columbia. "Everything the MMA community was used to fighting against, all the education we bestowed on the ignorant, was used against us ... by one of our own," said Ferraro. Patry vehemently denies any involvement with the SUAF situation, saying he was working 20-hour days on TKO 14 at the time. True, the event was non-sanctioned, but seven events had already taken place in the same city and the local government was fully aware and approved SUAF to take place. On December 5, 2003, just one day before showtime, the Canadian government shut down the event. "British Columbia can no longer hold events, and December 6 will always be known as 'black Friday' to Canadian MMA fans," said Ferraro. After the SUAF incident, there was never any mention of Patry and Pavelich working together and MFC never promoted again.

A new fight promotion, Apex Championship Fighting, emerged in 2004 with Alex Caporicci, a former TKO financial backer, at the helm. With shows set in Patry's backyard of Montreal, problems have already emerged as the TKO promoter strong-armed one fight team out of putting talent on the Apex card. TKO is still running shows today, but tension remains high, forcing promotions to fight amongst themselves instead of focusing on what's important.

Nothing behind the scenes will keep a fresh crop of fighters from making a name for themselves. Three TKO stars, David Loiseau, Georges St. Pierre and Patric Cote, recently made it to the UFC. The country produces more and more fighters every year, ready for the big leagues. "Canadians have always done well at sports you can train indoors at because of our harsh winters," said Donald Boswell, who heads up the Calgary combat sports commission. "Fighting and competing hard has always been part of being a Canadian. For a country with such a small population, I believe our pugilistic record speaks for itself."

Showdown, the company founded by Ferraro, along with partners Danny Yen, Paul Mitchell and Mike McNeil, keeps the scene alive in Ontario, running the country's only MMA store and magazine of the same name. Ontario is the mecca for the sport in Canada, just as California is in the States, and the comparison extends to sanctioning. "Ontario has the greatest concentration of MMA athletes and fans," said Yen. "And yet our fighters have to drive six hours to the nearest sanctioned province [Quebec] to compete when they live only thirty minutes away from each other." Boswell believes Ontario is close to giving MMA a trial run, much like Quebec did in 1998. "The recent fiasco in British Columbia showed us you have to do it right from the get go," he said.

Canada boasts one of the highest per-capita audiences for the sport. TKO has started releasing DVDs, and managed to keep its pay-per-view deal, despite losing some sponsors and owing money according to Rodley. Canadian pay-per-view and free television frequently broadcast shows from other countries as well. Rodley concluded, "After the events of the last several years, we all know who is who in the Canadian MMA scene. I think the scene is blessed with some great minds from coast to coast which could only mean that the sky is the limit for MMA in the great white north."

APPENDIX

THE BEST OF TANK ABBOTT

L OVE HIM OR hate him, David "Tank" Abbott was never at a loss for words. During three interviews with Abbott (all of which took place via phone from an undisclosed bar), he had plenty to say and talked for hours. From his UFC appearances and interviews conducted for this book, here are some of his more revealing quotes:

On growing up

I was brought up during Reaganomics, and there were a lot of people who shouldn't have had money, but did. At that time, I had a lot of resentment toward that because my parents didn't think the same way I did. So I was like, "Who the fuck are these guys?" I hung around with their group because they saw me as an asset. I was like their trained pet who would beat the hell out of anyone who got too close. But they didn't realize that they were my trained pet because I was enjoying all of their stuff – climbing on their boats, going out partying, doing their women because I'm their trained chimp.

How much of Tank is David Abbott?
Both of them are me. If you cross my path, you're fucked brother.

Tank says that he is the first one to have a real fight in the octagon. Well, tell that to Andy Anderson, who lost sight out of one eye (see Chapter 8).

That was a joke and a half! Those guys couldn't even hold a candle to my jock strap, brother! That is ridiculous! They couldn't even trim my toenails and you're telling me that "Oh, they had a real – FUCK!" I've seen two drunks have a real fight in a bar! And you're telling me that was a real fight! It's because they didn't have an interest in fighting the Gracies, but they were absolute garbage! Those guys are trash! Do you understand what I'm saying to you or not? For the first five shows of the Ultimate Fighting, it was the biggest joke, professional work – all to put the Gracies over and to sell their stupid, fucking martial arts that any stupid, average guy could learn. So you are telling me that two jokers that might as well be throwing water balloons at each other are being tough guys? They were the absolute jokers of the century! For you to say that these guys ...

(The Author) *No, I'm not saying it was any kind of great match with great technique, but it was a no-holds-barred match.*
Yeah, so is my mother and grandmother when they go at it! It doesn't make any difference, it's still girls fighting. But please don't tell me about two doughboys, pieces of shit that were set up for the Gracies to beat. That was a joke! Those are not fighters! They are absolute jokers, but if you want to use them as fighters, go ahead, but you are terribly, terribly wrong!

Have you ever got your ass kicked on the street?
Yeah. There have been three or four times where I've gotten the living fucking piss kicked out of me. I got beat up by four Samoans one time. I couldn't sleep for three days because I couldn't put my head down. The cops called me and said, "Hey, let's put these guys down," and I said, "Hey man, it's my turn for my ticket to get punched."

Fighting and Fame

I have 13 arrests for various convictions for fighting in public to attempted murder. I have four convictions ... I have served seven months in prison because bottom line is this: I'm not a bully; there are two willing participants that want to fight and then someone ends up on the short end of the stick. But when someone ends up on the short end of the stick so many times, they have to finally say that someone has a problem because you have so many pencil-pushing jackoffs who want to cause a problem. Modern society has adopted this philosophy that explains it and this is it: we are the weak and we are going to band together against people who can impose their will against us. That's why all the fuckers in Ultimate Fighting—they are not fighters, they are ultimate jokers. They are ultimate posers, every single one of them, and the biggest one is Ken Shamrock. He's not a fighter; he's a joke. Let me explain something to you. I'm in the professional wrestling business. You want to know what the number one fucking claim by professional wrestling is? I want to be famous for something that's easy! Ken Shamrock wants to be famous, and that's his whole motivation in life. He was a professional wrestler before he ever got into professional fighting. He's an absolute jokeaholic. He's a steroided, 180lb joke. He ain't nothing but a joke. He had two times to fight me and he ran! And you want to know what? A fighter does not care about losing. This is supposed to be about real fucking fighting, and this is supposed to be about doing jail time for your passion. I am Nelson Mandela of fucking no-holds-barred, but no one seems to get that because they all want to fucking live vicariously through a joker that says if you own my book of tools, you can be tough too. It's a joke!

Pre-fight Interview for UFC VI

My name is Tank Abbott. I'm going to be the most athletic person that has ever stepped into the octagon. That, coupled with my experience, will definitely make me the UFC VI champ.

Watching tape of his win over Paul Varelans at UFC VI

I'm starting to get sexually aroused so you better take that off.

Talking about his suspension at UFC X

When I count days, I'm counting days to get out of a cage. Now I'm counting days, 70 and running, to get back into a cage. You've seen the Discovery Channel. You've seen some animals rip apart a gazelle. That's what's going to happen.

Jeff Blatnick asks Tank about respecting the traditional martial arts

Well that's for Don "The Dragonfly" Wilson and let him go do ... where's he at? He's probably making a Godzilla voiceover that you'll see at three in the morning.

On Shamrock vs Severn II

You saw Glamrock and you saw Freddie Mercury-lookalike or whatever. They fought for 27 minutes and they all hid behind a second clock of a hand. They didn't go out there to fight. When I go in there, I'm not going in there to win. I'm going out there to fight!

After defeating Cal Worsham at Ultimate Ultimate '96

My fire is basically all about fighting. I'm a warrior ... if I wouldn't be in the octagon, I'd be in a bar, I'd be in an intersection – fighting.

After knocking out Steve Nelmark at Ultimate Ultimate '96

I'm healthy ... I'm like fire through bushes, baby. I do all my talking in the ring. It ended up the way it should. He was staggering, but he wasn't hurt. That's all part of the fight game. If you get on Queer Street, you make a right turn and get back to Main. I was just on him and not letting him turn.

Tony Blauer asks Tank if this is retribution for getting into the finals again at Ultimate Ultimate '96

I just come here to fight and it don't matter. Win or lose, I still put a ... there's an ass-kicking either way. One goes on me or the other person. I'm not part of the quick-tap club ... I go out there to bang.

Bruce Beck asks Tank about Shamrock

He's appropriately named Sham-rock. He's a fake. He's a fraud. He's a sham.

BAS RUTTEN: THE FLYING DUTCHMAN

WITH HIS SINISTER smile and mesmerizing eyes, the bald, charismatic Bas Rutten can not only claim to be the most famous European mixed martial artist, but also a Renaissance man with a carefree way of juggling everything life has to offer. He kicks ass too.

Rutten's trademark jumping splits and aggressive fighting style started with a twelve-year-old boy wandering into a French cinema to catch a glimpse of Bruce Lee in *Enter the Dragon*. He grew up in Holland with very conservative parents and was not allowed to partake in any type of martial arts. As a young teen, he faced constant taunting from other children because he suffered badly from the skin condition eczema. "My hands were so bad that I couldn't even grip a pen at times," said Rutten, who often wore gloves to protect them. He had bad asthma to boot.

Rutten's parents finally allowed him to take up tae kwon do at age 14. As the skin disease cleared up, he set out for revenge on those who had persecuted him. "After two weeks, I broke somebody's nose in a street fight and that was it, no more martial arts." Moving out of the house at age 20, Rutten took up kyokushinkai karate and tae kwon do, subsequently earning black belts in both. He enjoyed performing katas because the breathing exercises helped to control his asthma.

Balancing his college work, Rutten became a cook specializing in French cuisine before working as a bouncer, which paid more money in less time and allowed him to take better classes at a neighboring college. It also afforded him more time to train and he eventually took up Thai boxing as a more effective form of street defense than his traditional training. One of his training partners was 15-year-old Peter Aerts, who went on to become one of K-1's greatest stars. Rutten participated in his first Thai boxing match just three weeks after training and knocked his opponent out in the first round.

Rutten won 14 straight matches, but also found the rough and tumble streets of Amsterdam an irresistible attraction. He often spent nights in jail after rousing, drink-soaked parties, and had effectively given up the sport until an unlikely New Year's celebration at age 26. Drunk and out of hand, Rutten unknowingly agreed to take on well-known stand-up fighter Frank Lobman two months later. The promoters reminded him four weeks before the fight; Rutten had completely forgotten. "I realized that I had said yes, so I started training. At that time, I had not trained in four years, so I couldn't even finish my warm-up with rope skipping." Rutten lost by TKO.

In an effort to set things straight, he stepped up his training to fight top Dutch kickboxer Rene Rooze. Rutten dominated the first round, but Rooze developed a case of Tysonitis and bit a hole in his ear during the second round. "I told him to let go, he didn't, so I kneed him in the groin as hard as I could, and the whole audience started to fight," said Rutten, who had brought 30 bouncer friends to watch. The ensuing brawl ended the fight.

His final match came on the heels of a four-day sentence in jail. "One day before the fight [against France's Alexes Burger], they turned me loose, but I had caught an infection in one of my balls. I decided to fight anyway. I knocked the guy down three times during the first round, but I couldn't come out to the second round because I was cramped."

Rutten decided to retire after that second loss, realizing his fans were no longer with him. He found work doing martial arts shows around Holland, where he used his athleticism and uncanny comedic timing to entertain live audiences. The shows turned out to be so popular that Rutten soon found himself on Dutch TV and then European TV. "There were a lot of acrobatic jumps and kicks and stuff like that. We made it very funny."

Chris Dolman approached Rutten at one show and asked if he would consider trying out for Rings. Rutten resisted at first, not wanting to make the nearly two-hour drive to Amsterdam from his home in Idolan to train. He worked out with Dolman a handful of times and, as luck would have it, he was at the right place at the right time on one particular night. Pro wrestlers Masakatsu Funaki and Minoru Suzuki were scouting for their new shoot promotion, Pancrase, and wanted to see if Dolman had any notables in his midst. "One of the Rings Holland guys tried to put the pressure on me to show off in front of them and I ended up kicking him in the head and sending him to the hospital for stitches," said Rutten. "Five weeks later and I was fighting in Pancrase."

On September 21, 1993, Rutten made his MMA debut in the inaugural Pancrase event against Ryushi Yanagisawa, but first he had to take care of a little problem. Though his asthma had been attributed to stress while competing in Holland, Rutten felt relaxed in Japan, but needed an extra reminder. "I was always really relaxed until somebody hit me, and then I totally lost it. That's not good because sometimes you have to fight more than one round. That's dangerous because you can lose all your power." So before stepping into the ring, Rutten painted large Rs on his wrists. Since Pancrase was open-hand fighting, he would be able to see the Rs to reference "rustick", which means "relax" in Dutch. "The next time that somebody hit me, I look at my hands and say to myself, 'Relax Bas, relax, relax.'" Rutten knocked out Yanagisawa in 43 seconds and completed his new career start in a unique fashion. Taking a tip from his days as a martial arts performer, Rutten leapt up and did the splits, repeating it to each corner. The crowd went wild. "I had so much adrenaline in my body that I just jumped up [and it] became my trademark after that. Sometimes I did it for fun, but never in the ring."

If Rutten wanted to become the next big thing, he needed to learn submission fighting, something he was unfamiliar with until Pancrase founder Funaki submitted him in his third match. "They called me for a meeting and I thought, *that's it*. That's when I thought they were going to ask me to start doing fixed fights," said Rutten, who had heard the rumors about Japanese promotions. "Instead, they invited me to dinner and gave me a book and told me to study it." Yoshiaki Fujiwara penned the book, which described in great detail the submission holds he had learned from Karl Gotch.

Rutten was well on his way to becoming a superstar, but after losing once to Frank Shamrock and twice to Ken Shamrock, he swore he would never lose again and started grappling twice a day. From April 1995 to September 1998, he won 18 matches and had one draw. On September 1, 1995, Rutten won his first King of Pancrase title, and after besting such luminaries as Maurice Smith, Frank Shamrock and Guy Mezger, he defeated Pancrase founder Funaki on September 7, 1996, to win his second KOP title. "He was incredible and it took a lot of conditioning to beat him," said Rutten.

Of course, the wild side of Bas Rutten came out every once in awhile. Visiting Sweden in 1997, he found himself inebriated in a local pub where everyone knew who he was. "The bouncers there were called Mafia Bouncers and they pushed me between two doors into the marble stairway, the fire escape. They told me to leave and I said okay, but [I needed] to tell my friend that I was leaving and that I'll be gone. One guy started pushing my chest with his finger and I told him not to touch me." One more push created the swell of anger within him. Then one of the bouncers poked Rutten in the eye. "While I was holding my eye, he poked my other eye too. That's when I knocked him out and then all hell broke loose. I ended up fighting five bouncers and that was pretty rough. Three of them ended up in the hospital; they were pretty hurt. I had an instructional series at the time, so in the newspaper they put the picture demonstrating my street defense."

After winning the King of Pancrase for the third time, Rutten had accomplished all his goals in Japan. A meeting with UFC matchmaker John Perretti gave him the opportunity to test his skills in the US. "I fought guys who had won in the UFC and became champions, so I thought that it isn't much of a difference," said Rutten. On January 8, 1999, he fought Tsuyoshi Kosaka at UFC 18 and knocked him out after an exhausting war. He earned a shot at the heavyweight title against Kevin Randleman at UFC 20. The gruelling match that followed was nearly cut short four minutes in when it appeared Randleman had won by cut. "What many don't know is that I have a silicon nose," said Rutten, who kept going and won by a slim decision. This match went on to become one of the most controversial bouts in UFC history, forcing SEG to implement five-minute rounds to structure the judging process. Today, the UFC uses five five-minute rounds for title bouts and three five-minute rounds for non-title matches.

Riddled with injuries, Rutten took some time off and, with the UFC losing the pay-per-view battle at the time, he wasn't missing anything. He stayed in America and found he liked it much more than Holland. Today, he lives there with his wife Karin and his two daughters. He turned to acting, taking parts in Sammo Hung's short-lived martial arts series *Martial Law*, and in 2002 played opposite Pancrase founder Funaki, fighting him to a duel in the Japanese co-promotion, *Shadow Fury*.

Rutten shows no signs of slowing down and is still the life of the party. He attended a fight in Hawaii in May 2002, and after a drunken but relatively tranquil evening, he returned to his hotel room. With so much liquior in his system, Rutten took a shower before bedtime. "When I got out, for some reason, I knocked out the toilet with my head," laughed Rutten. "The whole fucking thing exploded into a hundred pieces. It looked like a ritual killing with blood everywhere." Tired and out of his mind, Rutten simply threw some blankets down and passed out. The next morning, he woke up to find a new toilet had been fitted. Apparently his fight with the porcelain god had flooded the entire 35th floor of the hotel. Security entered his room, the hotel cleaned everything up, replaced the toilet, and on top of that, gave everyone on the floor a complimentary breakfast for their toubles. Rutten kept a piece of the broken toilet as a souvenir.

Rutten went on to serve as color commentator for Pride Fighting Championships and to release *Bas Rutten's Big Books of Combat*, an illustrated look at the techniques that made him famous. He continues to act in low budget action films, even starring as the lead in *The Eliminator*, in which he fights Marco Ruas. Rest assured, no matter where he is, Bas Rutten is flying high.

75 SELECTED EVENT RESULTS

KEY

How was the match stopped?

TO	Tap Out
RS	Referee Stoppage
TWL	Corner throws in the towel
DS	Doctor Stoppage
DRW	Draw
D	Decision
NOC	No Contest
KO	Knock out
DQ	Disqualification

What was the match stopped with?

S	Strikes (punch, kick, knee, elbow)
RNC	Rear Naked Choke (RC – Rear Choke)
GC	Guillotine Choke
AB	Arm Bar
FC	Forearm Choke, Front Choke, Reverse Choke
AC	Arm Choke, Arm Triangle, Cross Arm Choke, Side Choke
KL	Key Lock, Arm Lock, Americana, Kimura, Hammer Lock
HH	Heel Hook, Ankle Lock
TC	Triangle Choke
NC	Neck Crank
KB	Knee Bar
BN	Broken Nose
O	Fighter Fatigue
C	Cut, Injury

All shows took place in continental USA, unless otherwise noted.
Organizations do not have universal times for rounds, so only the total fight time is tallied. (UFC uses five minute rounds, while Pride has one ten-minute round and one or two five-minute rounds)

10/30/84 Vale Tudo No Maracanãzinho (Brazil)

Eugenio Tadeu defeated Renan Pitanguy	5:02	KO
Marco Ruas drew with Fernando Pinduka	20:00	DRW
Ignacio Aragao defeated Bruce Lucio	2:27	TO (RNC)
Marcelo Behring defeated Flavio Molina	3:30	RS (S)
Rei Zulu defeated Sergio Batarelli	2:24	TO (GC)

09/21/93 Pancrase (Japan)

Minoru Suzuki defeated Katsuomi Inagaki	3:25	TO (RNC)
Bas Rutten defeated Ryushi Yanagisawa	0:43	KO
Takaku Fuke defeated Vernon White	1:19	TO (AB)
Yoshiki Takahashi defeated George Weingeroff	1:23	KO
Ken Shamrock defeated Masakatsu Funaki	6:15	TO (RNC)

11/12/93 Ultimate Fighting Championship

Gerard Gordeau defeated Teila Tuli	0:26	DS (C)
Kevin Rosier defeated Zane Frazier	4:16	TWL (S)
Royce Gracie defeated Art Jimmerson	2:10	TO (O)
Ken Shamrock defeated Pat Smith	1:49	TO (HH)
Gerard Gordeau defeated Kevin Rosier	0:57	TWL (S)
Royce Gracie defeated Ken Shamrock	1:08	TO (RC)
Jason DeLucia defeated Trent Jenkins	0:52	TO (RNC)
Royce Gracie defeated Gerard Gordeau	1:40	TO (RNC)

03/11/94 UFC 2

Scott Morris defeated Shawn Daugherty	0:20	TO (GC)
Pat Smith defeated Ray Wizard	0:58	TO (GC)
Johnny Rhodes defeated David Levicki	14:58	TO (S)
Freek Hamaker defeated Thaddeus Luster	4:52	TO (KL)
Orlando Weit defeated Robert Lucarelli	1:19	TWL (S)
Remco Pardoel defeated Alberto Cerro Leon	9:51	TO (FC)
Jason DeLucia defeated Scott Baker	6:41	TO (TC)
Royce Gracie defeated Minoki Ichihara	5:07	TO (TC)
Pat Smith defeated Scott Morris	0:41	KO
Johnny Rhodes defeated Fred Ettish	3:05	TO (RNC)
Remco Pardoel defeated Orlando Weit	1:28	KO
Royce Gracie defeated Jason DeLucia	1:04	TO (AB)
Pat Smith defeated Johnny Rhodes	1:06	TO (GC)
Royce Gracie defeated Remco Pardoel	1:29	TO (GC)
Royce Gracie defeated Pat Smith	1:16	TO (S)

07/29/94 Japan Open: Vale Tudo '94 (Japan)

Bud Smith defeated Chris Bass	0:54	RS (S)
Jan Lomulder defeated Kenji Kawaguchi	2:59	KO
David Levicki defeated Kazuhiro Kusayanagi	1:20	RS (S)
Rickson Gracie defeated Yoshinori Nish	2:58	TO (RNC)
Rickson Gracie defeated David Levicki	2:40	RS (S)
(Jan Lomulder dropped out due to injury)		
Rickson Gracie defeated Bud Smith	0:39	TO (S)

09/09/94 UFC 3

Keith Hackney defeated Emmanuel Yarbrough	1:59	TO (S)
Ken Shamrock defeated Christophe Leininger	4:49	TO (S)
Harold Howard defeated Roland Payne	0:46	KO
Royce Gracie defeated Kimo Leopoldo	4:40	TO (AB)
Ken Shamrock defeated Felix Lee Mitchell	4:35	TO (RNC)
(Royce Gracie dropped out due to injury)		
(Ken Shamrock dropped out due to injury)		
Steve Jennum defeated Harold Howard	1:28	TO (S)

12/16/94 UFC 4

Joe Charles defeated Kevin Rosier	0:14	TO (AB)
Marcus Bossett defeated Eldo Dias Xavier	4:55	RS (S)
Royce Gracie defeated Ron Van Clief	3:51	TO (RNC)
Keith Hackney defeated Joe Son	2:44	TO (C)
Steve Jennum defeated Melton Bowen	4:47	TO (AB)
Dan Severn defeated Anthony Macias	1:45	TO (FC)
Royce Gracie defeated Keith Hackney	5:34	TO (AB)
(Steve Jennum dropped out due to injury)		
Dan Severn defeated Marcus Bossett	0:54	TO (FC)
Guy Mezger defeated Jason Fairn	2:13	TO (S)
Royce Gracie defeated Dan Severn	15:49	TO (TC)

01/01/95 Cage Fight Tournament (Germany)

Rene Rozen defeated Andre Oetelaer	2:28	TWL (S)
Oswald Verlinden defeated Maduro	2:17	TO (FC)
Ed De Kruif defeated Bob Schrijber	4:20	TO (FC)
Rudi De Loos defeated Bob Schrijber	2:26	TO (RNC)
(Verlinden and Rozen dropped out due to injury)		
Ed De Kruif defeated Rudi De Loos	0:50	TO (RNC)

04/07/95 UFC 5

Dave Beneteau defeated Asbel Cancio	0:21	TO (S)
Guy Mezger defeated John Dowdy	2:02	RS (S)
Jon Hess defeated Andy Anderson	1:23	RS (S)
Todd Medina defeated Larry Cureton	2:55	TO (FC)
Oleg Taktarov defeated Ernest Verdecia	2:22	TO (AC)
Dan Severn defeated Joe Charles	1:39	TO (RNC)
Dave Beneteau defeated Todd Medina	2:13	TO (S)
Dan Severn defeated Oleg Taktarov	4:21	DS (C)
Royce Gracie drew with Ken Shamrock	36:06	DRW
Dan Severn defeated Dave Beneteau	3:03	TO (KL)

04/20/95 Japan Open: Vale Tudo '95 (Japan)

Craig Pittman defeated Wayne Emmons	2:48	TO (AC)
Yuki Nakai defeated Gerard Gordeau	28:12	TO (HH)
Todd Hays defeated Houichiro Kimura	2:55	TO (GC)
Rickson Gracie dftd Yoshihisa Yamamoto	20:47	RS (RNC)
Kenji Kawaguchi dftd Tommy Walkingstick	6:29	TO (AB)

Yuki Nakai defeated Craig Pittman	17:30	TO (AB)
Enson Inoue defeated Rene Rozen	6:41	TO (RNC)
(Todd Hays dropped out due to injury)		
Houichiro Kimura defeated Wayne Emmons	6:05	TO (GC)
Rickson Gracie defeated Houichiro Kimura	2:07	TO (RNC)
Rickson Gracie defeated Yuki Nakai	6:22	TO (RNC)

07/14/95 UFC 6

Joel Sutton defeated Jack McClaughlin	1:58	TO (S)
Anthony Macias defeated He-Man Gipson	3:06	TO (S)
Tank Abbott defeated John Matua	0:18	KO
Paul Varelans defeated Cal Worsham	1:04	RS (S)
Pat Smith defeated Rudyard Moncayo	1:09	TO (RNC)
Oleg Taktarov defeated Dave Beneteau	0:57	TO (GC)
Tank Abbott defeated Paul Varelans	1:51	RS (S)
Oleg Taktarov defeated Anthony Macias	0:12	TO (GC)
Ken Shamrock defeated Dan Severn	2:15	TO (GC)
Oleg Taktarov defeated Tank Abbott	17:47	TO (RNC)

09/08/95 UFCF (Hawaii)

Kimo Leopoldo defeated Fred Floyd	0:47	TO (RNC)
Carl Franks defeated Marcus Bossett	8:00	TO (AB)
John Lewis defeated Thomas Puckett	1:45	TO (AB)
Todd Bjornethun defeated Orlando Weit	5:43	TO (TC)

09/08/95 UFC 7

Scott Bessac defeated David Hood	0:37	TO (GC)
Joel Sutton defeated Geza Kahlman Jr	1:42	DS (C)
Onassis Parungao defeated Francesco Maturi	5:35	TO (S)
Paul Varelans defeated Gerry Harris	1:07	TO (S)
Mark Hall defeated Harold Howard	1:41	TO (S)
Remco Pardoel defeated Ryan Parker	3:05	TO (FC)
Marco Ruas defeated Larry Cureton	3:23	TO (HH)
Paul Varelans defeated Mark Hall	1:01	TO (KL)
Marco Ruas defeated Remco Pardoel	12:27	TO (P)
Ken Shamrock drew with Oleg Taktarov	35:00	DRW
Marco Ruas defeated Paul Varelans	13:17	RS (S)

10/07/95 World Combat Championship

Phil Benedict defeated Jerry Bell	0:36	TO (RNC)
Fred Floyd defeated Jerry Flynn	3:02	TO (GC)
Renzo Gracie defeated Ben Spijkers	2:48	TO (RNC)
Erik Paulson defeated Sean McCully	5:17	TO (S)
Bart Vale defeated Mike Bitonio	7:10	TO (TC)
James Warring defeated Jerome Turcan	2:35	TO (S)
Renzo Gracie defeated Phil Benedict	2:08	TO (S)
James Warring defeated Erik Paulson	16:08	TWL (S)
Renzo Gracie defeated James Warring	2:47	TO (FC)

11/18/95 Extreme Fighting

Ralph Gracie defeated Makoto Muraoko	0:43	RS (RNC)
Igor Zinoviev defeated Harold German	0:43	TO (S)
Gary Myers defeated Tom Glanville	2:28	TO (S)
Mario Sperry defeated Rudyard Moncayo	2:41	TO (S)
Conan Silveira defeated Victor Tatarkin	2:28	TWL
Alfonso Alcaraz defeated Robert Loyer	2:27	DS (C)
Carlson Gracie Jr drew with John Lewis	20:00	DRW
Conan Silveira defeated Gary Myers	4:25	TO (GC)
Igor Zinoviev defeated Mario Sperry	11:37	DS (C)

12/16/95 Ultimate Ultimate '95

Joe Charles defeated Scott Bessac	4:38	TO (KL)
Mark Hall defeated Trent Jenkins	5:29	TO (AB)
Tank Abbott defeated Steve Jennum	1:16	TO (O)
Dan Severn defeated Paul Varelans	1:01	TO (AC)
Oleg Taktarov defeated Dave Beneteau	1:22	TO (HH)
Marco Ruas defeated Keith Hackney	2:39	TO (RNC)
Dan Severn defeated Tank Abbott	20:00	D
Oleg Taktarov defeated Marco Ruas	20:00	D
Dan Severn defeated Oleg Taktarov	33:00	D

02/16/96 UFC 8

Sam Adkins defeated Keith Mielke	2:48	TO (S)
Don Frye defeated Thomas Ramirez	0:10	KO
Paul Varelans defeated Joe Moreira	10:00	D
Jerry Bohlander defeated Scott Ferrozzo	9:05	TO (GC)
Gary Goodridge defeated Paul Herrera	0:13	RS (S)
Don Frye defeated Sam Adkins	0:48	TO (S)
Gary Goodridge defeated Jerry Bohlander	5:33	RS (S)
Ken Shamrock defeated Kimo Leopoldo	4:24	TO (KB)
Don Frye defeated Gary Goodridge	2:14	TO (S)

03/30/96 International Fighting Championships (Russia)

Dimitri Eleseev defeated Justin Martin	6:50	RS (S)
Ruslan Kriviy defeated Peter Khmelev	4:15	TO (S)
Richard Heard defeated Igor Ahkmedov	0:51	TO (GC)
John Lober defeated Eric Hebestreit	3:39	TO (RNC)
John Dixson defeated Alexander Mandrk	2:30	TO (GC)
Igor Guerus defeated Gerry Harris	0:15	RS (S)
Paul Varelans defeated Valery Nikulin	5:20	TWL (S)
Igor Vovchanchyn defeated Fred Floyd	13:40	TO (S)
John Dixson defeated Igor Guerus	2:27	TO (GC)
Igor Vovchanchyn defeated Paul Varelans	6:20	RS (S)
Igor Vovchanchyn defeated John Dixson	6:18	TO (S)

04/05/96 Universal Vale Tudo Fighting (Japan)

Johil De Oliveira defeated Akira Nagase	10:00	DS (S)
Ebeneezer Fontes defeated Naohisa Kawamura	3:17	KO

Todd Medina defeated Antonio Carlos Ribeiro	6:06	TO (GC)
Michael Stam defeated Marcelo Mendes	17:47	TWL (O)
Wallid Ismail defeated Dennis Kefalinos	2:19	TO (RNC)
Carlos Barretto defeated Mikhail Illioukhine	13:10	TO (RNC)
Hugo Duarte defeated Dieusel Berto	1:28	TO (KL)
Pedro Otavio defeated Koji Kitao	5:32	TO (S)

04/21/96 Cage Fight Tournament 2 (Netherlands)

Rick Anderson defeated Sean McCully	5:15	TO (GC)
Eduardo Rocha defeated Alexander Zalski	20:00	D
Willie Peeters defeated Allen Harris	2.18	RS (S)
Hubert Numrich defeated Tim Tawak	3:50	RS (S)
Eduardo Rocha defeated Rick Anderson	2:16	TO (S)
Willie Peeters defeated Hubert Numrich	2:20	RS (S)
Willie Peeters defeated Eduardo Rocha	3:00	TO (S)

04/26/96 Extreme Fighting 2 (Canada)

Nigel Scantelbury drew with Jason Canals	15:00	DRW
John Lewis defeated Jim Teachout	0:52	TO (S)
Igor Zinoviev defeated Steve Faulkner	0:44	TO (RNC)
Ralph Gracie defeated Steve Nelson	0:44	TO (S)
Jean Riviere defeated Carlos Newton	7:22	TO (O)
Conan Silveira defeated Carl Franks	1:17	RS (S)

05/17/96 UFC 9

Steve Nelmark defeated Tai Bowden	7:25	RS (S)
Cal Worsham defeated Zane Frazier	3:17	TO (S)
Rafael Carino defeated Matt Anderson	5:33	RS (S)
Mark Schultz defeated Gary Goodridge	12:00	DS (C)
Mark Hall defeated Koji Kitao	0:47	DS (BN)
Don Frye defeated Amaury Bitetti	9:30	RS (S)
Dan Severn defeated Ken Shamrock	31:00	D

06/28/96 Super Brawl (Hawaii)

Jay R Palmer defeated Andras Szarka	7:59	TWL (S)
Haygar Chin defeated Hiroki Noritsugi	5:04	TO (RNC)
Chris Charnos defeated Jesse Matilla	1:34	TO (AB)
Jerry Bohlander defeated Alan Schaible	2:09	TO (RNC)
Tra Telligman defeated Brian Matapua	2:03	TO (S)
Jay R Palmer defeated Haygar Chin	20:00	D
Jerry Bohlander defeated Chris Charnos	8:25	TO (RNC)
Tra Telligman defeated Walt Darby	2:09	TO (S)

07/07/96 Japan Open: Vale Tudo '96

Alex Cook defeated Tomoaki Hayama	16:23	RS (AC)
Mushtaq Abdullah defeated Sanae Kikuta	6:27	TO (FC)
Ed De Kruif defeated Joe Estes	0:53	TO (RNC)
Todd Bjornethun defeated Eric Laven	6:53	RS (S)

Dan Severn defeated Doug Murphy	3:23	TO (KL)
John Lewis drew with Rumina Sato	24:00	DRW
Igor Zinoviev defeated Enson Inoue	0:44	RS (S)
Royler Gracie defeated Noboru Asahi	5:07	TO (RNC)

07/12/96 UFC 10

Geza Kahlman Jr defeated Dieusel Berto	5:57	RS (S)
Sam Adkins defeated Felix Lee Mitchell	10:00	D
Don Frye defeated Mark Hall	10:23	RS (S)
Brian Johnston defeated Scotty Fiedler	2:25	RS (S)
Mark Coleman defeated Moti Horenstein	2:43	TO (S)
Gary Goodridge defeated John Campatella	1:27	TO (S)
Don Frye defeated Brian Johnston	4:38	TO (S)
Mark Coleman defeated Gary Goodridge	7:00	TO (O)
Mark Coleman defeated Don Frye	11:36	RS (S)

08/04/96 World Vale Tudo Championship (Japan)

Fred Floyd defeated Dennis Crowell	1:44	TO (FC)
Michael Pacholik defeated Denilson Maia	4:52	TO (S)
David Hood defeated Todd Butler	9:37	TO (O)
Richard Heard defeated Scott Groff	1:05	TO (S)
Oleg Taktarov defeated Joe Charles	4:42	TO (KB)

Fred Floyd vs Michael Pacholik (Pacholik dropped due to injury)

Richard Heard defeated David Hood	4:26	TO (HH)
Marco Ruas defeated Steve Jennum	1:45	TO (S)
Richard Heard defeated Fred Floyd	1:58	TO (RNC)

09/20/96 UFC 11

Roberto Traven defeated David Berry	1:33	TO (RNC)
Scott Ferrozzo defeated Sam Fulton	1:45	TO (S)
Mark Coleman defeated Julian Sanchez	0:44	TO (NC)
Brian Johnston defeated Reza Nasri	0:30	RS (S)
Tank Abbott defeated Sam Adkins	2:26	TO (FC)
Jerry Bohlander defeated Fabio Gurgel	15:00	D
Mark Coleman defeated Brian Johnston	2:20	TO (S)
Scott Ferrozzo defeated Tank Abbott	18:00	D

Mark Coleman wins Scott Ferrozzo & Roberto Traven both dropped out due to injury

10/11/96 Super Brawl 2 (Hawaii)

Maurice Corty defeated Llewelyn Poomaihealani 1:33TO (AB)		
Jay R Palmer defeated Brian Gassaway	4:04	TO (S)
David Paalhui defeated Katsuhisa Fuji	0:53	RS (S)
Pete Williams defeated Donald De La Cruz	6:11	RS (S)
Joe Charles defeated Wes Gassaway	3:24	RS (S)
Jay R Palmer defeated Maurice Corty	2:26	KO
David Paalhui defeated Jesse Matilla	6:09	TO (AB)
Pete Williams defeated Joe Charles	1:38	TO (KB)
Vitor Belfort defeated Jon Hess	0:15	RS (S)

10/18/96 Extreme Fighting 3

Joao Roque defeated Abdelaziz Cherigui	4:02	TO (AB)
Todd Bjornethun defeated Rudyard Moncayo	2:50	TO (HH)
John Lewis drew with Johil De Oliveira	15:00	DRW
Matt Hume defeated Erik Paulson	10:44	DS (C)
Ralph Gracie defeated Ali Mihoubi	1:34	TO (AB)
Allan Goes defeated Anthony Macias	3:52	TO (O)
Igor Zinoviev drew with John Lober	15:00	DRW
Murakami Kazunari defeated Bart Vale	4:37	RS (S)
Maurice Smith defeated Conan Silveira	11:36	RS (S)

11/10/96 WVC 2 (Brazil)

Vernon "Tiger" White defeated Kees Besems	2:09	TO (HH)
Yuri Oulianitski defeated Hubert Numrich	0:25	TO (AB)
Pedro Rizzo defeated Nicklaus "Nicco" Hill	1:45	TO (S)
Richard Heard defeated Michael Tielrooy	1:07	TO (RNC)
(Heard dropped out due to injury)		
Tiger White defeated Yuri Oulianitski	1:50	KO
Pedro Rizzo defeated Michael Tielrooy	0:19	TO (KL)
Marco Ruas drew with Oleg Taktarov	31:00	DRW
Pedro Rizzo defeated Tiger White	6:32	KO

11/17/96 U-Japan

Paul Varelans defeated Shinji Katase	0:31	TO (S)
Becky Levi defeated Yoko Takahashi	2:13	TO (S)
Dave Beneteau defeated Pat Smith	1:10	TO (O)
Wallid Ismail defeated Katsumi Usuda	3:10	TO (RNC)
Don Frye defeated Mark Hall	5:29	TO (FC)
Dan Severn defeated Mitsuhiro Matsunaga	1:29	TO (KL)
Sean Alvares defeated Yoji Anjoh	34:27	TO (S)
Kimo defeated Bam Bam Bigelow	2:15	RS (S)

11/22/96 Martial Arts Reality Superfighting

Tom Erikson dftd Alexander Khramstovskly	9:26	RS (S)
Murilo Bustamante defeated Chris Haseman	1:06	TWL (S)
Willie Peeters defeated Serge Narsisyan	5:03	TWL (S)
Juan Mott defeated Yasunori Matsumoto	5:20	KO
Carlos Barretto defeated Alexander Rafalski	1:00	TO (S)
Tom Erikson defeated Willie Peeters	0:31	TO (NC)
Murilo Bustamente defeated Juan Mott	1:09	TO (S)
Mario Sperry defeated Andry Dudko	4:14	TO (KL)
Murilo Bustamente drew with Tom Erikson	40:00	DRW
Renzo Gracie defeated Oleg Taktarov	1:03	RS (S)

11/23/96 Extreme Challenge

Travis Fulton defeated Clayton Miller	3:09	RS (S)
Tyrone Roberts defeated Rick Gravesen	3:59	KO
Paul Wells defeated Jason Godsey	11:05	TO (GC)
Brian Dunn defeated Allen Porter	0:59	TO (GC)
Jesse Jones defeated Scott Gonyo	0:10	KO

Dave Strasser defeated Rolondo Higueros	8:32	DS (C)
Dennis Reed defeated Matt Anderson	10:34	TO (O)
Jeremy Horn defeated Gary Myers	2:06	TO (AB)
Pat Miletich defeated Earl Loucks	7:00	TO (KL)
Dan Severn defeated Steven Goss	1:53	TO (RNC)

12/07/96 Ultimate Ultimate '96

Mark Hall defeated Felix Lee Mitchell	1:45	RS (S)
Steve Nelmark defeated Marcus Bossett	1:37	TO (GC)
Tai Bowden defeated Jack Nilsson	4:46	TO (S)
Ken Shamrock defeated Brian Johnston	5:49	TO (FC)
Don Frye defeated Gary Goodridge	11:20	TO (O)
Tank Abbott defeated Cal Worsham	2:52	TO (S)
Kimo defeated Paul Varelans	9:09	TO (S)
Tank Abbott defeated Steve Nelmark	1:05	KO
Don Frye defeated Mark Hall	0:20	TO (HH)
Don Frye defeated Tank Abbott	1:23	TO (RNC)

01/17/97 Super Brawl 3 (Hawaii)

Pat Miletich defeated Jason Nicholson	15:00	D
Raynell Cooper defeated Taro Obata	1:17	RS (S)
(Miletich dropped out due to injury)		
Doug Murphy defeated Duke Pa'aaina	3:08	TO (RNC)
Pete Williams defeated John Renfro	2:55	TO (AB)
Raynell Cooper defeated Jason Nicholson	0:24	TWL (S)
Danny Bennett defeated Jay R Palmer	13:53	KO
John Lober defeated Frank Shamrock	30:00	D

01/19/97 WVC 3 (Brazil)

Mestre Hulk defeated Zane Frazier	2:06	KO
Mark Kerr defeated Paul Varelans	2:07	RS (S)
Fabio Gurgel defeated Pat Smith	0:45	TO (O)
Michael Pacholik defeated Nobuhiro Tsurumaki	1:26	TO (S)
Mark Kerr defeated Mestre Hulk	2:29	DQ
Fabio Gurgel defeated Michael Pacholik	4:56	TO (S)
Pedro Rizzo defeated Richard Heard	13:14	TO (S)
Mark Kerr defeated Fabio Gurgel	30:00	D

02/02/97 Rings Holland – The Final Challenge (Netherlands)

Ron van Gellekom dftd John van Wanrooy 10:00	D	
Gilbert Yvel defeated Ron van Leeuwen	4:06	RS (S)
Hans Nyman defeated Lee Hasdell	5:35	TO (GC)
Peter Dijkman defeated Iouri Bekichev	2:25	TO (RNC)
Willie Peeters defeated Sergei Sousserov	4:51	KO
Valentijn Overeem defeated Masayuki Naruse	3:58	DS (C)
Joop Kasteel defeated Mistuya Nagai	5:12	KO
Kiyoshi Tamura defeated Andre Mannaart	2:11	TO (RNC)
Bob Schrijber defeated Toon Stelling	6:01	RS (S)
Pedro de Palm vs Dick Vrij		NOC

02/08/97 UFC 12

Nick Sanzo defeated Jackie Lee	0:48	RS (S)
Jerry Bohlander defeated Rainy Martinez	1:24	TO (S)
Yoshiki Takahashi defeated Wallid Ismail	15:00	D
Scott Ferrozzo defeated Jim Mullen	8:17	RS (S)
Vitor Belfort defeated Ira Telligman	1:17	RS (S)
Jerry Bohlander defeated Nick Sanzo	0:35	TO (O)
Vitor Belfort defeated Scott Ferrozzo	0:52	RS (S)
Mark Coleman defeated Dan Severn	2:59	TO (NC)

02/14/97 World Fighting Federation

Matt Lindland defeated Karo Davtyan	6:31	RS (S)
Dan Bobish defeated Joe Charles	4:42	TO (C)
Hugo Duarte defeated Steve Seddon	0:28	TO (RNC)
Oleg Taktarov defeated Chuck Kim	0:22	TO (GC)
Tom Erikson defeated Davin Wright	0:43	TWL (S)
Gokor Chivichyan defeated Bell Maeda	0:51	TO (AB)

03/03/97 UVF 6 (Brazil)

Fernando Cerchiari defeated Douglas Aquino	1:12	TO (S)
Carlos Barretto defeated Geza Kahlman Jr	2:57	TO (GC)
Daniel Bobish defeated Jucimar Hypolito	0:05	KO
Kevin Randleman defeated Ebeneezer Braga	20:00	D
Mario Neto defeated Gary Goodridge	6:09	TO (O)
Carlos Barretto defeated Dan Bobish	8:13	TO (TC)
Kevin Randleman defeated Mario Neto	11:19	TO (S)
Carlos Barretto defeated Kevin Randleman	22:22	RS (TC)

03/22/97 World Cage Fight Championship (Australia)

Neil Bodycote defeated Simon Sweet	5:49	TO (GC)
Mario Sperry defeated Vernon "Tiger" White	15:00	D
Elvis Sinosic defeated Mathew Rocca	0:40	TO (S)
Chris Haseman defeated Hiriwa Te Rangi	0:54	TO (O)
Mario Sperry defeated Neil Bodycote	0:47	TO (S)
Chris Haseman defeated Elvis Sinosic	2:44	TO (O)
Mario Sperry defeated Chris Haseman	1:10	TO (S)

03/28/97 Extreme Fighting 4

Gary Myers drew with Tom Glanville	15:00	DRW
Allan Goes defeated Todd Bjornethun	0:46	TO (TC)
Erik Paulson drew with Paul Jones	15:00	DRW
Kevin Jackson defeated John Lober	6:12	TO (AC)
Matt Hume defeated Pat Miletich	5:00	DS (BN)
Kenny Monday defeated John Lewis	9:12	RS (S)
Maurice Smith defeated Murakami Kazunari	4:23	KO

05/30/97 UFC 13

Jack Nilsson defeated Saeed Hosseini	1:23	RS (S)
Tito Ortiz defeated Wes Albritton	0:31	TO (S)

Guy Mezger defeated Christophe Leininger	12:00	D
Enson Inoue defeated Royce Alger	1:40	TO (AB)
Steve Graham defeated Dmitrei Stepanov	1:30	TO (KL)
Randy Couture defeated Tony Halme	1:00	TO (RNC)
Guy Mezger defeated Tito Ortiz	3:00	TO (GC)
Randy Couture defeated Steve Graham	3:13	RS (S)
Vitor Belfort defeated Tank Abbott	0:53	RS (S)

06/15/97 Brazil Open '97

Fabiano Lopes defeated Paulo Arun	20:00	D
Pedro Otavio defeated Paulao Paulao	4:19	TO (S)
Dan Henderson defeated Crezio De Sousa	5:24	RS (S)
Eric Smith defeated Jose "Pele" Landi Jons	20:00	D
Kevin Randleman defeated Homan De Neve	2:21	TO (S)
Tom Erikson defeated Pantera Negra	2:30	RS (S)
Dan Henderson defeated Eric Smith	0:29	RS (GC)
Tom Erikson defeated Kevin Randleman	1:11	KO
Carlos Barretto defeated Paul Varelans	2:33	RS (S)

07/06/97 International Vale Tudo Championship (Brazil)

Egidio Amado defeated Lucio Carvalho	5:30	TO (S)
Gary Goodridge dftd "Monstro" Augusto Santos	0:32	TO (NC)
Cal Worsham defeated Aluisio Neto	0:25	TO (GC)
Pedro Otavio defeated Brian Keck	18:24	TO (RNC)
Andre Cardoso defeated John Gnap	0:30	RS (S)
Gary Goodridge defeated Cal Worsham	0:43	TO (FC)
Pedro Otavio defeated Andre Cardoso	8:41	TO (HH)
Dan Severn defeated Ebeneezer Braga	7:11	RS (S)
Gary Goodridge defeated Pedro Otavio	16:15	TO (S)

07/27/97 UFC 14

Alex Hunter defeated Sam Fulton	2:32	TO (S)
Anthony Fryklund defeated Donnie Chappell	1:27	TO (FC)
Joe Moreira defeated Yuri Vaulin	15:00	D
Kevin Jackson defeated Todd Butler	1:29	TO (S)
Mark Kerr defeated Moti Horenstein	2:32	RS (S)
Dan Bobish defeated Brian Johnston	2:11	TO (FC)
Kevin Jackson defeated Anthony Fryklund	0:44	TO (RNC)
Mark Kerr defeated Dan Bobish	1:48	TO (O)
Maurice Smith defeated Mark Coleman	21:00	D

9/26/97 Pentagon Combat (Brazil)

Marcelo "Tigre" defeated "Buda"	4:27	TO (RNC)
Rony Rústico defeated José Henrique "Rafkhal"	3:50	TO (S)
Ricardo Morais defeated Sergio "Muralha"	0:16	TO (S)
Oleg Taktarov defeated Sean Alvares	0:52	KO
Murilo Bustamante defeated Jerry Bohlander	5:39	KO
Renzo Gracie vs Eugenio Tadeu NOC *(riot occurred during fight)*		

10/11/97 Pride (Japan)

Murakami Kazunari defeated John Dixson	1:34	TO (AB)
Gary Goodridge defeated Oleg Taktarov	4:57	KO
Renzo Gracie drew with Akira Shoji	30:00	DRW
Koji Kitao defeated Nathan Jones	2:14	TO (KL)
Kimo drew with Dan Severn	30:00	DRW
Rickson Gracie defeated Nobuhiko Takada	4:47	TO (AB)

10/17/97 UFC 15

Alex Hunter defeated Harry Moskowitz	10:00	D
Dwane Cason defeated Houston Dorr	3:43	RS (S)
Mark Kerr defeated Greg "Ranger" Stott	0:20	RS (S)
Dave Beneteau defeated Carlos Barretto	12:00	D
Randy Couture defeated Vitor Belfort	8:17	RS (S)
Mark Kerr defeated Dwane Cason	0:54	TO (RNC)
Maurice Smith defeated Tank Abbott	8.09	TO (S)

11/01/97 Cage Fight Tournament 3 (Russia)

Ronny Rivano defeated Nikita Abramov	4:42	TO (FC)
Serguey Bytchkov defeated Rodney Faverus	6:00	D
Oleg Tsygolnik defeated Pedro De Palm	0:57	TO (RNC)
Gilbert Yvel defeated Serguey Tunic	1:16	RS (S)
Bob Schrijber defeated Emil Sroka	0:54	TO (S)
Ruslan Kerselyn defeated Colorado Lopez	0:09	TO (S)
Wendy van Maren drew with Marina Nikolaeva	6:00	DRW
Loes Scholte Aalbes drew with Elena Paulova	6:00	DRW
Irma Verhoeff defeated Trina Iknatovic	2:59	RS (S)
Serguey Bytchkov defeated Ronny Rivano	2:51	TO (HH)
Gilbert Yvel defeated Oleg Tsygolnik	1:02	TO (O)
Bob Schrijber defeated Ruslan Kerselyn	2:54	RS (S)

11/29/97 Japan Open: Vale Tudo '97

Jutaro Nakao defeated Steve Nelson	13:31	TO (TC)
Hayato Sakurai drew with Marcelo Aguilar	24:00	DRW
Kenji Kawaguchi defeated Jan Lomulder	19:49	TO (RNC)
Ucyuu Tatsumi drew with Joao Roque	24:00	DRW
Carlos Newton defeated Erik Paulson	0:41	TO (AB)
Tom Erikson defeated Ed De Kruijf	0:37	RS (S)
Rumina Sato defeated John Lewis	9:23	TO (AB)
Frank Shamrock defeated Enson Inoue	15:17	DQ

12/21/97 UFC Japan

Tra Telligman defeated Brad Kohler	10:10	TO (AB)
Conan Silveira vs Kazushi Sakuraba	NOC	
Tank Abbott defeated Yoji Anjoh	18:00	D
Frank Shamrock defeated Kevin Jackson	0:16	TO (AB)
Vitor Belfort defeated Joe Charles	4:04	TO (AB)
Kazushi Sakuraba defeated Conan Silveira	3:40	TO (AB)
Randy Couture defeated Maurice Smith	21:00	D

10/25/98 Japan Open: Vale Tudo '98

Caol Uno defeated Ricardo Botelho	12:03	TO (S)
Vladimir Matyushenko dftd Kenji Kawaguchi	3:10	RS (S)
Brandon Lee Hinkle defeated Masanori Suda	5:26	KO
Frank Trigg defeated Jean Jacques Machado	10:20	TWL (C)
Noboru Asahi drew with Joao Roque	18:00	DRW
Hayato Sakurai defeated Sergei Bytchkov	4:59	TO (AB)
Andre Pederneiras defeated Rumina Sato	4:20	KO
Enson Inoue defeated Randy Couture	1:39	TO (AB)

05/29/99 Shooto 10th Anniversary (Japan)

Hiroyuki Abe defeated Yoshiyuki Takayama	10:00	D
Izuru Takeuchi defeated Ahmed Lazizi	10:00	D
Dave Menne defeated Dennis Hallman	15:00	D
Matt Hughes defeated Akihiro Gono	15:00	D
Tetsuji Kato defeated Jutaro Nakao	15:00	D
Carlos Newton defeated Kenji Kawaguchi	5:00	TO (AB)
Hayato Sakurai defeated Marcelo Aguiar	15:00	D
Caol Uno defeated Rumina Sato	14:02	TO (RNC)

09/07/99 Superbrawl 13 (Hawaii)

Lincoln Tyler defeated Dain Agbayani	1:41	TO (HH)
Wayne Fisher defeated Kevini Maumau	3:48	RS (S)
John Marsh defeated Travis Fulton	7:48	TO (HH)
Josh Barnett defeated Juha Tuhkasaari	3:32	TO (AB)
Heath Herring defeated Rocky Batastini	1:00	TO (RNC)
Bobby Hoffman defeated Ricco Rodriguez	3:13	KO
Cheynne Padeken defeated Jay R Palmer	6:58	DS (C)
Lance Gibson defeated Akihiro Gono	15:00	D
Marcos De Silva defeated Ronald Jhun	7:19	TO (RNC)
Josh Barnett defeated John Marsh	4:23	TO (KL)
Bobby Hoffman defeated Heath Herring	10:00	D
Dave Menne defeated Jutaro Nakao	15:00	D
Josh Barnett defeated Bobby Hoffman	15:00	D
Ray Cooper defeated Danny bennett	2:43	TO (AB)

09/24/99 UFC XXII: There Can Be Only One Champion

Jens Pulver defeated Alfonso Alcarez	10:00	DRW
John Lewis defeated Lowell Anderson	10:13	TWL (S)
Matt Hughes defeated Valeri Ignatov	15:00	D
Chuck Liddell defeated Paul Jones	3:53	RS (S)
Brad Kohler defeated Steve Judson	0:30	KO
Jeremy Horn defeated Jason Godsey	2:08	TO (AL)
Tim Lajcik drew with Ron Waterman	15:00	DRW
Frank Shamrock defeated Tito Ortiz	19:42	TO (S)

02/26/00 Rings King of Kings Final 1999 (Japan)

Renato Sobral defeated Mikhail Illoukhine	10:40	TO (AB)
Dan Henderson defeated Gilbert Yvel	10:00	D

Rodrigo Nogueira defeated Andrei Kopylov	10:00	D
Kiyoshi Tamura defeated Renzo Gracie	10:00	D
Bobby Hoffman defeated Zaza Tkeshelashvili	0:34	KO
Dan Henderson defeated Rodrigo Nogueira	10:00	D
Renato Sobral defeated Kiyoshi Tamura	10:00	D
Dan Henderson defeated Renato Sobral	10:00	D

03/05/00 2 Hot 2 Handle (Netherlands)

Andrey Semenov defeated Goksel Sahinbas	3:28	RS (S)
Vadim Kuvatov defeated Michael Tielrooy	2:10	TO (AL)
Habib Ben Sallah defeated Sergei Zavadsky	2:33	RS (S)
Ronny Rivano defeated Marco Holkamp	9:30	RS (S)
Valentijn Overeem defeated Dennis Reed	0:28	TO (GC)
Alistair Overeem defeated Can Sahinbas	2:21	KO
Jose "Pele" Landi-jons dftd Martijn de Jong	10:00	D
Alexandre Ferreira defeated Moti Horenstein	2:43	TO (KL)
Gilbert Yvel defeated Brian Dunn	0:21	RS (S)
Heath Herring defeated Rene Rooze	3:20	DQ
Bob Schrijber defeated Hugo Duarte	3:34	RS (S)

05/01/00 Pride Grand Prix Finals 2000 (Japan)

Igor Vovchanchyn defeated Gary Goodridge	10:14	RS (S)
Kazushi Sakuraba defeated Royce Gracie	90:00	TWL (O)
Mark Coleman defeated Akira Shoji	15:00	D
Kazuyuki Fujita defeated Mark Kerr	15:00	D
Guy Mezger defeated Masaaki Satake	15:00	D
Igor Vovchanchyn defeated Kazushi Sakuraba	15:00	TWL (O)
Mark Coleman defeated Kazuyuki Fujita	0:02	TWL (O)
Ken Shamrock defeated Alexander Otsuka	9:43	RS (S)
Mark Coleman defeated Igor Vovchanchyn	18:09	TO (S)

05/26/00 Colosseum 2000 (Japan)

Yuki Kondo defeated Saulo Ribeiro	0:22	TWL (S)
Genki Sudo drew with Andre Pederneiras	15:00	DRW
Mario Sperry defeated Hiromitsu Kanehara	10:00	D
Kiyoshi Tamura defeated Jeremy Horn	10:00	D
Rickson Gracie defeated Masakatsu Funaki	12:49	RS (RNC)

06/02/00 Universal Combat Challenge: New Beginning (Canada)

Phil Hughes defeated Roger Pena	4:07	TO (RNC)
Donald Ouimet vs Sylvain Martineau	3:26	TWL (S)
Matt Rocca defeated Shawn Tompkins	8:50	RS (S)
Steve Vigneault defeated Jeff Davis	0:15	RS (S)
Justin Bruckmann defeated David Loiseau	3:04	TO (AB)
J.F. Bolduc defeated Joel Leblanc	1:39	TO (GC)
Wagnney Fabiano defeated Charles Nestor	20:00	D
Stephan Potvin defeated Rob Tallack	20:00	D
Claudionor Fontinelle dftd Dirk Waardenburg	5:30	TO (AB)
Elvis Sinosic drew with Dave Beneteau	20:00	DRW

08/27/00 Pride 10: Return of the Warriors (Japan)

Vitor Belfort defeated Daijiro Matsui	20:00	D
Wanderlei Silva defeated Guy Mezger	3:45	KO
Ricco Rodriguez defeated Giant Ochiai	6:03	TO (FC)
Gilbert Yvel defeated Gary Goodridge	0:26	KO
Mark Kerr defeated Igor Borisov	2:06	TO (NC)
Igor Vovchanchyn defeated Enson Inoue	10:00	RS (S)
Masaaki Satake defeated Murakami Kazunari	6:58	RS (S)
Kazuyuki Fujita defeated Ken Shamrock	6:45	TWL (O)
Ryan Gracie defeated Tokimitsu Ishizawa	2:16	RS (S)
Kazushi Sakuraba defeated Renzo Gracie	19:42	RS (KL)

11/17/00 UFC 28: High Stakes

Ben Earwood defeated Chris Lytle	10:00	D
Mark Hughes defeated Alex Steibling	10:00	D
Jens Pulver defeated John Lewis	0:15	KO
Andrei Arlovski defeated Aaron Brink	0:54	TO (AB)
Josh Barnett defeated Gan McGee	9:32	RS (S)
Renato Sobral defeated Maurice Smith	15:00	D
Randy Couture defeated Kevin Randleman	14:13	RS (S)

02/08/01 Warriors War (Kuwait)

Muhssen Terkawa defeated Steve Fordie	1:11	TO (RNC)
Maromegob defeated Lopes Moreno	0:34	KO
Antonio Tello defeated Khaled Mubarak	8:40	TO (AC)
Dave Menne defeated Carlos Newton	10:00	D
Kareem Barklaev defeated Derso Lema	10:00	D
Jose "Pele" Landi Jons defeated Matt Hughes	4:15	KO
Dave Menne defeated Maromegob	10:00	D
Kareem Barklaev dftd Jose "Pele" Landi Jons	5:59	RS (S)
Dave Menne defeated Kareem Barklaev	10:00	D

02/24/01 Rings King of Kings Final 2000 (Japan)

Hiromitsu Kanehara defeated Dave Menne	13:24	RS (S)
Rodrigo Nogueira defeated Volk Han	10:00	D
Randy Couture defeated Tsuyoshi Kosaka	10:00	D
Valentijn Overeem dftd Yoshihisa Yamamoto	0:45	TO (AB)
Alistair Overeem dftd Vladimer Tchanturia	1:06	TO (RNC)
Rodrigo Nogueira dftd Hiromitsu Kanehara	5:27	TO (RNC)
Valentijn Overeem defeated Randy Couture	0:56	TO (GC)
Ryushi Yanagisawa defeated Wataru Sakata	10:00	D
Renato Sobral defeated Kiyoshi Tamura	10:00	D
Rodrigo Nogueira defeated Valentijn Overeem	1:20	TO (AC)

09/28/01 UFC 33: Victory in Vegas

Din Thomas defeated Fabiano Iha	15:00	D
Ricardo Almeida defeated Eugene Jackson	4:06	TO (TC)
Jutaro Nakao defeated Tony DeSouza	10:00	KO
Dave Menne defeated Gil Castillo	25:00	D

Matt Serra defeated Yves Edwards	15:00	D
Chuck Liddell defeated Murilo Bustamante	15:00	D
Jens Pulver defeated Dennis Hallman	25:00	D
Tito Ortiz defeated Vladimir Matyushenko	25:00	D

10/11/01 Rings 10th Anniversary (Japan)

Gustavo Machado defeated Chris Haseman	15:00	D
Ricardo Arona defeated Jeremy Horn	10:00	D
Bobby Hoffman defeated Mikhail Illoukhine	10:00	D
Fedor Emelianenko defeated Renato Sobral	10:00	D
Hirotaka Yokoi defeated Ricardo Fyeet	2:34	TO (AB)
Bazigit Atajev defeated Aaron Brink	1:09	KO
Ricardo Arona defeated Gustavo Machado	1:29	KO
Tsuyoshi Kosaka dftd Koba Tkeshelashvili	2:17	KO
Matt Hughes defeated Hiromitsui Kanehara	10:00	D

Fedor Emelianenko wins as Hoffman dropped out

11/03/01 Pride 17: Championship Chaos (Japan)

Renzo Gracie defeated Michiyoshi Ohara	20:00	D
Quinton Jackson defeated Yuki Ishikawa	1:52	KO
Dan Henderson defeated Murilo Rua	15:00	D
Semmy Schilt defeated Masaaki Satake	2:18	KO
Mario Sperry defeated Igor Vovchanchyn	2:52	TO (AC)
Tom Erikson defeated Matt Skelton	1:11	TO (C)
Nobuhiko Takada drew with Mirko Filipovic	15:00	DRW
Rodrigo Nogueira defeated Heath Herring	20:00	D
Wanderlei Silva defeated Kazushi Sakuraba	10:00	DS (C)

07/13/02 UFC 38: Brawl at the Royal Albert Hall (UK)

Evan Tanner defeated Chris Haseman	15:00	D
Renato Sobral defeated Elvis Sinosic	15:00	D
Phillip Miller defeated James Zikic	15:00	D
Genki Sudo defeated Leigh Remedios	6:38	TO (RNC)
Mark Weir defeated Eugene Jackson	0:10	KO
Ian Freeman defeated Frank Mir	4:35	RS (S)
Matt Hughes defeated Carlos Newton	18:37	TO (S)

08/28/02 Pride: Shockwave—only MMA matches listed (Japan)

Wanderlei Silva defeated Tatsuya Iwasaki	1:16	RS (S)
Jerrel Venetiaan vs Daijiro Matsui	15:00	D
Gary Goodridge defeated Lloyd Van Dams	3:39	RS (S)
Antonio Rodrigo Nogueira defeated Bob Sapp	14:03	TO (AB)
Mirko Filipovic defeated Kazushi Sakuraba	15:00	DS (C)

11/22/02 UFC 40: Vendetta

Phillip Miller defeated Mark Weir	9:50	TO (RNC)
Vladimir Matyushenko defeated Travis Wiuff	4:10	RS (S)
Andrei Arlovski defeated Ian Freeman	1:25	KO
Robbie Lawler defeated Tiki Ghosen	1:29	RS (S)

Carlos Newton defeated Pete Spratt	1:45	TO (KL)
Matt Hughes defeated Gil Castillo	5:00	DS
Chuck Liddell defeated Renato Sobral	2:59	KO
Tito Ortiz defeated Ken Shamrock	15:00	TWL (O)

01/25/03 UCC 12: Adrenaline (Canada)

Samuel Guillet defeated George Peters	7:10	KO
Stephane Vigneault defeated Shane Rice	10:00	D
Joel Pigeon defeated Dirk Waardenburg	1:38	RS (S)
Dany Laflamme defeated Shawn Peters	15:00	D
Kultar Gill defeated Donald Ouimet	1:51	TO (RNC)
George St. Pierre defeated Thomas Denny	9:45	DS (C)
Steve Vigneault defeated Jermaine Andre	15:00	D
David Loiseau defeated Anthony Fryklund	4:24	DS (C)
Mark Hominick defeated Stephane Laliberte	4:43	TO (AB)
Jason Black defeated John Alessio	15:00	D
Duane Ludwig defeated Jens Pulver	1:13	KO

03/16/03 Pride 25: Body Blows (Japan)

Rogerio Nogueira dftd Kazuhiro Nakamura	13:30	TO (AB)
Akira Shoji defeated Alex Steibling	20:00	D
Alexander Otsuka defeated Kenichi Yamamoto	20:00	D
Anderson Silva defeated Carlos Newton	6:26	KO
Dan Henderson defeated Shungo Oyama	3:27	KO
Antonio Schembri defeated Kazushi Sakuraba	6:07	KO
Quinton Jackson defeated Kevin Randleman	7:00	KO
Fedor Emelianenko defeated Rodrigo Nogueira	20:00	D

09/26/03 UFC 44: Undisputed

Hermes Franca defeated Caol Uno	7:46	KO
Nick Diaz defeated Jeremy Jackson	12:04	TO (AB)
Josh Thomson defeated Gerald Strebendt	2:45	RS (S)
Karo Parisyan defeated Dave Strasser	3:52	TO (KL)
Rich Franklin defeated Edwin Dewees	3:35	RS (S)
Jorge Rivera defeated David Loiseau	15:00	D
Tim Sylvia defeated Gan McGee	1:54	KO
Andrei Arlovski dftd Vladimir Matyushenko	2:14	KO
Randy Couture defeated Tito Ortiz	25:00	D

04/02/04 UFC 47: It's On

Genki Sudo defeated Mike Brown	3:31	TO (AB)
Jonathan Wiezorek defeated Wade Shipp	4:39	RS (S)
Mike Kyle defeated Wes Sims	4:59	KO
Nick Diaz defeated Robbie Lawler	6:31	KO
Andrei Arlovski defeated Wesley Correira	6:15	RS (S)
Yves Edwards defeated Hermes Franca	15:00	D
Chris Lytle defeated Tiki Ghosen	6:55	TO (FC)
Chuck Liddell defeated Tito Ortiz	5:38	KO

MMA DIRECTORY

Fight Promotions

Apex Championship Fighting . . . . . . .www.apexfighting.com
Cage Rage . . . . .www.cagerage.tv
Cobra Fighting Federation . . . . .www.thecobra.com
Euphoria Mixed Fighting
    Championship . . . . .www.euphoriamfc.com
European Vale Tudo . . . . .www.europeanvaletudo.com
Extreme Challenge . . . . .www.extremechallenge.tv
Fight Festival . . . . .www.fightfestival.com
Freestyle Fighting Championships . . .www.ffc.tv
Future Brawl .www.superbrawl.tv
Gladiator Challenge . . . . .www.gladiatorchallenge.com
Grapplers Quest . . . . .www.grapplersquest.com
Hook n' Shoot . . . . .www.fightworld.com
International Fighting
    Championships USA . . . . .www.ifc-usa.com
International Vale Tudo
    Championships . . . . .www.valetudo.com.br
K-1 . . . . .www.k-1usa.net
King of the Cage . . . . .www.kingofthecage.com
Lords of the Ring . . . . .www.lordsko.com
M-1 Mix Fight . . . . .www.mixfight.ru
North American Grappling
    Association . . . . .www.nagafighter.com
Pancrase . . . . .www.pancrase.co.jp
Pit Fighting Championships . . . . .www.pitfc.com
Pride Fighting Championships . . . . . .www.pridefc.com
Pride & Glory . . . . .www.prideandglory.org.uk
Rage in the Cage . . . . .www.rageinthecage.com
Reality Combat . . . . .www.globalsportsent.com
Ring of Fire . . . . .www.rof-mma.com
Rings Holland . . . . .www.rings.nl
Rumble on the Rock . . . . .www.rumbleontherock.net
Shooto . . . . .www.x-shooto.jp
Sportfight . . . . .www.sportfight.tv
TKO Communications . . . . .www.tkozone.tv
Too Hot To Handle . . . . .www.mixfight.com
Total Combat Mexico . . . . .www.totalcombat.org
Ultimate Fighting Championship . . . .www.ufc.tv

Universal Aboveground Fighting . . . .www.uagf.com
World Extreme Cagefighting. . . . . www.wec.tv
World Freestyle Fighting
    Championships. . . . . www.wffchampionships.com
Xtreme Entertainment . . . . www.xtremefight.com
ZST . . . . www.zst.jp

General News/Forums

ADCC News. www.adcombat.com
Aggression TV . . . . www.aggressiontv.com
Brazilian Jiu-jitsu . . . . www.bjj.org
Cage Warriors. . . . . www.cagewarriors.com
Combat Ultimate . . . . www.combatultime.com
Fight Link . . . . www.fightlink.com
Fight Game TV, The. . . . . www.thefightgame.tv
Fighter Girls . . . . www.fightergirls.com
Fight News . . . . www.ufcfightnews.com
Fight Sport . . . . www.fightsport.com/fightsport/news/
                                            news.htm
Fight Training.com. . . . . www.fighttraining.com
Fight World. . . . . www.fightworld.com
Full Contact Fighter . . . . www.fcfighter.com
Gracie Family . . . . www.gracie.com
Inside Fighting . . . . www.insidefighting.com
International Union of Pankration . . . www.chez.com/pancrace
In the Guard . . . . www.intheguard.com
Max Fighting . . . . www.maxfighting.com
MMA Fighter . . . . www.mmafighter.com
MMA Fighting . . . . www.mmafighting.com
MMA News . . . . www.mmanews.com
MMA Ring Report . . . . www.mmaringreport.com
MMA Shooter. . . . . www.mmashooter.com
MMA Weekly . . . . www.mmaweekly.com
On the Mat . . . . www.onthemat.com
Peter Lockley Gallery. . . . . www.sportsshooter.com/peterlockley
Sherdog's MMA Site . . . . www.sherdog.com
Shoto Martial Arts . . . . www.shoto.com
Showdown Combat Sports . . . . www.showdowncombatsports.com
Submission Fighting UK . . . . www.sfuk.net
Susumu's Gallery. . . . . www.susumug.com
Texas MMA. . . . . www.txmma.com
Total Martial Arts UK . . . . www.totalmartialarts.co.uk
U-Fighting. . . . . www.ufighting.com
Underground Forum . . . . www.mma.tv
Who's Who in the Cage. . . . . www.fighters.itgo.com
Wrestling Observer, The . . . . www.wrestlingobserver.com
Xtreme Fighting Championship . . . . . www.xfc.com.au

Fight Wear/Merchandise/Misc.

Bad Boy Fightwear. . . . . www.badboy.com.br
Damage Wear . . . . www.damagewear.com
Dragon Skinz . . . . www.dragonskinz.com
Fighter's Notebook . . . . www.fightersnotebook.com
Grappler Gear. . . . . www.grapplergear.com
House of Pain Ironwear. . . . . www.houseofpainironwear.com
Howard Combat Kimonos . . . . www.howardliu.com
Hybrid Fightwear . . . . www.provinggroundz.com
MMA Gear . . . . www.mmagear.com
MVP Sportsbook (on-line gambling) . www.mvpsportsbook.com
Nikko Sports. . . . . www.nikko-sportsvideo.com
Olympic Sports Book. . . . . www.thegreek.com
Optic Feed (T shirt designs) . . . . www.opticfeed.com
Pain Inc. . . . . www.teampaininc.com
Rage Athletic Wear. . . . . www.rage-athleticwear.com
Red Nose . . . . www.rednosextreme.com.br
Serious Pimp. . . . . www.seriouspimp.com
Showdown Wear . . . . www.showdownfightwear.com
Sinister Clothing. . . . . www.sinisterclothing.com
Tap Out . . . . www.inyaface.com
The Octagon . . . . www.theoctagon.com
World Martial Arts. . . . . www.groundfighter.com

Fighter/MMA Personality Websites

Andre, Jermaine . . . . www.jermaineandre.com
Belfort, Vitor . . . . www.vitorbelfort.com.br
Blauer, Tony . . . . www.tonyblauer.com
Bobish, Dan. . . . . www.danbobish.com
Bravo, Eddie . . . . www.thetwister.tv
Brennan, Chris . . . . www.chrisbrennan.com
Buffer, Bruce . . . . www.bufferzone.net
Castro, Ulisses . . . . www.ulissescastro.com
Coenen, Marloes. . . . . home.planet.nl/~websitemarloes/
Couture, Randy . . . . www.ufcchamp.com
Denny, Thomas. . . . . www.thomasdenny.com
Emelianenko, Fedor. . . . . www.fedor.bel.ru/index_eng.shtml
Filipovic, Mirko . . . . www.free-zd.hinet.hr/webxtra/
Freeman, Ian. . . . . www.ianthemachine.com
Goodridge, Gary . . . . www.bconnex.net/~bigdaddy/power.htm
Gracie, Renzo . . . . www.renzogracie.com
Gracie, Rickson. . . . . www.rickson.com
Gracie, Royce . . . . www.roycegracie.tv
Gurgel, Fabio . . . . www.fabiogurgel.com.br
Herring, Heath . . . . www.heathherring.cjb.net
Iha, Fabiano . . . . www.fabianoiha.com

Ismail, Wallid . . . . www.valetudo.com.br/wallid.htm
Jackson, Quinton . . . . www.rampagejackson.com
Johnston, Brian . . . . www.brianjohnstononline.com
LeBell, Gene . . . . www.genelebell.com
Leininger, Christophe . . . . www.leiningerdojo.com
Lewis, John . . . . www.lewisjiujitsu.com
Liddell, Chuck . . . . www.chuckliddell.com
Lister, Dean. www.deanlister.com
Menjivar, Ivan. . . . . www.ivanmenjivar.com
Mezger, Guy . . . . www.guymezger.com
Miletich, Pat . . . . www.patmiletich.com
Moore, Homer . . . . www.homertherockmoore.com
Newton, Carlos . . . . www.carlosnewton.com
Nogueira, Antonio Rodrigo . . . . www.minotauro.net
Ortiz, Tito . . . . www.titoortiz.com
Pardoel, Remco. . . . . www.pardoelsports.com
Petruzelli, Seth . . . . www.silverbackseth.com
Randleman, Kevin . . . . www.kevinrandleman.com
Ritch, Shannon www.shannonthecannon.50megs.com
Rivera, Jorge . . . . www.jorgerivera.tv
Rodriguez, Ricco . . . . www.riccorodriguez.com
Rua, Murilo. . . . . www.muriloninja.com
Rutten, Bas . . . . www.basrutten.tv
Quadros, Stephen. . . . . www.stephenquadros.com
Sakuraba, Kazushi . . . . www.takada-dojo.com
Salaverry, Ivan . . . . www.ivansalaverry.com
Serra, Matt . . . . www.serrajitsu.com
Severn, Dan . . . . www.the-beast.com
Shamrock, Frank . . . . www.frankshamrock.com
Shamrock, Ken . . . . www.kenshamrock.com
Silva, Wanderlei . . . . www.wanderleisilva.com.br
Sperry, Ze Mario. . . . . www.virtuacomm.com/zemario
Stevenson, Joe. . . . . www.joestevenson.com
Sudo, Genki . . . . www.genkisudo.com
Takada, Nobuhiko . . . . www.takada-dojo.com
Taktarov, Oleg. . . . . www.olegt.com
Thomas, Din . . . . www.dinthomas.com
Toughill, Erin . . . . www.erintoughill.com
Trigg, Frank . . . . www.franktrigg.com
Vovchanchyn, Igor . . . . www.vovchanchyn.kharkov-ua.com
White, Vernon. . . . . www.geocities.com/vernon_tiger_white
Yvel, Gilbert . . . . www.hurricaneyvel.com

REFERENCES

Barry, Dan. "Outcast Gladiators Find a Home: New York." *New York Times.* January 15, 1997.

Barry, Dan. "Giuliani to Try to Prevent 'Extreme Fighting' Match. *New York Times.* January 16, 1997.

Barry, Dan. "Commission Approves Rules For Sport of Ultimate Fighting." *Metropolitan Desk.* January 31, 1997.

Barry, Dan. "Seasoned Lobbyist Gave No Quarter In Quest to Legitimize Bloody Sport." *New York Times.* February 7, 1997.

Barry, Dan. "Rules Upheld, So a Bout Leaves New York." *New York Times.* February 7, 1997.

Bash, Alan. "Brawls punch up pay-per-view numbers." *USA Today Life.* April 7, 1995.

Bunk, Tom. "The Extremely Ultimate Fights." *MAD Magazine.* August 1996.

Brunt, Stephen. "Sign of the Apocalypse: Call it Ultimate Fighting." *Toronto Globe.* December 4, 1995.

Cavalcanti, Keo. "The History of Kudokan Judo." judoinfo.com/jhist.htm

Chen, Jim (M.D.). "Masahiko Kimura. The Man Who Defeated Helio Gracie." 1996.

Corcoran, John & Farkas, Emil. *The Original Martial Arts Encyclopedia.* California: Pro-Action Publishing, 1993.

Crompton, Paul. *The Complete Martial Arts.* New York: McGraw-Hill Publishing Company, 1989.

Finnegan, Michael. "Big brawl has Pataki on ropes." *DKA News.* September 16, 1995.

Friend, Tad. "Getting Medieval." *New York.* February 19, 1996.

Gorsuch, Mark. "Mitsuyo Maeda Biography"—based on review of *A Lion's Dream: The Story of Mitsuyo Maeda* by Kohyama, Norio. April 1998.

Gross, Josh. "Rodrigo Nogueira." *Ultimate Athlete.* November 2001.

Gross, Josh. "Wanderlei Silva—The Axe Murderer." *Ultimate Athlete.* December 2001.

Hamilton, Kendall. "Brawling over brawling." *Newsweek.* November 27, 1995.

Hanania, Joseph. "No Mercy: The 'Ultimate Fighting Championship V' returns tonight on pay-per-view TV." *Los Angeles Times.* April 7, 1995.

Henican, Ellis. "Selling Blood Sport." Newsday. February 9, 1997.

Jordan, Pat. "BAD." *Playboy.* September 1989.

Kagan, Paul. "It's Bloody, It's Violent, It's PPV's Newest Hit." *The Pay TV Newsletter.* January 31, 1995.

Kano, Jigaro & Lindsay, T. "Jujitsu." *Transactions of the Asiatic Society of Japan, Volume 15.* 1887.

Kano, Jigaro. *Kodokan Judo.* Japan: Kodansha International, 1957.

Kessler, Sandra E. "Shotokan, Taekwondo and Kung Fu Challenge Jujutsu." *Black Belt*. April 1994.

Kriegel, Mark. "Gentlemen, start your bleeding." *Esquire*. March 1996.

Lane, Randall. "It's live, it's brutal." *Forbes*. May 22, 1995.

Lee, Bruce. *Tao of Jeet Kune Do*. California: Ohara Publications, 1975.

Linderman, Larry. "Fast Forward Section." *Penthouse*. October 1994.

Logan, Greg. "SPECIAL REPORT: Concussions in Sports/Damaging Blows for Boxing." Newsday. July 10, 1996.

Marks, John. "Whatever it takes to win." *U.S. News & World Report*. February 24, 1997.

McBride, Clay. "The Ultimate Fighting Championship II: Fighter biographies." *WOW Promotions*. 1994.

McBride, Clay. "The Ultimate Fighting Championship: various articles." *Martial Arts Legends Magazine*. 1994.

McBride, Clay. "The UFC Special Section." *Martial Arts Ultimate Warriors*. February 1995.

Meerman, Wiggert. "Lee Murray: British Bad Boy." *Ultimate Athlete*. January 2003

Meyrowitz, Robert. "A Survival Guide for Producers." *Multichannel News*. April 3, 1995.

Minzesheimer, Bob. "N.Y. deals blow to Extreme Fighting." *USA Today*. February 6, 1997.

Mitchell, Paul. *The Overlook Martial Arts Handbook*. New York: The Overlook Press, 1988.

Newfield, Jack. "Should We Let Boxing Die?" *Parade*. May 2, 2004.

Paul Newport, John. "Blood Sport." *Details*. March 1995.

Plummer, William. "Blood Sport." *People Weekly*. March 11, 1996.

Poliakoff, Michael. *Combat Sports in the Ancient World : Competition, Violence, and Culture*. Connecticut: Yale University Press, 1995.

Postell, Robin & Coleman, Jim. "Ultimate Fighting Championship Fails To Live Up To Its Billing." *Black Belt*. April 1996.

Rist, Curtis. "Hit-Com Pay-per-view mega-brawl has socko ratings." *Newsday*. August 31, 1994.

Rosato, Bill. "BOX: Sweden to review 30 year old boxing ban." *AAP Sports News (Australia)*. December 16, 1999.

Rosenberg, Howard. "'Ultimate' Lives Up to Name.'" *Los Angeles Times*. November 15, 1993.

Ruibal, Sal. "Fatalities infrequent but devastating." *USA Today Sports*. December 13, 2000.

Sokolove, Michael. "Bloodbath." *Philadelphia Inquirer*. February 25, 1996.

Stone, Andrea. "Fans see fun in brawls where anything goes." *USA Today*. December 19, 1995.

Umstead, Thomas. "Three Events Boost Early April PPV Revenues." *Multichannel News*. April 17, 1995.

Umstead, Thomas. "Operators Struggle Again With UFC Time Overrun." *Multichannel News*. September 18, 1995.

Umstead, Thomas. "InterMedia Nixes 'Ultimate Fighting'-Type Events." *Multichannel News*. January 1, 1996.

Umstead, Thomas. "SEG Gets Clearance in N.Y. for Ultimate Events." *Multichannel News*. November 18, 1996.

Umstead, Thomas. "UFC Prospers Despite Dwindling Support." *Multichannel News*. February 26, 1996.

Van Gelder, Lawrence. "Promoter Postpones 'Ultimate Fight' in Manhattan." *Metropolitan Desk*. February 6, 1997.

Warner, Gene. "Crowd-pleasing attraction triggers heated debate." *Buffalo News*. January 27, 1997.

Weiner, Stewart. "Fast Forward Section." *Penthouse*. December 1993.

Weiss, Al & Weiss, David. *The Official History of Karate in America*. California: Pro-Action Publishing, 1997.

White, Nadia. "Arizona senator: Stop 'bloody' fight in Casper." *Casper Star Tribune*. June 12, 1996.

Will, George. "'Extreme' Fighting: Just Today's Ultimate." *Newsday*. November 26, 1995.

Yan, Ellen. "Gov.: No Sport About Ultimate Fighting." *Newsday*. January 18, 1997.